W9-ACC-628

Unix System Administration Guide

Unix System Administration Guide

**Levi Reiss
and Joseph Radin**

Osborne McGraw-Hill

Berkeley New York St. Louis San Francisco
Auckland Bogotá Hamburg London Madrid
Mexico City Milan Montreal New Delhi Panama City
Paris São Paulo Singapore Sydney
Tokyo Toronto

Osborne **McGraw-Hill**
2600 Tenth Street
Berkeley, California 94710
U.S.A.

For information on translations or book distributors outside of the U.S.A., please write to Osborne **McGraw-Hill** at the above address.

Unix System Administration Guide

1234567890 DOC 99876543

ISBN 0-07-881951-2

Acquisitions Editor	**Project Editor**	**Indexer**
Jeffrey M. Pepper	Nancy McLaughlin	Valerie Robbins
Associate Editor	**Copy Editor**	**Computer Designer**
Vicki Van Ausdall	Paul Medoff	Lance Ravella
Technical Editor	**Proofreaders**	**Cover Design**
Harley Hahn	Zoe Borovsky	Mason Fong
	Charissa Hogeboom	

To our wives and children: Noga, Sami, and Maya Reiss and Sara, Gal, and Nurit Radin

Contents at a Glance

Part III
A Fundamental Application

Part IV
Appendixes

Contents

Part II
System Administration

5 Users and Accounts 95

6 System Administrator-User Communication 145

Part III
A Fundamental Application

Part IV
Appendixes

Acknowledgments

A computer book is never the sole product of one or two authors, and *Unix System Administration Guide* is no exception. We wish to thank the excellent Osborne McGraw-Hill team for their tireless efforts culminating in this text. Jeff Pepper played a more than active role, signing us and directing the project from its inception to the final stages. Vicki Van Ausdall kept in constant contact with us. Every page reflects her input. Special thanks go to Nancy McLaughlin, who headed the project on a day-to-day (and we mean day-to-day) basis, and to Paul Medoff for extensive copy editing. Their numerous clarifications helped us all. Harley Hahn was our technical reviewer. We want to thank him for his many minor, and occasional major, corrections. Our heartfelt appreciation goes to the design team for a beautiful, highly functional text, designed with you, the reader, in mind. Additional thanks go to Todd Hatcher, of Hamilton/Avnet, and Otto Gygax for their aid with this project. Final appreciation goes to our wives, Noga Reiss and Sara Radin, for their infinite patience and valuable input at all stages of the process. We often flew the material by them, and if it didn't fly, you don't see it. As is customary, the authors acknowledge their sole responsibility for any errors.

Preface

Given the increasing popularity of Unix systems, the importance of the system administration activity, and the complexity of Unix system administration tasks, it is safe to assume that you, the potential reader of this text, will find yourself choosing from a variety of Unix system administration books. The natural question arises: Why ours?

We propose several answers, whose order of importance depends on you, the Unix system administrator.

Our text is most definitely "hands-on," providing extensive C language programs and shell scripts in almost every chapter. All shell scripts and programs were tested under both System V and BSD Unix. (The scripts are written in the three major script programming languages, Korn shell, Bourne shell, and C shell.)

We feel that the system administration activity cannot be run on a "black box" basis.

Whether or not the system administrator chooses to apply manufacturer-supplied scripts, he or she must know what the scripts are doing, both generally and specifically. Learning to master scripts is an essential part of the system administrator's training.

A unique feature of our book is test scripts, covering all important system administration functions. These scripts enable the system administrator, or in many cases a trusted assistant, to learn before doing. With this approach, the system administrator can use his or her regular account for testing, and use the root account only for the final (production) activities. By the way, this is in accordance with the generally accepted Unix system administration practice of limiting the use of the root account, because of its complete system privileges and the ensuing potential for disaster.

Successful completion of this book means that you will be able to administer a multi-user Unix system, with the occasional aid of technical personnel. While our text is written at the beginning-to-intermediate level, the last chapter presents a relatively advanced application that you can modify to meet special requirements. After reading this book, you will be able to pick up any of the system's numerous manuals and fly (or in some cases crawl) with it.

HARDWARE AND SOFTWARE USED FOR THIS BOOK

The scripts in this book were written in the Korn, Bourne, and C shell programming languages. All of the programs were written in the C programming language. The Bourne shell scripts will run under the C shell after minor modifications. All scripts and programs appearing in this book were developed and tested on an IBM-compatible, 33 MHz 486 computer, with 8 MB of memory and a 210 MB hard disk running Unix System V. They were tested on a SPARC workstation running SunOS Release 4.1.1., which is based on BSD Unix.

NAMING CONVENTIONS USED IN THIS BOOK

All Unix commands, file names, and directory names appear in boldface. Shell and C language functions are identified as such. Variables are italicized, but flags and options that you enter as such are set in standard (Roman) type. Boolean operators appear in upper case. New terms appear in italics when they are first defined. Unix commands are assumed to be in the **/etc** directory unless otherwise specified.

....
HOW THIS BOOK IS ORGANIZED

The book is divided into three sections plus three appendixes. The introductory section, composed of four chapters, introduces Unix, the **vi** text editor, shell programming (Korn Shell, Bourne Shell, and C Shell), and the Unix kernel. This section presents what you need to get started in Unix system administration. The applications section, composed of ten chapters, describes in detail major Unix system administration activities. Almost every chapter includes multiple shell scripts and C language programs. The final chapter consists of a user-friendly interface to Unix, providing menu-driven access to system administration shell scripts and C language programs. A discussion of each of the chapters and appendixes follows.

Chapter 1, "Introduction"   The first chapter takes you on a quick tour of both Unix and system administration. It presents a rapid version of Unix's dynamic history, telling how Unix rose from an operating system of interest only to computer professionals to become significant for computer of all sizes. Then it introduces key Unix terms that you should know right from the beginning. The third section discusses some of the advantages of the Unix operating systems. The fourth and final section discusses what Unix system administrators do. Don't be disturbed if the list of duties is long.

Chapter 2, "The vi Editor"   The chapter examines the most important features of the widely Unix program editor **vi**, ranging from special keys and cursor movement commands to the various text manipulation commands to insert, delete, modify, move, and search for text. The chapter concludes by showing you how to customize **vi** to meet your special needs.

Chapter 3, "Shell Programming"   Chapter 3 introduces shell programming, the process by which system administrators and others create custom programs known as shell scripts that automatically execute a series of commands. It discusses in detail three shell programming languages, the Korn shell, the Bourne shell, and the C shell, which are applied in subsequent chapters.

Chapter 4, "Kernel Overview"   The kernel is the part of the operating system that resides in memory after the system has been booted. It is the core of the operating system. Chapter 4 presents in detail information that system administrators need to know to get the job done.

Chapter 5, "Users and Accounts"   Chapter 5 discusses the theory and practice of adding and removing user accounts, which is a time-consuming task in most installations. After explaining passwords, password selection, and the contents of the **passwd** file, the chapter provides several methods of automating the user account creation and removal processes. Once you have completed Chapter 5, you will have several options: using shell scripts to manage user accounts yourself; supplying C language programs to your assistant to manage user accounts, without compromising system security; or applying vendor-supplied scripts or programs where available.

Chapter 6, "System Administrator—User Communication"

Computer users often have a lot to say to each other, whether the information is of a strictly business or a personal nature. System administrators also have a constant need to keep in touch with their users. Chapter 6 presents several common, easy-to-use UNIX features that enhance interuser or system administrator communication.

Chapter 7, "File System Backup and Restoration"   It is difficult to over-

estimate the importance of file system backup and restoration. Anyone who has ever lost a file should realize the value of correctly designed and executed backup procedures. Users will hold you, the system administrator, responsible whenever they cannot restore lost files. Chapter 7 may be the most important one in this book. Keeping your file system backed up at all times is absolutely essential.

Chapter 8, "Unix File Systems"   The file system is an integral part of any Unix

system. Keeping the file system in running order is a crucial responsibility of the system administrator. As you will see in Chapter 8, you are not alone. In many instances, the work is semiautomatic. You may only have to answer Yes to a few questions, and Unix will repair the file system to the best of its ability. However, for those (hopefully) rare instances in which the Unix system cannot repair itself, you will have to master the principles and commands discussed in this important chapter.

Chapter 9, "Unix Startup and Shutdown"   The system administrator is re-

sponsible for starting and shutting down the computer system on a scheduled or an emergency basis. Unlike booting a DOS system, which may be done with the flick of a switch, initiating or terminating Unix is a complex process. Doing it incorrectly can be dangerous to your file system. Chapter 9 examines the principles of system startup and then looks at how a widely used microcomputer version of Unix implements system startup, including system administrator installation options and error messages.

Chapter 10, "System Peripherals"   A major responsibility of the system ad-

ministrator is installing and maintaining printers. (You can gauge the importance of printers by noting what happens when a printer is unavailable!) Unix provides several printer control commands, each of which offers numerous options. Chapter 10 provides shell scripts for adding and removing a line printer from the Unix system. The chapter concludes with a brief examination of other system peripherals, including the terminal and the mouse.

Chapter 11, "Network Administration"   One reason for Unix's importance is its networking facilities, which can link computing services across a campus or across the globe. As you might assume, the system administrator plays a major role in setting up, monitoring, and reorganizing computer networks. Besides presenting the theory and practice of Unix networking and its impact on the system administrator, Chapter 11 presents a C language program for monitoring the network, and shell scripts for reconfiguring the network.

Chapter 12, "Security Management"   Security is one of the most critical tasks of the system administrator. Proper security costs money and causes inconvenience. However, security breaches cost even more, in terms of both money and inconvenience. Convince your users of these truths and half the security battle is won. The system administrator's most important security task is establishing an effective security environment—convincing users of the importance of maintaining security 24 hours a day. Chapter 12 provides specific guidelines for maintaining account security, dealing with attacks on physical security—including natural disasters, handling specific network security problems, and auditing the system.

Chapter 13, "X Window System Administration"   The X Window System provides windowing services on Unix systems. Briefly stated, appropriate use of X combines the power of Unix with the user-friendliness of Macintosh (or, in the eyes of some, MS-Windows or OS/2.) In many installations, the system administrator is responsible for administering the X Window System. This relatively long chapter presents what the system administrator needs to know to manage X.

Chapter 14, "Tuning and Troubleshooting"   As system administrator, you are responsible for ensuring that the system runs, and doesn't crawl, stumble, or sputter. Chapter 14 presents system report commands that provide specific information on what the system is doing. You can use this information to tune the system, increasing productivity and user satisfaction.

Chapter 15, "A User-Friendly Interface"   The final chapter consists of a user-friendly interface to Unix, providing menu-driven access to system administration shell scripts and C language programs. Except for the testing option, which consists of C language programs that add or remove a pseudo user, all menu options must be executed by the system administrator with the root password. Most shell scripts in Chapter 15 are written in the Korn shell, but can easily be modified to run under the Bourne shell. Use the interface presented here as the starting point, and then add or modify different options as required.

Appendix A, "Major Unix Commands"   The first appendix contains commands of interest to Unix system administrators. In many cases it refers back to the chapter in which the command was introduced. Every attempt was made to be generic, but because Unix is not 100% compatible across platforms (what is?), on occasion the command version refers to Unix V. Several BSD commands are discussed. Use the **man** command described in Appendix A to access online documentation for your Unix implementation.

Appendix B, "Korn Shell and Bourne Shell Commands"   Appendix B

describes the major Korn shell and Bourne shell commands. All commands listed are available in the Korn shell, and most are also available in the Bourne shell.

Appendix C, "C Shell Commands"   The final appendix describes the major C

shell commands.

PART ONE

The Unix System

Unix System

- History

- Basic Unix Definitions

- Advantages of Unix Systems

- System Administration

Administration Guide

CHAPTER 1

Introduction

Welcome to Unix system administration. This rapidly developing area combines two separate but interrelated computer fields. Unix has become a major operating system for computers of all sizes. System administration is a special type of administrative activity that involves getting a computer system to meet the needs of a user community effectively and efficiently. Successful Unix system administration requires mastering both the Unix operating system and system administration. While this profession is definitely people-oriented, it requires considerable technical skill as well.

This book addresses Unix system administrative duties in great detail. Most chapters contain practical Unix scripts that you can enter into the computer and apply to your Unix system. The final chapter presents a menu-driven interface program that makes it easier for the system administrator to perform necessary tasks.

This introductory chapter takes you on a quick tour of both Unix and system administration. The first section presents a rapid version of Unix's dynamic history. It explains how Unix has risen from being an operating system of interest only to computer professionals to being significant for computers of all sizes. The second section introduces key Unix terms that you should know right from the beginning. The third section discusses some of the advantages of the Unix operating system, advantages that have helped put it where it is today and where it will be tomorrow. The fourth and final section discusses what Unix system administrators do. (Don't be disturbed if the list of duties seems long.)

Roll up your sleeves; it's time to begin.

HISTORY

An *operating system* is the control program that manages the hardware and software resources of a computer system. It provides the interface between the computer hardware and those who use the computer, including technical people, such as computer programmers and system administrators, and non-technical users. In the short but active history of computers, significant hardware advances such as more powerful processors, disks, and monitors have led, albeit sometimes after considerable delay, to operating systems that are more powerful and easier to use than their predecessors. The evolution of the Unix operating system is shown in Figure 1-1.

Initial Versions of Unix

In 1965 Bell Telephone Laboratories, commonly known as Bell Labs, the research arm of AT&T, joined General Electric and Project Mac of the Massachusetts Institute of Technology to develop an operating system called Multics. Multics was designed with the goal of enabling large numbers of users to access the computer simultaneously, sharing or not sharing their data as required. As is so often the case, the system took much longer to build than had been originally planned. In 1969 Bell Labs withdrew its representatives from the Multics team.

This move left high-level computer scientists at Bell Labs, including Ken Thompson, Dennis Ritchie, and Rudd Canaday, without a project—but not for long. They located a small DEC PDP-7 minicomputer on which to continue operating system development. The Unix operating system is now available on all sizes of computers ranging from microcomputers to supercomputers. Unix is the operating system of choice for scientists and engineers, and is making major inroads in commercial computing. But we are getting ahead of the story.

For every computer scientist interested in operating systems in and of themselves, hundreds if not thousands of individuals are interested in the applications administered by the operating systems. By 1971 Bell Lab's Legal Department relied on a Unix application for their specialized word processing. The application ran on a DEC PDP-11, a larger minicomputer than the original PDP-7. This early version of Unix took up 16K

FIGURE 1-1

The evolution of Unix

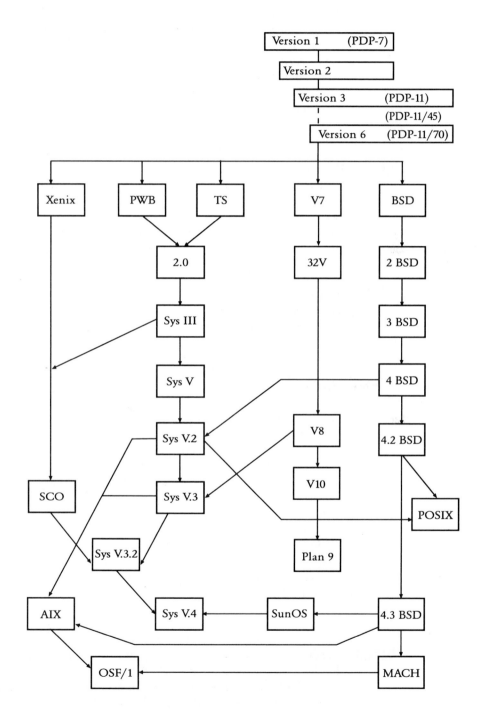

of memory, and the word processing program took up 8K. The computer disk was 512K, with individual files limited to 64K on disk. Given these sizes, it shouldn't be too surprising that Unix is available on microcomputers.

Another early Unix application was used for updating telephone directory listings, intercepting calls to numbers that had been changed. According to one of its major architects, Unix spread through Bell Labs because people loved to use it. Over the years the number of people who love using Unix has grown substantially.

Unix was originally programmed in assembly language, a programming language intimately linked to the particular platform on which it runs. Reprogramming an operating system written in assembly language to run on an even slightly different computer is a major task. In 1973 the major portion of Unix was rewritten in the C programming language to give it portability, unlike any other operating system at that time. *Portability* is the ability to move software from one hardware platform to another, without major recoding. Eventually, Unix was running on widely divergent computer hardware. The two major Unix versions, AT&T UNIX and BSD Unix are discussed briefly below.

System V Unix

In 1956, the United States Department of Justice issued a consent decree that accorded American Telephone & Telegraph, the mother company of Bell Labs, the right to provide telecommunications products to Bell Telephone Companies and telecommunications services to the nation. This landmark judgment denied AT&T the right to sell software. AT&T accorded licensees the right to use UNIX, and provided them with a computer tape and manuals, but did not provide any technical support. Due in part to the absence of technical support, UNIX licensees were mostly engineering firms and academic and research institutions, as opposed to businesses and administrative organizations.

As UNIX gained popularity in engineering and research circles, an increasing number of business users wanted to join in. In 1980 AT&T transferred UNIX marketing responsibility from Bell Labs to Western Electric, its manufacturing and supply arm. In 1982 System III, the first version of UNIX oriented toward commercial users, was released. (Arguably, calling this version System I would have reduced sales; potential customers might have chosen to wait for a later version, more likely to be free of bugs.) In 1983 the new, improved System V was introduced. (System IV had been restricted to internal AT&T use.) At the time of this writing, the most recent version is System V, Release 4.2. This release is marketed by Unix System Laboratories (USL), which was recently purchased by Novell.

Berkeley Unix

No history of Unix would be complete without discussing the major role played by the University of California, Berkeley. In January 1974, Berkeley's Computer Science department, Mathematics department, and Statistics department began using Unix on a PDP-11/45 minicomputer.

In early 1977, a Berkeley graduate student Bill Joy put together the first Berkeley Software Distribution (BSD) version of Unix, which included a Pascal interpreter and **ex**, a program editor. With the advent of screen addressable cursors on cathode ray tubes (CRTs), this editor evolved into the **vi** (short for visual) program editor, which is detailed in Chapter 2. The **vi** editor is available on both BSD and System V.

A major event in the development of BSD Unix occurred in the late 1970s, when the Defense Advanced Research Projects Agency succeeded in networking several major research centers that were equipped with platforms from different hardware vendors. Unix provides extensive networking services, available to most large computer systems whether they are Unix-based or not. Many Unix networking concepts and techniques can be seen in popular microcomputer-based local-area networks (LANs).

Microcomputer Versions of Unix

Microcomputer Unix is not a recent phenomenon; in 1980 Microsoft released XENIX 2.3, which was originally restricted to a single user. Today's microcomputer users can choose from several variants of Unix, most of which are based on System V. The most popular microcomputer based version of Unix is SCO Unix V.3.2 Release 4, distributed by the Santa Cruz Operation. This company also distributes SCO XENIX.

The microcomputer Unix market is exploding. UNIXWORLD magazine estimates that PC-based Unix systems sales were 350,000 in 1992, and predicts that sales will expand to 1.4 million in 1996.

Hardware requirements vary from one version of Unix to another. According to USL, the minimum hardware configuration for running Unix System V Release 4.2 is a 16-MHz 386SX processor with 4MB of memory and a 60MB hard disk. USL recommends 6MB of memory and an 80–120MB hard disk for a "typical client running several applications." Interestingly enough, these suggested values are smaller than the minimum values for previous releases of Unix System V.

BASIC UNIX DEFINITIONS

This section introduces key Unix terminology to be used throughout the text. The glossary at the back of the book defines these terms, and many others, more concisely.

Account   An *account* is a computerized record of all the information required for a user to log in to a given Unix system. Chapter 5 describes how the system administrator creates, modifies, and deletes user accounts.

Block Device   A *block device* is a peripheral unit that processes physical data organized in blocks, typically multiples of 512 bytes. The most common block device is a hard disk.

Bourne Shell   The *Bourne shell* was the standard command interpreter for System V Unix. Some of the scripts in this text are written in the Bourne shell. The dollar sign ($) is the Bourne shell input prompt; it indicates that the Bourne shell is awaiting your input.

C Shell   The *C shell* is a Unix command interpreter whose syntax resembles the C programming language. It is the standard command interpreter for BSD Unix. Some of the scripts in this text are written in the C shell. The percentage sign symbol (%) is the C shell prompt; it indicates that the C shell is awaiting your input.

Character Device   A *character device* is a peripheral unit that transfers data one or more characters at a time. Examples of character devices include modems and terminals.

Configuration File   A *configuration file* is a text file containing formatted information. An example of a Unix configuration file is **/etc/passwd**, the user account database.

Daemon   A *daemon* is a Unix process that runs in the background (while other tasks are being processed). Examples of daemons include **init**, the process that initiates user logins and starts other daemons, and **cron**, the process that keeps an eye on the system clock and periodically starts processes placed in its own configuration file.

Device Driver   A *device driver* is a program that controls a specific device, such as a laser printer. The device driver serves as an interface between the kernel (defined below) and the users.

Device File   A *device file* can be a character file or a block file. (Some physical devices are represented by a character device file and a block device file.) Device files are identified by two numbers: the *major device number* and the *minor device number*. The major device number identifies the associated device driver. The minor device number informs the device driver of the actual physical unit.

Directory   A *directory* can be thought of as a group of files. Unix adopts a hierarchical structure, meaning that a given directory may include one or more subdirectories.

File   A *file* is a named collection of data stored on disk. Examples of files include application programs (such as an organization's payroll), shell scripts (such as one that might remove a user's system privileges), and data (such as a record of an organization's physical inventory). Unix provides the system administrator with substantial control over user files.

Inode   *Inode* (short for index node) describes a file in great detail. The inode for a given file indicates the file's owner, size, type, and permissions (the information indicating who is allowed to access the file, as well as any restrictions on this file access), a list of the physical disk blocks that compose the file, and the number of links. It also includes three access times: the time that the file was last accessed, the time that the file was last modified, and the time that the inode itself was last accessed.

Kernel   The *kernel* is the part of the operating system that resides in memory after the system is booted (started). It is a resource manager, handling system hardware efficiently and effectively. The Unix kernel was designed to be small, approximately 500K. Chapter 4 discusses the kernel in greater depth.

Korn Shell   The *Korn shell* is now the standard command interpreter for System V Unix. It integrates the best aspects of the Bourne shell and the C shell. Some of the scripts in this text are written in the Korn shell. The dollar sign ($) is the Korn shell input prompt; it indicates that the Korn shell is awaiting your input.

Nested Subdirectory   A directory within a directory is known as a *nested subdirectory*. Unix places no limit on the depth of nested subdirectories.

Process   A *process* is an executing program. In contrast to most microcomputer operating systems, such as MS-DOS, Unix is designed for multiprocessing; this means that several programs can function under Unix at the same time. Appropriate system calls create, kill, and synchronize processes. The operating system carefully mediates interaction among processes.

Root Directory   The *root directory,* also called the *root,* is the primary Unix directory; it is not subordinate to any other directory. The system administrator has access to the root directory upon demand. Users may have limited access to the root directory.

Script   A *script* is a file containing Unix commands. Scripts are written for one of three shells: the Korn shell, the Bourne shell, or the C shell. Chapter 3 shows you how to program scripts.

Shell   The *shell* is the command interpreter program that serves as an interface between users and the operating system itself. The most widely used Unix shells are the Korn shell, the Bourne shell, and the C shell. Chapter 3 introduces these three shells and explains how to write programs for them.

System Call   A *system call* is a program request addressed to the kernel. Common activities such as accessing a file or reading the system clock require system calls.

ADVANTAGES OF UNIX SYSTEMS

It is no accident that Unix has achieved such a position of prominence in the competitive computer marketplace, or more exactly, marketplaces. In terms of sheer power and flexibility, it outstrips both MS-DOS and MS-Windows. At the same time, Unix can be easier to use than the proprietary minicomputer and mainframe computer operating systems. Among the major advantages of the Unix operating system are its portability—the ability to run Unix applications on a variety of hardware platforms. Unix also allows multitasking, which lets a user perform several tasks at the same time, and a multi-user environment that can serve more than one user simultaneously; extensive software; and X Window, which allows for display of graphics interfaces. These advantages are discussed in detail below.

Portability

Previous operating systems were intimately linked to a single computer or narrowly defined family of computers. Changing computers meant changing operating systems and heavily modifying or abandoning existing applications. Unix broke new ground by being portable. In part because Unix is mostly written in the C programming language, instead of assembly language, Unix is portable. It is relatively simple to move Unix and applications running under Unix from one computer to another, perhaps widely divergent, architecture. This portability enables installations to acquire a computer running Unix without worrying too much about being a prisoner of the manufacturer. When the installation outgrows the computer, it may be able to acquire another Unix computer, and adapt its applications to the new equipment.

Multitasking

Unlike MS-DOS, Unix was designed with *multitasking* in mind. Multitasking means that the computer system can perform several tasks simultaneously. Even on a stripped down version of Unix, users can answer their electronic mail, calculate travel expenses with an electronic spreadsheet, and pop the results of these calculations into their expense report using a word processor. Such multitasking is not readily available with MS-DOS but is available with MS-Windows and OS/2.

Multi-User Environment

Unlike MS-DOS, MS-Windows, or OS/2, Unix is a multi-user system. A *multi-user* operating system supports several users simultaneously. It allocates resources and protects them from each other, but allows them to share data when desired. While a single-user system may not require a system administrator, every multi-user system must have a system administrator to function effectively.

Extensive Software

Many MS-DOS users are hesitant to switch to Unix. They simply don't want to give up their familiar applications such as WordPerfect and Lotus 1-2-3. No worry. Popular MS-DOS programs are available on Unix, often in keystroke compatible versions. Unix implementations such as SCO Open Desktop include an MS-DOS mode. This provides full access to all familiar services including running programs and formatting diskettes. However, Unix software often goes beyond the MS-DOS versions. For example, Unix Lotus lets user display and process up to 26 active spreadsheets at any given time. Unix Lotus allows access to most Unix databases. Finally, once they get the hang of Unix many MS-DOS devotees will switch to Unix applications.

X Window System

Ever since the introduction of the Apple Macintosh, numerous computer specialists and non-technical users have preferred a graphical user interface (GUI) to the uninformative character interface supplied by MS-DOS and the Unix shells. The most widely used GUI on DOS computers is MS-Windows, also a product of the Microsoft Corporation. Unix has adopted a standard for GUIs, the X Window system, which was developed at the Laboratory for Computer Science at the Massachusetts Institute of Technology. Unlike MS-Windows, which is a commercial product, the heart of the X Window system is distributed freely.

Two widely used commercial toolkits make X Window easier to use. The OSF/Motif toolkit, often called Motif, is the most widely used. It provides an attractive interface similar to Microsoft Windows. Motif was developed through the Open Software Foundation (OSF), a consortium founded in 1988 by several major hardware vendors, including IBM, DEC, and Hewlett-Packard. The major competitor to OSF/Motif is the Open Look graphical user interface distributed by AT&T and Sun Microsystems. The authors' previous book, *X Window Inside & Out* (Berkeley, Osborne/McGraw-Hill, 1992) presents the theory of X Window systems and includes working X Window programs.

SYSTEM ADMINISTRATION

A single person, or occasionally a team of people, must have the final say on allocating resources among users and resolving the inevitable conflicts. The final section of this chapter introduces Unix system administration.

System Administration Duties

In short, the Unix system administrator is the person ultimately responsible for keeping Unix users happy. Successful system administration requires both technical competence and a mastery of interpersonal skills. The following list of system administration duties is not complete, but does serve as a starting point. Depending on organizational policy and the magnitude of the system, the system administrator may not have to perform all these duties; however, she or he must assure that everything gets done. Would-be system administrators need not despair. While this incomplete list is long, there are several tools to help system administrators. In addition to presenting system administration issues, this text contains numerous ready-to-run scripts to execute various system administration tasks.

Adding and Removing User Accounts

The Unix system is too precious a resource to be made available to all individuals on demand. The system administrator is responsible for creating accounts for authorized users and removing accounts for users who are no longer authorized. Like many other system administration tasks, adding and removing user accounts is partially technical and partially political. Should a student lose computer privileges for playing a game, sending a dirty joke to other users, or attempting to crash the system? The system administrator must decide. Chapter 5 addresses the theory and practice of adding and removing user accounts.

Communicating with the Users

The system administrator must communicate the installation's Unix strategy and tactics to the users. If policy states that users must change passwords every six months, the system administrator should warn them, preferably not at the last minute. Many systems display the latest news bulletin the first time the user logs in on any day. Chapter 6 discusses these and related issues in greater depth, culminating in useful scripts.

Backing Up and Restoring Files

The three certainties of life in the computer age are: death, taxes, and losing files, but generally not in that order. The system administrator must institute and enforce a file backup policy that works. The system administrator can select hardware and software to aid in this process. Different levels of backups should be executed on a daily, weekly, and monthly basis. Chapter 7 presents scripts that make backups much easier to perform. Chapter 8 discusses what the system administrator needs to know about Unix file organization, and about customizing file organization to maximize performance.

Starting Up and Shutting Down the System

Unix is not the same as MS-DOS. When an MS-DOS system crashes you can simply turn the computer off and on again. In contrast, when a Unix system goes down, it must be painstakingly rebuilt. This process should not be attempted by untrained individuals. From time to time the system must be shut down—for example, to perform scheduled maintenance or to change the hardware configuration. Chapter 9 points you on the road to startup/shutdown success.

Changing the Hardware Configuration

The system administrator plays a key role in hardware selection and installation. He or she monitors system performance and documents the need for new hardware. When new hardware is acquired, the system administrator is responsible for its physical installation and subsequent testing. Chapter 10 discusses a variety of hardware issues and presents useful scripts.

Communicating with Other Systems

The days of the personal computer sitting isolated in its corner are over. Computers running the Unix operating system are rarely used alone. These systems may be connected to other Unix-based computers or to computers running other operating systems such as DEC's VMS and Macintosh's System 7. Chapter 11 describes procedures for connecting Unix to other platforms, Unix-based or not, and provides valuable tips and scripts.

Security Management

The more valuable the computer system, the more costly to repair any efforts that are made to undermine it. The system administrator is a watchdog, using electronic tools to defend the computer system against assault and subversion. The battle never ends, because as system security software and hardware become more powerful, potential violators become better armed and more determined. Chapter 12 forges one weapon in the system administrator's arsenal.

Administering the X Window System

The X Window system is a complicated client-server based system. Successful implementation of the X Window system requires a unified user interface, regardless of the specific application or designer. Such interfaces do not come about by accident; they require active administration. In spite of the technical and administrative demands of X Window systems, more and more Unix-based systems are installing them. Expect to spend much of your time and energy getting X Window to run and to perform efficiently. The information in Chapter 13 will save you countless hours and headaches (especially if applied in conjunction with the communication techniques presented in Chapter 11).

System Troubleshooting and Tuning

A major portion of system administrators' time and effort is spent troubleshooting and fine-tuning the system. Typically, when tuning needs to be done, the users will complain. Perhaps the new network controller has trouble recognizing input from such-and-such a location. Perhaps the latest version of a manager's favorite graphics program is just too slow. Whatever the problem and whatever its cause, the system administrator is expected to find the answer, and fast. Chapter 14 will supply some of the answers and point you on the road to others.

Partially Automating System Administration

This text concludes with Chapter 15, which presents a menu-driven interface program that makes it easier for the system administrator to perform necessary tasks. System administrators can apply this program as is or modify it to meet their installation's specific needs. When properly customized, this interface may enable trusted assistants to perform some routine system administration tasks.

Surveying System Administrators

The above list of system administrator duties is long, but incomplete. The question arises, "How do typical system administrators actually spend their working days?" The simplest response is that there is no such thing as a typical system administrator. But the question is still worth asking, because the more we know about the system administrator's real duties, the easier it is to optimize the workload.

In perhaps the first formal attempt to determine how system administrators really spend their time, a survey was held at the 1991 Usenix Large Installation System Administration (LISA) Conference. Among the survey results were the following: The average Unix system administrator reported working 42.6 hours a week. Of this time, over 25% was spent on people-management responsibilities, such as dealing with users (16.7%). Other major duties included various software-related activities (22.5%), networking activities (12.6%), and hardware-related activities (11.3%), as well as system-management (10.5%). Backing up and restoring files took only 5.8% of an average Unix system administrator's time.

The survey attempted to calculate the average number of users served by a system administrator. It was not possible to determine a meaningful average, but two "typical" values were cited frequently: about 50 users per administrator, and about 16 users per administrator. One site, however, reported an incredible 1800 users for a single system administrator!

....

Chapter Summary

An *operating system* is the control program that manages the hardware and software resources of a computer system. In 1965 Bell Telephone Laboratories, commonly known as Bell Labs, the research arm of AT&T, joined General Electric and Project Mac of the Massachusetts Institute of Technology to develop an operating system called Multics. In 1969 Bell Labs withdrew its representatives from the Multics team. By 1971 Bell Lab's Legal Department relied on a Unix application, running on a DEC PDP-11, for their specialized word processing. Unix was originally programmed in assembly language, a programming language intimately linked to the particular platform on which it runs. In 1973 the major portion of Unix was rewritten in the C programming language.

The consent decree issued by the United States Department of Justice in 1956 accorded AT&T the right to provide telecommunications products to Bell Telephone Companies, and telecommunications services to the nation. This landmark judgment denied AT&T the right to sell software. As UNIX gained popularity in engineering and research circles, an increasing number of business users wanted to join in. In 1980, AT&T transferred UNIX marketing responsibility from Bell Labs to Western Electric, its manufacturing and supply arm. In 1983 the new, improved System V was introduced. At the time of this writing, the most recent variety is System V, Release 4.2. This release is marketed by AT&T's Unix System Laboratories (USL), which was recently purchased by Novell.

No history of Unix would be complete without discussing the major role played by the University of California, Berkeley. In January 1974, Berkeley's Computer Science, Mathematics, and Statistics departments began using Unix on a PDP-11/45 minicomputer. In early 1977, Berkeley graduate student Bill Joy put together the first Berkeley Software Distribution (BSD) version of Unix, which included a Pascal interpreter and ex, a program editor. A major event in the development of BSD Unix occurred in the late 1970s, when the Defense Advanced Research Projects Agency succeeding in networking several major research centers equipped with platforms from different hardware vendors.

Microcomputer Unix is not a recent phenomenon; in 1980 Microsoft released XENIX 2.3, which was originally restricted to a single user. Today's microcomputer users can choose from several commercial variants of Unix, most of which are based on System V. The microcomputer Unix market is exploding. Hardware requirements vary from one Unix version to another.

Advantages of Unix Systems   It is no accident that Unix has achieved such a position of prominence in the competitive computer marketplace, or more exactly, marketplaces. In terms of sheer power and flexibility it outstrips both MS-DOS and MS-Windows. At the same time, Unix can be easier to use than the proprietary minicomputer and mainframe computer operating systems. Among the major advantages of the Unix operating system are portability—the ability to run Unix applications on a variety of hardware platforms; multitasking, which allows a user to perform several tasks at the same time; a multi-user environment, the ability to serve more than one user simultaneously; extensive software; and X Window, which allows for display of graphics interfaces.

System Administration   A single person, or occasionally a team, must have the final say on allocating resources among users and resolving the inevitable conflicts. Among the duties of a system administrator are the following: adding and removing user accounts, communicating with users, backing up and restoring files, starting up and shutting down the system, communicating with other systems, security management, administering the X Window system, changing the hardware configuration, debugging the system, and perhaps automating these system administration tasks.

Unix System

- Editor Modes

- Basic vi Operations

- File Editing

- vi Command Line Options

- vi Environment Options

Administration Guide

CHAPTER 2

The vi Editor

System administrators spend a major portion of their time writing or modifying scripts, which are files containing Unix commands that help automate system administration tasks. A *program editor,* also called an *editor,* is a software tool for creating and modifying scripts and programs. This chapter presents **vi**, the most widely used Unix program editor.

The chapter describes the editor modes that determine how the editor handles the input received. It shows you how to set the terminal type, start the editor, quit the editor, and write and read files.

In addition, the chapter examines the most important features of **vi**, ranging from special keys and cursor movement commands to the various text manipulation commands for inserting, deleting, modifying, moving, and searching for text. The chapter concludes by showing you how to customize **vi** to meet your special needs. Tables summarize cursor movement commands, text insertion commands, text deletion commands, text modification commands, text movement commands, and search commands.

INTRODUCTION

In the late 1970s Bill Joy, perhaps the key individual in the development of BSD (Berkeley System Distribution) Unix, created the **vi** editor. Within a few years **vi** became the most widely used Unix editor. The name **vi** is short for visual; **vi** is a full-screen editor. It is available on almost every version of Unix. After a short training period, individuals can use **vi** to create and modify programs and scripts in the Unix environment. Unlike word processors, **vi** does not do text formatting, and cannot import graphics. Because it was specifically designed for program editing, you should use **vi** (or another editor such as **emacs**) instead of a word processor when editing programs and scripts.

Among other operations, **vi** can read and write files, insert and delete text, locate one or more occurrences of specified text within a given document, substitute one character string for another, and move a block of text from one location to another. You'll find that **vi** is a powerful, relatively easy-to-use tool for coding scripts. It will enable you to focus on the scripts themselves, rather than the mechanics of coding the scripts. All self-respecting Unix system administrators should have **vi** or an alternative editor in their toolbox. Because the system administrator has complete access to the Unix system, it is absolutely necessary that he or she master the editor. A seemingly minor mistake in a script can have serious consequences. As the authors know from bitter experience, rebuilding the system can take several hours or more.

EDITOR MODES

The editor *mode* (or state) determines how the editor handles the input it receives. Potentially critical errors occur when the user is unaware of the current editor mode. Working with **vi** requires that you recognize each mode and know how to navigate efficiently from one mode to another. There are two modes in **vi**: command mode and input mode.

 Command mode is used to enter commands—for example, to search for a character string or quit the file.

Input mode is used to enter text into the file.

By itself, **vi** always starts in command mode. You switch back and forth among the modes as required, using input mode to enter data and command mode to edit it. When you have completed editing a file, you may save it and access another file or end the editing session. Before examining the basic **vi** operations let's see how to switch among modes.

Switching Modes

Several commands change from command mode to input mode. For example, the command **a** (append) places **vi** in input mode and specifies that the input text will be inserted after the cursor. The command **A** places **vi** in input mode and specifies that the input text will be placed at the end of the current line.

To change from input mode to command mode, simply press the ESC key.

Mode Errors

Each **vi** mode has its own set of commands. When you work with this editor, you must know at all times which mode you are in, or else you risk making costly errors. Suppose that you think you're in input mode but, in reality, you are in command mode. You enter the characters **:wq**. Instead of entering some text, you have overwritten the file and quit the **vi** editor.

On the other hand, suppose that you think you're in command mode but you are really in input mode. You want to quit the editor, first saving the file. You enter three characters **:wq**. Instead of performing the desired operations, you have added three characters to your text. Until you have developed the ability to sense your mode automatically, use the **set showmode** or **:set showmode** command, if available in your version of Unix, to display the current mode on the screen.

BASIC vi OPERATIONS

This section presents the **vi** operations that you must know. First you will learn how to indicate your terminal type. Next you will see how to start **vi**. This section then shows you how to write (save) a file, read (reload) the file, and switch from one file to another. It concludes by showing you the right way to exit **vi**. Nobody, not even a system administrator, should exit the editor by simply pressing a computer's Off button.

Setting the Terminal Type

The port you connect to will default to a given terminal type, depending on the installation. If your terminal is different, which may be the case if it is not hardwired, you will have to set the terminal type yourself. Popular terminal type designations include **ansi**, **vt100**, and **xterm**, the latter for the X Window System environment. You must enter the terminal type information correctly or risk generating illegible output, or perhaps no output at all. The exact command you should enter depends on the shell you are using.

Korn Shell or Bourne Shell

One way to handle the terminal setting is to enter two commands such as the following:

```
$ TERM=ansi
$ export TERM
```

The dollar sign ($) is the *Korn shell input prompt* or the *Bourne shell input prompt*. It indicates that the selected shell is awaiting your input. Do *not* enter the $. The first command sets the **TERM** environment variable to the standard terminal type **ansi**. The second line makes the global **TERM** environment variable available to any of your subshells, and to any of your programs running within one of your subshells.

Instead of typing these two lines every time you log in to Unix, you should include them in a special file called **.profile**, which Unix executes automatically after a successful login. The **.profile** file is discussed in Chapter 5.

C Shell

One way to handle the terminal setting is to enter the following line:

```
% setenv TERM ansi
```

The percent sign symbol (%) is the *C shell input prompt,* indicating that the C shell is awaiting your input. Do *not* enter the %. This line sets the **TERM** environment variable to the standard terminal type **ansi**.

Instead of typing this line every time you log onto Unix, you should include it in a special file called **.login**, which Unix executes automatically after a successful login. The **.login** file is discussed in Chapter 5.

Starting vi

Usually **vi** is invoked with a command such as the following:

vi *filename*

Here, *filename* obeys standard Unix file naming conventions (discussed in Chapter 4). If *filename* already exists, the editor will access that file and will position the cursor at the beginning of its first line. If *filename* does not currently exist, the editor will create an empty file with that name and will position the cursor at the upper left-hand corner of the screen.

When **vi** is active, the screen shows as much of the file as possible. A single line at the bottom of the screen displays control information. Blank lines at the end of the file include a tilde (~) in the leftmost column.

The following command invokes the **vi** editor, starting at the top of an unnamed file.

```
vi
```

Of course, to save this file you must give it a name, as discussed later in this section.

Unlike many word processing programs, you can tell **vi** that you want to work on a series of files, as in the following example:

```
vi filename1 filename2
```

In this case the editor first processes the file **filename1** and then the file **filename2**. It is possible to switch back and forth between two (or more) files. However, **vi** will not let you edit two or more files simultaneously.

Suppose that you wish to append data to the end of the file **abc**. You could start **vi** with that filename, and then move the cursor to the end of the file. (The cursor and navigation commands will be discussed shortly.) The following command starts **vi** at the end of the file **abc**.

```
vi +$ abc
```

The **vi** editor stores information in a special memory area known as a *buffer*. Lines within the buffer are numbered, but the line numbers do not appear on the display. The following command starts **vi** in line 10 of the file **abc**.

```
vi +10 abc
```

Recovering from a System Crash

When your system crashes or you are disconnected, for example, due to a power failure, it is possible to recover the file that you were editing. First, restore the file system, as explained in Chapter 7. Then, access the directory that was active when the system went down. Finally, activate **vi** with the -r option and the name of the file being edited. For example:

```
vi -r abc.txt
```

You can use **vi** -r to see if any files are available for recovery.

BSD notifies a user who has experienced this sort of accident by sending a mail message the next time the user logs into the system.

Quitting vi

The simplest way to exit **vi** is by entering the command **:q**, which will return you to the shell. If you have not made any changes to the file, **vi** accepts this command. However, if you have made changes but have not saved them (which would not be surprising, since the appropriate procedure is first described in the following section), **vi** rejects the **:q** command. In this case, you have a choice: either save these changes by writing them to disk, or enter the command **:q!** which overrides the standard **vi** protection against file loss. The ! (Unix calls this character a *bang*) tells the system to go ahead and exit **vi** anyway. Use it judiciously.

Learn how to enter and exit **vi**, saving files as desired while your files are still small. Don't wait until your files are full-sized to find that you have misunderstood and must create a large script from scratch because you accidentally exited **vi**. You can protect yourself by mastering the various options described below for writing files.

Writing Files

Because the contents of the **vi** buffer are stored in memory, they will be lost if you exit Unix either intentionally or by accident—for example, due to a power failure. Therefore it is extremely important to write (save) the buffer contents to disk on a regular basis. Failure to do so can have disastrous consequences. And there is no excuse not to save regularly—the procedure is quite simple: you enter the command **:w**. This command writes the file to disk, overwriting any previous file contents, but not affecting the buffer contents.

The command **:w** saves the file under its current name. To save the file under a different name, such as **newfile**, enter the command **:w newfile**. If no such file presently exists, the **vi** editor saves the file and indicates the file size. If a file by that name already exists, **vi** tells you so, and does not update the file. To update the existing file, enter the command **:w! newfile**; here, once again, the bang (!) overrides the standard **vi** protection against overwriting a file.

File Saving Strategies

Suppose that you are developing a lengthy script called **myscript** and, as is usually preferred, you want to test the script stage-by-stage rather than attempting to debug the entire script. You don't want to overwrite a given stage until you are sure that the next stage is working properly. (One of the most frustrating activities that computer specialists face is trying to reconstruct a lost version that "worked.")

Start **vi** with the filename **myscript1**, and save the first stage with the command **:w**, as discussed above. Then continue to create the second stage. Save this script and exit **vi** with the following commands:

```
:w myscript2
:q
```

Note   The command :zz can be used to replace the commands :w and :q.

Test the second stage of this script. Depending on your test results, apply one of the three file saving policies described below.

▰ The test is totally positive. The second stage works. In this case, you restart **vi** with the command **vi myscript2** and proceed to work on stage three. When you are ready to test stage three, exit **vi** with the commands **:w myscript3** and **:q**.

▰ The test is partially positive. The second stage is not yet complete. In this case, you restart **vi** with the command **vi myscript2** and continue to work on stage two. When you are ready to retest stage two, exit **vi** with the commands **:w myscript2** and **:q**. This saves the updated version of stage two.

▰ The test is quite negative. The second stage is so far from working that you must return to the first stage and try again. Document these unsuccessful changes so that you don't make the same mistakes twice. Then restart **vi** with the command **vi myscript1**. When you are ready to retest stage two, exit **vi** with the commands **:w! myscript2** and **:q**. This saves the updated version of stage two.

In summary, **vi** offers you several strategies for writing your files. It's up to you to choose the correct command to meet your specific needs.

Switching Files

Suppose that you have invoked the **vi** editor with a list of files, as discussed previously.

```
vi filename1 filename2
```

The command **:n** switches from one file to another, provided that the changes in the first file have been saved. Assuming that changes are written to disk, the first time this command is entered, **vi** switches from the file **filename1** to the file **filename2**. The second time this command is entered, **vi** switches from the file **filename2** to the file **filename1**.

The command **:n!** switches from one file to another, whether or not the buffer has been written. As always, use caution when entering commands that include the bang (!) character.

Reading Files

The command **:r** reads the named file into the buffer. This command can be used to merge several files. For example, suppose that the two script segments **newscript1** and **newscript2** have been separately tested. They can be combined into the script **newscript** with the following procedure:

- ☑   Type **vi newscript1**.
- ☑   Move the cursor to the beginning of the last line.
- ☑   Press ESC-O.
- ☑   Press ESC.
- ☑   Press SHIFT and type **:r newscript2**.
- ☑   Press SHIFT and type **:w newscript**.

Note

While this procedure can seem a bit long, master it and you may save precious hours when building large scripts.

Placing a line number before the **r** reads (places) the file after the given line. For example, the following command

```
:20r abc
```

reads the file **abc** into the buffer after line 20.

Figure 2-1 shows a screen full of a script segment. When completed, this script will set the system time. The last line of the screen reads in the remaining script segment, whose name is **stjr2**.

Figure 2-2 shows a screen full of the completed script. After the **vi r**(ead) command terminates successfully, the screen contents scroll upward, making room for the **stjr2** script segment.

In Figure 2-3 the last line **:w stjr** shows the command that writes (saves) this completed script. After the file is successfully written, the last line of the screen indicates the filename, the number of lines, and the number of characters written. When it has finished writing the **stjr** file, the system generates the following message:

```
"stjr" 53 lines, 1375 characters
```

FIGURE 2-1

Reading a file

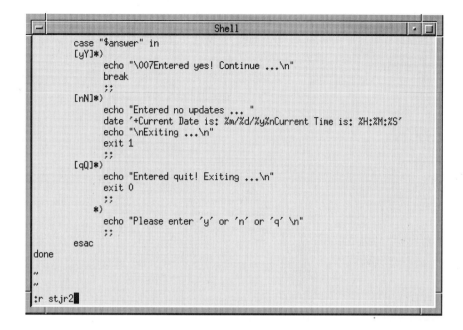

```
                case "$answer" in
        [yY]*)
                echo "\007Entered yes! Continue ...\n"
                break
                ;;
        [nN]*)
                echo "Entered no updates ... "
                date '+Current Date is: %m/%d/%y%nCurrent Time is: %H:%M:%S'
                echo "\nExiting ...\n"
                exit 1
                ;;
        [qQ]*)
                echo "Entered quit! Exiting ...\n"
                exit 0
                ;;
            *)
                echo "Please enter 'y' or 'n' or 'q' \n"
                ;;
        esac
done

~
~
:r st.jr2
```

FIGURE 2-2

A script after a
successful read

```
        [qQ]*)
                echo "Entered quit! Exiting ...\n"
                exit 0
                ;;
            *)
                echo "Please enter 'y' or 'n' or 'q' \n"
                ;;
        esac
done


if [ $log_name = "root" ]
then
        echo "\nSetting Time ...\n"
        rtc=no
        # If we have a real-time clock, synchronize system clock to it.
        cat /dev/clock > /dev/null 2>&1 && {
                rtc=yes
                date `/etc/setclock` > /dev/null
        }
        echo "\nSystem Time is `date`"
        echo "\nEnter new time ([YearMonthDay]HourMin): \c"
        while
                read date
```

FIGURE 2-3

FIGURE 2-3

Writing (saving) a file

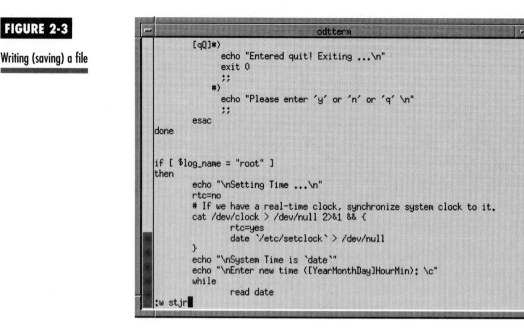

```
        [qQ]*)
                echo "Entered quit! Exiting ...\n"
                exit 0
                ;;
        *)
                echo "Please enter 'y' or 'n' or 'q' \n"
                ;;
        esac
done


if [ $log_name = "root" ]
then
        echo "\nSetting Time ...\n"
        rtc=no
        # If we have a real-time clock, synchronize system clock to it.
        cat /dev/clock > /dev/null 2>&1 && {
                rtc=yes
                date `/etc/setclock` > /dev/null
        }
        echo "\nSystem Time is `date`"
        echo "\nEnter new time ([YearMonthDay]HourMin): \c"
        while
                read date
:w st.jr
```

FILE EDITING

It is imperative that Unix system administrators become experts in file editing, using **vi** or an alternative editor. A simple editing mistake in a script can cause untold damage, even wiping out user files if the system is poorly protected. Furthermore, routine changes should be entered rapidly. This section introduces the special keys and cursor movement commands that enable people to edit files rapidly in **vi**. It then presents the actual commands used to insert, delete, modify, move, and locate text. The section concludes with an examination of **vi** options that enable the system administrator or individual users to customize the editor.

Tip

It will be more valuable to master a subset of the commands that meets your needs than to acquire a half-baked familiarity with all the commands in this chapter.

Special Keys

Like any other program editor or word processor, **vi** uses its own set of special keys to perform useful operations. There are two sets of special keys, one for command mode and another for input mode.

Command Mode

The special keys active in the command mode include ESC, DEL (or CTRL-C), /, ?, and :. These keys are described below:

- ESC   Used to cancel partially formed commands.

- DEL   (The same as CTRL-C on most terminals.) Generates an interrupt, telling the editor to stop what it is doing. Used to abort any command that is executing.

- /   Used to specify a string to be searched for. The slash appears on the last line as a prompt for a search string.

- ?   Used to specify a string to be searched for. The question mark appears on the last line as a prompt for a search string. It is used to search backward in a file instead of forward in the case of the slash (/).

- :   Used to access an **ex** command such as **r** (read) and **w** (write). **ex** is a program editor associated with the **vi** editor.

Input Mode

The special keys active in the text mode include ESC, ENTER, BACKSPACE, CTRL-U, and CTRL-W. These keys are described below:

- ESC   Used to change to command mode.

- ENTER   Used to start a new line.

- BACKSPACE   Backs up the cursor one character on the current line. The last character typed before the BKSP is removed from the input buffer, but remains displayed on the screen.

- CTRL-U   Moves the cursor back to the first character of the insertion and restarts insertion. Some systems use CTRL-X instead.

- CTRL-W   Moves the cursor back to the first character of the last inserted word.

Cursor Movement Commands

A major aspect in editing efficiency is mastery of the cursor movement commands. Many of **vi**'s cursor movement commands can be executed with a variety of different keystrokes, depending on your specific terminal. For example, the cursor control keys such as the RIGHT ARROW key are not available on some older terminals. Over a period of time you will develop your own strategy for moving the cursor rapidly and effortlessly. Table 2-1 lists and briefly describes the major cursor movement commands. Test all of these

	Keystroke	Action	Comments
TABLE 2-1	l or SPACEBAR	Moves right	Count allowed.
Cursor Movement Commands	RIGHT ARROW	Moves right	Cannot move cursor past end of current line.
	h or BACKSPACE	Backspace	Count allowed.
	LEFT ARROW	Moves left	Cannot move cursor past beginning of current line.
	+ or ENTER	Next line	Moves cursor to beginning of next line.
	j or CTRL-N or LF or DOWN ARROW	Next line	Moves cursor to same column in next line.
	k or CTRL-P or UP ARROW	Previous line	Moves cursor to same column in previous line. Count allowed.
	–	Previous line	Moves cursor to beginning of previous line. Count allowed.
	0 or ^	Beginning of line*	
	$	End of line	If count, moves cursor forward count –1 lines.
	G	Goto Line	Moves cursor to beginning of specified line. If no line number is specified, moves cursor to beginning of last line.
	w or W	Word Forward	Moves cursor to beginning of next word.†
	b or B	Back Word	Moves cursor backward to beginning of current word.†
	e or E	End	Moves cursor to end of word.†
	(,)	Sentence	Moves cursor to beginning (or end) of current sentence.
	[,]	Section	Moves cursor to beginning (or end) of current section.
	{ , }	Paragraph	Moves cursor to beginning (or end) of current paragraph.
	%	Match	Moves cursor to matching parenthesis, delimiter bracket, or brace.
	H	Home	Moves cursor to upper-left corner of screen.
	M	Middle Screen	Moves cursor to beginning of screen's middle line.
	L	Lower Screen	Moves cursor to lowest line on screen.

*The 0 always moves the cursor to the first character of the current line. The caret (^) moves to the first character on a line that is not a tab or a space. It is useful for editing files that have a great deal of indentation, such as programs and scripts.

† The lowercase commands w, b, and e consider a word to be a string of alphanumeric characters separated by punctuation or whitespace (i. e. tab, newline, or space). The uppercase commands W, B, and E consider a word to be a string of non-whitespace characters.

commands and note which ones work on your system. Many commands, such as l, provide a *count* parameter indicating the number of repetitions. For example, l7 means move the cursor 7 spaces forward.

Text Insertion Commands

Text insertion commands add text to the editing buffer. The location at which the text is entered depends on the specific command. To exit input mode, press the ESC key. Table 2-2 lists and briefly describes the major text insertion commands.

Text Deletion Commands

Text deletion commands delete text, saving this text in a buffer. A count may be used in specifying the text to be deleted. Deleted text is placed on a stack of buffers numbered 1 to 9. The most recently deleted text is placed in a special delete buffer, called the *unnamed buffer*. Deleted text may be accessed with the **put** command described in the Text Movement section below. Table 2-3 lists and briefly describes the major text deletion commands.

Text Modification Commands

Text modification commands change specified text, in effect deleting the initial version and replacing it with a new modified version. Pay particular attention to the **Undo** (u and U) commands, which can roll back the effect of many different **vi** commands. Table 2-4 lists and describes briefly the major text modification commands.

TABLE 2-2

Text Insertion Commands

User Input	Action	Comments
i *text* ESC	Insert	Places new text before cursor. Press ENTER for a new line.
I *text* ESC	Insert	Places new text at beginning of current line.
a *text* ESC	Append	Places new text after cursor.
A *text* ESC	Insert	Places new text after end of current line.
o *text* ESC	Open New Line	Creates new line below current line.
O *text* ESC	Open New Line	Creates new line above current line.

TABLE 2-3

Text Deletion Commands

User Input	Action	Comments
x	Delete	Deletes character beneath cursor.
x	Character	Deletes count to right.
X	Delete	Deletes character left of cursor.
X	Character	Deletes count to left.
dd	Delete	Deletes whole lines.
D	Delete	Deletes text from cursor to end of current line.
d [cursor movement]	Delete	Deletes object delimited by cursor movement.

Note

The [and] symbols serve to delimit cursor movement. Do not enter them.

Figure 2-4 shows a screen full of a test script that simulates removing a user's account from the system. Because it is not the final version, it uses a test directory containing pseudo users.

The last line command, shown here,

```
:1,$ s/dirjrp/dirpd/g
```

substitutes a directory named **dirpd** for a directory named **dirjrp**. The **g** denotes that the substitution applies to the entire (1,$) (global) editing buffer. Figure 2-5 shows the results of this substitution.

TABLE 2-4

Text Modification Commands

User Input	Action	Comments
u	Undo	Undoes last Insert or Delete command.
U	Undo	Restores current line to state it was in when cursor originally moved to line.
.	Repeat	Repeats last Insert or Delete command that changed contents of editing buffer.
cc [cursor movement] text ESC	Change	Replaces text object defined by cursor movement with specified text.
C text ESC or cc text ESC	Change	Replaces entire lines.
r char	Replace	Overstrikes characters. Stays in command mode.
R text ESC	Replace	Overstrikes to end of current line. Enters input mode.
s text ESC	Substitute	Replaces count characters.
S text ESC	Substitute	Replaces count lines.

FIGURE 2-4

A substitution command

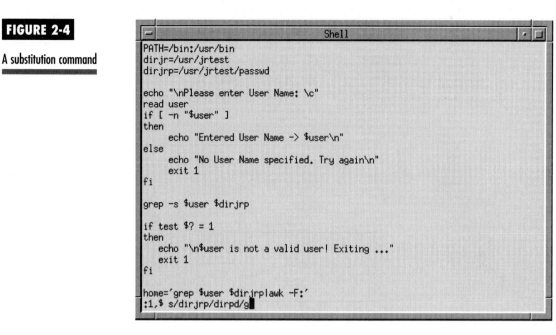

```
PATH=/bin:/usr/bin
dirjr=/usr/jrtest
dirjrp=/usr/jrtest/passwd

echo "\nPlease enter User Name: \c"
read user
if [ -n "$user" ]
then
     echo "Entered User Name -> $user\n"
else
     echo "No User Name specified. Try again\n"
     exit 1
fi

grep -s $user $dirjrp

if test $? = 1
then
   echo "\n$user is not a valid user! Exiting ..."
   exit 1
fi

home='grep $user $dirjrplawk -F:'
:1,$ s/dirjrp/dirpd/g
```

FIGURE 2-5

Results of substitution

```
dirjr=/usr/jrtest
dirpd=/usr/jrtest/passwd

echo "\nPlease enter User Name: \c"
read user
if [ -n "$user" ]
then
     echo "Entered User Name -> $user\n"
else
     echo "No User Name specified. Try again\n"
     exit 1
fi

grep -s $user $dirpd

if test $? = 1
then
   echo "\n$user is not a valid user! Exiting ..."
   exit 1
fi

home='grep $user $dirpdlawk -F:'
```

Text Movement Commands

Text movement commands move text in and out of the named buffers a–z and out of the delete buffers 1–9 and the unnamed buffer. Combine a **delete** command and a **put** command to perform a cut and paste operation, transferring text from one location to another. Combine a **yank** command and a **put** command to perform a copy and paste operation, copying text from one location to another, while retaining the original copy. Table 2-5 lists and briefly describes the major text movement commands.

Search Commands

Search commands traverse the editing buffer either forward or backward looking for a specified pattern. They wrap around the beginning (or the end) of the buffer. Search commands may be repeated, changing search direction upon request. A related command marks text for subsequent reference. Table 2-6 lists and briefly describes the major search commands.

VI COMMAND LINE OPTIONS

Not everyone wants to use **vi** in exactly the same way. For example, in sensitive situations, users may want to encrypt their files to keep them hidden from prying eyes. Individual users or the system administrator can customize their use of **vi** by invoking **vi** options from the command line. Major **vi** command line options are shown below.

-x encryption option   Encrypts the file as it is being written; the file will require an encryption key in order to be read.

-c command   Begins editing by executing the specified editor command (usually a search or positioning command).

-r file   Retrieves the last saved version of the named file. (Used in recovering after an editor or system crash.)

-L   Lists the names of all files saved as a result of an editor or system crash. Files may be recovered with the -r option.

-R   Sets a read-only option so that files can be viewed but not edited.

TABLE 2-5

Text Movement Commands

User Input	Action	Comments
" *text* p	Put	Copies delete buffer to editing buffer after current line.
" *text* P	Put	Copies delete buffer to editing buffer above current line.
" *letter* y [cursor movement]	Yank	Copies delimited text in editing buffer to designated buffer.
" *letter* yy or " *letter* Y	Yank	Copies count lines to designated buffer.

TABLE 2-6

Search Commands

User Input	Action	Comments
/ *pattern* / ENTER	Search	Searches forward for specified pattern.
/ *pattern* ? ENTER	Search	Searches backward for specified pattern.
n	Next String	Repeats last search (in the same direction).
N	Next String	Repeats last search (in the opposite direction).
f *char*	Find Character	Searches forward on current line for specified character.*
F *char*	Find Character	Searches backward on current line for specified character.*
;	Find Character	Repeats last f or F command.
,	Find Character	Reverses direction of last character search.
t *char*	To Character	Moves cursor forward to position just after specified character.*
T *char*	To Character	Moves cursor backward to position just before specified character.
;	To Character	Repeats last character search.
,	To Character	Reverses direction of last character search.
m *letter*	Mark	Marks location in editing buffer.†
' *letter*	To Mark	Moves cursor to beginning of marked line.†
` *letter*	To Mark	Moves cursor to exact location of mark.†

*The f, F, t, and T commands provide the useful ; and , parameters. Type ; to repeat the most recently entered of these commands. Type , to repeat the most recently entered of these commands, reversing the search direction.

†When using mark and the other commands, distinguish carefully among the following: " (two quotes), " (two back quotes), 'x (quote letter), and `x (back quote letter). Do not confuse " (two quotes) with " (double quote).

VI ENVIRONMENT OPTIONS

A number of options can be set to affect the **vi** environment. These can be set with the **:set** command while editing, with the *EXINIT* environment variable, or in the **vi** start-up file, **.exrc**. This file normally sets the user's preferred options so that they do not need to be set manually each time **vi** is invoked.

There are two kinds of environment options: switch options and string options. A *switch option* is either on or off. A switch is turned off by prefixing the word *no* to the name of the switch within a set command. *String options* are strings of characters that are assigned values with the syntax *option=string*. Multiple options may be specified on a line. The switch and string options are listed below:

autoindent, ai (Default: noai)   Can be used to ease the preparation of structured program text. For each line created by an *append, change, insert, open,* or *substitute* operation, **vi** looks at the preceding line to determine and insert an appropriate amount of indentation. To move the cursor back to the preceding tab stop, press CTRL-D. To move the cursor back to the beginning of the line, press 0-CTRL-D.

autowrite, aw (Default: noaw)   Causes modified buffer contents to be automatically written to the current file when you give a *next, rewind, tag,* or *!* command, or a CTRL-^ (switch files) or CTRL-] (tag go to) command.

beautify, bf (Default: nobeautify)   Causes all control characters except *tab, newline,* and *formfeed* to be discarded from the input. A complaint is registered the first time a *backspace* character is discarded. *beautify* does not apply to command input.

directory, dir (Default: dir=/tmp)   Specifies the directory in which **vi** should place the editing buffer file. If the directory does not have write permission, the editor will exit abruptly when it fails to write to the buffer file.

errorbells, eb (Default: noeb)   Causes error messages to be preceded by a sound, usually a beep. If possible, the editor always places the error message in inverse video instead of making noise.

hardtabs, ht (Default: ht=8)   Gives the settings for terminal hardware tabs.

ignorecase, ic (Default: noic)   Maps uppercase characters in the text to lowercase. See **vi** manual for exceptions.

list (Default: nolist)   Causes all characters to be displayed, including *tab* and *newline* characters.

mesg (Default: nomesg)   Causes write permission to the terminal to be turned on while you are in visual mode. The default *nomesg* setting prevents people from writing to your screen with the Unix **write** command and scrambling your screen as you edit.

number, n (Default: nonumber)   Causes all lines to be displayed with their line numbers.

showmatch, sm (Default: nosm)   When a) or } is typed, moves the cursor to the matching (or { for one second (at most) if this matching character is on the screen.

showmode (Default: noshowmode)   Causes the message "input mode" to appear on lower right corner of the screen when insert mode is activated. (This useful option is not available on all Unix implementations.)

slowopen (Default: noslowopen)   Postpones update of the display during insertion of text.

term (Default=value of shell TERM variable)   Indicates the output device terminal type.

terse (Default: noterse)   Shortens error diagnostics for the experienced user.

warn (Default: warn)   Causes a warning to appear if there has been "[No write since last change]" before a shell escape command (!).

Setting vi Options

Figure 2-6 shows all the current **vi** option settings. Toward the top of the screen, the line shown here sets these **vi** options when the user logs on the system, executing a startup file called **.login**. (This code must be typed on a single line in the **.login** file.)

```
setenv EXINIT 'set ai sw=4 report=20 bf sm showmode
               terse nowarn'
```

These options are displayed when the command **:set all** is executed. Setting the **ai** option turns on the **autoindent** parameter, while the **autoprint** parameter is on by default, and the **autowrite** parameter is off by default.

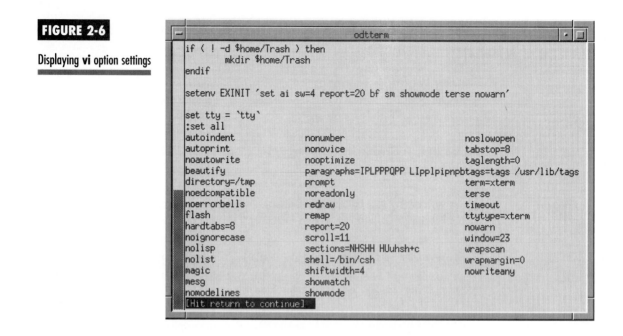

```
─                                odtterm                              ▪ □
if ( ! -d $home/Trash ) then
        mkdir $home/Trash
endif

setenv EXINIT 'set ai sw=4 report=20 bf sm showmode terse nowarn'

set tty = `tty`
:set all
autoindent              nonumber                noslowopen
autoprint               nonovice                tabstop=8
noautowrite             nooptimize              taglength=0
beautify                paragraphs=IPLPPPQPP LIpplpipnpbtags=tags /usr/lib/tags
directory=/tmp          prompt                  term=xterm
noedcompatible          noreadonly              terse
noerrorbells            redraw                  timeout
flash                   remap                   ttytype=xterm
hardtabs=8              report=20               nowarn
noignorecase            scroll=11               window=23
nolisp                  sections=NHSHH HUuhsh+c wrapscan
nolist                  shell=/bin/csh          wrapmargin=0
magic                   shiftwidth=4            nowriteany
mesg                    showmatch
nomodelines             showmode
[Hit return to continue]
```

Figure 2-7 shows the **vi** startup **.exrc** file that sets the user's preferred **vi** options.

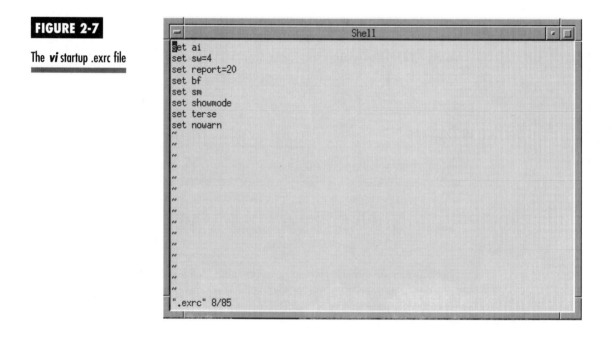

```
─                                 Shell                               ▪ □
set ai
set sw=4
set report=20
set bf
set sm
set showmode
set terse
set nowarn
~
~
~
~
~
~
~
~
~
~
~
~
~
~
~
~
".exrc" 8/85
```

Chapter Summary

In the late 1970s Bill Joy, associated with BSD Unix, created **vi**, which soon became the most widely used Unix editor. This full-screen editor is available on almost every version of Unix. After a relatively short training period, individuals can apply **vi** to create and modify programs and scripts in the Unix environment. Because it was specifically designed for program editing, you should use **vi** (or another editor) instead of a word processor when editing programs and scripts.

Among other operations, **vi** can read and write files, insert and delete text, locate one or more occurrences of specified text within a given document, substitute one character string for another, and move a block of text from one location to another. Because the system administrator has complete access to the Unix system, it is absolutely necessary that he or she master the editor. A seemingly minor mistake in a script can have serious consequences, perhaps necessitating rebuilding the system, which can take several hours or more.

Editor Modes   The editor mode determines how the editor handles the input it receives. Potentially critical errors occur when the user is unaware of the current editor mode. There are two modes in **vi**. Command mode is used for entering commands, such as those that search for a character string or quit the file. Input mode is used for entering text into the file.

Basic vi Operations   Most versions of Unix cannot sense the terminal type automatically. Popular terminal type designations include **ansi**, **vt100**, and **xterm** (for the X Window System environment). You must enter the terminal type information correctly or risk generating illegible output, or perhaps no output at all. The exact code you should enter depends on the shell you are using.

Usually **vi** is invoked with a command such as **vi filename**, where *filename* obeys standard Unix file naming conventions as discussed in Chapter 4. When **vi** is active, the screen shows as much of the file as possible. A single line at the bottom of the screen displays control information. Each blank line at the end of the file has a tilde (~) in the leftmost column.

The simplest way to exit **vi** is by entering the mode command **:q**, which returns you to the shell if the file has not been changed since the last file save. Otherwise either save your changes by writing them to disk, or enter the command **:q!**, which overrides the standard **vi** protection against file loss.

The command **:w** saves the file under its current name. To save the file under a different name, such as **newfile**, enter the command **:w newfile**, which verifies whether a file by that name already exists. The command **:n** switches from one file to another, provided that the changes in the first file have been saved. The command **:n!** switches from one file to another, whether or not the buffer has been written. The command **:r** reads the named file into the buffer. This command can be used to merge several files.

File Editing   Like any other program editor or word processor, **vi** uses its own set of special keys to perform useful operations. The special keys active in the command mode include ESC, DEL (CTRL-C), /, and ?. The special keys active in the text mode include ESC, ENTER, BACKSPACE, CTRL-U, and CTRL-W.

A major aspect of efficient editing is mastery of the cursor movement commands, many of which can be executed with a variety of different keystrokes, depending on your specific terminal. Text insertion commands add text to the editing buffer. The location at which the text is entered depends on the specific command. To exit input mode, press the ESC key. Text deletion commands delete text, saving the text in a buffer. Text may be specified as one or several (count) characters, one or several lines, or a block of text.

Text modification commands change specified text, in effect deleting the initial version and replacing it with a new modified version. The **Undo** (**u** and **U**) commands can roll back the effect of many different **vi** commands. Text movement commands move text in and out of the named buffers a–z and out of the delete buffers 1–9 and the unnamed buffer. These commands may be combined to perform cut-and-paste or copy-and-paste operations. Search commands traverse the editing buffer either forward or backward looking for a specified pattern.

vi Command Line Options   Not everyone wants to use **vi** in exactly the same way. For example, in sensitive situations, users may want to encrypt their files to hide them from prying eyes. Individual users or the system administrator can customize their use of **vi** by invoking **vi** options from the command line.

vi Environment Options   A number of options can be set to affect the **vi** environment. These can be set with the **:set** command while editing, with the *EXINIT* environment variable, or in the **vi** start-up file, **.exrc**. This file normally sets the user's preferred options so that they do not need to be set manually each time **vi** is invoked.

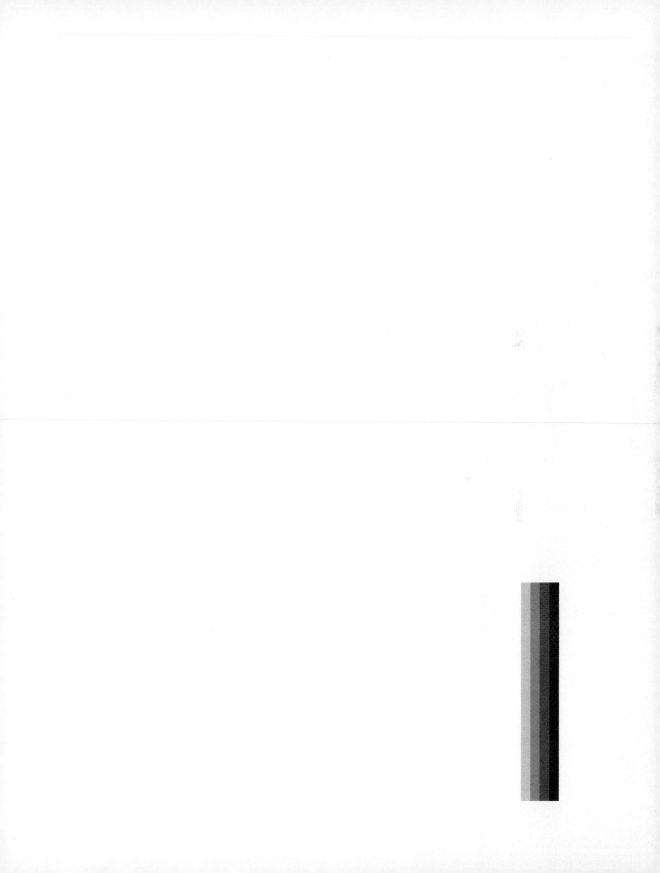

Unix System

- Unix System Commands

- Programming Structures and Commands

Administration Guide

CHAPTER 3

Shell Programming

This chapter introduces shell programming, the process by which system administrators and others create custom programs, known as shell scripts, that automatically execute a series of commands. The chapter presents four categories of Unix commands: file and directory management commands, text processing commands, system status commands, and software maintenance commands.

Control structures provide the mechanism by which commands are linked in order to meet processing needs. For example, the **if** structure provides the execution of alternate commands depending on a given condition. (*If the user in question has a top security rating, let her access such and such a file; if not, print a warning message.*) Other control structures handle a series of **if**s or repeat selected commands. As might be expected, the exact rules for employing control structures vary from one shell programming language to another. Sometimes the changes are minor, and sometimes they are not. The chapter explains other common programming language commands and features, and their relevance to system administrators. It concludes with an examination of important Korn shell and C shell programming language features that are absent from the Bourne shell programming language.

INTRODUCTION

The shell is the Unix user interface. People can interact with the shell via a standard command programming language that executes commands read from a terminal or a file. This chapter will discuss in detail the three most commonly used shell programming languages: the Korn shell, the C shell, and the Bourne shell. It introduces *command history,* which allows previously typed commands to be accessed and repeated either as they are or with modifications, and *aliasing,* which allows commonly used commands to be identified with a name of your own choice. These two features are available with the C shell and the Korn shell.

The Bourne shell was the original standard shell programming language for AT&T UNIX. It still remains a major shell programming language.

The C shell originated with BSD Unix, but is now widely available. It resembles the C programming language, the language in which virtually all of Unix is written.

The Korn shell attempts to combine the best features of the Bourne shell and the C shell. As of Release 4, the Korn shell is the standard System V shell programming language.

Bourne shell programs may be run under the Korn shell without modification. All Bourne shell programs included in this text will run, as they are, under the Korn shell. Of course, Korn shell programs that use features such as aliasing will not run under the Bourne shell. In general, you will have to convert C shell programs to run under other languages, and vice versa.

For the time being, let's focus on the similarities rather than the differences between these shell programming languages. No matter which shell is used, the shell commands may include predefined programs, such as **cp** (which copies files). The commands may also include custom programs, known as scripts. A *script* is a series of commands, similar to a batch file in MS-DOS systems. One of the responsibilities of the system administrator is to develop scripts that enable users to execute complicated tasks with a single command. First let's look at the standard Unix system commands.

UNIX SYSTEM COMMANDS

The Unix system provides a wide variety of commands that address common system needs, both for system developers and system administrators. These commands are the same no matter which shell is used. This section examines major commands in four categories:

- ☑ File and directory management commands, such as **cp** (which copies files).
- ☑ Text processing commands, such as **grep** (which searches a file or files for a given pattern).
- ☑ System status commands, such as **du** (which summarizes disk usage).
- ☑ Software maintenance commands, such as **tar** and **cpio** (which are used to back up and restore files).

Some of the commands, such as **mkdir**, provide *exit codes,* which are numeric values indicating errors or successful completion (e.g., exit code = 0).

Note | The commands presented in this chapter are widely used, but their specific functions and available arguments may differ from one Unix implementation to another.

File and Directory Management Commands

File management commands enable the system administrator to copy, find, rename, move, and erase files. Directory management commands are used to change, remove, list, and rename directories. Access to file and directory management commands is often restricted to the system administrator. The major Unix file and directory management commands are summarized in Table 3-1. These commands are then discussed in detail.

TABLE 3-1

Major Unix File and Directory Management Commands

Command	Description
cd	Changes the working directory
rmdir	Removes directories
rm	Removes files or directories
ls	Displays information about directory contents
find	Locates specified files
mkdir	Makes a directory
mv	Moves or renames files and directories
cp	Copies files

The cd Command

The **cd** command changes the working (default) directory. It has the following syntax:

cd [*directory*]

The specified *directory*, if any, becomes the new working directory; otherwise, the shell parameter *$HOME* is used. The individual who issues this command must have permission to search all directories on the path to the proposed working directory.

The rmdir Command

The **rmdir** command removes directories. It has the following syntax:

rmdir [-p] [-s] *directories*

rmdir removes the entries for one or more subdirectories from a directory, if the individual issuing the command has the right to remove the directory. A directory must be empty before it can be removed.

Note

Refer to Appendix A for available options and other details about the commands listed in this chapter.

The rm Command

The **rm** command removes files or directories. It has the following syntax:

rm [-fri] *files*

rm removes the entries for one or more files from a directory. If an entry being removed is the last link to the file, then the file is destroyed.

The ls Command

The **ls** command gives information about directory contents. It has the following syntax:

ls [-ACFRabcdfgilmnopqrstux] [*names*]

For each directory named, **ls** lists the contents of that directory; for each file named, **ls** repeats its name and any other information requested. By default, the output is sorted alphabetically. When no argument is given, the current directory is listed. When several arguments are given, the arguments are first sorted appropriately; file arguments are processed before directories and their contents.

Figure 3-1 shows the output generated by an **ls** -al command. This listing includes information about files (permissions, owners, groups, size, and date) and directories.

The find Command

The **find** command finds files. It has the following syntax:

find *pathname-list expression*

The **find** command is used to find files matching specified selection criteria, for further processing.

The following command searches for files named *chapter1* in the current directory and all directories below it and sends the pathname of any such files it finds to the standard output:

```
find . -name chapter1 -print
```

FIGURE 3-1

Output generated by an
ls command

```
 ─                                    Shell                              ▲ □
JR: /usr/gproject/jr_adm >> ls -al
total 136
drwxr-xr-x   5 gproject group         912 Oct 13 21:34 .
drwxr--r--   6 gproject group         608 Oct 12 20:33 ..
-rwxr-xr-x   1 gproject other        1945 Oct 05 20:17 addjr
-rwxr-xr-x   1 gproject other         687 Oct 05 20:17 cnjr
-rwxr-xr-x   1 gproject other         709 Oct 05 20:17 fkjr
-rw-r--r--   1 gproject other         780 Sep 17 01:45 frsct
-rwxr-xr-x   1 gproject group       20761 Oct 05 20:18 getchjr
-rw-rw-rw-   1 gproject other          90 Sep 07 19:29 getchjr.c
-rwxr-xr-x   1 gproject other       20833 Oct 05 20:18 getsjr
-rw-rw-rw-   1 gproject other         116 Sep 21 23:50 getsjr.c
-rwxr-xr-x   1 gproject other         865 Oct 12 23:01 jbjr
drwxr-xr-x   2 gproject group         448 Oct 12 20:24 jr_com
drwxr-xr-x   2 gproject other         464 Oct 06 23:37 jr_net
-rw-r--r--   1 gproject group         348 Sep 10 00:22 makefile
-rwxrwxrwx   1 gproject other        3612 Sep 20 16:42 menucshfr
-rwxrwxrwx   1 gproject other         571 Oct 05 20:18 menucshjr
-rw-r--r--   1 gproject other         538 Sep 15 00:56 menujr
-rwxr-xr-x   1 gproject other         836 Oct 05 20:18 rmjr
-rw-r--r--   1 gproject other         334 Sep 17 01:45 screen_menu
-rwxr-xr-x   1 gproject other        1374 Oct 05 20:18 stjr
drwxr-xr-x   2 gproject group         112 Oct 13 21:33 test
JR: /usr/gproject/jr_adm >> ▮
```

The mkdir Command

The **mkdir** command makes (creates) a directory. It has the following syntax:

mkdir [-m *mode*] [-p] *dirnames*

Standard directory entries (the files ., indicating the directory itself, and .., indicating the parent directory) are made automatically. **mkdir** cannot create these entries by name. The command returns exit code 0 if all directories given in the command line are successfully created. Otherwise, it prints a diagnostic and returns a nonzero exit code stored in *errno*.

The mv Command

The **mv** command moves or renames files or directories. It has the following syntax:

mv [-f] *file1 file2*

mv [-f] *directory1 directory2*

mv [-f] *files directory*

mv moves (changes the name of) **file1** to **file2** (or **directory1** to **directory2**). If **file2** already exists, it is removed before **file1** is moved.

The cp Command

The **cp** command copies files. It has the following syntax:

cp *file1 file2*

cp *files directory*

The **cp** command will copy **file1** to **file2**, unless the files are identical. It will also copy one or more specified files to an existing directory.

Text Processing Commands

Text processing commands enable the system administrator to search files for a pattern, to list the differences between two files, and to edit system scripts. The major Unix text processing commands are listed in Table 3-2, and then discussed in detail.

TABLE 3-2

Major Unix Text Processing Commands

Command	Description
grep, egrep, fgrep	Searches a file for a pattern
sed	Invokes the stream editor
awk	Invokes pattern scanning and processing language
diff	Compares two text files
vi	Invokes the vi editor

The grep Commands

The **grep**, **egrep**, and **fgrep** commands search files for specified patterns. These commands have the following syntax:

grep [-bchilnsvy] [-e *expression*] [*files*]

egrep [-bchlnv] [-e *expression*] [*files*]

fgrep [-bclnvxy] [-f *expfile*] [*files*]

These three commands search the input files (or standard input if no files are specified) for lines matching a pattern. Normally, each matching line is copied to the standard output. If more than one file is being searched, the name of the file in which each match occurs is also written to the standard output along with the matching line. The command shown here

```
grep '[Ss]omeone' textfile
```

finds all lines containing the word *someone* in the file **textfile**, whether the initial *s* is uppercase or lowercase.

The following command

```
grep -i someone textfile
```

also finds all lines containing the word *someone* in the file **textfile**, whether the initial *s* is uppercase or lowercase. In addition it finds words such as *sOmeone* and *SOMeoNe*.

Tip

grep is a powerful text processing tool. Learn to use it.

The sed Command

The **sed** command invokes the stream editor, which combines some of the best features of **vi** and **grep**. **sed** is not interactive. It reads a line of input, attempts to make a substitution, and writes a line of output. Because it doesn't use any buffer, it may edit files that are too large for other editors.

The awk Command

The **awk** command is used for pattern processing. It scans one or more input files for lines that match specified patterns. When a match is found, an action is taken, such as printing or performing calculations. While **awk** is not easy to learn, mastering it can save you countless hours of repetitive editing.

The diff Command

The **diff** command compares two text files. It has the following syntax:

diff [-befh] *file1 file2*

diff indicates which lines would have to be changed in two files to bring them into agreement. Except in rare circumstances, **diff** finds the smallest sufficient set of file differences. If **file1** or **file2** is a hyphen (-), the standard input is used. If **file1** or **file2** is a directory, **diff** uses the file in that directory with the same name as the specified file. For example:

```
diff /tmp/dog dog
```

compares the file named **dog** in the **/tmp** directory with the file **dog** in the current directory.

The vi Command

The **vi** command invokes the program editor discussed in detail in Chapter 2.

System Status Commands

System status commands enable the system administrator to obtain the system date and time, to gather statistics on system usage, to display the current environment variables, to terminate a process, and to display information about process status and the working directory, to set or display terminal characteristics, to determine who is using the system, and to send and receive mail. The major Unix system status commands are summarized in Table 3-3. These commands are then discussed in detail.

The *date* Command

The **date** command displays and sets the date. It may have the following syntax (the **date** syntax varies with system implementation):

date [*mmddhhmm*[*yy*]] [+*format*]

If no argument is given, or if the argument begins with +, the current date and time are displayed, as defined by the locale. Otherwise, the current date is set. The first *mm* is the month number; *dd* is the day number in the month; *hh* is the hour number (24-hour system); the second *mm* is the minute number; *yy*, which is optional, is the last 2 digits of the year number. For example:

```
date 10080045
```

sets the date to Oct 8, 12:45 AM, if the local language is set to English. The current year is the default if no year is mentioned. Internally the system operates in GMT. **date** takes care of the conversion to and from local standard and daylight times.

If the argument begins with +, the user controls **date** output. All output fields are of fixed size (zero padded if necessary). Each field descriptor is preceded by a percent sign (%), and will be replaced in the output by its corresponding value.

TABLE 3-3

Major Unix System Status
Commands

Command	Description
date	Displays and sets the date
du	Summarizes disk usage
env	Sets the environment for command execution
kill	Signals or terminates a process
ps	Reports the status of a process
pwd	Prints the name of the working directory
stty	Sets the options for a terminal
who	Lists the names of the people on the system
id	Prints the names and IDs of users and groups
mail	Sends and reads mail

A single percent sign is encoded as %%. All other characters are copied to the output without change. The string is always terminated with a newline character.

The line

```
date '+DATE: %m/%d/%y%nTIME: %H:%M:%S'
```

generates output such as:

```
DATE: 08/01/93
TIME: 14:45:05
```

The du Command

The **du** command summarizes disk usage. It has the following syntax:

du [-afrsu] [*names*]

du gives the number of 512-byte blocks contained in all files and subdirectories for each directory and file specified by the *names* argument. The block count includes the indirect blocks of the file. If *names* is missing, the current directory is used. A file with two or more links is only counted once.

The env Command

The **env** command sets an environment for command execution. It has the following syntax:

env [-] [*name* =*value*] ... [*command* [*args*]]

env obtains the current environment, modifies it according to its arguments, then executes the command with the modified environment. Arguments of the form *name=value* are merged into the inherited environment before the command is executed. The – flag causes the inherited environment to be ignored completely, so that the command is executed with exactly the environment specified by the arguments. If no command is specified, the environment is printed, one *name=value* pair per line.

The kill Command

The **kill** command terminates a process. It has the following syntax:

kill [-*signo*] *processids*

kill sends signal 15 (terminate) to the specified process (or processes). This will normally kill processes that do not catch or ignore the signal. To kill a process you must own it, unless you are the system administrator. If the first argument is a signal number preceded by -, that signal is sent instead of the terminate signal. In particular "kill -9 ..." is a sure kill.

The ps Command

The **ps** command reports the status of a process. It has the following syntax:

ps [*options*]

ps prints certain information about active processes. Entering **ps** without any options calls up information about processes associated with the current terminal. (See Chapter 14 for a list of available options and other information about this command.)

Figure 3-2 shows output of the **ps** command. For example, this figure shows two separate **csh** processes and the **cron** daemon.

Note	The situation can change while ps is running; the picture it gives is only a close approximation of reality. Some data, printed for defunct processes, is liable to be irrelevant.

FIGURE 3-2

Output generated by a **ps** command

```
=                                Shell                              
JR: /usr/gproject/jr_adm >> ps
     UID  PID PPID C    STIME TTY      TIME COMMAND
    root    0    0 0 23:04:24 ?       0:00 sched
    root    1    0 0 23:04:24 ?       0:02 /etc/init
    root    2    0 0 23:04:24 ?       0:01 vhand
    root    3    0 0 23:04:24 ?       0:00 bdflush
    root  293    1 0 21:24:33 01      0:01 -csh
  gprojec  294    1 0 21:24:33 02      0:01 -csh
    root  266    1 0 21:24:25 ?       0:00 strerr
    root  182    1 0 21:24:13 ?       0:00 /etc/logger /dev/error /usr/adm/m
essages /usr/adm/hwconfig
    root  230    1 0 21:24:19 ?       0:00 /etc/cron
    root  259    1 0 21:24:23 ?       0:00 cpd
    root  236    1 0 21:24:20 ?       0:00 /usr/lib/lpsched
    root  261    1 0 21:24:24 ?       0:00 slink
    root  271    1 0 21:24:26 ?       0:00 inetd
    root  295    1 0 21:24:33 03      0:00 /etc/getty tty03 m
    root  273    1 0 21:24:27 ?       0:00 routed
    root  276    1 0 21:24:28 ?       0:02 rwhod
    root  296    1 0 21:24:33 04      0:00 /etc/getty tty04 m
    mmdf  281    1 0 21:24:31 ?       0:00 /usr/mmdf/bin/deliver -b -clocal
    root  297    1 0 21:24:33 05      0:00 /etc/getty tty05 m
    root  298    1 0 21:24:34 06      0:00 /etc/getty tty06 m
--More--
```

The pwd Command

The **pwd** command prints the working directory name. It has the following syntax:

pwd

pwd prints the pathname of the working (current) directory.

The stty Command

The **stty** command sets the options for a terminal. It has the following syntax:

stty [-a] [-g] [*options*]

stty sets terminal I/O options for the current standard input device, and reports selected option settings. **stty -a** reports all option settings. **stty** -g outputs the current terminal settings as a list of twelve hexadecimal numbers separated by colons. This output may be used for restoring settings as required. **stty** -g generates more compact output than **stty** -a.

The following shell script uses **stty** -g to store the current terminal settings, then turns off character echo while reading a line of input. The stored terminal values are then restored.

```
#!/bin/sh
# @(#) -current terminal settings store script
echo "Enter your secret code: \c"
old='stty -g'
stty -echo intr ^a
read code
stty $old
```


The who Command

The **who** command lists information about current system users. It has the following syntax:

who [-uATHldtasqbrp] [*file*]

who can list each user's name, terminal line, login time, and the elapsed time since activity occurred on the line; it also lists the process ID of the command interpreter (shell) for each current user. The *am i* and *am I* options identify the invoking user. With the appropriate options, **who** can list logins, logoffs, reboots, and changes to the system clock, as well as other processes spawned by the init process.

The id Command

The **id** command prints user and group IDs and names. It has the following syntax:

> id

The **id** command displays the user and group IDs (see Chapter 5) and the corresponding names of the invoking process. The **id** command is not available for BSD Unix.

The mail Command

The **mail** command sends and receives mail. It has the following syntax:

> mail [*options*] [*name ...*]

mail provides commands to facilitate saving, deleting, and responding to messages that are read. For sending mail, **mail** allows editing, reviewing, and other modification of a message as it is entered. This command, or a replacement, must be a part of any self-respecting system administrator's toolkit. It is discussed in detail in Chapter 6.

Software Maintenance Commands

Software maintenance commands enable developers to display a list of symbols and a memory dump. They also enable the system administrator to back up and restore files. The major Unix software maintenance commands are summarized in Table 3-4. The **cpio** and **tar** commands are discussed in detail in Chapter 7.

The nm Command

The **nm** command prints name lists of common object files. It has the following syntax:

> nm [-oxhvnefurpVT] *filenames*

The **nm** command displays the symbol table of each common object file, filename. The *filename* argument may be a relocatable or absolute common object file, or it may be an archive of relocatable or absolute common object files.

TABLE 3-4

Major Unix Software
Maintenance Commands

Command	Description
nm	Prints name lists of common object files
od	Displays files in octal format
tar	Archives files
cpio	Copies file archives in and out

The od Command

The **od** command displays files in various formats. It has the following syntax:

od [-bcdox] [*file*] [[+]*offset*[.][b]]

od displays a file in one or more formats, as specified by the first argument. The default first argument is *-o* (octal).

The tar Command

The **tar** command archives files. It has the following syntax:

tar [*key*] [*files*]

tar saves and restores files to and from an archive medium, which is typically a storage device such as floppy disk or tape. Its actions are controlled by the *key* argument, a string of characters containing, at most, one function letter and possibly one or more function modifiers. Other command arguments are files (or directory names) specifying the files to be backed up or restored.

Note

As a system administrator, you will use the tar command extensively, and will be responsible for mastering it in detail. A seemingly "small" error can have disastrous consequences. For example, a critical consideration when creating a tar volume involves the use of absolute or relative pathnames. Chapter 7 and Appendix A discuss the tar command in detail. Keep them as ready references when backing up or restoring files.

The cpio Command

The **cpio** command copies file archives in and out. It has the following syntax:

cpio -o[acBvV] [-C *bufsize*] [[-O *file*] [-K *volumesize*] [-M *message*]]

cpio -i[BcdmrtTuvVfsSb6k] [-C *bufsize*] [[-I *file*]
    [-K *volumesize*] [-M *message*]] [*pattern ...*]

cpio -p[adlmuvV] *directory*

cpio -o (copy out) reads the standard input to obtain a list of pathnames, and copies those files onto the standard output, together with pathnames and status information.

cpio -i (copy in) extracts files from the standard input, which is assumed to be the product of a previous **cpio -o**. Only files with names that match specified patterns are selected.

cpio -p (pass) reads the standard input to obtain a list of pathnames of files that are conditionally created and copied into the destination directory tree, based upon selected options.

Note	As a system administrator, you will use the cpio command extensively, and will be responsible for mastering it in detail. A seemingly "small" error can have disastrous consequences. Chapter 7 and Appendix A discuss the cpio command in detail. Keep them as as ready reference when backing up or restoring files.

PROGRAMMING STRUCTURES AND COMMANDS

A *simple command* is a sequence of nonblank words separated by tabs or spaces. The first word specifies the command to be executed. With some exceptions, the remaining words are passed as command arguments.

A *pipeline* is a sequence of one or more commands separated by a vertical bar. Each command's standard output (except for the last command) is connected by a pipe to the standard input of the next command. Each command runs as a separate process; the shell waits for the last command to terminate. Pipelines reduce the need for intermediate files.

All Unix shell programming languages provide *control structures* that combine individual instructions or commands in order to express common programming needs. For example, you may wish to perform one set of activities under normal circumstances, and another set of activities when an error condition is discovered. This common situation may be expressed with the **if** control structure (discussed below). The exact implementation will differ, but the general principles remain the same. Table 3-5 summarizes several useful programming structures and commands.

	Command	Structure or Description
TABLE 3-5	if	Executes alternate commands depending on a condition. Korn shell and Bourne shell if terminate with fi. C shell if terminates with endif.
Commonly Used Programming Structures and Commands	case	Evaluates a character string and determines which list of commands to execute. Korn shell and Bourne shell case terminate with esac. C shell case uses breaksw and terminates with endsw.
	while	Repeats a series of commands as long as a given condition is TRUE. Also known as a while loop. Korn shell and Bourne shell while use do and terminate with done. C shell while terminates with end.
	for	Korn shell and Bourne shell structure that repeats a series of commands a predetermined number of times. Terminates with done.
	foreach	C shell structure that repeats a series of commands a predetermined number of times. Terminates with end.
	exit	Stops a script and returns to the shell.
	break	Leaves a structure, such as case, but remains in script.
	read	Reads data from standard input. Korn shell and Bourne shell only.
	set	Reads data from standard input. C shell only.
	echo	Displays data on standard output.

Generic if Control Structure

The **if** control structure enables the shell script to do different things in different circumstances depending on a condition (or conditions) that is either TRUE or FALSE. When the condition is TRUE the commands following the condition are executed. In the simplest form of the **if** command, when the condition is FALSE no commands are executed. In a slightly more complex form of the **if** command (**if...then...else**) when the condition is FALSE an alternate set of commands is executed. The exact coding of the **if** command depends on the shell programming language.

The Korn Shell and Bourne Shell if Control Structure

The simplest form of the Korn shell and Bourne shell **if** command is shown here:

if *expression* then
  command list
fi

If the *expression* variable is TRUE, all commands between **then** and **fi** (**if** spelled backwards) are executed. If *expression* is FALSE, commands between **then** and **fi** are skipped. Indentation is often used to show that *command list* "belongs to" the **if...fi** control structure.

Sometimes it is useful to execute one set of commands when *expression* is TRUE and another set of commands when *expression* is FALSE. In this case, use the version of the **if** command shown here:

if *expression* then
  command list1
else
  command list2
fi

If *expression* is TRUE, the commands in *command list1* are executed. If *expression* is FALSE, the commands in *command list2* are executed. Notice the use of indentation, as in the first version of the **if** command.

Consider the following code segment from a script that adds a user to the system:

```
echo "Please enter User Name: \c"
read user
if [-n "$user" ] then
  echo "Entered User Name -> $user\n"
else
  echo "No User Name specified. Try again\n"
  exit 1
fi
```

The first line tells the operator what to do; namely to enter the user name. The second line reads the input and stores it in a variable named *user*. The third line tests the user name. (This test is described in detail in Chapter 5.) If a user name has been entered (expression is TRUE), the script so informs the operator. If no user name has been entered (expression is FALSE), the script so informs the operator and sets the *exit status* variable to 1. A nonzero value of this variable is used to indicate the presence of an error.

The C Shell if Control Structure

The simplest form of the C shell **if** command is shown here:

if *expression* then
  command list
endif

If *expression* is TRUE, all commands between **then** and **endif** are executed. If the *expression* is FALSE, commands between **then** and **endif** are skipped. Indentation is often used to show that the *command list* "belongs to" the **if...endif** control structure.

Sometimes it is useful to execute one set of commands when *expression* is TRUE and another set of commands when *expression* is FALSE. In this case, use the version of the C shell **if** command shown below.

```
if expression then
    command list1
else
    command list2
endif
```

If *expression* is TRUE, the commands in *command list1* are executed. If *expression* is FALSE, the commands in *command list2* are executed. Notice the use of indentation, as in the first version of the **if** command. For an example of this command, see the end of the section entitled "The Korn Shell and Bourne Shell If Control Structure," and change the final line from **fi** to **endif**. (If only all conversions were so simple!)

Generic case Control Structure

The **case** control structure can be thought of as a complex **if** control structure. It evaluates a character string and determines which list of commands to execute. The exact coding of the **case** structure depends on the shell programming language.

The Korn Shell and Bourne Shell case Control Structure

When using either the Korn shell or the Bourne shell, the **case** control structure starts with a **case** statement and ends with the **esac** operator (*case* spelled backwards.) Its syntax is as follows:

```
case word in
    pattern1 )
       command list1
    ;;
    pattern2 )
       command list2
    ;;
esac
```

If the character string *word* matches *pattern1,* the script executes the commands denoted by *command list1.* If the character string *word* matches *pattern2,* the script executes the commands denoted by *command list2.* Note the use of the double semicolon (;;) to terminate each command list. The **esac** operator terminates the **case** control structure for both the Korn shell and the Bourne shell.

The following code is extracted from a script that manages the system date and time. This script is presented in detail in Chapter 15.

```
echo "\nDo you want to set new date/time ? [y/n/q] \c"
read answer
case "$answer" in
  [yY]*)
    echo "Entered yes! Continue ...\n"
    break
    ;;
  [nN]*)
    echo "Entered no updates ... "
    date '+Current Date is: %m/%d/%y%nCurrent Time is:
        %H:%M:%S'
    echo "\nExiting ...\n"
    exit 1
    ;;
  [qQ]*)
    echo "Entered quit! Exiting ...\n"
    exit 0
    ;;
  *)
    echo "Please enter 'y' or 'n'or 'q' \n"
    ;;
esac
```

The first line prompts the terminal operator to enter information, and the second line accepts this input. The first segment of the **case** structure generates output when the terminal operator has entered either **y** or **Y** (for Yes).

The **break** statement causes execution to resume after the **esac** statement marking the end of the **case** structure. If either **n** or **N** is entered (for No), two lines are output and the **exit** variable is set to 1. If either **q** or **Q** is entered (for Quit), a single line is output, and the **exit** variable is set to 0. If none of these patterns is recognized, the system requests that the terminal operator enter an acceptable value. This additional entry is handled by the **while** control structure, discussed later in this chapter.

The C Shell case Control Structure

The C shell **case** control structure starts with a **switch** statement and ends with the **endsw** operator. The syntax of the C shell **case** control structure is shown here:

```
switch (word)
   case pattern1
      command list1
   breaksw
   case pattern2
      command list2
   breaksw
   default:
      command list3
   breaksw
endsw
```

If the character string *word* matches *pattern1,* the script executes the commands denoted by *command list1*. If the character string *word* matches *pattern2* the script executes the commands denoted by *command list2*. If the character string *word* does not match any pattern the commands after **default:** (in this case, *command list3*) are executed. Note the use of the **breaksw** statement to terminate each command list and the **endsw** operator to terminate the C shell **case** structure. Figure 3-3 shows part of a C shell script that uses the **case** structure.

Generic while Control Structure

The **while** control structure, also known as a *while loop,* repeats a series of commands while (as long as) a given condition is TRUE. This control structure is used when the number of repetitions is not known in advance. The exact coding of the **while** structure depends on the shell programming language.

The Korn Shell and Bourne Shell while Control Structure

The Korn shell and Bourne shell **while** control structure repeats a series of instructions an indeterminate number of times. The commands to be repeated are enclosed within **do** and **done** statements. The syntax is shown here:

```
while expression
do
   command list
done
```

```
                                        Shell
        echo "Format floppy under Operating System [uU]nix/[dD]os? \c"
        stty raw
        set ops = `getchjr`
        stty -raw
        echo ""
        echo ""
        switch ($ops)
          case [uU]:
                  set mod = 1
                  set dcase = 0
                  breaksw
          case [dD]:
                  set mod = 0
                  set dcase = 1
                  breaksw
          default:
                  echo "Wrong selection! Please enter 'u' or 'd': \n"
                  set good = 0
                  set devcase = 0
                  breaksw
        endsw
```

First the *expression* is evaluated. If it is TRUE, the command list is executed, and then *expression* is evaluated again. If *expression* is FALSE, control passes to the command following the **done** statement. Sooner or later *expression* must be FALSE; if not, an infinite loop occurs and execution stops, perhaps necessitating rebooting the system. Whenever you write a script using the **while** structure, check it carefully by hand to make sure that the loop terminates.

You saw part of a shell script, for managing the system date and time, that illustrated the **case** control structure as used in the Korn shell and the Bourne shell. The script segment shown in Figure 3-4 now includes a **while** loop to request terminal operator input as long as this input has not been furnished.

This particular loop has no expression that stops loop repetition. Instead the **break** command executes when the terminal operator enters **y** or **Y**, and the **exit** command executes when the terminal operator enters **n**, **N**, **q**, or **Q**. Until the terminal operator enters one of these six characters, the loop repeats.

The C Shell while Control Structure

The C shell **while** control structure repeats a series of instructions an indeterminate number of times. The commands to be repeated are enclosed within **while** and **end** statements. The syntax is shown here:

The Korn shell and Bourne
shell **while** control structure

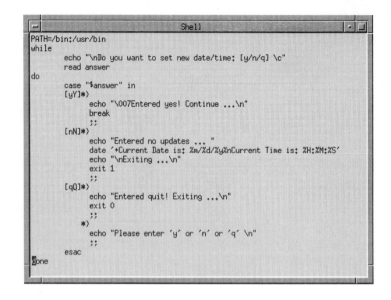

```
PATH=/bin:/usr/bin
while
        echo "\nDo you want to set new date/time: [y/n/q] \c"
        read answer
do
        case "$answer" in
        [yY]*)
                echo "\007Entered yes! Continue ...\n"
                break
                ;;
        [nN]*)
                echo "Entered no updates ... "
                date '+Current Date is: %m/%d/%y%nCurrent Time is: %H:%M:%S'
                echo "\nExiting ...\n"
                exit 1
                ;;
        [qQ]*)
                echo "Entered quit! Exiting ...\n"
                exit 0
                ;;
            *)
                echo "Please enter 'y' or 'n' or 'q' \n"
                ;;
        esac
done
```

```
while expression
      command list
end
```

First the *expression* is evaluated. If it is TRUE, the command list is executed, and then *expression* is evaluated again. If the *expression* is FALSE, control passes to the command following the *end* statement. Sooner or later, *expression* must be FALSE; if not, an infinite loop occurs and execution stops, perhaps necessitating rebooting the system. Whenever you write a script using the **while** control structure, check it carefully by hand to make sure that the loop terminates.

Generic for Control Structure

The control structure that executes one or a series of commands for a predetermined number of repetitions is commonly called the **for** structure. Its exact form depends on the programming shell used.

The Korn Shell and Bourne Shell for Control Structure

The Korn shell and Bourne shell **for** structure is shown next:

```
for name [in word ...]
do
    command list
done
```

When the shell encounters the **for** control structure, it sets the variable *name* to the first value in the word list and executes all commands between **do** and **done**. It then sets the variable *name* to the next value in the word list and executes all commands between **do** and **done**. Execution ends when there are no more words in the list. Figure 3-5 illustrates a shell script that uses the **for** structure to send mail to a series of users. Figure 3-6 illustrates the output of this shell script when the specified user types the **mail** command. The **mail** command is discussed in greater detail in Chapter 6.

The C Shell for Control Structure

The C shell **foreach** control structure is shown here:

```
foreach name (word list)
    command list
end
```

When the C shell encounters the **foreach** control structure, it sets the variable *name* to the first value in the word list and executes all commands between **foreach** and **end**. It then sets the variable *name* to the next value in the word list and executes all commands between **foreach** and **end**. Execution ends when there are no more words in the list.

Additional Programming Commands

Several programming commands have already been used in shell scripts. Sometimes the exact command depends on the programming shell used. These commands include the **exit** command for leaving a script, the **break** or **breaksw** command for leaving a **case** statement, the **read** or **set** command for reading data from the standard input, and the **echo** command for displaying data on the standard output.

The exit Command

The **exit** command stops a script and returns control to the shell. Its syntax is shown here.

```
exit [n]
```

A shell script applying **for** control structure

```
csh script to notify all users to logout for a weekly backup
# the message will be mailed to all users defined in the usr_names
# each user will be notified that there is mail
# by typing mail the user will read the message
# from the System Administrator
# Usage: wbk_mess
set usr_names = (jradin gproject)
foreach user ($usr_names)
    echo "        ==================== \
        Message from \
    System Administrator \
        to $user \
    ==================== \
    Today at 4.30 pm - weekly backup on your computer. \
    Please finish your tasks and you should logout at 4.15 pm. \
    At 4.20 pm - weekly department meeting in the conference \
    room #5. \
    You are invited to a lecture to be held Monday at 10 am \
    in the conference room #2: \
    Subject - Users and System Administrator. \
    Have a nice weekend ...\
    == End of Message ==" | mail $user
end
"wbk_mess" 23/886
```

FIGURE 3-6

Receiving mail

```
Message  1:
From root Wed Oct 14 23:33:41 1992
From: root@jradin.UUCP (Superuser)
X-Mailer: SCO System V Mail (version 3.2)
To: gproject
Date: Wed, 14 Oct 92 23:33:40 EDT
Message-ID:  <9210142333.aa01545@jradin.UUCP>
Status: R

    ====================
        Message from
    System Administrator
        to gproject
    ====================
    Today at 4.30 pm - weekly backup on your computer.
    Please finish your tasks and you should logout at 4.15 pm.
    At 4.20 pm - weekly department meeting in the conference
    room #5.
    You are invited to a lecture to be held Monday at 10 am
    in the conference room #2:
    Subject - Users and System Administrator.
    Have a nice weekend ..
    == End of Message ==
&
```

The exit status is specified by n. If n is omitted, the exit status is that of the last command executed. An end-of-file will also cause the shell to exit.

The break and breaksw Commands

The **break** command is used to leave a Korn shell or Bourne shell **case** control structure without returning to the shell. This command may also be used to leave the **for** structure shell and the **while** loop.

The **breaksw** command is used to leave a C shell **case** control structure without returning to the shell.

The read Command

In the Korn shell and the Bourne shell the **read** command is used to set a variable, or a group of variables, with data entered at the terminal. Normally this data entry is prompted with an **echo** command.

The set Command

In the C shell the **set** command is used to read a line of input. Use **$<** on the right-hand side of the **set** command. Preceed the **set** with **echo**. An example is shown here:

```
echo "Do you want to set the new date/time? [y/n/q]"
set answer = $<
```

See the Input/Output Redirection section for more details.

The echo Command

The **echo** command displays strings to the standard output, which by default is the terminal. It is often used to prompt input, as in the following example:

```
echo "Do you want to set new date/time? [y/n/q] \c"
read answer
```

Additional Shell Programming Features

This section includes useful programming features that are available with the three programming shells. These features include comments, exit status, and input and output redirection. This section also includes a table describing major shell parameters.

Comments

A word beginning with # causes that word and all the following characters up to a newline to be ignored. Liberal use of comments make your shell scripts easier to understand. If you can't find the time to place comments in your scripts, where will you find the time to understand and debug your uncommented scripts?

Exit Status

Errors detected by the shell, such as syntax errors, cause the shell to return a nonzero exit status. If the shell is being used non-interactively, execution of the shell file is abandoned. Otherwise, the shell returns the exit status of the last command executed. (See the **exit** command above.)

Input/Output Redirection

Before a command is executed, its input and output may be redirected by use of a special notation interpreted by the shell. The following notations may appear anywhere in a simple command, or may precede or follow a command. They are not passed on to the invoked command; substitution occurs before the word or digit is used:

- ◪ *<filename* Use the designated *filename* as standard input (file descriptor 0).

- ◪ *>filename* Use the designated *filename* as standard output (file descriptor 1). If the file does not exist, it is created; otherwise, it is truncated to zero length.

- ◪ *>>filename* Use the designated *filename* as standard output. If the file exists, output is appended to it (by first seeking the end-of-file); otherwise, the file is created.

- ◪ *<<[-]word* The shell input is read up to a line that is the same as *word*, or to an end-of-file. The resulting document becomes the standard input. See your manual for more information.

- ◪ *<&digit* The standard input is duplicated from a file descriptor digit.

- ◪ *>&digit* The standard output is duplicated from a file descriptor digit.

◪   <&-   The standard input is closed. If this operator is preceded by a digit, the file descriptor created is that specified by the digit (instead of the default 0 or 1).

◪   >&-   The standard output is closed. If this operator is preceded by a digit, the file descriptor created is that specified by the digit (instead of the default 0 or 1).

For example, ... **2>&1** creates file descriptor 2 that is a duplicate of file descriptor 1. If a command is followed by **&**, the default standard input for the command is **/dev/null**. Otherwise, the environment for the execution of a command contains the file descriptors of the invoking shell, as modified by input/output specifications.

Command History and Aliases

Command history provides the ability to access and modify previously entered commands, rather than having to enter each command from scratch. *Aliasing* provides the ability to refer to a command by several names. These two features are absent from the Bourne shell, but are provided with the C shell and the Korn shell, as discussed below.

C Shell Command History and Aliasing

The C shell provides the opportunity to see the commands executed during a session. This feature is useful when you don't remember exactly what you've done. The C shell maintains the list of commands internally. You can list them, and then either access a desired command by number or search for it. The C shell **alias** command allows you to change command names. Use it to customize your command line environment. The **.cshrc** file often contains the aliases.

Korn Shell Command History and Aliasing

The Korn shell saves the last 128 commands entered in a history list, whose size can be changed if required. This history list is a file that can be edited using **vi** or **grep** with some restrictions. The Korn shell provides sophisticated command history operations that should be mastered by busy system administrators to save time and energy. In addition to user-defined aliases, the Korn shell defines its own aliases to improve system performance. Because user-defined aliases exist only during a given session, you may wish to place **alias** commands in your **ENV** file.

Figure 3-7 illustrates the use of the **history** command. When this command is entered the system generates a numbered list of previous commands. In this case the user wished to access the find command (number 6 in the history buffer) and so entered **!6**. Then the user modified the command several times, without having to type it in full.

FIGURE 3-7

The **history** command

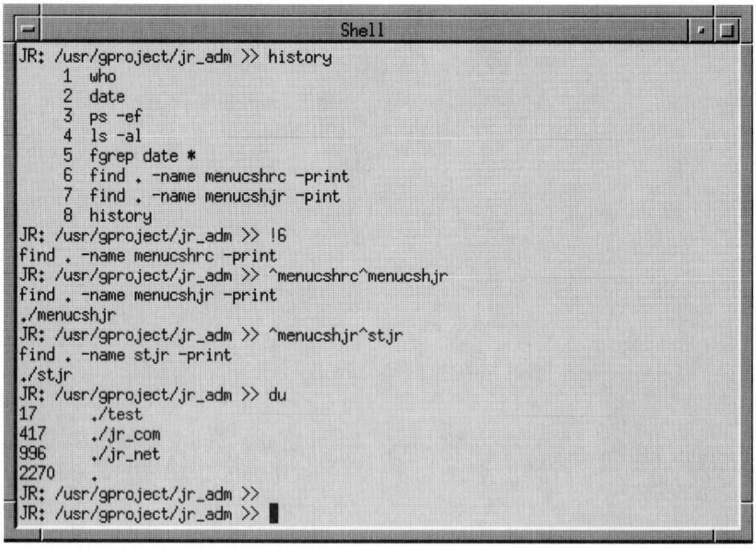

```
┌─┬────────────────────────────── Shell ──────────────────────────┬▲─□┐
│ JR: /usr/gproject/jr_adm >> history                                   │
│        1   who                                                        │
│        2   date                                                       │
│        3   ps -ef                                                     │
│        4   ls -al                                                     │
│        5   fgrep date *                                               │
│        6   find . -name menucshrc -print                              │
│        7   find . -name menucshjr -pint                               │
│        8   history                                                    │
│ JR: /usr/gproject/jr_adm >> !6                                        │
│ find . -name menucshrc -print                                         │
│ JR: /usr/gproject/jr_adm >> ^menucshrc^menucshjr                      │
│ find . -name menucshjr -print                                         │
│ ./menucshjr                                                           │
│ JR: /usr/gproject/jr_adm >> ^menucshjr^stjr                           │
│ find . -name stjr -print                                              │
│ ./stjr                                                                │
│ JR: /usr/gproject/jr_adm >> du                                        │
│ 17      ./test                                                        │
│ 417     ./jr_com                                                      │
│ 996     ./jr_net                                                      │
│ 2270    .                                                             │
│ JR: /usr/gproject/jr_adm >>                                           │
│ JR: /usr/gproject/jr_adm >> █                                         │
└───────────────────────────────────────────────────────────────────┘
```

If the alias for **ls** were "ls -l" the command "ls /usr" would map to "ls -l /usr". Similarly, if the alias for "lookup" were "grep \!^ /etc/passwd" then "lookup bill" would map to "grep bill /etc/passwd".

Chapter Summary

The shell is the Unix user interface. People can address the shell via a standard command programming language that executes commands read from a terminal or a file. The Bourne shell was the original standard shell programming language for AT&T UNIX. The C shell resembles the C programming language, in which virtually all of Unix is written. The Korn shell attempts to combine the best features of the Bourne shell and the C shell. As of Release 4 the Korn shell is the standard System V shell programming language. A script is a series of commands similar to a batch file in MS-DOS systems. One of the duties of the system administrator is to develop scripts that enable users to execute complicated tasks with a single command.

Unix System Commands   The Unix system provides a wide variety of commands that address common system needs, both for systems developers and system administrators. These commands are the same no matter which shell is used. File management commands enable the system administrator to copy, find, rename, move, and erase files. Directory management commands are used to change, remove, list, and rename directories. Text processing commands enable the system administrator to search files for patterns, to list the differences between two files, and to edit system scripts. System status commands enable the system administrator to obtain the system date and time, to gather statistics on systems usage, to display the current environment variables, to terminate a process, to display information about process status and the working directory, to set or display terminal characteristics, to determine who is using the system, and to send and receive mail. Software maintenance commands enable developers to display a list of symbols and a memory dump. They also enable the system administrator to back up and restore files.

File and Directory Management Commands

This chapter considers the following file and directory management commands: **cd**, which changes the working directory, **rmdir**, which removes directories, **rm**, which removes files or directories, **ls**, which gives information about directory contents, **find**, which locates files for further processing, **mv**, which moves or renames files or directories, and **cp**, which copies files.

Text Processing Commands

This chapter considers the following text processing commands: **grep**, **egrep**, and **fgrep**, which search a file for a pattern, **sed**, which combines some of the best features of **vi** and **grep**, **awk**, used for pattern processing, **diff**, which compares two text files, and **vi**, which invokes the program editor discussed in Chapter 2.

System Status Commands

This chapter considers the following system status commands: **date**, which prints and sets the date, **du**, which summarizes disk usage, **env**, which sets the environment for command execution, **kill**, which terminates a process, **ps**, which reports process status, **pwd**, which prints the working directory name, **stty**, which sets the options for a terminal, **who**, which lists who is on the system, and **id**, which prints user and group IDs and names.

Software Maintenance Commands

This chapter considers the following maintenance commands: **nm**, which prints a name list of the common object file, **od**, which displays files in octal format, **tar**, which archives files, and **cpio**, which copies file archives in and out. The latter two software maintenance commands are of particular interest to system administrators.

Programming Structures and Commands   This chapter considers four programming control structures: The **if** control structure is used to execute alternate commands depending on a condition or conditions. The **case** control structure can be thought of as a complex **if** control structure. It evaluates a character string and determines which list of commands to execute. The **while** control structure repeats a series of commands while (as long as) a given condition is TRUE. This control structure is used when the number of repetitions is not known in advance. The **for** control structure executes a command or a series of commands for a predetermined number of repetitions. The Korn shell and Bourne shell control structures have the same syntax, while the syntax of C shell control structures differs somewhat.

The **exit** command stops a script and returns control to the shell. The **break** command is used to leave a Korn shell or Bourne shell **case** statement without returning to the shell. This command may also be used to leave the **for** structure and the **while** loop. The **breaksw** command is used to leave a C shell **case** statement without returning to the shell. In the Korn shell and the Bourne shell, the **read** command is used to set a variable or variables with data entered at the terminal. In the C shell the **set** command is used to read a line of input. The **echo** command displays strings to the standard output, by default the terminal.

Comments and input output redirection are useful programming features available in all the shell programming languages. The C shell and the Korn shell offer two important features absent from the Bourne shell. Command history enables you to access previously typed commands to repeat them, either as they are or with modifications. Aliasing enables you to identify commonly used commands with a name of your own choice.

Unix System

- Unix Files and Directories

- The Kernel File Subsystem

- The Process Control Subsystem

- Client-Server Architecture

Administration Guide

CHAPTER

4

Kernel Overview

Chapter 1 defined the kernel as the part of the
operating system that resides in memory after
the system is booted. The kernel is the core of
the operating system. Most users have no
interest in interfacing with the kernel; they
simply want to get their work done, as painlessly
as possible. In contrast, the system administrator
is responsible for fine-tuning the kernel, making
the necessary adjustments to increase computer
system efficiency in light of the organization's
specific computing needs.

The kernel can be divided into two basic
subsystems: the file subsystem and the process
control subsystem. The *file subsystem* is responsible for accessing and managing user and system
files. The *process control subsystem* is responsible
for the management of processes (executing programs) and the resources that these processes require. Before examining how the kernel handles
these two functions, let's look at Unix files and
directories from a user's point of view.

UNIX FILES AND DIRECTORIES

A word of caution to MS-DOS users: Unix and MS-DOS often employ the same terms, but not necessarily with the same precise meaning. Despite some similarities between Unix and MS-DOS, these two operating systems are quite different. This should come as no surprise; while MS-DOS is a single-user system, Unix is a multi-user system.

Chapter 1 defined a file as a named collection of data stored on a medium such as disk. Unix handles peripheral devices, such as disks and terminals, as if they were files. Unix considers a file to be simply a group of data bytes. However, both users and programs may provide a structure to aid in interpreting the data contained within a file. For example, a special ASCII character known as *newline* marks the end of each line of text. Programs can process this character as if it were a regular character, such as *X* or *a*.

A *directory* is a special file that contains a list of filenames, along with information describing each listed file. Chapter 3 introduced directory management commands; for example, the **mkdir** command, which makes a directory.

File Hierarchy

The relationship between Unix files and directories is known as the *file hierarchy*. Depicted graphically, as in Figure 4-1, this hierarchy resembles an upside-down tree. The root is

FIGURE 4-1

File hierarchy

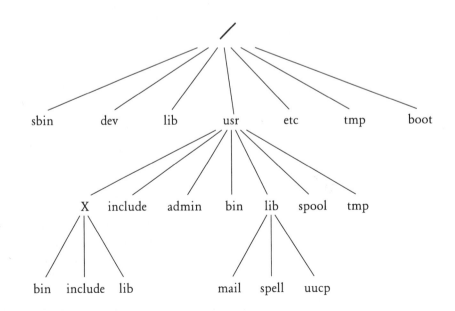

found at the top of the file hierarchy. Subordinate to the root are several directories. Table 4-1 shows some major Unix directories, along with representative subdirectories and files, listed according to the Unix System V Release 4 file hierarchy. If you are working with an older version of Unix System V or with BSD Unix consult your system manual for the correct directory names. (Many systems use **/bin** for executable files and **/usr** for user files.)

The Path

Knowledge of the file hierarchy is often necessary for accessing a given file. The complete filename includes the *path,* which describes the exact location of the file. For example, consider the toy program **aquarium**, which displays moving fish on the background of an X Window System screen. (This system is discussed in detail in Chapter 13.) Assuming that the X Window System has been installed, you can access this program from anywhere within Unix by entering the following line:

TABLE 4-1

Major Unix Directories and
Sample Files

Path	Contents of Directory
/boot	Boot files
/dev	Files associated with hardware devices
/dev/dsk	Disk devices
/etc	Machine-specific administration files
/etc/Backup	List of backup directories
/home	User home directories
/install	Add-on packages (e.g., word processors, etc.)
/lib	Points to /usr/lib, libraries and shared libraries
/sbin	Administrative commands
/shlib	Shared libraries
/tmp	Temporary files
/usr	Files that don't change
/usr/adm	Accounting controls
/usr/admin	Administration menus for add-on packages
/usr/bin	Executable user commands
/usr/lib	Libraries and shared libraries
/usr/X	X Window System support tools
/usr/X/bin	X Window System executable files

```
/usr/X/bin/aquarium
```

This line specifies the complete path. The initial slash (/) accesses the **root** directory. The **usr** accesses the **usr** directory, the directory of files that don't change. The **/X** accesses the X Window System subdirectory. The **/bin** accesses the X Window System executable files. And **aquarium** accesses the executable file (program) of the same name. Depending on where you are in the Unix system, you may be able to use an abbreviated path, saving time and reducing the likelihood of error.

Suppose that you are already working in the **/usr/X/bin** directory and either **/usr/X/bin** or . (the current directory) is in your environment path. Then you need only type

```
aquarium
```

to start viewing the fish.

Unix Naming Conventions

When naming Unix files and directories, it is very important to follow some specific rules, known as *naming conventions*. An installation may supplement Unix's naming conventions with naming conventions of its own. As system administrator, you may be asked to develop and enforce local naming conventions.

The most important Unix naming convention, and the one most likely to cause difficulty, is the distinction between uppercase and lowercase letters. Unlike MS-DOS, which considers **myfile** and **MYFILE** to be the same, Unix considers these two files to be distinct. If you encounter a system message such as: *File not found,* check your spelling and capitalization very carefully.

In Unix V Release 4 and later, some implementations allow filenames with a maximum of 14 characters, whereas others allow a maximum of 256 characters. This character count includes a period (.), if used. The period may designate the *extension,* possibly indicating the file type. The period can also be used as a word separator within the name of a file or directory.

The character slash (/) cannot be used in filenames. Do not start filenames with a minus sign (–). To avoid possible misunderstanding when writing scripts, you should also avoid using the following characters in filenames: ampersand (&), asterisk (*), backslash (\), dollar ($), exclamation point (!), piping symbol (|), and semicolon (:). Also, don't cause yourself unnecessary complications by assigning your own files Unix directory names, such as **usr**. Don't call a file **USR**, for example, even though Unix would consider the names **usr** and **USR** to be completely different.

■■■■■■■■■■■■■■■■■■■■■■■

THE KERNEL FILE SUBSYSTEM

The kernel accesses the physical data stored on magnetic media, such as disks, via the file subsystem. The contents of a given storage unit may be divided into several logical groups known as *file systems*. A file system is composed of a series of data blocks, each of whose size is a multiple of 512 bytes. It contains control information and the file data itself. The rest of this section provides an overview of file systems. (They are discussed in still greater detail in Chapter 8.)

File Subsystem Data Structures

The file subsystem includes three data structures that describe each file and associated user access. These data structures are the file descriptor table, associated with a particular process; the file table, associated with the kernel as a whole; and the inode, unique for each file.

The File Descriptor Table

A user *file descriptor table* is associated with each process, and identifies all open files for that process. Each entry contains an integer, called the *file descriptor,* that identifies the file. File operations such as reading a file, writing a file, determining a file's status, and closing a file make use of the file descriptor.

The File Table

The *file table* indicates the starting address of the next user read or write operation for each file, and initial access rights to the file. When a process creates a new file or opens a presently existing file, the kernel allocates an entry in the file table.

The Inode

A file may have several names, but is described by only a single inode. When a process references a file by name, the kernel accesses the inode after verifying the process' permission. During the chain of events leading to file access, the inode is copied to memory, where it may undergo transformation. Let's examine the inode contents on disk and in memory.

The inode on disk does not change during file processing. It contains the following fields:

- **File owner identifier.** This field identifies both the individual owner and the group owner, several associated users who are given access to the file. Remember, the system administrator may access all files, regardless of who owns them.

- **File type.** Unix provides the following file types: regular, directory, character or block special, and pipes.

- **File access permissions.** With respect to file access permission, Unix considers three categories of users: the owner, the group, and other users. File access permission is discussed in greater detail in Chapters 5 and 12.

- **File access information.** This field includes the time when the file was last modified, when it was last accessed, and when the associated inode was last modified.

- **Number of links.** The number of names that the file has in the directory hierarchy.

- **List of data addresses for the file.** It is unusual that a large file occupy a single contiguous (uninterrupted) area on disk.

- **File size.** The size of the file in bytes.

The inode in memory contains all information of the inode on disk. In addition, it contains the following fields:

- **The status of the inode in memory.** This indicates the following:

  1. whether the inode is locked—in other words, whether the associated file is unavailable for processing.

  2. whether a process is waiting for the inode to become unlocked.

  3. whether the memory-based version of the inode is different from the corresponding disk-based version.

  4. whether steps have been taken to grant the user access to data as a file, rather than only as a series of blocks on disk.

- **A number identifying the file system associated with this file.**

- **The inode number, indicating the inode's relative position on disk.**

- **Pointers to other memory-based inodes.**

- **A count indicating the number of instances of the file that are active.**

Accessing a File

When the file subsystem encounters a file open, read, or write command, it accesses the user file descriptor table, extracts information to find the associated entry in the file table, and then accesses the appropriate inode entry. Finally, the file subsystem extracts inode information that will enable it to access the physical file, provided that the user has the necessary access permission. The relationship between these three data structures is shown in Figure 4-2.

THE PROCESS CONTROL SUBSYSTEM

The kernel manages executing programs, also called processes. This section examines the relationship between user processes and the kernel. It then describes process management functions.

Kernel-User Interaction

A *system call* requests that the kernel carry out operations for the calling process, exchanging data between the kernel and the process. When a process executes a system call, the process changes from user mode to kernel mode. A *user mode* process can access

FIGURE 4-2

File subsystem data structures

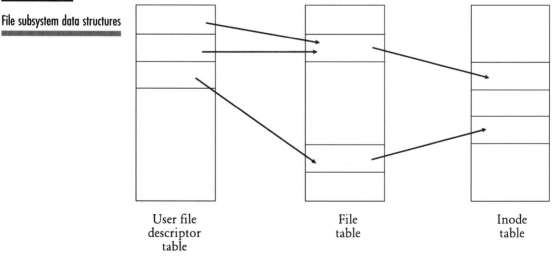

User file   File   Inode
descriptor   table   table
table

only instructions and data associated with that given process. Some instructions are unavailable to user mode processes. A *kernel mode* process may access instructions and data anywhere within the system. Kernel mode processes may execute any and all instructions.

Although the system runs both kernel mode and user mode processes, they are not independent. Kernel mode processes run with a single goal in mind: to support user mode processes, carrying out tasks that user mode processes could not, or should not, do themselves. The next section provides detailed examples of kernel mode processes.

Kernel Mode Management Functions

The kernel mode supports user mode processes. Major kernel mode management functions include controlling process execution, allocating memory for processes, scheduling processes, and managing process resource access.

Controlling Process Execution

The kernel's process control subsystem creates, terminates, coordinates, or suspends processes. It does so by invoking system calls, such as **fork** (which creates a new process called a *child process*), **exit** (which terminates execution of a process), and **wait** (which synchronizes process execution—for example, instructing the system to start process A when process B terminates).

Allocating Memory for Processes

Because a typical Unix system involves numerous processes that attempt to be active at the same time, the kernel is often required to apportion memory. It may have to determine which process or processes should be suspended so that another process can be loaded into memory. System administrators should review statistics on memory usage (for example, **vmstat**) and waiting time, and then fine-tune the kernel to improve performance. System tuning and related subjects are discussed in detail in Chapter 14.

Scheduling Processes

It is pointless to load a process into memory if the process cannot access the *central processing unit* (CPU), which is the part of the computer that actually executes program instructions. If the hardware contains a single CPU, as is usually the case, then only one process can be active at any given time. The kernel must decide when to activate and when to suspend individual processes. This decision, and the resulting activities, must take place efficiently; after all, when a kernel process is active, no user processes are active.

Even if the system administrator did not write the scheduling program, she or he will have to explain to unhappy users why they cannot have instant access to the system at all times.

Managing Resource Access For Processes

This function is quite similar to handling CPU access. After all, the CPU can be considered a resource—certainly a major resource. The kernel is responsible for allocating resources such as disk drives, tape drives, and terminals to processes on demand. It determines when a resource is no longer needed by a given process, and allocates the resource to another process.

CLIENT-SERVER ARCHITECTURE

Processes often need to communicate with one another. One commonly used technique is called a *pipe,* which causes the output of one process to become the input of another process. Other communications methods include sending formatted data, known as *messages,* and sharing memory among processes. This chapter presents an example of an increasingly popular means of interprocess communication: client-server architecture.

Client-server architecture divides the processing of an application between a client, which processes data locally and maintains a user interface, and a server, which handles database and computing-intensive processing. The client typically runs on a relatively small computer, such as a microcomputer or an engineering workstation. The server computer is usually, but not always, more powerful. Under client-server architecture, the client requests a service from the server and then waits for a response. The server listens for the client request, accepts it, and then carries it out.

Figure 4-3 shows one implementation of client-server architecture. This model contains three levels: the device layer, the protocol layer, and the socket layer, all described below.

▰   The *device layer* consists of the kernel routines called device drivers that control the operation of peripheral devices. For example, Ethernet is a widely used communications technology that supplies the physical link between the clients and the server across the network.

▰   The *protocol layer* consists of the communications protocol TCP/IP (Transmission Control Protocol/Internet Protocol). This transfers data to or from the socket layer.

▰   The *socket layer* provides the interface to system calls. Both the client and the server communicate with a *socket,* one end of a communications path. As the

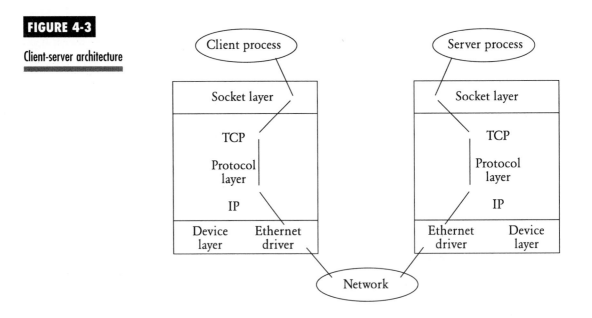

FIGURE 4-3

Client-server architecture

data moves from the socket level to TCP/IP, and then to Ethernet, the system automatically affixes communications control data. While sockets were originally restricted to BSD Unix, they have been added to Unix System V.

The Server Process

The server process, as shown in the following program, creates a stream socket and binds the socket name to the socket descriptor. In the file **/etc/services** you can specify a predefined socket name associated with a number called a port; otherwise, by activating the **getsockname** system call (shown in this program), you will find the port number bound to the socket. The server forks (creates) a child process and waits to communicate with the client through the same port. Then the server invokes the **listen** system call and waits for incoming requests. The **accept** system call sleeps until a connection request from the client is detected through the port; it then returns a new socket descriptor in response to the request. Now you can read and write from the new socket, thus talking to the socket on the client side. (Only a **write** system call is shown in this program.)

```
# include <stdio.h>
# include <signal.h>
# include <sys/types.h>
# include <sys/socket.h>
# include <sys/time.h>
# include <netinet/in.h>
```

```
# include <netdb.h>

struct sockaddr_in sin = { AF_INET };

main(argc, argv)
  int argc;
  char** argv;
{
  char buff[2048];
  int num, nnum, nlen, nsk, sk;

/*
  We establish the end point of a communication link.
*/

  if ((sk = socket(AF_INET, SOCK_STREAM, IPPROTO_TCP)) < 0) {
    perror("socket");
    exit(1);
  }
  printf("Created socket with sk = %d\n", sk);
/*
  We associate a name with the socket descriptor sk.
  The sin points to a structure that specifies a
  communication domain identifier and protocol
  specified in the previous system call, and nlen
  is the length of the sin structure.
*/

  nlen = sizeof(sin);
  if (bind(sk, &sin, nlen) < 0) {
    perror("bind");
    exit(2);
  }
  printf("Bind OK\n");

/*
  We retrieve the port number bound by the
  previous system call.
*/

  if (getsockname(sk, &sin, &nlen) < 0) {
    perror("getsockname");
    exit(3);
  }
```

```
    printf("You should activate: client %u\n\n",
            ntohs(sin.sin_port));

/*
  Now we fork a child. If the child is forked successfully
  then we exit the child process in order not to interfere
  with the communication traffic of the other process.
*/

  if (fork()) {
    printf("Forked child OK Exit now ...\n");
    exit(0);
  }

/*
  We specify the internal queue length to handle up to 5
  incoming messages.
*/

  if (listen(sk, 5) < 0) {
    perror("listen");
    exit(4);
  }
  printf("Listen OK\n");

/*
  Now we can accept requests toward the socket through
  the port number. Accept returns new socket descriptors
  for the incoming requests.
*/

  if ((nsk = accept(sk, &sin, &nlen)) < 0) {
    perror("accept");
    exit(5);
  }
  printf("\nWe established connection on the new
            socket %d\n", nsk);

  num = 0;
  sleep(3);
```

```
/*
   Now we can write to the new socket, thus talking to
   the socket on the client side.
*/

   for (;;) {
     nnum = htonl(num);
     write(nsk, &nnum, 4);
     num++;
   }
}
```

Output from this program is shown in the inner window of Figure 4-4. The server program is activated from the command line. It must be activated before any attempt is made to activate the client program. The server program generates several messages—for example, showing the number of the port to be used when activating a client. This relatively simple program provides no regular mechanism for stopping the client-server application. To stop the application you, the system administrator, must activate the **ps** command discussed in Chapter 3 and find the PID (Process IDentification) of the **server** program (see Figure 3-2). Then you enter **kill**, followed by the PID. This kills the server program, which causes the client program to terminate.

FIGURE 4-4

A client-server example

The Client Process

The client process, as shown in the next program, creates a socket and connects to the remote port given by the server program, and to the remote host name. The remote host name in this program is **localhost** (the same computer); it can be found in the file **/etc/hosts**. In order to use another remote host name on your network (not on the same computer), you should examine the **/etc/hosts** file for the proper name. Now you can read and write, thus communicating with the server side. (Only **read** system call is shown in this program.)

```
# include <stdio.h>
# include <signal.h>
# include <errno.h>
# include <sys/types.h>
# include <sys/socket.h>
# include <sys/time.h>
# include <netinet/in.h>
# include <netdb.h>

extern errno;
struct timeval zero = { 0, 0 };

main(argc, argv)
  int argc;
  char** argv;
{
  struct hostent* ht;
  struct sockaddr_in sin;
  char buf[2048];
  int i, sk;
  int num, nnum, sw;

  if (argc != 2) {
    fprintf(stderr, "Use: %s port#[first run server]\n",
            argv[0]);
    exit(0);
  }

/*
  We establish the end point of a communication link.
*/

  if ((sk = socket(AF_INET, SOCK_STREAM, IPPROTO_TCP)) < 0) {
    perror("socket");
    exit(1);
```

```
  }
  printf("Socket %d created.\n", sk);

/*
  We connect to the server through a remote port and a
  remote host. Here we are using the same computer
  (localhost). The remote port we got from the command line
  by running first the server program.
*/

  if (!(ht = gethostbyname("localhost"))) {
    printf("ERROR: Not valid host name\n");
    exit(2);
  }
  bzero(&sin, sizeof(sin));
  sin.sin_family = AF_INET;
  bcopy(ht->h_addr, &sin.sin_addr, ht->h_length);
  sin.sin_port = htons(atoi(argv[1]));
  if (connect(sk, &sin, sizeof(sin)) < 0) {
    printf("ERROR: Not valid connection\n");
  }
  printf("Connection established\n");

  num = 0;
  sw = 0;

/*
  Now we can read data sent by the server program.
*/

  while (read(sk, &nnum, 4) == 4) {
    nnum = ntohl(nnum);
    if (num != nnum) {
      printf("read %d bytes but expected %d bytes\n",
             nnum, num);
      num = nnum;
    }
    else
      num++;
    if (!(nnum % 50))
    {
      if (nnum == 0)
        fprintf(stderr, "\Client reads data from the
                server...\n\n");
```

```
        else
        {
          if (sw == 0)
            fprintf(stderr, "JR");
          else
            fprintf(stderr, "LR");
          }
        }
        if (!(nnum % 1850))
        {
          if (sw == 0)
            ++sw;
          else
            sw = 0;
            fprintf(stderr, " UAG\n");
        }
      }
    }
```

Output from this program is shown in the outer window of Figure 4-4. The client program is activated from the command line by entering the program name and the port number, which is obtained by running the server program. The client program generates several messages, and then generates repetitive output until the server program is killed.

Chapter Summary

Unix Files and Directories   Unix handles peripheral devices, such as disks and terminals, as if they were files. Unix considers a file to be simply a group of data bytes. A directory is a file that contains a list of filenames and information describing each file. The relationship between Unix files and directories is the file hierarchy, which can be visualized as an upside-down tree. The complete filename includes the path, which describes the exact location of the file in the file system. When naming Unix files and directories, it is important to follow some specific rules, known as naming conventions. The most important Unix naming convention, and the one most likely to cause difficulty with MS-DOS users, is the distinction between uppercase and lowercase letters. In Unix V Release 4 and later, some implementations allow filenames with a maximum of 14 characters, whereas others allow a maximum of 256 characters. The character slash (/) cannot be used in filenames. Do not start a filename with a minus sign (–). It is suggested that you not use the following characters in filenames:

ampersand (&), asterisk (*), backslash (\), dollar ($), exclamation point (!), piping symbol (|), and semicolon (:) to avoid possible misunderstanding when writing scripts.

The Kernel File Subsystem   The kernel accesses the physical data stored on magnetic media such as disk via the file subsystem. The contents of a given storage unit may be divided into several logical groups known as file systems. The file system is composed of a series of data blocks whose size is a multiple of 512 bytes. The file subsystem includes three data structures that describe each file and associated user access. These data structures are the file descriptor table, associated with a particular process; the file table, associated with the kernel as a whole; and the inode, unique for each file. When the file subsystem encounters a file open, read, or write command, it accesses the user file descriptor table, extracts information to find the associated entry in the file table, and then accesses the appropriate inode entry. Finally the file subsystem extracts inode information enabling it to access the physical file, provided, of course, that the user has the necessary access permission.

The Process Control Subsystem   The kernel manages executing programs, also called processes. A system call requests the kernel to carry out operations for the calling process, exchanging data between the kernel and the process. The kernel mode supports user mode processes. Major kernel mode management functions include controlling process execution, allocating memory for processes, scheduling processes, and managing process resource access.

Client-Server Architecture   Processes often need to communicate with one another. Pipes are one method of interprocess communication in which the output of one process becomes the input to another process. Another is client-server architecture that divides processing of an application between a client, which processes data locally and maintains a user interface, and a server, which handles database and computing-intensive processing. The client typically runs on a relatively small computer, such as a microcomputer or an engineering workstation. The server computer is usually, but not always, more powerful. Under the client-server architecture, the client requests a service from the server and then waits for a response. The server listens for the client request, accepts it, and then carries it out.

 The BSD model (now available with Unix System V) is one implementation of the client-server architecture. This model includes three levels: (1) The device layer consisting of the kernel routines, called device drivers, that control the operation of peripheral devices, and Ethernet, a widely used communications technology that supplies the physical link between the clients and server across the network. (2) The protocol layer consisting of the communications protocol, TCP/IP, that transfers data to or from the socket layer. (3) The socket layer providing the interface to system calls.

PART TWO

System Administration

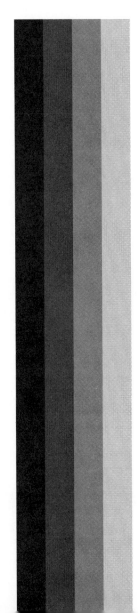

Unix System

- The Superuser
- Passwords and Groups
- Adding and Removing Users
- A nuser Shell Script
- A ruser Shell Script
- A C Language nuser Program
- A C Language Program for Setting a Password
- A C Language ruser Program

Administration Guide

CHAPTER

Users and Accounts

This long chapter is of extreme importance to system administrators. It discusses the theory and practice of adding and removing user accounts, a time-consuming task in most installations. After explaining passwords, password selection, and the contents of the **passwd** file, the chapter provides several methods of automating the processes of creating and removing user accounts. When you have finished reading this chapter, you will have the choice of using shell scripts to manage user accounts yourself, or supplying your assistant with C language programs for managing user accounts, without compromising system security. Be sure that you (and your assistant, if you have one) work through the test procedures before actually creating or removing user accounts.

THE SUPERUSER

Unix is a multi-user operating system. Under normal circumstances, users can access Unix without fear of interference from other users. Normally User A will not have to worry about errors in User B's programs; these errors will be trapped by Unix before they can damage User A's files or programs. If worst comes to worst, User B's program will crash without affecting User A. Of course, things don't always work as they are supposed to, especially if User B is a knowledgeable individual intent on wreaking mischief or doing damage. Security considerations are discussed in Chapter 12.

The system administrator is not bound by the constraints affecting most users. She or her delegate has the right and, in fact, the obligation to intervene when a user is abusing the system. For example, many installations have a clear policy denying user privileges to individuals running programs generating racist or sexist output. The system administrator must be able to kill a runaway process. She or he is also responsible for creating user accounts. To accomplish such tasks requires privileged system access. This access is available via the superuser account.

The *superuser* is a privileged account associated with the user name *root*. The superuser has complete access to all commands and files on a given Unix system. Among the activities restricted to the superuser are the following:

- Modifying the root directory for a process
- Changing file ownership
- Setting the system clock
- Increasing or decreasing resource usage limits
- Creating device files
- Specifying the network interface
- Shutting down the system

The above activities, and many others, require that the system administrator have superuser privileges. These privileges come at a cost. Because superusers are allowed to do anything, their errors can have major consequences. The system will not stop them as it stops mere mortals. Therefore, system administrators should perform routine work with a regular account, not with a superuser account. Furthermore, the password security considerations discussed in the next section must be applied rigorously for the superuser account. A word of warning to system administrators: Don't forget your superuser password, or you may need to reinstall the entire system.

* *
# PASSWORDS AND GROUPS

A *password* is a secret code by which a user identifies himself or herself to the system. While there is no strategy for selecting unbreakable passwords, by following the password selection guidelines in this chapter, you will make it much harder for individuals to obtain unauthorized access to the system. When creating an account, the system administrator enters manually, by shell script or by C language, the fields of the file containing the passwords. For passwords to maintain their security value, they must be changed from time to time. This chapter discusses options available for changing passwords.

Unix recognizes the importance of work groups by providing for groups of users who share files. You will learn how to create and modify such groups. You will also master the commands that assign user ownership, assign group ownership, and assign access permissions.

Password Selection

Passwords form the first line of defense for system security. Unfortunately, users tend to view passwords as an annoyance rather than a means of enhancing their own protection. As system administrator you are responsible for installing passwords, monitoring password usage, and establishing a climate in which users view passwords as an essential component of system security. Unix provides you with tools for these first two objectives; the third relies on your administrative and political skills.

Guidelines for Creating Passwords

The whole idea behind assigning passwords is to block unauthorized individuals from accessing the system. In these days of worldwide computer networks accessed by a single telephone call, every user must realize that protecting his or her own password goes far beyond personal considerations.

There is no magic formula for selecting a password that cannot be broken. Many criminals and pranksters are able to write a program generating thousands of potential passwords. Chapter 12 discusses how to fight against such programs. Carefully chosen passwords will discourage some amateurs and make it harder for professionals to break the system. Users should avoid the following passwords:

◢ A user's name, or the name of anyone in their family or entourage. Anybody who so desires can probably find out your pet's name, for instance, without arousing suspicion.

- All names associated with your company and its products.

- Birthdays, anniversaries, and social security numbers belonging to you, family, friends, or associates.

- The names of famous people or places. The best policy, in fact, is to avoid names altogether.

- English-language words. Many people feel that no words belonging to any human language should be used, although exceptions may be made for extinct languages. Some programs attempting unauthorized access use a dictionary file to generate potential passwords.

- Easily guessed numbers such as 9999 or 9876. Of course, the number on your license plate could easily be guessed.

- Simple modifications of any excluded password.

The question arises what is an acceptable password? Consider the password *69FDjtPo*. This password clearly does not belong to any of the excluded categories mentioned above. It does, however, have several drawbacks. It is hard to remember and hard to type. A user might feel the need to write it down, effectively destroying its worth as a password. The user would be likely to type such a password slowly, enabling interested parties to follow the keystrokes from afar. And finally once a password is published it is useless. In conclusion, a password should be hard to guess but easy to remember and type.

A password example that follows these guidelines is *i4getU2Day*. Of course, now that it is published, you shouldn't use it.

The passwd File and Shadow Password Files

The **passwd** file is a list of users recognized by the system. It is found in the **/etc** directory. Each line in this file is associated with a single user. This file can be edited with any available editor, such as **vi**. It is standard practice to copy the **passwd** file before editing it to enable easy recovery in case of errors.

For extra security, some Unix implementations provide *shadow password files,* used for storing encrypted passwords. Shadow password files are accessible only by the superuser. One possible name is **/etc/shadow**.

/etc/passwd file entries each contain seven fields, separated by colons, as shown in Figure 5-1.

Consider the first and last entries in the file, each shown here:

```
root:*:0:1:Superuser:/:bin/csh
```

and

FIGURE 5-1

An /etc/password file

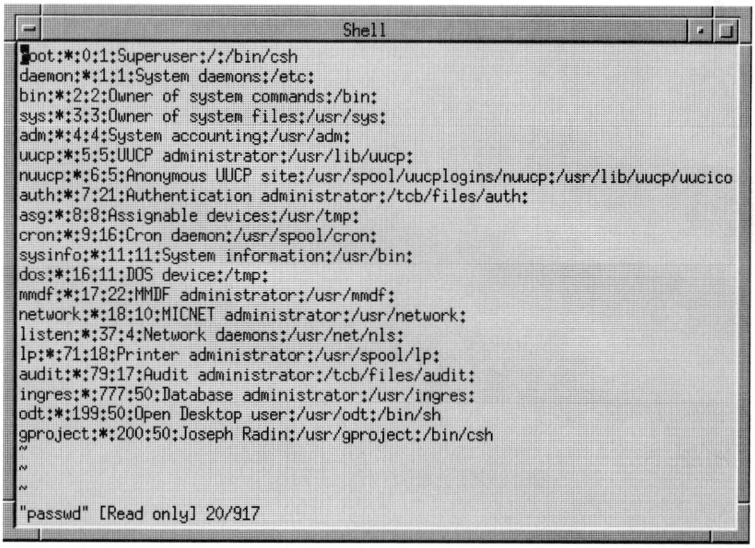

```
-                                    Shell                              ▾ □
root:*:0:1:Superuser:/:/bin/csh
daemon:*:1:1:System daemons:/etc:
bin:*:2:2:Owner of system commands:/bin:
sys:*:3:3:Owner of system files:/usr/sys:
adm:*:4:4:System accounting:/usr/adm:
uucp:*:5:5:UUCP administrator:/usr/lib/uucp:
nuucp:*:6:5:Anonymous UUCP site:/usr/spool/uucplogins/nuucp:/usr/lib/uucp/uucico
auth:*:7:21:Authentication administrator:/tcb/files/auth:
asg:*:8:8:Assignable devices:/usr/tmp:
cron:*:9:16:Cron daemon:/usr/spool/cron:
sysinfo:*:11:11:System information:/usr/bin:
dos:*:16:11:DOS device:/tmp:
mmdf:*:17:22:MMDF administrator:/usr/mmdf:
network:*:18:10:MICNET administrator:/usr/network:
listen:*:37:4:Network daemons:/usr/net/nls:
lp:*:71:18:Printer administrator:/usr/spool/lp:
audit:*:79:17:Audit administrator:/tcb/files/audit:
ingres:*:777:50:Database administrator:/usr/ingres:
odt:*:199:50:Open Desktop user:/usr/odt:/bin/sh
gproject:*:200:50:Joseph Radin:/usr/gproject:/bin/csh
~
~
~
"passwd" [Read only] 20/917
```

```
gproject:*:200:50:Joseph Radin:/usr/gproject:/bin/csh
```

Each entry contains the following fields:

- ◪ Login name
- ◪ Encrypted password
- ◪ UID number
- ◪ Default GID number
- ◪ GCOS field
- ◪ Home directory
- ◪ Login shell

These entries are described in the following sections.

The Login Name

The *login name* is the name by which a user identifies herself or himself to the system. It is also known as the *user name*. Login names must be unique and must not exceed eight characters. Login names are often composed of lowercase letters and numbers. Because the login name is used for communication between users, it should be chosen for convenience, not for security.

Many systems employ the user's first initial and last name as the login name. Of course, the system administrator or her agent must devise a policy to handle the inevitable complications, including long names and potential duplicate names. Particular care must be taken with installations that use several Unix (or other) operating systems. Users will want to log into each computer system with the same login name. This is one instance in which users and system administrators see things the same way. Furthermore, different users should not have the same login name on different systems, or the likelihood of a security breach is increased.

The first entry in Figure 5-1 sets the login name to *root,* the login name of the superuser. The last entry sets the login name to *gproject,* for a user without superuser privileges.

The Encrypted Password

The encrypted password is set using the **passwd** program. For manual user account creation only, the encrypted password field is initially set to *. This value prevents everyone, including the intended user, from accessing the new account before the account creation process is completed. Before terminating the manual account creation process, the system administrator removes the * and then sets the initial password by activating the **passwd** program.

Caution	DO NOT leave the encrypted password field blank!

If the password field is set to the value ,.. (manually or by shell script), Unix will force the new user to enter a password at the initial login.

All entries in Figure 5-1 show an asterisk (*) in the encrypted password field. In this particular Unix implementation, the encrypted password appears on the shadow file for additional security.

The UID Number

The *UID number,* also called *user ID number,* is a unique integer between 0 and 32767. It identifies a login name throughout a network. UIDs lower than 100 are commonly reserved for system usage. Entries in the **/etc/passwd** file are usually maintained in order of the UID number. When an individual leaves the organization, the associated UID number should be retired; this will prevent problems when files are restored.

The first entry in Figure 5-1 sets the UID number to *0,* the UID number of the superuser. The last entry sets the UID number to *200.*

The Default GID Number

The *default GID number,* also called the *default group ID number,* is a unique integer between 0 and 32767. It indicates the collection of users (the *group*) to which the login user belongs, in the absence of an alternative specification.

The first example sets the default GID number to *1*. The second example sets the default group for *gproject* to 50. The **chgrp** command could be used to change the group to another value, such as 20.

The GCOS Field

The *GCOS field* contains personal information for each user. The system administrator defines this field according to system needs, and communicates this information to the user. In the sample situation shown in Figure 5-1, the system administrator requests that the user supply four information items: the full user name, office number, office telephone extension, and home phone. The **finger** program available with most Unix systems can process these fields if they are separated by commas.

In the first example, the GCOS field is *Superuser.* This can be interpreted as follows: The full user name is *Superuser,* and the system administrator has not supplied additional information.

In the second example, the GCOS field is *Joseph Radin.* For security reasons, no other information is included.

The Home Directory

The *home directory* is the directory in which users are placed when they log into the system. In the first example, the home directory is */.* The home directory of the superuser is the root. In the second example the home directory is **/usr/gproject.**

The Login Shell

The *login shell* is the shell initially available to the user. The most common shells are the Bourne shell (**/bin/sh**), the C shell (**/bin/csh**), and the Korn shell (**/bin/ksh**). On most System V implementations, the Korn shell is the default shell.

Both examples from Figure 5-1 set the login shell to **/bin/csh,** the C shell.

Changing Passwords

Sooner or later, individual passwords tend to lose their effectiveness. Perhaps a user has let a colleague access his account, just once. Perhaps a malicious program has finally discovered a user's password by sheer determination. Many organizations require that users change their passwords on a predetermined basis.

The Unix V command **passwd**, whose options appear in Table 5-1, provides an option for setting the minimum and maximum password life, in days, for individual users. For example, the command

```
passwd -n7 -x91 lreiss
```

specifies that user lreiss must change his password after a maximum of 91 days (about three months). Once the password has been changed, the new password must remain in force for a minimum of seven days. It is common practice to send warning messages to users before they are actually required to change their password.

System administrators may expect some resistance from users who are required to change their passwords. Furthermore, some users will make a minimum change in their password; for example, changing *69FDjtPo* to *69FDjtPO* or *69FDjtoP*.

Groups

In Unix, a *group* is a collection of users who share files or other system resources. Groups are an important tool for improving system security. Group membership is defined via two mechanisms: the **passwd** file (the fourth parameter), previously discussed, or the **group** file presented below.

Many Unix V implementations accord the user membership in only one active group at any given time. At login time, the group is set to the user's default group (often noted in the associated **passwd** file entry). The user enters the **newgrp** command to change the active group. The **id** command can be used at any time to determine the user's active group.

TABLE 5-1

The **passwd** Command Aging Options

Option	Purpose
-x	Specifies maximum password lifetime, in days. *-1* provides an unlimited lifetime.
-n	Specifies minimum password lifetime, in days.
-f	Forces user to change password at next login.
-l	Locks account so that user cannot log in.
-s	Lists password data for a single user.
-a	When used with the -s option, lists password data for all users.
-d	Deletes password for user. AVOID THIS OPTION.

BSD Unix allows a user to belong to several groups at once. This enables users to access all files for which they are authorized, without having to issue a special command. The primary group has a special meaning only for accounting purposes.

The group File

The **/etc/group** file lists the system's groups. Each entry has the following syntax (no spaces allowed):

group-name: * : *GID*: *additional-users*

In this command, *group-name* is a unique name that identifies the group, the asterisk (*) is coded to maintain compatibility with older Unix systems, *GID* is the group identification number discussed in the **passwd file** section, and *additional-users* is a list of user names and group names that also belong to the group being identified. It is not necessary to specify those users whose group membership has already been coded in the **/etc/passwd** file. Sample entries appear below:

```
stats:*:10:lreiss,jkeenan,pgodena,root
system:*:20:jradin,rzuric,ttippett,root
```

> **Note** | See your Unix system manual for commands that manipulate the /etc/group file.

Changing Ownership and Permissions

Unix provides several commands that enable the system administrator to change user and group ownership of files, directories, and devices, and to accord access permissions for owners, group owners, and other users. The **chown** command assigns user ownership, the **chgrp** command assigns group ownership, and the **chmod** command assigns access permissions. Correct use of these commands and their corresponding system calls can increase system security and efficiency.

The chown Command

The **chown** command is used to change ownership of a file or a directory. It employs the following syntax:

chown *logname filename*

In this command, *logname* is the login name identifying the user gaining ownership and *filename* is the name of the file or directory whose ownership is changed.

Consider the following **chown** command:

```
chown gproject /user/jrtest/gproject
```

This command assigns ownership of the **/usr/jrtest/gproject** directory to the login name of the user, identified as gproject. C language programs can employ the **chown** system call, whose effect is the same.

The chgrp Command

The **chgrp** command changes the group ownership of files, directories, and devices. It employs the following syntax:

chgrp *groupid filename*

In this command, *groupid* is the group identification number designating the group gaining ownership and *filename* is the name of the file, directory, or device whose group ownership is changed.

The following **chgrp** command:

```
chgrp 10 /usr/jrtest/gproject
```

assigns group ownership of the **/usr/jrtest/gproject** directory to the group whose ID is 10. C language programs can employ the **chgrp** system call whose effect is the same.

The chmod Command

The **chmod** command and the corresponding **chmod** system call use bits to provide three separate file permissions. The permission code 4 (binary 100) accords read permission; the permission code 2 (binary 10) accords write permission, and the permission code 1 (binary 1) accords execute permission. These permissions may be granted separately or together. For example, a permission code of 7 (binary 111) accords read, write, and execute permission (7 equals 4 + 2 + 1). A permission code of 3 (binary 11) accords write and execute permission (3 equals 2 + 1). Finally, a permission code of 0 accords no permission for the designated file.

The **chmod** command sets file protection for three categories of users:

- The owner, perhaps set by the **chown** command or system call
- The group owner, perhaps set by the **chgrp** command or system call
- Others

The following command sets permissions on the file **abc**. It accords the user full (read, write, and execute) permission, accords the group write and read permission, and accords other users no permission.

```
chmod 730 abc
```

The superuser has full permission on all files when using the root password.

Symbolic modes express permissions without the bother of using bits and remembering the order in which permissions are specified (owner, group, and other). The exact syntax may differ from one system to another. The following abbreviations are often used: **r** for read, **w** for write, and **x** for execute, **u** for user or owner, **g** for group, and **o** for other. The **+** is used to add permission, and the **–** is used to remove permission. Consider a few examples:

```
chmod g+r abc
```

accords the group read permission on the **abc** file.

The command

```
chmod u-w abc
```

removes write permission from the owner (user) of the **abc** file.

While the meaning of file read, write, and execute permissions should be clear, the associated directory permissions may require explanation. Don't forget that a directory is a file describing other files.

▰ Directory read permission accords the right to see the filenames in the specified directory. It does not accord the right to issue a **cd** command to access the directory.

▰ Directory write permission accords the right to modify directory contents, even if no write permission is accorded for the individual files in this directory.

Caution | *Grant directory write permission with care.*

▰ Directory execute permission accords the right to access the directory with the **cd** command and to use the directory name within the pathname.

ADDING AND REMOVING USERS

A time-consuming but relatively mundane task for system administrators is adding and removing users from the system. These tasks cannot only be automated by the use of system scripts; with the aid of C language programs, they can also be assigned to assistants without compromising system security.

Adding Users

The system administrator is responsible for adding users to the system. A user is not necessarily an individual; for example, a user might be an automated process, such as a program generating system usage statistics. No matter who (or what) the user is, the general process of adding a user to the system is the same. Some steps, such as determining user identification and entering this data into the **/etc/passwd** file, are mandatory. Other steps, such as copying initialization (startup) files into the user home directory, save time for the user and consequently save time and effort for the system administrator. The steps involved in adding a user to the system are listed here:

- ◪ Specify a login name, a user ID, and a default user group.
- ◪ Enter the above user data into the **/etc/passwd** file.
- ◪ Assign an initial password to this account.
- ◪ Set associated user account parameters, such as password lifetime.
- ◪ Create a user home directory.
- ◪ Set or copy initialization files.
- ◪ Assign ownership of the home directory and initialization files.
- ◪ Create a user **mail** file in the system mail directory.
- ◪ Provide access to other system facilities.
- ◪ Define secondary group memberships.
- ◪ Test the new account.

Prior to creating a new user account, the system administrator should have an up-to-date listing of the **/etc/passwd** and **/etc/group** files. It usually saves time to create several new user accounts at one sitting. This chapter presents shell scripts and C language programs that automate the processes of creating and deleting user accounts, including test versions. Make sure that you understand the creation or deletion process and apply the appropriate test version before actually creating or deleting any user accounts.

Specifying User Identification Data

The system administrator specifies the user name, the user ID, and the default group for each user. The user name is coded according to the installation's rules—for example, with the user's first initial followed by the last name, to a maximum of eight characters. The user ID is generally assigned in sequence. All user identification information should be available before the system administrator starts to access the computer, especially if more than one user is created at a given sitting.

Adding User Identification Data to the passwd File

The system administrator accesses the **passwd** file, manually or by running a shell script to create a new user and enter the data determined in the previous step. The password field must be set to *, either manually or via a shell script that prevents others from accessing the **passwd** file entry. This procedure is mandatory; it protects the password file if the system administrator is called away from the terminal during the account creation process.

Assigning an Initial Password

The system administrator has the option of entering the initial password. Then the user can modify this password, and may be obliged to change it on a regular basis.

Setting Associated User Account Parameters

The system administrator might set the password aging parameters according to the installation policy. Additional information entered at this step might allocate resources such as memory, disk space, and permission to use magnetic tape.

Creating a User Home Directory

The **mkdir** command creates a user home directory. This home directory must be the same as the one specified in the **/etc/passwd** file. On some systems, the home directory is located within a separate file system.

Setting or Copying Initialization Files

The system administrator is responsible for creating standard initialization files for users, and for storing these files in the appropriate user directory. Sometimes the system administrator will set the files; on other occasions she might copy them from default locations, which might vary from one Unix implementation to another.

The appropriate initialization files are copied into the user's home directory. For a user running the Bourne shell or the Korn shell, the initialization file is **.profile**. For a user running the C shell, the initialization files are **.login** and **.cshrc**. The shell scripts presented in the following section show sample contents of initialization files.

Assigning Home Directory and File Ownership

This directory and any files belonging to this directory must be assigned to the specified user. Recall that the **chown** command changes the file and directory ownership. Recall that the **chgrp** command changes group ownership.

Creating a User Mail File

The system administrator creates a user mail file in the system mail directory. Mail is discussed in detail in Chapter 6.

Providing Access to Other System Facilities

This step may include assigning access to the print queue. (See Chapter 10 for more details on printing.)

Defining Secondary Group Memberships

The system administrator can edit the **/etc/group** file or manipulate it with commands such as **groupadd** to add secondary group memberships for the given user.

Testing the Account Creation Process

The system administrator must test the account creation process before releasing it. Failure to test this process is an invitation to serious trouble, perhaps affecting the security of the entire system. The first **Nuser** shell script presents one testing strategy.

Removing Users

In theory, removing users from the system is much simpler than adding users to the system. The key point to remember is to back up the users' data before removing them. The backup process is discussed in detail in Chapter 7.

Always test the procedure for removing users before applying it to real users. This chapter includes a test shell script for removing users, along with a shell script and a C language program for removing a live user.

A nuser TEST SHELL SCRIPT

The Bourne shell script presented in this section is used to test the installation of a new pseudo user account on your system. To practice this script, specify a pseudo user name and ID, and the user's required shell. The script creates a test directory where you can check the script. Next, the test script creates a mail subdirectory within the test directory, to verify the mail usage. Then you need to specify the user's first and last name. This test script checks to see that the individual who runs it does not have superuser (system administrator) access permission. If she does, the script generates error messages and terminates.

After accepting information about the new pseudo user, the script updates the **passwd** file in the test directory by creating an entry for her. It creates the new pseudo user's home directory, and sets the proper group and ownership. Then the script changes the default directory to the newly created home directory. The script installs the appropriate startup files (.**login**, .**profile**, and .**cshrc**) and the terminating file (.**logout**), enabling the pseudo user to access either the Korn shell or the C shell. The next step is assigning the proper group and ownership for the startup and terminating files. The script also changes the mod (write and read permissions) of the newly created user directory. Finally, the script displays a message saying that the new pseudo user has been added to the system.

After successfully testing this script several times, you can install the final version, which will add new users to your actual system. The first line automatically invokes the Bourne shell command interpreter, even if you are using the C shell. Replace this line with #!/bin/ksh for Korn shell scripts, and with #!/bin/csh for C shell scripts.

The second line provides program identification displays by executing **what** (see Appendix A) followed by the script name.

```
#!/bin/sh
#@ (#) adding new pseudo user test script
```

The following code prompts the system administrator to enter a pseudo user name. The script either displays a message to confirm successful entry, or displays an error message and terminates. The first line sets the current user name. If your system does not provide **whoami**, jump to the beginning of Chapter 15 for a C language version.

```
log_name = 'whoami'
echo "\nPlease enter Pseudo User Name: \c"
read user
```

```
if [ -n "$user" ]
then
  echo "Entered Pseudo User Name -> $user\n"
else
  echo "No Pseudo User Name specified. Try again\n"
  exit 1
fi
```

The following code prompts the system administrator to enter a pseudo user ID. The script displays a message to confirm successful entry or sets the pseudo user ID to the default value.

```
echo "Please enter Pseudo User ID: \c"
read uid
if [ -n "$uid" ]
then
  echo "Entered Pseudo User ID -> $uid\n"
else
  echo "No Pseudo User ID specified.
        Using default user id -> 999\n"
  uid=999
fi
```

The following code prompts the system administrator to enter a pseudo group ID. The script displays a message to confirm successful entry or sets the pseudo group ID to the default value.

```
echo "Please enter Pseudo Group ID: \c"
read gid
if [ -n "$gid" ]
then
  echo "Entered Pseudo Group ID -> $gid\n"
else
  echo "No Pseudo Group ID specified.
        Using default group id -> 50\n"
  gid=50
fi
```

The following code prompts the system administrator to enter the shell programming language (Korn or C shell). Appropriate messages are then displayed. (The default language is the Korn shell.)

```
echo "Please enter shell to be used[ksh(Korn shell)
      or csh(C shell)]: \c"
read ush
```

```
if [ -n "$ush" ]
then
  echo "Entered Shell -> $ush\n"
else
  echo "No Shell specified. Using default Korn shell\n"
  ush=ksh
fi
```

The following eight lines are used to test the script. First the script creates the **jrtest** directory for testing purposes. The user directory will be a subdirectory under this test directory. The first time this script executes, it creates a test directory. Subsequent executions notify the system administrator that the test directory exists. Once you have verified this script, you can remove these lines.

```
dirjr=/usr/jrtest
if [ -s $dirjr ]
then
  echo "Directory $dirjr exists\n"
else
  echo "Directory $dirjr not exist! Making ...\n"
  mkdir $dirjr
fi
```

The following eight lines are also used to test the script. First the script creates the **jrtest/mail** directory for testing purposes. The user directory to be created is a subdirectory under this mail directory. The first time this script executes, it creates a test directory. Subsequent executions notify the system administrator that the test directory exists. Once you have verified this script, you can remove these lines.

```
dirjrm=/usr/jrtest/mail
if [ -s $dirjrm ]
then
  echo "Directory $dirjrm exists\n"
else
  echo "Directory $dirjrm not exist! Making ...\n"
  mkdir $dirjrm
fi
```

The following code prompts the system administrator to enter the user's first and last names.

```
echo "Please enter user's first and last name: \c"
read comment
```

The following code ensures that the individual executing this script does not have superuser permission. Superuser permission terminates the script.

```
if [ $log_name != "root"]
then
  echo "\nAdding Pseudo User $user ...\n"
```

The following code updates the **passwd** file in the test directory by creating an entry for the new user.

```
echo "$user:*:$uid:gid:$comment:
      $dirjr/$user:/bin/$ush" >> $dirjr/passwd
```

The following code creates a subdirectory for the new user, subordinate to the test directory.

```
mkdir $dirjr/$user
```

The following code is a comment, not a functioning command. It is not possible to assign directory ownership to a pseudo user. However, you can remove the comment symbol and examine the ensuing error message.

```
#  chown $user $dirjr/$user
```

The following code prompts the system administrator to enter a real user name for the system employed. The script either displays a message to confirm successful entry, or sets the real user name to a default value.

```
echo "\nPlease enter Real User Name: \c"
read realuser
if [ -n "$realuser" ]
then
  echo "Entered Real User Name -> $realuser\n"
else
  echo "No Real User Name specified.
        Using default user name -> root\n"
  realuser=log_name
fi
```

The following code assigns directory ownership to a real user who is not a new user within the system. This avoids the error message associated with the attempt to assign directory ownership to a pseudo user.

```
chown $realuser $dirjr/$realuser
```

The following code sets the group ID of the user directory under the test directory.

```
chgrp $gid $dirjr/$user
```

The following code sets the default directory to be the user directory under the test directory.

```
cd $dirjr/$user

cat > tempo << EOF
#!/bin/sh
```

The following code creates the **.profile** startup file in the user directory under the test directory.

```
  cat > .profile <<'End of .profile'
  :
#  start of profile
  SHELL=/bin/sh
  HOME=$dirjr/$user
  PATH=/bin:/usr/bin:/usr/hosts:/usr/local:/etc
  export PATH SHELL HOME
  date
#  end of profile
End of .profile
```

The following code creates the **.login** startup file in the user directory under the test directory.

```
  cat > .login <<'End of .login'
#  start of login
  stty dec
  umask 0
  set ignoreeof mail=(0 $dirjrm/$user)
  tset -s -Q -m 'unknown:?wy75' > /tmp/tset\$\$
  source /tmp/tset\$\$
  alias cmdx chmod +x
  set path=(. /bin /usr/bin /usr/hosts /usr/local /etc)
  set prompt="'uname -n' \\!% "
  set history=150
  date
#  end of login
End of .login
```

The following code creates the **.cshrc** startup file in the user directory under the test directory.

```
cat > .cshrc <<'End of .cshrc'
#  start of cshrc
set prompt="CSH: 'uname -n' \\!% "
set path=(. /bin /usr/bin /usr/hosts /usr/local /etc)
set history=150
alias h history
#  end of cshrc
End of .cshrc
```

The following code creates the **.logout** terminating file in the user directory under the test directory.

```
cat >.logout <<'End of .logout'
#  start of logout
clear
#  end of logout
EOF

sh tempo
rm tempo
touch $dirjrm/$user
```

The following code sets read and write permissions for the user file under the test mail directory.

```
chmod 660 $dirjrm/$user
```

The following code sets the ownership of the newly created startup and terminating files and the mail file under the test mail directory. The **chown** command in the following code requires the real user name.

```
chown $realuser .profile .login .cshrc .logout
chown $realuser $dirjrm/$user
```

The following code sets the group ID of the newly created startup and terminating files.

```
chgrp $gid .profile .login .cshrc .logout
```

The following code sets the group ID to the value *mail* for the newly created mail file under the test mail directory.

```
chgrp mail $dirjrm/$user
```

The following code is a comment, not a functioning command. It is not possible to assign a password to a pseudo user. However, you can remove the comment symbol and examine the ensuing error message.

```
#   passwd $user
```

The following code informs the superuser that the new user has been added to the system.

```
echo "\nAdded $user!\n"
else
  echo "Cannot execute - not a root user!\n"
fi
```

FINAL VERSION OF THE nuser SHELL SCRIPT

This final Bourne shell script version installs a new user account in your system. This version should be used only after you have verified the test version and made any necessary changes.

```
#!/bin/sh
# @(#) adding new user script = final version
log_name = 'whoami'

echo "\nPlease enter User Name: \c"
read user
if [ -n "$user" ]
then
  echo "Entered User Name -> $user\n"
else
  echo "No User Name specified. Try again\n"
  exit 1
fi
echo "Please enter User ID: \c"
read uid
if [ -n "$uid" ]
then
  echo "Entered User ID -> $uid\n"
else
  echo "No User ID specified.
```

```
             Using default user id -> 999\n"
    uid=999
fi
echo "Please enter Group ID: \c"
read gid
if [ -n "$gid" ]
then
  echo "Entered Group ID -> $gid\n"
else
  echo "No Group ID specified.
          Using default group id -> 50\n"
  gid=50
fi
echo "Please enter shell to be used
       [ksh(Korn shell) or csh(C shell)]: \c"
read ush
if [ -n "$ush" ]
then
  echo "Entered Shell -> $ush\n"
else
  echo "No Shell specified.
          Using default Korn shell\n"
  ush=ksh
fi
dir=/usr
dirm=/usr/spool/mail
echo "Please enter user's first and last name: \c"
read comment
if[ $log_name = "root" ]
then
  echo "\nAdding $user ...\n"
# The following echo command has been set on two lines
# because of typesetting constraints. The actual passwd file
# entry occurs on a single line.
  echo "$user:*:$uid:$gid:$comment:
          $dir/$user:/bin/$ush" >> /etc/passwd
  mkdir $dir/$user
  chown $user $dir/$user
  chgrp $gid $dir/$user
  cd $dir/$user

# Most systems include scripts that will be copied to
# this directory, for example, you might enter the following
# commands:
```

```
# cp /etc/profile .profile
# cp /etc/cshrc .cshrc
# This would replace the following lines:

  cat > tempo << EOF
  !/bin/ksh
  cat > .profile <<'End of .profile'
  :
#  start of profile
  SHELL=/bin/ksh
  HOME=$dir/$user
  PATH=/bin:/usr/bin:/usr/hosts:/usr/local:/etc
#  eval 'tset -m ansi:ansi -m :\?ansi -e -s -Q'
  export TERM PATH SHELL HOME
  date
#  end of profile
  End of .profile
  cat > .login <<'End of .login'
#  start of login
  stty dec
  umask 0
  set ignoreeof mail=(0 $dirm/$user)
#  tset -s -Q -m 'unknown:?wy75' > /tmp/tset\$\$
  source /tmp/tset\$\$
  alias cmdx chmod +x
  set path=(/bin /usr/bin /usr/hosts /usr/local /etc)
  set prompt="'uname -n' \\!% "
  set history=150
  date
#  end of login
  End of .login
  cat > .cshrc <<'End of .cshrc'
#  start of cshrc
  set prompt="'uname -n' \\!% "
  set path=(/bin /usr/bin /usr/hosts /usr/local /etc)
  set history=150
  alias h history
# end of cshrc
  End of .cshrc
  cat >.logout <<'End of .logout'
#  start of logout
  clear
#  end of logout
  EOF
```

```
    sh tempo
    rm tempo

# The remaining lines in this script are not replaced by
# the copied scripts but must be entered

    touch $dirm/$user
    chmod 622 $dirm/$user
    chown $user .profile .login .cshrc .logout $dirm/$user
    chgrp $gid .profile .login .cshrc .logout
    chgrp mail $dirm/$user
    passwd $user
    echo "\nAdded $user!\n"
else
    echo "Cannot execute - not a root user!\n"
    echo "Check your permissions!\n"
fi
```

Note

You may choose to assign a trusted assistant responsibility for adding new users to the system. If so, you can change the user name root in the appropriate if statement to the assistant's user name, and set the correct permissions.

A ruser TEST SHELL SCRIPT

This Bourne shell script is used to test the removal of a pseudo user account from your system. To test the script itself, specify a pseudo user name to be removed. This test script checks to see that the individual attempting to run it does not have superuser access permission. If she does, the script generates an error message and terminates.

After verifying that the designated user has an account in the test directory, this script removes the user name from the **passwd** file. Next, it removes all user files in the test directory. It also removes the mail file in the mail subdirectory under the test directory, and then removes the mail subdirectory itself. Then it removes the user home directory.

The script removes all startup files (**.login**, **.profile**, and **.cshrc**) and the terminating file (**.logout**). Finally the test script displays a message saying that the pseudo user account has been removed. After successfully testing this script you can install its final version, together with the final version of the **addjr** script that adds new users to the system.

```
#!/bin/sh
# @(#) removing pseudo user test script
log_name = 'whoami'
```

This script is tested in the **jrtest** directory; the **passwd** file is placed in the test directory.

```
dirjr=/usr/jrtest
dirjrp=/usr/jrtest/passwd
```

The following code prompts the system administrator to enter a pseudo user name. The script either displays a message to confirm successful entry, or displays an error message and terminates.

```
echo "\nPlease enter Pseudo User Name: \c"
read user
if [ -n "$user" ]
then
  echo "Entered Pseudo User Name -> $user\n"
else
  echo "No Pseudo User Name specified. Try again\n"
  exit 1
fi
grep -s $user $dirjrp
if test $? = 1
then
  echo "\n$user is not a valid user! Exiting ..."
  exit 1
fi
home='grep $user $dirjrp|awk -F:'
```

The following code ensures that the individual who executes this script does not have superuser access permission. Superuser permission terminates the script.

```
if[ $log_name! = "root" ]
then
  echo "\nRemoving $user ...\n"
```

The following code updates the **passwd** file in the test directory by removing the entry for the user. The old **passwd** file is kept as a backup.

```
cp $dirjrp $dirjr/passwd.old
sed '/^'$user':/d' $dirjrp >/tmp/rm$$
mv /tmp/rm$$ $dirjrp
```

The following code recursively removes all files from the user directory under the test directory.

```
rm -rf $home
```

The following code removes the user mail file from the mail directory under the test directory.

```
rm -f $dirjr/mail/$user
```

The following code removes the mail directory under the test directory.

```
rmdir $dirjr/mail
```

The following code removes all startup and terminating files from the user directory under the test directory.

```
rm -f $dirjr/$user/.profile
rm -f $dirjr/$user/.login
rm -f $dirjr/$user/.cshrc
rm -f $dirjr/$user/.logout
```

The following code removes the user directory under the test directory.

```
rmdir $dirjr/$user
```

The following code informs the superuser who activated this script that the user has been removed from the system.

```
  echo "\n$user removed!\n"
else
  echo "Cannot execute - not a root user!\n"
  echo "Rerun as a regular user!\n"
esac
```

FINAL VERSION OF THE ruser SHELL SCRIPT

This final Bourne shell script version removes a user account from your system. This version should be used only after you have verified the test version and made any necessary changes.

```
#!/bin/sh
# @(#)removing user script = Final version
log_name = 'whoami'
dir=/usr
dirm=/usr/spool/mail
dirp=/etc/passwd
echo "\nPlease enter User Name: \c"
```

```
read user
if [ -n "$user" ]
then
  echo "Entered User Name -> $user\n"
else
  echo "No User Name specified. Try again\n"
  exit 1
fi

grep -s $user $dirp

if test $? = 1
then
  echo "\n$user is not a valid user! Exiting ..."
  exit 1
fi
home='grep $user $dirp|awk -F:'
if [ $log_name = "root" ]
then
  echo "\nRemoving $user ...\n"
  cp $dirp /tmp/passwd.old
  sed '/^'$user':/d' $dirp >/tmp/rm$$
  mv /tmp/rm$$ $dirp
  rm -rf $home
  rm -f $dirm/$user
  rm -f $dir/$user/.profile
  rm -f $dir/$user/.login
  rm -f $dir/$user/.cshrc
  rm -f $dir/$user/.logout
  rm -f $dir/$user/.exrc
  rm -f $dir/$user/.newsrc
  rmdir $dir/$user
  echo "\n$user removed!\n"
else
  echo "Cannot execute - not a root user!\n"
  echo "Check your permissions!\n"
esac
```

Note

You may choose to assign a trusted assistant responsibility for removing users from the system. If so, you can change the user name root in the appropriate if statement to the assistant's user name, and set the correct permissions.

A C LANGUAGE nuser PROGRAM

Several problems can occur when you use a shell script to add users. The script can be executed only by someone with the superuser permission. In busy centers, this restriction can lead to a dilemma. Either the already overworked system administrator must personally run the scripts for adding and removing users, or the system administrator must furnish a deputy with the superuser password so that the deputy can run the scripts. The first solution is often unacceptable because it is inefficient. The second solution is unacceptable for security reasons.

This dilemma can be resolved by using a C language program, such as the one presented in this section. The C language program requires a password, but it does not require the root password. The system administrator can issue his or her assistant a password for maintenance of users' accounts, a time-consuming but not particularly sophisticated activity. Furthermore, the assistant need not have access to the C language program (source) code; he or she can simply run the binary file. This flexibility provides an additional level of security, because the binary file is composed of 0s and 1s, and is thus illegible. Consequently, tampering is rendered virtually impossible.

In order for a trusted assistant to run the following program, the system administrator must edit the **/etc/group** file, adding to the root the assistant's login name, and must then issue the following commands:

```
chmod u+s addjrc
chmod u+s rmjrc
chown root addjrc
chown root rmjrc
```

The first line of Figure 5-2 shows that the assistant's login name is *gproject*. The remaining lines in this figure show other groups. The individual entries in Figure 5-3 show file permissions and ownerships after the above **chmod** and **chown** commands have been issued.

Prior to running the C language program, the system administrator must follow a test procedure similar to that used for the **nuser** shell script. This means creating a test directory, as well as pseudo users identified by test passwords. The complete test version of the C language **nuser** program is found in Chapter 15. After successfully testing the program several times, you can install the final version of the following program, making any necessary changes.

```
#include <stdio.h>
#include <string.h>
#include <sgtty.h>
#include <memory.h>
#include <sys/errno.h>
```

FIGURE 5-2

An **/etc/group** file

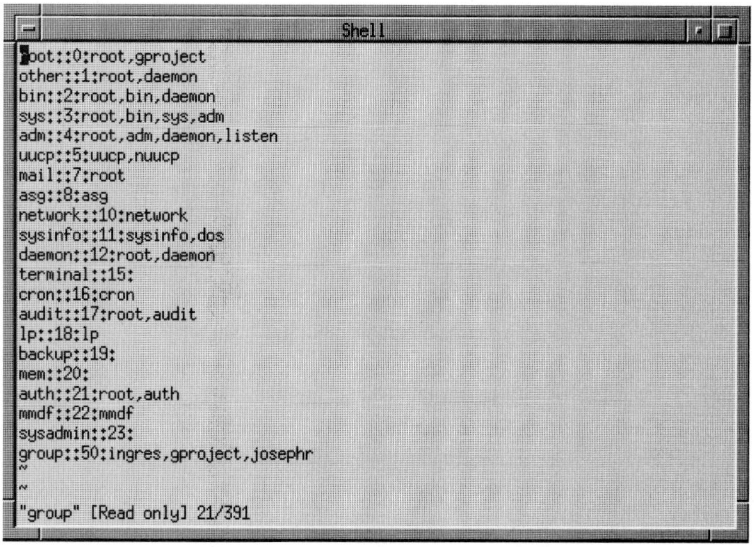

```
                              Shell
root::0:root,gproject
other::1:root,daemon
bin::2:root,bin,daemon
sys::3:root,bin,sys,adm
adm::4:root,adm,daemon,listen
uucp::5:uucp,nuucp
mail::7:root
asg::8:asg
network::10:network
sysinfo::11:sysinfo,dos
daemon::12:root,daemon
terminal::15:
cron::16:cron
audit::17:root,audit
lp::18:lp
backup::19:
mem::20:
auth::21:root,auth
mmdf::22:mmdf
sysadmin::23:
group::50:ingres,gproject,josephr
~
"group" [Read only] 21/391
```

FIGURE 5-3

File permissions and
ownerships

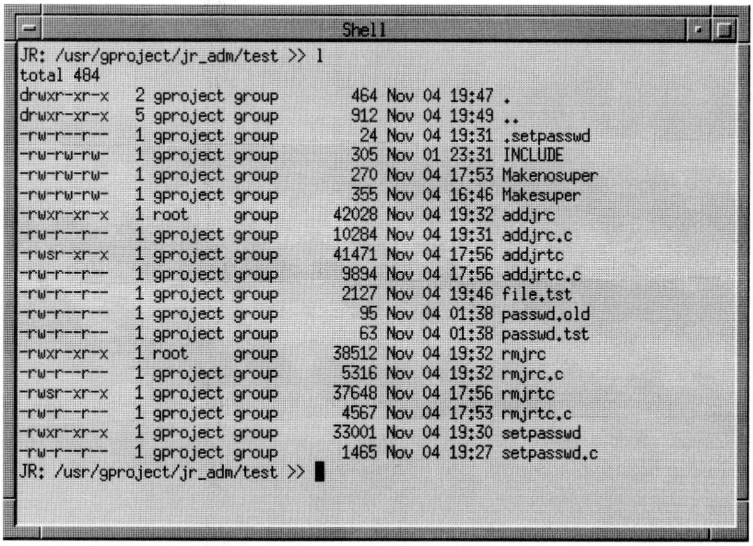

```
                              Shell
JR: /usr/gproject/jr_adm/test >> l
total 484
drwxr-xr-x   2 gproject group      464 Nov 04 19:47 .
drwxr-xr-x   5 gproject group      912 Nov 04 19:49 ..
-rw-r--r--   1 gproject group       24 Nov 04 19:31 .setpasswd
-rw-rw-rw-   1 gproject group      305 Nov 01 23:31 INCLUDE
-rw-rw-rw-   1 gproject group      270 Nov 04 17:53 Makenosuper
-rw-rw-rw-   1 gproject group      355 Nov 04 16:46 Makesuper
-rwxr-xr-x   1 root     group    42028 Nov 04 19:32 addjrc
-rw-r--r--   1 gproject group    10284 Nov 04 19:31 addjrc.c
-rwsr-xr-x   1 gproject group    41471 Nov 04 17:56 addjrtc
-rw-r--r--   1 gproject group     9894 Nov 04 17:56 addjrtc.c
-rw-r--r--   1 gproject group     2127 Nov 04 19:46 file.tst
-rw-r--r--   1 gproject group       95 Nov 04 01:38 passwd.old
-rw-r--r--   1 gproject group       63 Nov 04 01:38 passwd.tst
-rwxr-xr-x   1 root     group    38512 Nov 04 19:32 rmjrc
-rw-r--r--   1 gproject group     5316 Nov 04 19:32 rmjrc.c
-rwsr-xr-x   1 gproject group    37648 Nov 04 17:56 rmjrtc
-rw-r--r--   1 gproject group     4567 Nov 04 17:53 rmjrtc.c
-rwxr-xr-x   1 gproject group    33001 Nov 04 19:30 setpasswd
-rw-r--r--   1 gproject group     1465 Nov 04 19:27 setpasswd.c
JR: /usr/gproject/jr_adm/test >>
```

```
#define MYPASSWD "././setpasswd"
#define PASSWD_SIZE 24
int hidebuf[PASSWD_SIZE] = {11, 2, 5, 12, 7, 1, 3, 5,
                            10, 4, 8, 10, 11, 7, 5, 12,
                            2, 9, 3, 11, 6, 1, 9, 0};

#define DIR "/usr/"
#define DIRM "/usr/spool/mail/"
#define PASSWD "/etc/passwd"
#define DEFAULT_USER_ID "999"
#define DEFAULT_GROUP_ID "20"
#define DEFAULT_SHELL "ksh"
#define PROFILE ".profile"
#define LOGIN ".login"
#define LOGOUT ".logout"
#define CSHRC ".cshrc"
/*
Some of the following #define statements have been set on
two lines because of typesetting constraints. These
statements must be coded on a single line.
*/

#define PRFSTR1 "SHELL=/bin/sh"
#define PRFSTR2 "HOME="
#define PRFSTR3 "MAIL="
#define PRFSTR4 "PATH=/bin:/usr/bin:
                        /usr/hosts:/usr/local:/etc:."
#define PRFSTR5 "TERM="
#define PRFSTR6 "export TERM PATH SHELL HOME MAIL"

#define LINSTR1 "stty dec"
#define LINSTR2 "umask 0"
#define LINSTR3 "tset -s -Q -m 'unknown:?wy75'> /tmp/tset\$\$"
#define LINSTR4 "source /tmp/tset\$\$"
#define LINSTR5 "alias cmdx chmod +x"
#define LINSTR6 "set path=(. /bin /usr/bin
                            /usr/hosts /usr/local /etc)"
#define LINSTR7 "set history=150"

#define CSHSTR1 "set path=(. /bin /usr/bin
                            /usr/hosts /usr/local /etc)"
```

```
#define CSHSTR2 "set history=150"
#define CSHSTR3 "alias h history"

#define LOTSTR1 "clear"

int CheckPasswd();

int main()
{
char buf_1[256];
char tstbuf_1[80];
char tstbuf_2[80];
char keep_user[16];
char keep_gid[16];
char keep_uid[16];
char tmp_str[16];
char str[512];
int size;
FILE *fd;
int uid, sid;

  if (!CheckPasswd())
  {
    printf("\n Password is not valid. Please contact");
    printf("System Administrator!\n");
    printf("\n Program aborted!\n");
    exit(1);
  }
  uid = getuid();
  setuid(0);
  sid = getuid();

  printf("\n     Now you are in the superuser mode");
  printf("with the user id %d!\n", sid);
  printf("\nEnter new User :");
  gets(keep_user);
  if (strlen(keep_user) < 1)
  {
    printf("ERROR: NO USER ENTERED! Exiting ...\n");
    exit(1);
  }
  else
  {
```

```
      strcpy(tmp_str,"root");
      if (strcmp (tmp_str, keep_uid))
      {
        printf("ERROR:\n");
        printf("ROOT HAS ACTIVATED THIS PROGRAM!");
        exit(1);
      }
      else
      {
        printf("Continue with user %s\n", keep_user);
        strcpy(tstbuf_1,keep_user);
      }
    }
    printf("\nEnter user ID :");
    gets(keep_uid);
    if (strlen(keep_uid) < 2)
    {
      printf("WARNING: NO USER ID ENTERED!\n");
      printf("Using default value ...\n");
      strcpy(keep_uid,DEFAULT_USER_ID);
    }
    printf("\n");
    strcat(tstbuf_1,":");
    strcat(tstbuf_1,":");
    strcat(tstbuf_1,keep_uid);
    printf("\nEnter Group ID :");
    gets(keep_gid);
    if (strlen(keep_gid) < 2)
    {
      printf("WARNING: NO USER GROUP ENTERED!\n");
      printf("Using default value ...\n");
      strcpy(keep_gid,DEFAULT_GROUP_ID);
    }
    printf("\n");
    strcat(tstbuf_1,":");
    strcat(tstbuf_1,keep_gid);
    printf("\nEnter Full User Name :");
    gets(tstbuf_2);
    printf("\n");
    strcat(tstbuf_1,":");
    strcat(tstbuf_1,tstbuf_2);
    strcat(tstbuf_1,":");
    strcat(tstbuf_1,DIR);
```

```
strcat(tstbuf_1,keep_user);
printf("\nShell? [sh/csh] :");
gets(tstbuf_2);
if (strlen(tstbuf_2) < 2)
{
  printf("WARNING: NO SHELL ENTERED!\n");
  printf("Using default value ...\n");
  strcpy(tstbuf_2,DEFAULT_SHELL);
}
printf("\n");
strcat(tstbuf_1,":");
strcat(tstbuf_1,"/bin/");
strcat(tstbuf_1,tstbuf_2);
strcat(tstbuf_1,"\n");
size = strlen(tstbuf_1);
fd = fopen(PASSWD,"a");
if (!fd)
{
  printf("Cannot open file ! Exiting ...\n");
  exit(1);
}
else
{
  if(!fwrite(tstbuf_1,size,1,fd))
  {
    fclose(fd);
    printf("Cannot write to file %s! Exiting ...\n");
    exit(1);
  }

}
fclose(fd);
strcpy(tstbuf_1,"mkdir ");
strcat(tstbuf_1,DIR);
strcat(tstbuf_1,keep_user);
printf("Executing:  %s\n", tstbuf_1);
system(tstbuf_1);
strcpy(tstbuf_1,"chown ");
strcat(tstbuf_1,keep_user);
strcat(tstbuf_1," ");
strcat(tstbuf_1,DIR);
strcat(tstbuf_1,keep_user);
```

```
                    printf("Executing:  %s\n", tstbuf_1);
                    system(tstbuf_1);
                    strcpy(tstbuf_1,"chgrp ");
                    strcat(tstbuf_1,keep_gid);
                    strcat(tstbuf_1," ");
                    strcat(tstbuf_1,DIR);
                    strcat(tstbuf_1,keep_user);
                    printf("Executing:  %s\n", tstbuf_1);
                    system(tstbuf_1);
                    strcpy(tstbuf_1,DIR);
                    strcat(tstbuf_1,keep_user);
                    strcat(tstbuf_1,"/");
                    strcat(tstbuf_1,PROFILE);
                    fd = fopen(tstbuf_1, "w");
                    if (!fd)
                      printf("\nCannot open file %s\n",tstbuf_1);
                    else
                    {
                      strcpy(str,":");
                      strcat(str,"\n");
                      strcat(str,PRFSTR1);
                      strcat(str,"\n");
                      strcat(str,PRFSTR2);
                      strcat(str,DIR);
                      strcat(str,keep_user);
                      strcat(str,"\n");
                      strcat(str,PRFSTR3);
                      strcat(str,DIRM);
                      strcat(str,keep_user);
                      strcat(str,"\n");
                      strcat(str,PRFSTR4);
                      strcat(str,"\n");
                      strcat(str,PRFSTR5);
                      strcat(str,"\n");
                      strcat(str,PRFSTR6);
                      strcat(str,"\n");
                      size = strlen(str);
                      if(!fwrite(str,size,1,fd))
                      {
                        fclose(fd);
                        printf("\nCannot write to the file");
                      fclose(fd);
```

```
}
strcpy(tstbuf_1,DIR);
strcat(tstbuf_1,keep_user);
strcat(tstbuf_1,"/");
strcat(tstbuf_1,LOGIN);
fd = fopen(tstbuf_1, "w");
if (!fd)
  printf("\nCannot open file %s\n",tstbuf_1);
else
{
  strcpy(str,LINSTR1);
  strcat(str,"\n");
  strcat(str,LINSTR2);
  strcat(str,"\n");
  strcat(str,LINSTR3);
  strcat(str,"\n");
  strcat(str,LINSTR4);
  strcat(str,"\n");
  strcat(str,LINSTR5);
  strcat(str,"\n");
  strcat(str,LINSTR6);
  strcat(str,"\n");
  strcat(str,LINSTR7);
  strcat(str,"\n");
  size = strlen(str);
  if(!fwrite(str,size,1,fd))
  {
    fclose(fd);
    printf("\nCannot write to the file");
  }
  fclose(fd);
}
strcpy(tstbuf_1,DIR);
strcat(tstbuf_1,keep_user);
strcat(tstbuf_1,"/");
strcat(tstbuf_1,LOGOUT);
fd = fopen(tstbuf_1, "w");
if (!fd)
  printf("\nCannot open file %s\n",tstbuf_1);
else
```

```
{
  strcpy(str,LOTSTR1);
  strcat(str,"\n");
  size = strlen(str);
  if(!fwrite(str,size,1,fd))
  {
    fclose(fd);
    printf("\nCannot write to the file);
  }
  fclose(fd);
}
strcpy(tstbuf_1,DIR);
strcat(tstbuf_1,keep_user);
strcat(tstbuf_1,"/");
strcat(tstbuf_1,CSHRC);
fd = fopen(tstbuf_1, "w");
if (!fd)
  printf("\nCannot open file %s\n",tstbuf_1);
else
{
  strcpy(str,CSHSTR1);
  strcat(str,"\n");
  strcat(str,CSHSTR2);
  strcat(str,"\n");
  strcat(str,CSHSTR3);
  strcat(str,"\n");
  size = strlen(str);
  if(!fwrite(str,size,1,fd))
  {
    fclose(fd);
    printf("\nCannot write to the file);
  }
  fclose(fd);
}
strcpy(tstbuf_1,"touch ");
strcat(tstbuf_1,DIRM);
strcat(tstbuf_1,keep_user);
printf("Executing:  %s\n", tstbuf_1);
system(tstbuf_1);
strcpy(tstbuf_1,"chmod 660 ");
strcat(tstbuf_1,DIRM);
```

```
strcat(tstbuf_1,keep_user);
printf("Executing:  %s\n", tstbuf_1);
system(tstbuf_1);
strcpy(buf_1,"chown ");
strcat(buf_1,keep_user);
strcat(buf_1," ");
strcat(buf_1,DIR);
strcat(buf_1,keep_user);
strcat(buf_1,"/");
strcat(buf_1,PROFILE);
strcat(buf_1," ");
strcat(buf_1,DIR);
strcat(buf_1,keep_user);
strcat(buf_1,"/");
strcat(buf_1,LOGIN);
strcat(buf_1," ");
strcat(buf_1,DIR);
strcat(buf_1,keep_user);
strcat(buf_1,"/");
strcat(buf_1,CSHRC);
strcat(buf_1," ");
strcat(buf_1,DIR);
strcat(buf_1,keep_user);
strcat(buf_1,"/");
strcat(buf_1,LOGOUT);
strcat(buf_1," ");
strcat(buf_1,DIRM);
strcat(buf_1,keep_user);
printf("Executing:  %s\n", buf_1);
system(buf_1);
strcpy(buf_1,"chgrp ");
strcat(buf_1,keep_gid);
strcat(buf_1," ");
strcat(buf_1,DIR);
strcat(buf_1,keep_user);
strcat(buf_1,"/");
strcat(buf_1,PROFILE);
strcat(buf_1," ");
strcat(buf_1,DIR);
strcat(buf_1,keep_user);
strcat(buf_1,"/");
```

```
        strcat(buf_1,LOGIN);
        strcat(buf_1," ");
        strcat(buf_1,DIR);
        strcat(buf_1,keep_user);
        strcat(buf_1,"/");
        strcat(buf_1,CSHRC);
        strcat(buf_1," ");
        strcat(buf_1,DIR);
        strcat(buf_1,keep_user);
        strcat(buf_1,"/");
        strcat(buf_1,LOGOUT);
        printf("Executing:  %s\n", buf_1);
        system(buf_1);
        strcpy(buf_1,"chgrp ");
        strcat(buf_1,"mail");
        strcat(buf_1," ");
        strcat(buf_1,DIRM);
        strcat(buf_1,keep_user);
        printf("Executing:  %s\n", buf_1);
        system(buf_1);
        strcpy(buf_1,"/bin/passwd ");
        strcat(buf_1,keep_user);
        printf("Executing:  %s\n", buf_1);
        system(buf_1);
        printf("\n   New User < %s > entered to the");
        printf("Unix system!\n",keep_user);
        printf("\n");
        printf("\n");

        setuid(uid);
        printf("\n You are in the regular user mode.\n");
}

int CheckPasswd()
{
FILE *ffd;
char buf[80];
char *ptr;
int count;
char chr;
struct sgttyb tty;
char pwd[28];
```

```
gtty(fileno(stdin), &tty);
printf("\nPassword: ");
tty.sg_flags &= ~ECHO;
stty(fileno(stdin),&tty);
gets(buf);
tty.sg_flags |= ECHO;
stty(fileno(stdin),&tty);
printf("\n");
ffd = fopen(MYPASSWD, "rb");
if (!ffd)
  return (0);
if (!fread(&chr, 1, 1, ffd))
{
  fclose(ffd);
  return (0);
}
if (!fread(pwd, PASSWD_SIZE - 1, 1, ffd))
{
  fclose(ffd);
  return (0);
}
fclose(ffd);
ptr = pwd;
for (count = 0; count < PASSWD_SIZE; count++)
  *ptr++ -= (char)hidebuf[count];
  pwd[(int)chr - 32] = 0;
  if (strcmp(pwd, buf))
    return (0);
  return (1);
}
```

The following MAKE file was used to process this program in Unix V with SCO Open Desktop. The MAKE file for other Unix implementations will vary.

```
ROOT =
IROOT =
ETC = $(ROOT)/etc
BIN = $(ROOT)/usr/local/bin
TESTDIR = .
SHELL = /bin/sh
```

```
          REL =
          INCRT = $(IROOT)/usr/include
          BROOT = $(ROOT)
          I = $(INCRT)
          MORECPP =
          CFLAGS = -O -DLAI_TCP $(MORECPP) -I$(INCRT) $(REL)
                  -Di386 -DBUFFER_SIZE=8192
          LDFLAGS =
          LDLIBS =
          SOCKETLIB = -lsocket
          INS =
          INSDIR = $(BIN)
          LIBS =
          PROD = addjrtc rmjrtc

          install all: $(PROD)

          addjrtc: addjrtc.c
             $(CC) $(CFLAGS) -o $(TESTDIR)/addjrtc addjrtc.c $(LIBS)

          rmjrtc: rmjrtc.c
             $(CC) $(CFLAGS) -o $(TESTDIR)/rmjrtc rmjrtc.c $(LIBS)

          clean:
             -rm -f *.o

          clobber: clean
             -rm -f $(PROD)
```

A C LANGUAGE PROGRAM FOR SETTING A PASSWORD

The following program sets a password. It may be used by the system administrator to assign a password to an assistant, who will then be able to run the C language programs for adding and removing users.

```
#include <stdio.h>
#include <string.h>
#include <memory.h>

#define PASSWD "././.setpasswd"
#define PASSWD_SIZE 23
```

```
int hidebuf[PASSWD_SIZE] = {11, 2, 5, 12, 7, 1, 3, 5,
                            10, 4, 8, 10, 11, 7, 5, 12,
                            2, 9, 3, 11, 6, 1, 9};
char buf_1[80];
char buf_2[80];
char passwd[28];

int main()
{
FILE *fd;
int not_done, count, size;
char chr;

  not_done = 1;
  while (not_done)
  {
    printf("\nEnter Password [more than");
    printf("four characters]: ");
    gets(buf_1);
    size = strlen(buf_1);
    if (size < 4)
    {
      printf("Enter four characters or more.");
      printf("Exit program ... try again!\n");
      not_done = 0;
      exit(1);
    }
    if ((size > 3) && (size < PASSWD_SIZE - 1))
    {
      printf("Entered correct number of characters!\n");
      printf("Checking %s ... OK? [y/n] ", buf_1);
      gets(buf_2);
      printf("\n");
      if ((*buf_2 == 'y') || (*buf_2 == 'Y'))
      {
        strcpy(passwd, buf_1);
        not_done = 0;
      }
    }
  }
  for (count = size; count < PASSWD_SIZE; count++)
    passwd[count] = passwd[count % size];
  for (count = 0; count < PASSWD_SIZE; count++)
```

```
      passwd[count] += hidebuf[count];
  fd = fopen(PASSWD, "wb");
  if (!fd) return (1);
  chr = (char)(size + 32);
  if (!fwrite(&chr, 1, 1, fd))
  {
    fclose(fd);
    return (1);
  }
  if (!fwrite(passwd, PASSWD_SIZE, 1, fd))
  {
    fclose(fd);
    return (1);
  }
  fclose(fd);
  return (0);
}
```

A C LANGUAGE ruser PROGRAM

As was the case with adding users, there are several problems with using a shell script to remove users. This script must be run by someone who has superuser permission. The system administrator can apply the following C language program to assign an assistant the task of removing users; this can be done without compromising system security. As is customary, the system administrator or the designated assistant must follow a test procedure similar to that used in the **nuser** shell script and in the C language **nuser** program. The complete test version of the C language **ruser** program can be found in Chapter 15. After successfully testing the program several times, you can install the final version of the following program, making any necessary changes.

```
#include <stdio.h>
#include <string.h>
#include <sgtty.h>
#include <memory.h>
#include <sys/errno.h>

#define MYPASSWD "./.setpasswd"
#define PASSWD_SIZE 24

int hidebuf[PASSWD_SIZE] = {11, 2, 5, 12, 7, 1, 3, 5,
                            10, 4, 8, 10, 11, 7, 5, 12,
                            2, 9, 3, 11, 6, 1, 9, 0};
```

```c
#define DIR "/usr/"
#define DIRM "/usr/spool/mail/"
#define PASSWD "/etc/passwd"
#define PASSWDOLD "/etc/passwd.old"
#define PASSWDNEW "/etc/passwd.new"
#define PROFILE ".profile"
#define LOGIN ".login"
#define LOGOUT ".logout"
#define CSHRC ".cshrc"

int CheckPasswd();

int main()
{
char tstbuf_1[80];
char tstbuf_2[80];
char keep_user[16];
char user[16];
char tmp_str[16]
int size;
FILE *fd;
FILE *fdd;
char chr;
int i, found, first;
int entry_ok;
int uid, sid;

  if (!CheckPasswd())
  {
    printf("\n Password is not valid.");
            Please contact System Administrator!\n");
    printf("\n Program aborted!\n");
    exit(1);
  }
  uid = getuid();
  setuid(0);
  sid = getuid();

  printf("\n    Now you are in the superuser mode");
  printf("with the user id %d!\n", sid);
```

```
printf("\nEnter User to remove :");
gets(user);
if (strlen(user) < 1)
{
   printf("ERROR: NO USER ENTERED! Exiting ...\n");
   exit(1);
}
else
{
   strcpy(tmp_str,"root")
   if (stremp(tmp_str,user))
 {
     printf("ERROR! ATTEMP TO REMOVE ROOT!");
     exit(1)
 }
}
fd = fopen(PASSWD,"r");
if (!fd)
{
   printf(Cannot open the file! Exiting \n",PASSWD);
   exit(1);
}
fdd = fopen(PASSWDNEW,"w");
if (!fdd)
{
   printf(Cannot open the file! Exiting \n",PASSWDNEW);
   exit(1);
}
i = 0;
first = 0;
found = 0;
entry_ok = 0;
do
{
   chr = getc(fd);
   tstbuf_1[i] = chr;
   if (!first)
   {
     if (i < 16)
       keep_user[i] = chr;
```

```
    else
      printf("\n buffer overflow\n");

  }
  ++i;
  if ((chr == ':') && (!first))
  {
    --i;
    keep_user[i] = '\0';
    if (strcmp(user,keep_user) == 0)
    {
      found = 1;
      entry_ok = 1;
    }
    first = 1;
    ++i;
  }
  if (chr == '\n')
  {
    i = 0;
    first = 0;
    if (!found)
    {
      if (!fwrite(tstbuf_1,strlen(tstbuf_1),1,fdd))
      {
        printf("\nCannot write to the file\n");
                PASSWDNEW);
        fclose(fdd);
      }
      else
      {
        printf("\nUpdated the file %s\n",PASSWDNEW);
        found = 0;
      }
    }
} while (!feof(fd));
    fclose(fd);
    fclose(fdd);
    if (!entry_ok)
    {
      printf("ERROR: NO USER FOUND TO REMOVE!");
```

```
     exit(1);
}
printf("\n Removing User %s ...\n",user);
strcpy(tstbuf_1,"cp ");
strcat(tstbuf_1,PASSWD);
strcat(tstbuf_1," ");
strcat(tstbuf_1,PASSWDOLD);
printf("Executing:  %s\n", tstbuf_1);
system(tstbuf_1);
strcpy(tstbuf_1,"mv ");
strcat(tstbuf_1,PASSWDNEW);
strcat(tstbuf_1," ");
strcat(tstbuf_1,PASSWD);
printf("Executing:  %s\n", tstbuf_1);
system(tstbuf_1);
strcpy(tstbuf_1,"rm -rf ");
strcat(tstbuf_1,DIR);
strcat(tstbuf_1,user);
printf("Executing:  %s\n", tstbuf_1);
system(tstbuf_1);
strcpy(tstbuf_1,"rm -f ");
strcat(tstbuf_1,DIRM);
strcat(tstbuf_1,user);
printf("Executing:  %s\n", tstbuf_1);
system(tstbuf_1);
strcpy(tstbuf_1,"rm -f ");
strcat(tstbuf_1,DIR);
strcat(tstbuf_1,user);
strcat(tstbuf_1,"/");
strcat(tstbuf_1,PROFILE);
printf("Executing:  %s\n", tstbuf_1);
system(tstbuf_1);
strcpy(tstbuf_1,"rm -f ");
strcat(tstbuf_1,DIR);
strcat(tstbuf_1,user);
strcat(tstbuf_1,"/");
strcat(tstbuf_1,LOGIN);
printf("Executing:  %s\n", tstbuf_1);
system(tstbuf_1);
strcpy(tstbuf_1,"rm -f ");
```

```
          strcat(tstbuf_1,DIR);
          strcat(tstbuf_1,user);
          strcat(tstbuf_1,"/");
          strcat(tstbuf_1,LOGOUT);
          printf("Executing:  %s\n", tstbuf_1);
          system(tstbuf_1);
          strcpy(tstbuf_1,"rm -f ");
          strcat(tstbuf_1,DIR);
          strcat(tstbuf_1,user);
          strcat(tstbuf_1,"/");
          strcat(tstbuf_1,CSHRC);
          printf("Executing:  %s\n", tstbuf_1);
          system(tstbuf_1);
          strcpy(tstbuf_1,"rmdir ");
          strcat(tstbuf_1,DIR);
          strcat(tstbuf_1,user);
          printf("Executing:  %s\n", tstbuf_1);
          system(tstbuf_1);
          printf("User < %s > removed from
          printf("the Unix system\n",user);
          printf("\n");
          printf("\n");

          setuid(uid);
          printf("You are in the regular user mode.\n");

}

int CheckPasswd()
{
FILE *ffd;
char buf[80];
char *ptr;
int count;
char chr;
struct sgttyb tty;
char pwd[28];

  gtty(fileno(stdin), &tty);
  printf("\nPassword: ");
```

```
tty.sg_flags &= ~ECHO;
stty(fileno(stdin),&tty);
gets(buf);
tty.sg_flags |=~ECHO;
stty(fileno(stdin),&tty);
printf("\n");
ffd = fopen(MYPASSWD, "rb");
if (!ffd)
  return (0);
if (!fread(&chr, 1, 1, ffd))
{
  fclose(ffd);
  return (0);
}
if (!fread(pwd, PASSWD_SIZE - 1, 1, ffd))
{
  fclose(ffd);
  return (0);
}
fclose(ffd);
ptr = pwd;
for (count = 0; count < PASSWD_SIZE; count++)
  *ptr++ -= (char)hidebuf[count];
pwd[(int)chr - 32] = 0;
if (strcmp(pwd, buf))
  return (0);
return (1);
}
```

Chapter Summary

Superuser   The system administrator is not bound by the constraints affecting most users. He or she has privileged system access available via the superuser account; this is a privileged account associated with the user name *root*. The superuser has complete access to all commands and files on a given Unix system.

Passwords and Groups   A password is a secret code by which a user identifies himself or herself to the system. Passwords are the first line of defense in system security. When creating an account, the system administrator enters the seven fields of the **passwd** file in one of three ways: manually, through a shell script, or through a C language program. These seven fields include the login name, the encrypted password, the UID (user identification) number, the default GID (group identification) number, the GCOS (user identification) field, the user's home directory, and the login shell.

Unix recognizes the importance of work groups by providing for groups of users who share files. This chapter explains how to create and modify such groups, and surveys the commands used to assign user ownership, group ownership, and access permissions.

Adding Users   The system administrator is responsible for adding users to the system. Some steps, such as determining user identification and entering this data into the **/etc/passwd** file, are mandatory. Other steps, such as copying initialization (startup) files into the user home directory, save time for the user and, consequently, save time and effort for the system administrator.

The steps involved in adding a user include: specifying a login name, a user ID, and a default user group; entering the above user data into the **/etc/passwd** file; assigning an initial password to this account; setting associated user account parameters such as password lifetime; creating a user home directory; setting or copying initialization files; assigning ownership of the home directory and initialization files; creating a user **mail** file in the system mail directory; providing access to other system facilities; defining secondary group memberships; and testing the new account.

Removing Users   It is the system administrator's responsibility to remove user accounts when they are no longer needed. It is important to back up user files before removing them from the system. As is the case with adding user accounts, the system administrator might apply a shell script to remove accounts, or might provide an assistant with a C language program for removing accounts. This can be done without compromising system security.

Unix System

- Using Mail Facilities

- Applying the write command

- System News

Administration Guide

CHAPTER

System Administrator-User Communication

Computer users often have a lot to say to others, whether the information is strictly business or of a personal nature. System administrators also have the constant need to keep in touch with their users. This chapter presents several common, easy-to-use Unix features that enhance interuser or system administrator communication. These features include the **mail** and more sophisticated **mailx** commands, which transmit and read messages without disturbing a user's terminal session, the **write** command, which immediately displays a message on affected users' terminals, and the **news** command, by which the system administrator or an assistant can inform groups of users about items of interest.

USING MAIL FACILITIES

Unix provides several commands that enable a user to communicate with one or several other users who need not be logged into the same Unix-based computer. The **mail** command and the more sophisticated **mailx** command may inform the logged-in recipients that mail is available when their current command finishes executing. These commands inform off-line users that mail is available when they log into the system.

Sending Mail with the mail Command

Joseph can send a message to Sharon and Mickey with the following command:

```
$ mail sharon mickey
```

Here, sharon and mickey are the appropriate login names. The **mail** command waits for Joseph to compose the message. Joseph may compose short messages by directly typing in each message, then terminating it by pressing the CTRL-D key. The message includes the text that Joseph wishes to transmit, and identifying information known as the *header*. The header consists of the message size in bytes, and perhaps the message type, a *Subject:* line, and a *To:* line designating the recipient or recipients.

Longer messages should be composed with a text editor such as **vi** (see Chapter 2) and saved in a file. This procedure offers several advantages compared to directly typing the message at the **mail** prompt: When the message goes out it is clean; if you are a poor typist, your users will never have to know. In addition, the message is available for future reference, including possible corrections. For example, suppose that you send a half-page message calling a meeting, and the next day you are obliged to change the meeting room. If you have saved the message in a file, you can edit it to make the changes without having to retype the entire message.

The alternate option, simply sending a room change message, is insufficient. Users might not realize exactly which meeting you are talking about, and the initial convocation's useful information, such as the proposed agenda, will not be available at hand.

Invoke the text editor, specifying the message filename, as follows:

```
vi meeting
```

then compose the message, making any necessary corrections before saving it. Finally, send the message, redirecting the standard input (in other words, telling Unix to get its input from the **mail_file** file instead of from the keyboard), as follows:

```
mail sharon mickey < meeting
```

Receiving Mail with the mail Command

The **mail** command does not interrupt a user's work in progress. When a designated user's present command terminates, if he or she has issued the command **biff** y, the system displays the following message on the screen:

```
You have mail
```

If a designated user was not logged into the system when the mail message was sent, he or she will be so informed after successfully logging in. Users can read their mail, either immediately or later, using the **mail** command options described in the following section. The user's mail is available on a last in, first out basis.

mail Command Options

Table 6-1 presents the **mail** command options. These options are displayed when the user types a question mark (?) or an asterisk (*) in response to the question mark generated by the **mail** command. They are discussed in detail below.

TABLE 6-1

The **mail** Command Options

Option	Description
q	Quit
x	Exit without changing mail
p	Print
f *file*	Read (default filename mbox)
s *file*	Save (default filename mbox)
w *file*	Save without header
–	Print previous
d	Delete
+	Next (do not delete)
m *user*	Send mail to named user
! *commmand*	Execute named command

The q (Quit) Option

The *q* option quits the **mail** command. It removes deleted messages and returns the user to the system prompt. Typing CTRL-D at the prompt has the same effect.

The x (Exit) Option

The *x* option exits the **mail** command. It does not remove deleted messages. It returns the user to the system prompt *$*. Use this option if you have accidentally deleted messages that you wish to keep.

The p (Print) Option

The *p* option displays a message. Print messages that you may wish to refer to at a later date.

The f (File) Option

The *f* option reads a message from a named file. If no filename is supplied, it reads the **mbox** file.

The s (Save) Option

The *s* option saves a message in a named file. An example appears below.

```
? s nov10_meet
From joseph Wed Nov 8 13:13:34 1995
Don't forget the new hire meeting Nov 10 at 15:00
in my office!
?
```

This command saves the mail message from joseph in a file called **nov10_meet**. The system checks to see whether a file by that name presently exists. If no such file exists, the system creates one. If the file exists, the system appends this message to the end of the file. This message file is the recipient's file, placed in the user's mail directory. It is distinct from the sender's file.

After saving the message, the system displays the next message, if any. If no other mail messages are available, the system terminates the **mail** command, returning the user to the *$* prompt. This message is no longer available within the user's mail; however, it is available in the designated file. It is the user's responsibility to delete unneeded mail files periodically.

The w (Save Without Header) Option

The *w* option saves a message in a named file. It is identical to the *s* option, except that the *w* option does not save the header; for example:

```
From joseph Wed Nov 8 13:13:34 1995
```

In the following example the user did not specify a filename, so the default (**mbox**) file will be used.

```
? w
From joseph Wed Nov 8 13:13:34 1995
Don't forget the new hire meeting Nov 10 at 15:00
in my office!
?
```

This message is saved in a file called **mbox** within the user's home directory. If no such file exists, the **mail** command creates it. Otherwise, the **mail** command appends the message to this file.

The – (Print Previous) Option

The – option displays the previous message. This option is useful if you forget to display a given message before you read the next message.

The d (Delete) Option

The *d* option deletes a given message. Remember, if you have deleted a message and later change your mind, use the *x* option to exit the **mail** command without actually deleting any messages. Of course, a better policy is to watch what you are doing and only delete a message when you are certain that you no longer require it.

The + (Next) Option

The + option accesses the next **mail** command message. It does not delete the current message.

The m (Forward Mail) Option

The *m* option forwards a message to the named user. For example, assume that Sharon has just read Joseph's message concerning the November 10th meeting. She wants her assistant, Albert, to attend this meeting as well. She can forward this message with the following option:

```
? m albert
?
```

Albert will see the following mail message:

```
? mail
From joseph Wed Nov 8 13:13:34 1995
>From sharon Wed Nov 8 13:15:23 1995 forwarded
Don't forget the new hire meeting Nov 10 at 15:00
in my office!
?
```

Albert can use the appropriate **mail** options to save the forwarded message, with or without the header.

The ! (Execute Command) Option

The ! option executes a named Unix command. For example, if Albert wishes to answer Sharon's message upon receipt, he can enter the following:

```
? !mail sharon
I'll be at the Nov 10 meeting.
I'm bringing the resumes of the two applicants.
```

Note | You cannot change the directory from inside the mail command.

Graphical User Interface for the Mail Utility

Many Unix systems include the standard windowing system called X Window. System administration issues related to X Window are discussed in Chapter 13. (See also *X Window Inside & Out,* also by Reiss and Radin, Berkeley, Osborne McGraw-Hill, 1992, for a complete discussion of X Window.)

An experienced X Window system programmer working with a system administrator can develop a graphical user interface application for managing the mail utility. Figure 6-1 shows an example of such a graphical interface. This application can be assigned to the system administrator's assistant if she or he is temporarily given superuser access privileges. These privileges are limited to this application. When the application

FIGURE 6-1

A graphical user interface for the mail utility

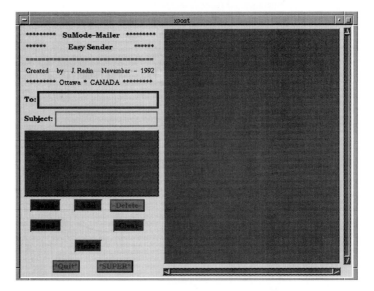

terminates, the assistant reverts to regular access privileges, and so system security is maintained.

The mailx Command

The more sophisticated **mailx** command is available with every Unix System V version. It is more powerful than the **mail** command and, consequently, is somewhat more difficult to master. However, given the importance of interuser communication, and system administrator-user communication, this command is important and should be mastered by every serious system administrator.

Sending a Mail Message with the mailx Command

Joseph can send a message to Sharon and Mickey with the **mailx** command, as follows:

```
$ mailx sharon mickey
Subject:
```

The command prompts Joseph to enter the subject. (The actual prompt is installation-dependent and can be modified by the system administrator.) After entering the subject, the message sender completes the message and sends it. The subject classification enables message recipients to answer their most important mail first. It also helps them avoid the situation of wading through dozens of messages to find the desired one.

Receiving a Mail Message with the mailx Command

Sharon types the **mailx** command to see a screen such as the following:

```
"/usr/mail/sharon": 2 messages 1 new 1 unread
 U  1 alice     Tue Nov 7 18:55    5/61 Budget Cuts
>N  2 joseph    Wed Nov 8 13:13    4/46 New Hire Meeting
```

Each message is described in a single entry containing several fields:

■ Message status, such as *U* for unread and *N* for new.

■ Reference number, such as *1*.

■ Sender login name, such as *alice*.

■ Date and time sent, such as *Tue Nov 7 18:55*.

■ Message length in lines and characters, such as *5* lines and *46* characters.

■ Subject, such as *Budget Cuts*.

The > in the first column identifies the current message. Note that Sharon has received a message that she has not yet read, concerning budget cuts. Sharon can read Joseph's message by entering this command:

```
mailx t2
```

The following sections discuss **mailx** command escapes and **mailx** commands. Some command escapes and some commands are available when you are composing a message; others are available when you are reading a message.

mailx Command Escapes

Table 6-2 presents the **mailx** *tilde escapes*. These escapes enable the user to leave the **mailx** command, execute an option, and then return to the command. For example, the *~v* escape invokes the **vi** editor for editing the message. Some **mailx** command escapes are available to message senders; others are available to message recipients.

	Escape	**Meaning**
TABLE 6-2	~~	Quote a tilde.
The **mailx** Command Escapes	~a, ~A	Autograph (insert 'sign' variable to identify a message).
	~b *users*	Add users to the Bcc list.
	~c *users*	Add users to the Cc list.
	~d	Read in dead.letter file.
	~e	Edit message with the designated editor.
	~m *messages*	Read in messages, shifted right by a tab.
	~f *messages*	Read in unshifted messages.
	~h	Prompt for the To list, the Subject, and the Co list.
	~p	Print the message buffer.
	~q, ~Q	Quit, save in $HOME/dead.letter.
	~x	Quit without saving.
	~r *file*	Read file into the message buffer.
	~s *subject*	Set subject.
	~t *users*	Add users to the To list.
	~v	Invoke the **vi** editor.
	~w *file*	Write a message on file.
	~.	End of input.
	~!*command*	Execute a shell command.
	~|*command*	Pipe the message through the command.

mailx Command Options

Table 6-3 presents the **mailx** command options. As shown below, the **mailx** command provides a wider variety of options than does the **mail** command. Furthermore, **mailx** command options may be more sophisticated than the corresponding **mail** command options. Some **mailx** commands are available to message senders, others are available to message recipients.

TABLE 6-3

The **mailx** Command Options

Option	Meaning
type *msglist*	Display messages.
next	Display type next message.
edit *msglist*	Edit messages.
from *msglist*	Display header lines of messages.
undelete *msglist*	Restore deleted messages.
save *msglist file*	Append messages to a file.
reply *message*	Reply to all recipients of a message.
Reply *msglist*	Reply to author(s) of messages.
preserve *msglist*	Preserve messages in the mailbox.
mail *user*	Send mail to the specified user.
quit	Quit, preserving unread messages.
xit	Quit, preserving all messages.
header	Print page of active message headers.[*]
!	Escape to the shell.
cd *directory*	Change to the specified directory. Change to home directory if none is specified.
list	List all commands without explanations.
top *msglist*	Print top 5 lines of messages.[†]
z	Display next page of 10 headers.
–	Display last page of 10 headers.

[*]mailx provides flexible, sophisticated message headers. See your system manual for more information.

[†]*msglist* is optional; it specifies messages by number, author, subject, or type. The default is the current message.

APPLYING THE write COMMAND

Unlike the **mail** command, which can communicate with anyone on a linked system, the **write** command requires that recipients be logged into the sender's system. Because the **write** command interrupts the recipient, it should be used with care.

Sending a Mail Message with the write Command

For example, Joseph could inform Sharon of the meeting with this message:

```
$ write sharon
Don't forget the new hire meeting Nov 10 at 15:00
in my office!
^D
$
```

If Sharon is not logged on, Joseph's screen will display a message such as one of the following:

```
$ write sharon
sharon is not logged on.
$
```

or

```
$ write sharon
Don't forget the new hire meeting Nov 10 at 15:00
sharon is not logged on.
$
```

The exact wording of the message will depend on the delay before the system determines that Sharon is not logged on. To avoid this problem, Joseph can issue the **who** command to obtain the list of active login names before issuing the **write** command.

```
$ who
root            tty01       Nov 08   20:34
gproject        tty02       Nov 08   20:31
joseph          tty05       Nov 08   09:42
```

Receiving a Mail Message with the write Command

If Sharon is logged on, and if she enters **write joseph** to establish a communications link, she will receive the message a line at a time. In the best case scenario, Sharon would receive the following message:

```
Message from joseph Wed Nov 8 13:13:34 1995
Don't forget the new hire meeting Nov 10 at 15:00
in my office!
EOF
```

Here, EOF (end of file) indicates message termination. However, receiving a message issued by the **write** command can disturb a recipient. Suppose that Sharon was working with a text editor when Joseph sent her the above message. The results could appear as follows:

```
Sharon's file  line 1
Message from joseph Wed Nov 8 13:13:34 1995
Sharon's file  line 2
Sharon's file  line 3
Don't forget the new hire meeting Nov 10 at 15:00
in my office!
Sharon's file  line 4
EOF
```

One can well imagine the change in Sharon's mood. She might want to retaliate by issuing her own **write** command to Joseph, sending him a long message. Guerrilla warfare via the **write** command is not suggested. Instead, Sharon can use the **mesg** command to prevent users other than the system administrator from writing to her screen.

The mesg Command

Sharon prevents users from writing to her screen by issuing the following command:

```
$ mesg n
```

which, in effect, says "no messages."

If Sharon issued the **mesg n** command before Joseph issued the **write** command, Joseph would see the following message:

```
Permission denied
```

Sharon could enable message receipt by issuing the following command:

```
$ mesg y
```

Note

A write command issued by the superuser overrides the mesg n command. However, the superuser should avoid sending too many write messages, as they can cause both technical and interpersonal problems. Remember that the more such messages sent, the fewer that users will act upon.

The command **mesg**, without any parameters, displays the current message permission status (y or n) on the screen, as shown here:

```
$ mesg
is y
```

Dialogue Considerations

The **write** command may be employed interactively between two users. However, such a dialogue can be complicated. For example, the delay in sending a message can be considerable, especially in a busy system. To smooth the dialogue, it's important that the users set up a protocol ahead of time. One commonly used protocol is described below.

1. The first user issues an initial **write** command announcing her readiness to communicate.

2. The second user issues an initial **write** command announcing his readiness to communicate.

3. The first user issues a **write** command to generate a message, terminated by the letter **o** (for *over*).

4. The second user waits for the letter **o** to be sure that the message is complete, and then issues a **write** command to generate a message, terminated by the letter **o** (for *over*).

5. Steps 3 and 4 are repeated as often as necessary. A user who wishes to terminate the dialogue issues a **write** command to generate a message, terminated by the letters **oo** (for *over and out*).

6. The other user continues to send messages as required. She or he terminates the final message with the letters **oo**.

7. Each user presses CTRL-D to break the physical connections between the two users.

The write all Command

The **wall** (write all) command issues a **write** command to all logged-in users. One common use of this command is to inform users of an unscheduled system backup. Unless the path contains **/etc**, enter **/etc/wall** to execute this command.

• •

SYSTEM NEWS

Nothing helps a system run better than proper communication between the system administrator and the system users. The concluding section of this chapter introduces two Unix features that promote such communication: the **news** command and the message of the day facility.

The news Command

The **news** command allows the system administrator or others to inform users of items of interest (see Figure 6-2.) Individual news items appear in a file that resides in the system directory **/usr/news**.

Reading News Items

Any user allowed to access a given Unix system can obtain the system news by issuing the **news** command. This command displays all news items that have not been previously accessed by the given user; the most recent news item is displayed first. The system decides

Output of the **news** command

```
                                        Shell
JR: /usr/gproject/jr_adm/test >> news

msg.tst (gproject) Wed Nov  4 22:23:23 1992

    News from the System Administrator (logged as a regular user gproject) :
    ======================================================================
    Several programs can be executed by a regular user with a special System
    Administartor permission and password.
    By executing these programs the regular user will be set temporarily to the
    super-user mode. After finishing the request in the super-user mode, the
    program will set this user to the regular mode (no super-user).

news.tst (root) Wed Nov  4 22:12:56 1992

    From the System Administrator: testing the news system!
    Any news files are kept in the /usr/news directory.
    You can insert new items in this directory.

JR: /usr/gproject/jr_adm/test >> █
```

whether or not to display a given news item by examining the date associated with the **.news_time** file in the user's home directory. By default, Unix displays only news items that have been modified after the date assigned to the **.news_time** file.

Users can obtain the name of available news files by issuing the **news** -n command, as shown here:

```
$ news -n
news: syschanges personnel decsched hockey
```

A user interested in the organization's hockey club could issue the following command to obtain required information without having to wade through other news items.

```
$ news hockey
hockey (the system) Thu Nov 9 08:55:55 1995
Don't forget that we're still trying to get together
a hockey league for Tues nights. Notify jill (2368) ASAP
$
```

An interesting option for forgetful users is the -a option. This displays all news items, independent of their modification dates.

Composing News Items

Individuals can create news items only if they have write permission on the system directory **/usr/news**. The filename should indicate the type of news to potential readers who issue the **news** -n command.

Don't forget to regularly delete old news items; they waste valuable disk space and user time.

Message of the Day

Most Unix systems provide a *message of the day* facility. The system administrator composes messages that appear on the screen whenever users log into the system. These messages appear in the **/etc/motd** file, which should be readable by all, but writable only by the system administrator. For the sake of users' sanity, it is important to keep messages short and to remove them on a regular basis. The message of the day facility should be restricted to crucial messages, such as one reminding users of a scheduled system shutdown.

Chapter Summary

System Communication Commands and Facilities   Unix provides several commands that enable a user to communicate with one or several other users who need not be logged into the same Unix-based computer. The **mail** command and the more sophisticated **mailx** command inform the logged-in recipients that mail is available when their current command finishes executing. These commands inform users when they log into the system that mail is available.

The message sent by the **write** command appears immediately on the recipient's monitor, provided that he or she is logged into the sender's system and has issued a **write** command to establish a communications link. The **mesg** command can prevent users other than the system administrator from writing to an individual's screen. To smooth the dialogue, it's important that the users set up a protocol ahead of time.

The **news** command allows the system administrator or others to inform users of items of interest. (See Figure 6-2.) The individual news items appear in a file that resides in the system directory **/usr/news**.

Most Unix systems provide a *message of the day* facility. The system administrator composes messages that appear on the screen whenever users log into the system. These messages appear in the **/etc/motd** file, which should be readable by all, but writable only by the system administrator.

Unix System

- Commands for Backing Up and Restoring Files

- A tar Backup Script

- A tar Restore Script

- A cpio Backup Script

- A cpio Restore Script

Administration Guide

CHAPTER

File System Backup and Restoration

It is difficult to overestimate the importance of file system backup and restoration. Anyone who has ever lost a file should realize the value of correctly designed and executed backup procedures. Users will hold you, the system administrator, responsible whenever they cannot restore lost files. The current chapter may be the most important one in this book. Keeping your file system backed up at all times is absolutely essential.

INTRODUCTION

System administrators have many different types of backup and storage media at their disposal. Interestingly enough, making backups too often is almost as bad as not making them often enough. For maximum efficiency, and minimum likelihood of lost files, you must choose a backup medium that's appropriate for your installation. This section concludes with advice on backups and restorations. If applying this advice means one less file lost, then this book may have more than paid for itself.

Types of Backups

As system administrator, not only do you need to know how to make backups, you also need to know when to make them. In one sense, the more often you back up the file system, the better protected you are against disaster. However, overkill is a definite possibility. Backups require time, energy, and file storage media. They can be disruptive because during the time that backups are being made, users should not access the file system. Furthermore, to restore a lost file, you must first find the appropriate file and reload it, without destroying any other files. You will have to choose what type of backups to make, and at what frequency.

A *full backup* copies the entire file system. Make a full backup when you first install the system and whenever you make important modifications to the system, such as installing a new central hard disk. Many installations will make a full backup periodically. A *partial backup* is a complete copy of any file system or directory tree. Be sure to make partial backups on a regular basis for frequently changing file systems and directories. An *incremental backup* includes copies of new files and files that have changed since the last backup. It's a good idea to make an incremental backup at least once every working day.

Storage Media

The system administrator has a wide variety of choices for the media on which to store the files. Choosing the appropriate storage medium (or media) for your installation makes the backup process much more convenient and, consequently, increases the possibility that the backups will actually be done and done correctly. The choices include conventional magnetic tape, floppy disk, cartridge tape, video tape, and WORM disks. Although systems are often distributed on CD-ROM, this medium cannot be used for backups because it is read-only.

Conventional Magnetic Tape

At one time, magnetic tape was the standard choice for backing up Unix file systems. However, between the dramatic increase in Unix systems on workstations and on microcomputers, and the equally dramatic decline in cost for mainframe and minicomputer hard disks, magnetic tape has lost its predominance. While it does offer rapid data transfer and relatively high storage capacity (perhaps 150MB), magnetic tape requires expensive, somewhat outdated equipment, along with a technical maintenance staff.

Floppy Disks

Floppy disks are a convenient medium for incremental backups, particularly for Unix systems serving only one user. They are inexpensive, offer a familiar technology, and are extremely portable (although their portability can be a disadvantage from the security point of view.) However, because of their relatively tiny storage capacity (usually a maximum of 1.44MB, but 2.88MB diskettes are gaining popularity), floppy disks are not a serious option for complete system backups, even for Unix systems serving only one user. They are often used for small incremental backups. When the capacity of floppy disks and related technologies increases substantially, they will become a more important storage option for all types of backups.

Cartridge Tape

Most workstations, and many microcomputer-based Unix systems, rely on cartridge tape as a backup medium. While more expensive than floppy disk drives, cartridge tape units are not costly, especially when you consider the time that they save and the cost of failing to back up the file system. Their storage capacity tends to be in the same range as conventional magnetic tapes, on the order of 150MB. Use cartridge tape for incremental backups of any system, and for full backups of Unix systems serving one user.

Video Tape

Because of their great storage capacity, which is measured in gigabytes instead of in megabytes, video tapes make unattended backups possible. However, at the time of this writing, video tape has not yet become a major storage option.

WORM Disks

WORM stands for write once, read many. A WORM disk is a relatively expensive laser disk with a storage capacity measured in gigabytes. Because it can only be written on a single time, there is no danger of losing its contents through an accidental overwrite. Furthermore, auditors tend to like WORM disks, because they know that the contents have not undergone tampering.

General Advice

One of the most frustrating experiences is to restore a file, only to find that it is unreadable or useless for other reasons. The following suggestions do not guarantee that you won't lose any files. However, applying them judiciously will decrease the likelihood of lost files, and make the backup and restore process work smoother.

- **Use shell scripts.**   This chapter includes four shell scripts for file system backup and restoration. These scripts are menu driven and provide a wide variety of options. However, you may choose to modify them to meet your specific needs.

- **Verify your backups.**   Practice restoring files to make sure your procedures and equipment work before you actually need them. Otherwise, a small hardware or software error could have disastrous consequences.

- **Label your backups.**   Don't make people guess about the contents of a given disk or cartridge. Labelling is only worthwhile if you have developed a clear, unambiguous file-naming scheme.

- **Document your backup and restoration processes.**   A few minutes completing logbook entries can save you countless hours of trying to piece together exactly what happened on the night of November 24th. Unix itself provides some of the documentation tools, for example, selected commands may generate a list of filenames.

COMMANDS FOR BACKING UP AND RESTORING FILES

System V Unix includes several commands for file system backup and restoration. The two most commonly employed commands, **tar** and **cpio**, are used for both backup and restoration. The **dd** command transfers raw data between devices. The **restore** command performs a Unix incremental file system restore of a previous backup. The **volcopy** command makes a literal copy of the entire file system. BSD Unix includes the **tar** command, the **dump** command to generate an incremental file system backup, and the **restor** command to perform an incremental file system restore.

Major System V Commands

One major System V file backup and restore command is **tar** (tape archive). Unless otherwise specified, **tar** puts each file back where it came from, creating needed directories along the way. You can use **tar** to move files from one directory to another. It allows you to replace archived files with different versions, and to append new files to the end of the archive. The following section provides the **tar** command syntax. The chapter includes a backup script and a restore script, each employing **tar**.

The more recent major System V file backup and restore command is **cpio** (copy input and output.) This command archives a list of input files to a single large output file. The **find** command and the **ls** are often employed to generate the filenames to archive. After presenting the **tar** command and the **cpio** command, this chapter compares these two Unix file system backup and restore commands. It also includes a backup script and a restore script, each employing **cpio**.

The tar command

The Unix System V **tar** command archives files. It has the following syntax:

tar [*key*] [*files*]

tar saves and restores files to and from an archive medium, typically a floppy disk or tape. Its actions are controlled by the *key* argument, a set of options that can be prefaced with a hyphen. Other command arguments are files or directory names specifying the files to be backed up or restored. A directory name refers to the files and all subdirectories for that directory.

Note	The r and u options of the tar command (both described next) cannot be used with tape devices.

A single letter specifies the key function portion. The most commonly used letters are described below:

r   Writes named files to the end of an existing archive.

x   Extracts named files from the archive. If a named file matches a directory whose contents had been written onto the archive, this directory is (recursively) extracted. The owner, modification time, and mode are restored (if possible). If no *files* argument is given, the entire contents of the archive are extracted. If the archive contains several files with the same name, the last one overwrites all earlier ones.

t Lists names of specified files whenever they occur on the archive. If no *files* argument is given, all names on the archive are listed.

u Adds specified files to the archive if they are not already there, or if they have been modified since last written on that archive. This option can be slow.

c Creates a new archive; it writes from the archive's beginning, not after the last file.

v (verbose) Displays the name of each file treated, preceded by the function letter and additional information.

w Displays the action to be taken, followed by the filename. Any word beginning with the letter *y* launches the action. Any other input means *no*.

f Defines the next argument as the archive medium name instead of using the default device (for SCO Unix, listed in **/etc/default/tar**.) Examples occur in the shell scripts at the end of this chapter.

b Defines the next argument as the blocking factor for archive records.

A critical consideration when creating a **tar** volume is the use of absolute or relative pathnames. *Absolute pathnames* specify the file location relative to the root directory (/); *relative pathnames* are relative to the current directory. Take pathnames into account when making a **tar** tape or disk. Backup volumes use absolute pathnames so that they can be restored to the proper directory. Use relative pathnames when creating a **tar** volume where absolute pathnames are unnecessary.

Consider the following **tar** command examples, as executed from the directory **/usr/target**:

```
tar cv /usr/target/arrow
tar cv arrow
```

The first command creates a **tar** volume with the absolute pathname **/usr/target/arrow**. The second yields a **tar** volume with a relative pathname: **./arrow**. (The ./ is implicit, shown here as an example; it should not be specified when retrieving the file from the archive.) When restored, the first example writes the file **arrow** to the directory **/usr/target** (if it exists and you have write permission), no matter what your working directory. The second example writes the file **arrow** to your current working directory.

The cpio command

The Unix System V **cpio** command copies file archives in and out. It has the following syntax:

cpio -o[acBvV] [-C *bufsize*] [[-O *file*] [-K *volumesize*] [-M *message*]]

cpio -i[BcdmrtTuvVfsSb6k] [-C *bufsize*] [[-I *file*] [-K *volumesize*] [-M *message*]]
    [*pattern ...*]

cpio -p[adlmuvV] directory

cpio -o (copy out)   Reads the standard input to obtain a list of pathnames, and copies those files onto the standard output together with pathname and status information. Output is padded to a 512-byte boundary by default.

cpio -i (copy in)   Extracts files from the standard input, which is assumed to be the product of a previous **cpio** -o. Only files with names that match patterns are selected. Patterns are regular expressions given in the filename-generating notation of **sh**.

Note

If cpio -i tries to create a file that already exists, and the existing file is the same age or newer, cpio issues a warning message and does not replace the file. (The -u option can be used to overwrite the existing file unconditionally.)

cpio -p (pass)   Reads the standard input to obtain a list of file pathnames that are conditionally created and copied into the destination directory tree based on the options coded.

The major options are listed below:

-B   Blocks input/output 5,120 bytes to the record. The default buffer size is 512 bytes when this and the -C options are not used. (-B does not apply to the pass option; -B is meaningful only with data directed to or from a character-special device.)

-c   Writes header information in ASCII character form for portability. Always use this option when the origin and destination machines are of different types.

-C *bufsize*   Blocks input/output with a positive integer number of bytes per record. The default buffer size is 512 bytes when this option, and the -B options, are not used. (-C does not apply to the pass option; -C is meaningful only with data directed to or from a character-special device.) When used with the -K option, *bufsize* is forced to be a 1K multiple.

-d Creates directories as needed.

-f Copies in all files except those in patterns. (Patterns are described in the paragraph explaining **cpio** -i.)

-I *file* Reads the contents of the specified file as input. For character-special devices, when the first medium is full, replace the medium and press ENTER to continue to the next medium. Use only with the -i option.

-k Attempts to skip corrupted file headers and I/O errors, if any. If you want to copy files from a medium that is corrupted or out of sequence, this option lets you read only those files with good headers.

-l Links files, whenever possible, rather than copying them. Can only be used with the -p option.

-m Retains previous file modification time. This option is ineffective on directories that are being copied.

-K *volumesize* Specifies the media volume size in 1K blocks. For example, a 1.2MB floppy disk has a volumesize of 1200. When using this option you must include the -C option with a *bufsize* multiple of 1K.

-O *file* Directs **cpio** output to the specified file. If you are using a character-special device, replace the first medium when full, and press ENTER to continue to the next medium. Use only with the -o option.

-v (verbose) Causes a list of filenames to be printed. When -v is used with the -t option (table of contents), the resulting output looks like that of an **ls** -l command.

-V (SpecialVerbose) Prints a dot for each file seen. This command assures the user that **cpio** is working without printing out all filenames.

The following example illustrates a **cpio** command for file backup:

```
find . -print | cpio - ocvB > /dev/rct0
```

This example finds all files in the current directory and pipes these filenames to **cpio**, which backs them up to a tape device.

The following example illustrates a **cpio** command for file restoration:

```
cpio - icdmB /usr/target/arrow < /dev/rct0
```

This example extracts the **arrow** file from the backup tape.

Comparing tar to cpio

System administrators should be familiar with the mechanics of both **tar** and **cpio**. Furthermore, they should have a good idea of each command's advantages and, consequently, of when each should be used. Compared to **cpio**, the main advantage of **tar** is its relatively simple syntax. As stated previously, **tar** can move files on the directory tree. It allows you to replace archived files with different versions and to append new files to the end of the archive. **tar** archives are often used to distribute software, especially over anonymous ftp, described in Chapter 11.

The **cpio** command has several advantages. It can back up files describing devices (see special files, defined in Chapter 8), as well as data files. **cpio** tends to be faster than **tar**; it also stores data more efficiently. Unlike **tar**, **cpio** will attempt to read a tape several times if it encounters difficulties. Furthermore, **cpio** will skip a bad area on the tape.

Additional System V Commands

The **dd** command transfers raw data between devices, generating an exact copy or converting the data on request. For example, it can convert data from the industry standard format ASCII to the IBM mainframe format EBCDIC, and vice versa. **dd** is often used to read tapes that are not in Unix format. The **backup** command saves files that may be extracted by the **restore** command. The **volcopy** command makes a literal copy of the entire file system, modifying the block size if required. This command executes rapidly, and verifies tape or disk labels to reduce the frequency of errors. However, it requires a separate tape for each file system.

The dd command

The Unix System V **dd** command converts and copies a file. It has the following syntax:

dd [*option ...*]

dd copies the specified input file to the specified output with possible conversions. The standard input and output are used by default. The input and output block size may be specified to take advantage of raw physical I/O.

The most important option values are described below:

if=*file*   Designates the input filename; standard input is the default.

of=*file*   Designates the output filename; standard output is the default.

ibs=*n*   Sets the input block size.

obs=*n*   Sets the output block size.

bs=*n*   Sets both the block size for both input and output, superseding ibs and obs.

cbs=*n*   Sets the conversion buffer size.

skip=*n*   Skips *n* input records before starting to copy.

seek=*n*   Seeks *n* records from the beginning of the output file before copying.

count=*n*   Copies only *n* input records.

conv=ascii   Converts EBCDIC to ASCII.

conv=ebcdic   Converts ASCII to EBCDIC.

The backup command

The **backup** command performs Unix backup functions. It has the following syntax:

backup [-t] [-p | -c | -f *files* | -u "*user1* [*user2*]"] -d *device*
backup -h

The **backup** utility is a front-end for **cpio**. Use **restore** to restore backups made with this utility. Do not use **backup** for routine system backups; instead, use the **sysadmsh** interface.

backup includes the following options:

-h   Produces a backup history, informing the user when the last complete and incremental/partial backups were done.

-c   Generates a complete backup, all files changed since system installation.

-p   Does an incremental/partial backup, only files modified since the last backup.

-f *files*   Backs up specified files. Filenames may contain characters to be expanded (i.e., *, .) by the shell. The argument must be in quotes.

-u   Backs up all files in the user's home directory. At least one user must be specified. If more than one user is specified, the argument must be in quotes. The argument "all" backs up all users' home directories.

-d   Specifies the backup device.

-t   Indicates that the backup device is a tape. -t must be used with the -d option when the tape device is specified.

A complete backup must be done before a partial backup can be done. Use raw devices instead of block devices. The program can handle multi-volume backups, prompting the user when it is ready for the next medium. It estimates the number of floppies/tapes needed to do the backup. Floppies *must* be formatted before the backup is done. Except for mini-cartridge tapes, tapes need not be formatted. If backup is done to tape, the tape must be rewound.

The restore command

The Unix System V **restore** command performs an incremental file system restore of a previous backup. It has the following syntax:

restore [-c] [-i] [-o] [-t] [-d *device*] [*pattern* [*pattern*] ...]

This utility acts as a front end to **cpio**, and thus reads **cpio** format tapes or floppies. This utility should only be used to restore backups made with the System V **backup** utility. The following options are available:

-c Complete restore. All files on the tape are restored.

-i Gets the index file off of the medium.

-o Overwrites existing files. If the file to be restored already exists it will not be restored unless this option is specified.

-t Indicates that the tape device is to be used. This option *must* be used with the -d option when restoring from tape.

-d *device* Indicates the raw device to be used.

Note

When end of medium is reached, the user is prompted for the next medium. Enter q to exit here. If the file already exists and an attempt is made to restore it without the -o option, the filename will be printed on the screen followed by a question mark. This file will not be restored.

The volcopy command

The Unix System V **volcopy** command makes a literal copy of the file system using a block size matched to the device. It has the following syntax:

volcopy [*options*] *fsname srcdevice volname1 destdevice volname2*

Options are:

-a Invokes a verification sequence requiring a positive operator response instead of the standard 10-second delay before the copy is made.

-s (default) Aborts if wrong verification sequence. The program requests length and density information if not given on the command line or not recorded on an input tape label.

fsname argument Represents the mounted name (e.g., **root**, **u1**, etc.) of the file system being copied. The *srcdevice* or *destdevice* should be the physical disk section or tape.

volname Represents the physical volume name, and should match the external label sticker. Such label names are limited to six or fewer characters.

srcdevice and *volname1*   Represent the device and volume from which the file system copy is extracted.

destdevice and *volname2*   Represent the target device and volume.

BSD Commands

The **tar** command is always available on BSD Unix. In addition, Berkeley Unix employs the **dump** command to generate an incremental file system backup and the **restor** command to perform an incremental file system restore. These two commands are described in detail below.

The dump command

The **dump** command generates an incremental file system dump for BSD Unix. It has the following syntax:

dump [*key* [*argument ...*]] [*file system*]

dump copies to a storage medium all files in the file system that were changed after a specified date. You should normally execute **dump** in the single-user mode.

key specifies the date and other options about the **dump**, and consists of characters from the set *0123456789adFfknosuWw*. Certain key letters require an argument. The argument list must be in the same order as the corresponding key letters. Failure to observe this convention can result in dumping the wrong file system to the wrong device, with potentially disastrous consequences.

The major key letters are as follows:

0–9   This number is the dump level. Level 0 means dump the entire file system. Level 1 dumps only those files that have been modified since the last level 0 dump. Level 2 dumps only those files modified since the last level 0 or 1 dump, whichever was later. Level 3 dumps only those files modified since the last level 0, 1, or 2 dump, whichever was latest, and so on.

a   Uses synchronous tape writes. You must use the *a* key letter if you dump to a device (such as a floppy disk) that does not support asynchronous reads and writes.

d   Interprets the corresponding argument as the tape density, expressed in bits per inch (bpi). This is used, with the tape size, to calculate the amount of data that can be stored on a single dump tape. The default density argument value is 1600.

F   Allows background dumps. If an error occurs, the dump process terminates.

f   Dumps to the device given by the corresponding argument.

s   Interprets the corresponding argument as the size of the dump tape, in feet. This size determines how much data can be stored on a single tape.

Note

The dump command requires operator intervention on the following conditions: end of tape, end of dump, tape write error, tape open error, or disk read error (if there are more than a threshold of 32). In addition to alerting all operators as required by the n key, dump interacts with the operator on the control terminal when it can no longer proceed, or when something is grossly wrong. Answer all questions posed by dump by typing yes or no, and then pressing ENTER.

Since making a full dump involves a lot of time and effort, **dump** checkpoints itself at the beginning of each volume (tape). If writing a given volume fails for some reason, **dump** requests operator permission to restart itself from the checkpoint after the old tape has been rewound and removed, and a new tape has been mounted. Periodically **dump** displays information about system activities, including usually low estimates of the number of blocks still to be written, the number of tapes needed, and the time to completion.

To perform a full, level 0 dump of disk **da0** to the 1/2-inch magnetic tape, type:

```
dump 0uo /dev/da0
```

The restor command

The **restor** command performs an incremental file system restore for BSD Unix. It has the following syntax:

restor *key* [*argument* ...] [*file system*]

restor reads magnetic tapes containing the output of the **dump** command. You can use it to restore all or part of a corrupted file system, or to retrieve individual files accidentally deleted or overwritten by users. (You can retrieve a file only if it was included in a previous dump. The version generated is the current version at the dump date.)

You must be in stand-alone mode to restore the root file system when executing **restor**. The stand-alone version of **restor** does not accept any arguments, and can be used only to restore the root file system. The r key letter option described below is implicit whenever you execute the stand-alone version of **restor**.

Only the superuser may restore a file system including special files. A command line argument error could result in destruction of a file system.

The key letters are described below:

f   Interprets the corresponding argument as the name of the dump tape device to be read.

F   Interprets the corresponding argument as the number of the dump to be read.

c   Reads the tape and compares it with the file system, but does not actually restore the file system. This provides a way to confirm the integrity of a dump immediately after performing it.

Note

restor reports on files by giving their inode number. Use the ncheck command, presented in Chapter 8, to convert this number to a file pathname.

r   Reads the tape and loads it into the file system, destroying the previous contents of the file system.

t   Prints the date the tape was written, together with the "dumped from" date, determined by the dump level and previous dump history. For example, if the dump captured all files modified since 10:58 on February 28, 1994 then that is the "dumped from" date.

T   Prints the date the tape was written, together with the "dumped from" date (see the t key letter); then prints the names and inode numbers of all the files and directories on the tape.

x or X   Extracts each file on the tape named by an argument, where each argument should be a pathname matching the name of a file in the dump. If the tape contains a dump of a mounted file system, the filenames in the dump do not contain the mount directory prefix. If the key letter is x, the extracted file is copied into the current directory and given a numeric name, that is the file's inode number. If the key letter is X, the file is restored to the appropriate directory; that is, **/usr/mydir/myfile** is restored as **/usr/mydir/myfile**.

The following command creates an empty file system on **/dev/ca0-**, destroying the existing file system, and then restores a complete dump to the same device.

Note

This command does not work if /dev/ca0 contains the root file system, since after the mkfs command, the restor program, like the rest of the root file system, would no longer exist.

```
mkfs /dev/ca0
```

If **/dev/ca0**is not the root device and is not mounted, then the following command restores the dumped file system to the disk:

```
restor r /dev/ca0
```

This command assumes that the dump tape is mounted on the default tape device, for example, **/dev/rmt0**. To restore a complete dump to the root file system, you must use the stand-alone versions of **mkfs** and **restor**. Consult your System Management Guide for information on these utilities. You can use a **dump** followed by a **mkfs** and a **restor** to change the size of a file system.

If you have dumped the file system on the default device whose name is system-specific, you can verify the dump with the following command. (This command does not copy any files to disk.)

```
restor cf /dev/da0
```

To obtain a table of contents from a dump tape mounted on the default tape device, and to place it in a file called **toc**, enter the following command:

```
restor T > toc
```

To extract a file named **/usr/mydir/myfile** from a dump tape mounted on the default tape device, execute the following command. The extracted file, if found, is placed in the current directory, in a file with a numeric name (inode number):

```
restor x /usr/mydir/myfile
```

Or you could use X to generate a file with the original name and path, as follows:

```
restor X /usr/mydir/myfile
```

A tar BACKUP SCRIPT

This Bourne shell script (also executable via the Korn shell) applies the **tar** command to perform an incremental backup covering the designated time period. Set the ownership of the script to root, and restrict permission to the owner (root). This script will be executed only by the system administrator, who will specify the backup medium and directory. This script prints an optional log file of archived files.

```
#!/bin/sh
# @(#) tar backup script

log_name='whoami'
```

```
tarinfo=/tmp/tblists
scr=backup_menu        #  backup menu follows this script
d=/usr/$log_name/menus
# The above line (d...) defines a location for your
# menus. If necessary, change the d definition.

# The following code verifies whether the individual
# executing this script has superuser permission.
# In the absence of such permission,
# the script is terminated.
if [ $log_name = "root" ]
then
  echo "\nPlease enter Directory Name: \c"
  read dirs
  if [-n "$dirs"]
  then
    echo "Entered Directory Name -> $dirs\n"
    if [! -d $dirs]; then
      echo "ERROR: $dirs - Not Directory. Try again\n"
      exit 1
    fi
  else
    echo "No Directory Name specified. Try again\n"
    exit 1
  fi

  echo "\nPlease enter Number[of days]: \c"
  read days
  if [-n "$days"]
  then
    echo "Entered Number -> $days\n"
  else
    days=1
    echo "No Number specified. Using default:
         number of days -> $days\n"
  fi
  echo "\n Doing incremental backup ...\n"

  cd $dirs

# The following find command generates the list of files
# to be backed up.
#
  find . -type f -mtime -$days -print > $tarinfo
```

```
cat $d/$scr | more

echo "\nPlease enter Device Name [/dev/]: \c"
read devs
if [-n "$devs"]
then
  echo "Entered Device Name -> /dev/$devs\n"
else
  echo "No Device Name specified.
        Cannot backup ... exiting\n"
  exit 1
fi

device=/dev/$devs

# tar options are:
# c creates a new archive and writes at the beginning of it
# v (verbose) displays names of files treated
# f next argument ($device) is archive name

tar cvf $device 'cat $tarinfo'

while
  echo "Print list of archived files before
        removing [y/n] \c"
  read answer
  do
    case "$answer" in
      [yY]*)
        echo "\nPrinting and Removing ...\n"
        lp $tarinfo
        rm $tarinfo
      break
      ;;
      [nN]*)
        echo "\nRemoving ...\n"
        rm $tarinfo
      break
      ;;
      *)
        echo "Please enter 'y' or 'n' \n"
      ;;
```

```
    esac
  done
else
        echo "Cannot execute - not a root user!\n"
        echo "Check your permissions!\n"
fi
```

Note

You may choose to assign backup duties to a trusted assistant. If so, you must change the user name root in the appropriate if statement to the assistant's user name, and set the correct permissions.

The source code for the **backup_menu**, used in several scripts, is shown here:

```
=================================================
0 1440K floppy/3-1/2"/drive 0
-------------------------------------------------
1 1200K floppy/5-1/4"/drive 0
-------------------------------------------------
2 720K floppy/3-1/2"/drive 0
-------------------------------------------------
3 720K floppy/5-1/4"/drive 0
-------------------------------------------------
4 1440K floppy/3-1/2"/drive 1
-------------------------------------------------
5 1200K floppy/5-1/4"/drive 1
-------------------------------------------------
6 720K floppy/3-1/2"/drive 1
-------------------------------------------------
7 720K floppy/5-1/4"/drive 1
-------------------------------------------------
8 QIC Cartridge tape
-------------------------------------------------
9 Mini-Cartridge tape
-------------------------------------------------
q[Q]    ----------------------->      QUIT
=================================================
```

A tar RESTORE SCRIPT

The following C shell script applies the **tar** command to the list and then restores one or more files from the selected media. Set the ownership of the script to root, and restrict permission to the owner (root). This script will be executed only by the system administrator.

```csh
#!/bin/csh
# @(#) tar restore script
set log_name = 'whoami'
set scr = backup_menu
set d = /usr/$log_name/menus
# The above line (d...) defines a location for your
# menus. If necessary, change the d definition.
set devcase = 1
if ($log_name == "root") then
  cat $d/$scr
  echo "          Enter selection    —>    \c "
  stty raw
  set answ = 'getch'# getch source code follows this script
  stty -raw
  echo ""
  echo ""
  set devcase = 1
  switch ($answ)
    case [qQ]:
      echo '          Exiting ...\n'
      exit 0
    breaksw
    case [0]:
      set med = /dev/rfd0135ds18
#    1440K floppy/3-1/2"/drive 0
    breaksw
    case [1]:
      set med = /devrfd096ds15
#    1200K floppy/5-1/4"/drive 0
    breaksw
    case [2]:
      set med = /dev/rfd0135ds9
#    720K floppy/3-1/2"/drive 0
    breaksw
    case [3]:
      set med = /dev/rfd096ds9
#    720K floppy/5-1/4"/drive 0
    breaksw
    case [4]:
      set med = /dev/rfd1135ds18
```

```
#   1440K floppy/3-1/2"/drive 1
    breaksw
    case [5]:
      set med = /dev/rfd196ds15
#   1200K floppy/5-1/4"/drive 1
    breaksw
    case [6]:
      set med = /dev/rfd1135ds9
#   720K floppy/3-1/2"/drive 1
    breaksw
    case [7]:
      set med = /dev/rfd196ds9
#   720K floppy/5-1/4"/drive 1
    breaksw
    case [8]:
      set med = /dev/rct0
#   QIC Cartridge tape
    breaksw
    case [9]:
      set med = /dev/rctmini
#   Mini-Cartridge tape
    breaksw
    default:
      set devcase = 0
      echo "\nNo device selected! Try again ..."
    breaksw
  endsw
  if ($devcase == 1) then
    echo "        Are you sure? [y/n]: \c"
    stty raw
    set resp = 'getch'
    stty -raw
    echo ""
    echo ""
    switch ($resp)
      case [yY]:
        echo "List of contents(before restoring) [y/n]? \c"
        set response = 'gets'#  gets source code follows this script
        switch ($response)
          case [yY]:
            echo "\nList of contents selected! Continue ..."

#  tar options are:
```

```
# t names of specified files listed as they occur on archive
# v (verbose) displays names of files treated
# f next argument ($med) is archive name

            tar tvf $med | pg -cnsp "RETURN for next ..."
        breaksw
        case [nN]:
          echo "\nNo List of contents selected!
                Continue ..."
        breaksw
        default:
          echo "Please enter 'y' or 'n' \n"
        breaksw
      endsw
      echo "List file(s) to be restored ..."
      echo "When done -> type RETURN twice"
      set files
      while (1)
        set file = 'gets'
        if ("$file" != "") then
          set files = "$files $file"
        else
          break
        endif
      end
      if ("$files" != "") then
        echo "Files to Restore: $files"
      else
        exit 0
      endif
      echo '        Restoring ...'
      echo "\n"
      cd /

# tar options are:
# x named files extracted from archive
# v (verbose) displays names of files treated
# f next argument ($med) is archive name

      tar xvf $med $files
    breaksw
    case [nN]:
```

```
      echo '          Exiting ...\n'
      exit 1
    breaksw
    default:
      echo "Wrong selection! Please enter 'y' or 'n'\n"
    breaksw
  endsw
endif
else
  echo "Cannot execute—not a root user!\n"
  echo "Check your permissions!\n"
endif
```

Note

To assign restoration duties to a trusted assistant, you must change the user name root in the appropriate if statement to the assistant's user name, and set the correct permissions.

The **getch** source code, used in several scripts, is shown here:

```
#include <stdio.h>

main()
{
  int c;

  c = getchar();
  putchar(c);
  return(0);
}
```

The **gets** source code, used in several scripts, is shown here:

```
#include <stdio.h>

main()
{
  int c;

  while ((c = getchar()) != '\n' && c !=EOF)
    putchar(c);
  putchar('\n');
}
```

A cpio BACKUP SCRIPT

The following Bourne shell script (also executable via the Korn shell) applies the **cpio** command to perform an incremental backup. Set the ownership of the script to root, and restrict permission to the owner (root). This script will be executed only by the system administrator, who will specify the backup medium and directory. This script prints an optional log file of archived files.

```
#!/bin/sh
# @(#) cpio backup script
log_name = 'whoami'
scr=backup_menu
d=/usr/$log_name/menus
# The above line (d...) defines a location for your
# menus. If necessary, change the d definition.
backuplogdir=/tmp/backup/logs

# The following code determines whether the person running the
# script has superuser permission. If not, a message is issued
# and the script terminates.
if [ $log_name = "root" ]
then
  if [-s $backuplogdir]
  then
    echo "Directory $backuplogdir for the backup
          logs exists\n"
  else
    echo "Directory $backuplogdir for the backup logs
          does not exist! Making ...\n"
    mkdir $backuplogdir
  fi

  echo "\nPlease enter Directory Name: \c"
  read dirs
  if [-n "$dirs"]
  then
    echo "Entered Directory Name -> $dirs\n"
    if [! -d $dirs]; then
      echo "ERROR: $dirs - Not Directory. Try again\n"
      exit 1
    fi
  else
    echo "No Directory Name specified ...
```

```
            setting the root directory!\n"
    dirs=/
fi
    echo "\n Doing incremental backup by using cpio ...\n"

cd $dirs

cat $d/$scr | more
    echo "\nPlease enter Device Name [/dev/]: \c"
    read devs
    if [-n "$devs"]
    then
      echo "Entered Device Name -> /dev/$devs\n"
    else
      echo "No Device Name specified.
             Cannot backup ... exiting\n"
      exit 1
    fi
    device=/dev/$devs

    touch cpio.curr
    echo "\n Doing backup of $dirs directory
          (log file -> $cpioinfo) ..."
    cpioinfo=backuplogdir/'date +%d$m'.blg
    date > $cpioinfo

# cpio options are:
# o output,
# c ASCII header information,
# a reset access times of input files after copying
# v (verbose) list of filenames,
# B blocked input/output

# The following find command generates the list of files
# to be backed up.
#
    find . -newer cpio.prev -print | cpio -ocavB >
        $device 2>>$cpioinfo
    mv cpio.curr cpio.prev

    while
      echo "Print log file of archived files [y/n] \c"
      read answer
```

```
        do
          case "$answer" in
            [yY]*)
              echo "\nPrinting Log File $cpioinfo ...\n"
              lp $cpioinfo
            break
            ;;
            [nN]*)
              echo "\nNo Printing Log File.\n"
            break
            ;;
        *)
          echo "Please enter 'y' or 'n' \n"
          ;;
        esac
        done
else
    echo "Cannot execute - not a root user!\n"
    echo "Check your permissions!\n"
fi
```

To assign cpio backup duties to a trusted assistant, you must change the user name root in the appropriate if statement to the assistant's user name, and set the correct permissions.

A cpio RESTORE SCRIPT

This C shell script applies the **cpio** command to list and then restore one or more files from the selected media. It allows the system administrator to specify the directory to which the files will be restored. This specification is quite important. For example, if you choose to restore to the default **/tmp** directory and do not move your files, they will be lost when the directory is cleaned. Set the ownership of the script to root, and restrict permission to the owner (root). This script will be executed only by the system administrator.

```
#!/bin/csh
# @(#) cpio restore script

set log_name = 'whoami'
set scr = backup_menu# file presenting menu options
set d = /usr/$log_name/menus
# The above line (d...) defines a location for your
```

```
# menus. If necessary, change the d definition.
set devcase = 1

if ($log_name = "root") then
  cat $d/$scr
  echo  "          Enter selection   —>    \c "
  stty raw
  set answ = 'getch'
  stty -raw
  echo ""
  echo ""
  set devcase = 1
  switch ($answ)
    case [qQ]:
      echo '          Exiting ...\n'
      exit 0
    breaksw
    case [0]:
      set med = /dev/rfd0135ds18
#     1440K floppy/3-1/2"/drive 0
    breaksw
    case [1]:
      set med = /dev/rfd096ds15
#     1200K floppy/5-1/4"/drive 0
    breaksw
    case [2]:
      set med = /dev/rfd0135ds9
#     720K floppy/3-1/2"/drive 0
    breaksw
    case [3]:
      set med = /dev/rfd096ds9
#     720K floppy/5-1/4"/drive 0
    breaksw
    case [4]:
      set med = /dev/rfd1135ds18
#     1440K floppy/3-1/2"/drive 1
    breaksw
    case [5]:
      set med = /dev/rfd196ds15
#     1200K floppy/5-1/4"/drive 1
    breaksw
    case [6]:
      set med = /dev/rfd1135ds9
```

```
#    720K floppy/3-1/2"/drive 1
    breaksw
    case [7]:
      set med = /dev/rfd196ds9
#    720K floppy/5-1/4"/drive 1
    breaksw
    case [8]:
      set med = /dev/rct0
#    QIC Cartridge tape
    breaksw
    case [9]:
      set med = /dev/rctmini
#    Mini-Cartridge tape
    breaksw
    default:
      set devcase = 0
      echo "\nNo device selected! Try again ..."
    breaksw
  endsw

  if ($devcase == 1) then
    echo "        Are you sure? [y/n]: \c"
    stty raw
    set resp = 'getch'
    stty -raw
    echo ""
    echo ""
# The program provides an optional list of contents
    switch ($resp)
      case [yY]:
        echo "List of contents(before restoring) [y/n]? \c"
        get response = 'gets'
        switch ($response)
          case [yY]:
            echo "\nList of contents selected! Continue ..."

# cpio options are:
# i input,
# c ASCII header information,
# v (verbose) list of filenames,
# t input table of contents
# B blocked input/output

            cpio -icvtB < $med
```

```
            breaksw
            case [nN]:
              echo "\nNo List of contents selected!
                    Continue ..."
            breaksw
            default:
              echo "Please enter 'y' or 'n' \n"
            breaksw
          endsw
          echo "List file(s) to be restored ..."
          echo "When done -> type RETURN twice"
          set files
          while (1)
            set file = 'gets'
            if ("$file" != "") then
#  restore individual selected files
              set files = "$files $file"
            else
              break
            endif
          end
          if ("$files" != "") then
            echo "Files to Restore: $files"
          else
            exit 0
          endif
          echo "\nSet  directory to which
                you want to restore: \c"
          set dirs = 'gets'
          if ("$dirs" != "") then
            echo "\nRestoring to $dirs"
            cd $dirs
          else
#  The following code sets the default directory to /tmp.
#  Specify your installation's default directory
            set dirs = /tmp
            echo "\nNo directory selected ...
                  Restoring to $dirs"
            cd $dirs
          endif
          echo '          Restoring ...'
          echo "\n"

#  cpio options are:
```

```
# i input,
# c ASCII header information,
# v (verbose) list of filenames,
# d directories created as needed
# m retain previous file modification time,
# u copy unconditionally
# B blocked input/output

        cpio -icvdmuB $files < $med
      breaksw
      case [nN]:
        echo '          Exiting ...\n'
        exit 1
      breaksw
      default:
        echo "Wrong selection! Please enter 'y' or 'n'\n"
      breaksw
    endsw
  endif
else
    echo "Cannot execute - not a root user!\n"
    echo "Check your permissions!\n"
endif
```

To assign cpio restoration duties to a trusted assistant, you must change the user name root in the appropriate if statement to the assistant's user name, and set the correct permissions.

Chapter Summary

A full backup copies the entire file system. Make a full backup when you first install the system and whenever you make important modifications to the system, such as installing a new central hard disk. A partial backup is a complete copy of any file system or directory tree. Make partial backups on a regular basis for frequently changing file systems and directories. An incremental backup is a copy of new files and files that have changed since the last backup. Make an incremental backup at least once each working day. Media choices for storing your data include conventional magnetic tape, floppy disks, cartridge tape, video tape, and WORM disks.

The following precautions increase the likelihood of successful file system backups and restorations: Use shell scripts. Verify your backups before you actually need them. Label your backups using a clear, unambiguous file-naming scheme. Finally, document your backup and restoration processes in a log book.

Commands   The most widely used System V Unix commands for file system backup and restoration are **tar** and **cpio**, used both for backup and for restoration. **dd** transfers raw data between devices. **restore** performs a Unix incremental file system restore of a previous backup. **volcopy** makes a literal copy of the entire file system. BSD Unix includes **tar**, **dump** to generate an incremental file system backup; **backup** to generate a backup; and **restor** to perform an incremental file system restore from a previous **dump** backup.

Unix System

- Manipulating Undamaged File Systems

- A Script for Checking File System Integrity

- Checking and Repairing File Systems

Administration Guide

CHAPTER

Unix File Systems

The file system is an integral part of any Unix system. Keeping the file system in running order is a primary responsibility of the system administrator. As you will see in this chapter, you are not alone. In many instances, much of the work involved in maintaining the file system is semiautomatic. You may only have to answer *Yes* to a few questions, and Unix will then repair your system to the best of its ability. However, for those (hopefully) rare instances when Unix cannot repair itself, you will have to master the principles and commands discussed in this important chapter.

INTRODUCTION

This section introduces basic vocabulary associated with the file system. It then examines the file system's basic components and their interrelationships. You must be familiar with this material before you can profitably examine your file systems, much less repair them.

Basic Vocabulary

The following terms have not yet been defined in this text. You will need to understand them to work with file systems. Other basic terms are discussed in greater detail in the following section.

Logical Disk   A *logical disk* is a simplified model of the physical (actual) disk. Neither the system administrator nor the users are usually interested in the details of the physical disk; however, the system administrator may need to know about the logical disk.

Partition   A *partition* is a segment of the logical disk. Dividing a logical disk into partitions improves its use (for example, by limiting the maximum disk space that a greedy user can reserve). The **/dev/dsk** logical disk may be divided into several partitions, such as **/dev/dsk/0s0**, **/dev/dsk/0s1**, etc. Partitions vary widely in size, and may overlap. They are described in a partition table.

File System Components

The file system includes several major components: data blocks, containing programs and data; the superblock containing system control information; inodes describing files and directories; and device drivers, programs that control hardware devices. These components and their interaction are described below.

Blocks and Superblocks

The *superblock* is a 512-byte area starting at byte number 512 of the file system. It contains valuable information including the file system name and size, the address of the first data block, the count and list of inodes, the count and list of free data blocks, and the time of last (superblock) update. A copy of the superblock is maintained in memory for increased efficiency. However, because the disk-resident copy of the superblock does not necessarily change whenever the memory-resident copy changes, you should not simply turn off the system. Doing so may cause system inconsistencies, requiring you to repair the file system with the **fsck** command, discussed later in this chapter.

Chapter 9 discusses the steps to take before turning off the system. In case of emergency, issue several **sync** commands. Why several? Because the **sync** command does not necessarily take effect immediately when issued; using several **sync** commands reduces the likelihood of lost information. This command writes the superblock and other system information to disk, in effect synchronizing the disk image and memory image of the system. The **cron** daemon automatically issues **sync** commands on a regular basis.

Inodes

A major component of Unix file systems is an *inode* (short for index node.) Chapter 4 presented inode contents. The inode on disk does not change during file processing. It contains the following fields: file owner identifier; file type, file access permissions; file access information, including the time when the file was last modified, when it was last accessed, and when the associated inode was last modified; the number of names that the file has in the directory hierarchy; the list of data addresses for the file; and the file size in bytes. The inode in memory contains all this information and other information, such as whether or not the file is locked (protected against simultaneous access by another process). Furthermore, the in-memory inode changes whenever the file system changes, for example, when a user creates a new file, reducing the number of free blocks in the file system. As is the case with the superblock, disk resident inodes are not necessarily updated immediately.

Inode 0 is used to mark a removed directory entry. Inode 1 was used by older versions of Unix to store bad blocks. It is now used only to maintain compatibility. Inode 2 describes the file system's **root** directory.

An inode may contain a directory name. In this case, it is said that the directory name is *linked* (or *hard linked*) to the inode number. More than one directory name may be linked to a given inode number. Thus you can refer to the same file (inode) by more than one name. Sometimes a given file must be executed from a specified directory. Instead of copying the file into that directory, simply link the file using the **ln** command. This generates a *symbolic link* (or *soft link*). The use of symbolic links saves time, and disk space.

Other Components

A *device driver* is a program that controls a specific device, such as a laser printer. Device drivers are defined in the **/dev** directory; this directory also contains inodes describing special file types, as discussed below.

A *block special file,* also known as a *block file,* moves data a block at a time between the file system and a block device, such as a disk drive. A *character special file,* also known as a *character file,* moves data a character at a time between the file system and a character device, such as a terminal. The first character in the output generated by the **ls** -l (long listing) command indicates the file type. A *b* indicates a block file. A *c* indicates a character file. A *d* indicates a directory file. A *p* indicates a *fifo* (first in, first out) file, which is a named pipe created by one process in order to communicate with other processes. A – indicates an ordinary (data) file.

MANIPULATING UNDAMAGED FILE SYSTEMS

This section deals with file systems that do not need repair. It describes the principles and commands involved in creating file systems, monitoring them, and reorganizing them.

Creating a file system involves two basic steps. After planning your file system, you issue the **mkfs** command to make the physical file system. Then you issue the **mount** command to link the new file system to the previously existing file system. Issue the **umount** command to unlink the new file system. In the hands of a knowledgeable system administrator the **df**, **du**, and **find** commands reveal potential problems before they become critical. The **fsstat** command reports on the status of the file system. The more heavily the system is used, the more rapidly its performance will degrade. The **dcopy** command reorganizes the file system, usually increasing its efficiency.

Creating a File System

It is necessary to create a file system prior to mounting a disk. This is done via the **mkfs** command, described below. The basic process is fairly easy. However, when system efficiency is a major issue, you may have to experiment some. For example, the partition size can affect system performance substantially. Whenever you use the **mkfs** command, make sure to create a new **lost+found** directory. This directory is required to run the **fsck** command, used in repairing file systems.

The mkfs Command

The **mkfs** command constructs a file system. It has the following syntax:

mkfs [-y | -n] [-f *fstype*] *special blocks* [: *inodes*] [*gap inblocks*]

mkfs constructs a file system by writing on the special file **special**, as specified by command line options. The -f option specifies the file system type.

Standard Options   If the *special* file appears to contain a file system, operator confirmation is requested before the data is overwritten.

-y   Writes over any existing data without question.

-n   Terminates **mkfs** immediately if the target contains an existing file system. The system reads block one from the target device (block one is the superblock) and determines whether the bytes are the same. If they are not the same, the block read is assumed to contain meaningful data, and confirmation is requested.

If the second argument is a digit string, the file system size is *blocks* interpreted as a decimal number. This indicates how many physical disk blocks the file system will occupy. The default number of *inodes* is approximately the number of logical blocks divided by 4.

Unix File System Options   -b *blocksize* specifies the *logical block size,* the number of bytes read or written by the operating system in a single I/O operation. Valid blocksizes are 512, 1024, and 2048. The default is 1024. If the -b option is used, it must appear last on the command line.

Mounting and Unmounting File Systems

Mounting a disk (or a diskette) links its file system with one of the installation's existing file systems. A file system must be mounted before it can be accessed. The place at which the mounted file system's **root** directory is inserted into the original file system is known as the *mount point. Unmounting* a disk reverses the mount operation; it breaks the link between the unmounted disk and the original, larger file system. When a file system contains an open file, or when it is the user's working directory (accessed via the **cd** command), it may not be unmounted. Generally, file systems are unmounted as part of the system shutdown process. The **mount** and **umount** commands are detailed next.

The mount Command

The **mount** command mounts a file structure. It has the following syntax:

mount [-v] [-r] [-f *fstyp*] *special device*

mount announces to the system that a removable file structure is present on the specified special device. The file structure is mounted at the specified directory. The specified directory must already exist, and it should be empty. It becomes the root of the newly mounted file structure. If the directory contains files, they will appear to have been removed while the special device is mounted and reappear when the special device is unmounted. The **mount** command is restricted to the superuser.

The **mount** command maintains a table of mounted devices. If **mount** is invoked without any arguments, it displays the name of each mounted device, and the directory on which it is mounted, whether the file structure is read-only, and the date it was mounted. **mount** has the following options:

-f *fstyp*   Specifies the file system type to be mounted. Its default is the root *fstyp*.

-r   Indicates that the file is to be mounted read-only. File structures that are physically write-protected, such as floppy disks with write-protect tabs, must be mounted in this way; otherwise, errors occur when access times are updated, whether or not any explicit write is attempted.

-v   Displays mount information in detail.

Note

The mount command does not check for file system integrity. To perform such a check, you must issue an fsck command prior to issuing a mount command.

The umount Command

The **umount** command dismounts a file structure. It has the following syntax:

umount *special device*

umount announces to the system that the removable file structure previously mounted on device *special device* is to be removed. Any pending I/O for the file system is completed, and the file structure is flagged clean. The **mount** and **umount** commands maintain a table of mounted devices. For a detailed explanation of the mounting process, see **mount** described previously.

Busy file structures cannot be dismounted with **umount**. A file structure is busy if it contains an open file or some user's working directory.

Note

umount issues a sync command to copy modified parts of the file system to disk before unmounting the file system. Remove the mount directory if the device is to be premanently unmounted.

Monitoring File Systems

Carefully monitoring the file system will reduce inevitable malfunctions, such as running out of disk space. The system administrator should be familiar with several monitoring commands. The **du** command summarizes disk usage. It returns the number of blocks contained in all files and directories recursively, within each specified directory and file. The **df** command reports the number of free disk blocks. It examines the counts in the superblocks and then prints the number of free blocks and free inodes available for all on-line file systems. These two commands are discussed in detail in Chapter 14. The **find** command locates files that meet specified selection criteria. Use it to identify files to be deleted. The **fsstat** command reports on the file system status. It lets you know if the file system needs checking (which could be done with the **fsck** command, described later in this chapter). However, even if it suggests that the file system has no problems, you still should issue **fsck** commands on a regular basis.

The find Command

The **find** command finds files. It has the following syntax:

find *pathname-list expression*

The **find** command locates files that match a certain set of selection criteria. It recursively descends the directory hierarchy for each pathname in the pathname-list (i.e., one or more pathnames) seeking files that match a Boolean expression.

Use this command to locate files that you may wish to delete. For example, core files are generated when a program aborts. These large files may be of use for program debugging, but should be deleted if they are not being used. The following command deletes all core files that have not been accessed in the last seven days:

```
find / -name core -atime +7 -exec rm {} \;
```

| Tip |

To avoid problems, inform users in writing about deleting files before you actually delete them.

The fsstat Command

The Unix System V command **fsstat** reports the file system status. It has the following syntax:

fsstat special_file

The **fsstat** command reports on the status of the file system on **special_file**. During system startup, this command determines whether the file system needs checking before it is mounted. **fsstat** succeeds if the file system is unmounted and if it appears to be clean. For the root file system, it succeeds if the file system is active and not marked bad. It generates the following exit codes:

0 if the file system is not mounted and appears to be clean (except for the root, where 0 means mounted and clean).

1 if the file system is not mounted and needs to be checked.

2 if the file system is mounted.

3 if the command fails.

Reorganizing File Systems

Over a period of time, the file system, especially the user file system, will become fragmented. As users create, enlarge, and remove files and directories, the system's free blocks become scattered. Accessing a file may require moving the physical access mechanism several times. BSD Unix provides the Fast File System for correcting fragmentation automatically. System V provides the **dcopy** command to correct fragmentation. Depending on system activity, you may wish to perform a **dcopy** every few days. This should be done when there are few users on the system—perhaps at night or on the weekend.

The dcopy Command

The Unix System V command **dcopy** copies Unix file systems for optimal access time. It has the following syntax:

dcopy [-sX] [-an] [-d] [-v]
    [-f*size*[:*isize*]] inputfs outputfs

The **dcopy** command copies the device file **inputfs** for the existing file system to the reorganized device file **outputfs**. For maximum optimization, **inputfs** should be the raw device and **outputfs** should be the block device. They should both be unmounted file systems.

    If no options are specified, **dcopy** copies files from **inputfs**, compressing directories by removing vacant entries, and spacing consecutive blocks in a file by the optimal rotational gap. See your system manual for available options.

dcopy catches **interrupts** and **quits**, and reports on their progress. To terminate dcopy, issue a **quit** signal followed by an **interrupt** or a **quit**.

A SCRIPT FOR CHECKING FILE SYSTEM INTEGRITY

The following Bourne shell script checks the file system integrity. Set the ownership of this script to root and restrict permission to the owner (root). This script will be executed only by the system administrator.

```
#!/bin/sh
# @(#) file system integrity check script
clnsys=/dev/root
log_name = 'whoami'

while
   echo "\nDo you want to check Filesystem Integrity: [y/n] \c"
   read answer
do
   case "$answer" in
     [yY]*)
        echo "\007Entered yes! Continue ...\n"
     break
     ;;
     [nN]*)
        echo "\nExiting ...\n"
        exit 0
     ;;
     *)
        echo "Please enter 'y' or 'n' \n"
     ;;
   esac
done
if [ $log_name = "root" ]
then
     echo "Start Filesystem check ...\n"
     /etc/fsck -y $clnsys
     rm -f /etc/downclean
     echo "\n"
     echo "Filesystem check - done!\n"
```

```
else
# this should not happen
    echo "Cannot execute - not a root user!\n"
    echo "Offending user is $log_name!\n"
    echo "You forgot to set proper permissions (root)!!\n"
fi
```

CHECKING AND REPAIRING FILE SYSTEMS

Sometimes the file system goes bad. Unix offers several tools for checking and repairing the file system when this happens. The main tool is the **fsck** program. Mastering the **fsck** command is necessary for keeping the file system, and consequently the computer system, in working order. Therefore, this command and its output are presented in great detail. When **fsck** denotes a problem with a given inode, you will have to run the **ncheck** command to determine the associated filename. This chapter concludes with a brief examination of **fsdb**, the file system debugger.

The fsck Program

The **fsck** (file system check) program is the Unix tool for uncovering and repairing file system inconsistencies. It should be used by system administrators on a regular basis. Because of its importance, this command is discussed in great detail.

Unlike many other commands, **fsck** is interactive. Whenever it runs into a potential problem, it asks you to choose from alternatives. The wrong choice can cause substantial damage to your file system. Before we examine this command in detail, here is an overview of the command's phases.

The Phases of fsck

The **fsck** program executes in eight well-defined phases. Each phase carries out specific tasks, and may generate error messages. You must respond to any error messages before proceeding to the next phase.

▟ **Initialization Phase** This phase invokes the command line options and opens the special device file. It validates the superblock by comparing the total size of the file system to the sizes in the inode list. If the total file system size is less than the sizes in the inode list, the superblock is corrupt.

▰   **Phase 1—Check Blocks and Sizes** This phase checks the inodes for valid size, file type, and block addresses, and for a nonzero link count. It also prepares data on block addresses, and inodes and their links to be employed in subsequent phases. For example, each inode is identified with an inode type, such as *directory*. If duplicate blocks are found, the file system is rescanned for more duplicate blocks. This rescanning is sometimes known as Phase 1B.

▰   **Phase 2—Check Pathnames** This phase checks all directory entries, starting with the root, for a valid inode (as determined in Phase 1). It completes the link counts for each inode.

▰   **Phase 3—Check Connectivity** This phase may (at the superuser's discretion) create a directory entry for a directory-type inode that currently is not connected to any directory.

▰   **Phase 4—Check Reference Counts** This phase may create directory entries for inodes whose type is not directory. The number of directory entries generated in Phase 2 must be equal to the sum of the inode link counts. The total number of inodes must be equal to the inode count appearing in the superblock.

▰   **Phase 5—Check Free List** The superblock contains a list of free blocks up to a maximum count of 50. If the file system contains more than 50 free blocks, the 50th address points to a block containing the addresses of the next 50 free blocks, etc. This phase checks the validity of the free list, making sure that no block addresses appear in the inodes. Except for bad blocks, all blocks in the file system must be in the free block list, or be allocated to an inode.

▰   **Phase 6—Salvage Free Block List** This phase reconstructs the free block list.

▰   **Cleanup Phase** After checking a file system, **fsck** performs a few cleanup functions.

Syntax and Options for fsck

The **fsck** command audits and interactively repairs inconsistent conditions for all supported file systems. If the file system is consistent, it reports the number of files, the number of blocks used, and the number of free blocks. If the file system is inconsistent, the operator is prompted for permission as each correction is attempted. Note that most corrective actions result in some loss of data. The amount and severity of data loss may be determined from the diagnostic output.

The **fsck** command has the following syntax:

fsck [*options*] [*file system*] ...

whose options are:

-b   When the root file system is being checked or modified, either remounts or reboots the system. Do a remount only if the damage was minor.

-C[*clustersize*]   Converts the named S51K file system into an AFS (Acer Fast File system). The -s option must also be included. The *clustersize* argument must be a power of 2 and less than 16 (8 is recommended). The potential increase in system performance provided by a fast file system is not immediately apparent; it can take effect only when new files are added to the file system. There is little or no benefit in transforming a file system that is nearly full. It is impossible to convert a file system that is within a few blocks of being full.

-y   Assumes a *yes* response to all questions asked by **fsck**. This option saves the system administrator time, but can cause headaches. For example, when **fsck** removes bad blocks, it will do so silently, so you won't know which blocks to restore.

-n   Assumes a *no* response to all questions asked by **fsck**; does not open the file system for writing. This option is recommended when hardware problems are suspected. You don't want **fsck** to make any changes to the file system in response to hardware errors.

-sb:c   Ignores the actual free list and (unconditionally) reconstructs a new one by rewriting the file system's superblock. The file system must be unmounted while this is being done. This option allows for creating an optimal free-list organization.

-S   Conditionally reconstructs the free list. This option is similar to -sb:c above, except that with the -S option, the free list is rebuilt only if no file system discrepancies are discovered. This option forces a *no* response to all questions asked by **fsck**. It is useful for forcing free list reorganization on uncontaminated file systems.

-t   If **fsck** cannot obtain enough memory to keep its tables, it uses a scratch file, specified in the *filename* argument. Coding -t*filename* (omitting the space after the t) is a recipe for disaster: **fsck** will use the entire file system as a scratch file and erase the entire disk.

-q (Quiet **fsck**)   Instructs **fsck** not to print size-check messages in Phase 1. If **fsck** so requires, counts in the superblock will be automatically fixed, and the free list salvaged. Because you want to know what **fsck** has found, this option should generally not be used.

-D   Checks directories for bad blocks. This option is useful after system crashes.

-f (Fast check)   Checks blocks and sizes (Phase 1) and checks the free list (Phase 5). The free list will be reconstructed (Phase 6) if necessary.

Summary of fsck Use

Consider the following points with respect to using **fsck**:

- Run this program on a regular basis during periods when system use is light, such as nights and weekends.

- Run this program only on unmounted file systems.

- Do not use the -q or -y options.

- Let **fsck** do it. Answer **Y** (for *Yes*) to most questions, except those pertaining to (1) the **lost+found** directory and (2) DUP TABLE overflow. In the first case, fix the **lost+found** directory manually, and then rerun **fsck**. In the second case, **fsck** terminates when you answer **N**. Regenerate **fsck** with a larger table size. (See your system manual for details.) Rerun **fsck**.

- Keep a record of files deleted in Phase 2 (Check Pathnames). You may have to restore these files from backups.

- If **fsck** finds and corrects errors, run it again to be sure that the file system is clean.

Error Messages in fsck

The **fsck** program generates different error messages at each phase of its operation. Unless you have run it with the -y option (not recommended), it waits for your response before continuing its operation.

General Errors

These three error messages may appear in any phase. In general you should regard them as fatal, stop the program, and investigate the cause of the problem.

- CAN NOT SEEK: BLK B (CONTINUE?)   The request for moving to a specified block number B in the file system has failed.

- CAN NOT READ: BLK B (CONTINUE?)   The request for reading from a specified block number B in the file system has failed.

- CAN NOT WRITE: BLK B (CONTINUE?)   The request for writing to a specified block number B in the file system has failed. The disk may be write-protected.

When one of these error messages appears, entering **N** (for *No*) terminates the program. (This is the recommended response.) Entering **Y** (for *Yes*) causes **fsck** to try to continue running the file system check program. Often, however, the problem persists. The error condition does not allow a complete check of the file system, so you should run **fsck** again to recheck the system.

Errors in the Initialization Phase

This phase checks the command syntax. Before performing the file system check, **fsck** sets up certain tables and opens some files. It terminates upon encountering initialization errors.

Errors in Phase 1—Check Blocks and Sizes

This phase checks the inode list. The meanings of Yes and No responses to **fsck** questions are as follows:

- CONTINUE?   No—Terminates the program. (This is the recommended response.) Yes—Continues with the program. This response means that a complete file system check is not possible. Run **fsck** again to recheck the file system.

- CLEAR?   No—Ignores the error condition. A No response is only appropriate if the user intends to take other measures to fix the problem. Yes—Deallocates inode by zeroing its contents. This may invoke the UNALLOCATED error condition in Phase 2 for each directory entry pointing to this inode.

Phase 1 may generate the following error or warning messages:

- UNKNOWN FILE TYPE I=I (CLEAR?)   The mode word of the inode I suggests that it is not a named pipe, special character inode, regular inode, or directory inode.

- LINK COUNT TABLE OVERFLOW (CONTINUE?)   An internal table, containing allocated inodes with a link count of zero, is full.

- B BAD I=I   Inode I contains block number B with a number lower than the number of the first data block in the file system or greater than the number of the last block in the file system. This error condition may invoke the EXCESSIVE BAD BLKS error condition in Phase 1 if inode I has too many block numbers outside the file system range. This error condition invokes the BAD/DUP error condition in Phase 2 and Phase 4.

- EXCESSIVE BAD BLOCKS I=I (CONTINUE?)   There are too many (usually more than 10) blocks whose number is lower than the number of the first data block in the file system or greater than the number of the last block in the file system associated with inode I.

- B DUP I=I   Inode I contains block number B, already claimed by another inode. This error condition may invoke the EXCESSIVE DUP BLKS error condition in Phase 1 if inode I has too many block numbers claimed by other inodes. This error condition invokes Phase 1B and the BAD/DUP error condition in Phase 2 and Phase 4.

- EXCESSIVE DUP BLKS I=I (CONTINUE?)   There are too many blocks (usually more than 10) claimed by other inodes.

- DUP TABLE OVERFLOW (CONTINUE?)   An internal table, containing duplicate block numbers, is full.

- POSSIBLE FILE SIZE ERROR I=I   The size of inode I does not match the actual number of blocks used by the inode. This is only a warning. The -q option suppresses this message.

- DIRECTORY MISALIGNED I=I   The directory inode size is not a multiple of 16. This is only a warning. The -q option suppresses this message.

- PARTIALLY ALLOCATED INODE I=I (CLEAR?)   Inode I is neither allocated nor unallocated.

Errors in Phase 2—Check Pathnames

This phase removes directory entries pointing to bad inodes found in Phase 1 and Phase 1B. The meaning of Yes and No responses to **fsck** questions follows:

▰ FIX?   No—Terminates the program since **fsck** will be unable to continue. Answer **Y** (yes) to change the root inode type to *directory.* If the root inode data blocks are not directory blocks, a very large number of error conditions are produced.

▰ CONTINUE?   No—Terminates the program. Yes—Ignores DUPS/BAD error condition in root inode and attempts to continue running the file system check. If the root inode is not correct, then a great number of additional error conditions might result.

▰ REMOVE?   No—Ignores the error condition. A No response is only appropriate if the user intends to take other measures to fix the problem. Yes—Removes duplicate or unallocated blocks.

Phase 2 may generate the following error messages:

▰ ROOT INODE UNALLOCATED. TERMINATING   The root inode (always inode number 2) has no allocated mode bits. This error condition indicates a serious problem; when it appears, the program stops.

▰ ROOT INODE NOT DIRECTORY (FIX?)   The root inode (usually inode number 2) is not directory inode type.

▰ DUPS/BAD IN ROOT INODE (CONTINUE?)   Phase 1 or Phase 1B has found duplicate blocks or bad blocks in the root inode (usually inode number 2) of the file system.

▰ I OUT OF RANGE I=I NAME=F (REMOVE?)   A directory entry F has an inode number I greater than the end of the inode list.

▰ UNALLOCATED I=I OWNER=O MODE=M SIZE=S MTIME=T NAME=F (REMOVE?)   A directory entry F has an inode I without allocated mode bits. The owner O, mode M, size S, modify time T, and filename F are printed. If the file system is not mounted, and if the -n option has not been specified, the entry will be removed automatically if it points to an inode whose character size is 0.

▰ DUP/BAD I=I OWNER=O MODE=M SIZE=S MTIME=T DIR=F (REMOVE?)   Phase 1 or Phase 1B has found duplicate blocks or bad blocks associated with directory entry F and directory inode I. The owner O, mode M, size S, modify time T, and directory name F are printed.

▰ DUP/BAD I=I OWNER=O MODE=M SIZE=S MTIME=T FILE=F (REMOVE?)   Phase 1 or Phase 1B has found duplicate blocks or bad blocks associated with file entry F, inode I. The owner O, mode M, size S, modify time T, and filename F are printed.

▰ BAD BLK B IN DIR I=I OWNER=O MODE=M SIZE=S MTIME=T   This message only occurs when the -D option is used. A bad block has been found in DIR inode I. Error conditions that are searched for within directory blocks are nonzero padded entries, inconsistent . and .. entries, and embedded slashes in the name field. This error message means that the user should subsequently either remove the directory inode if the entire block looks bad, or change (or remove) those directory entries that look bad.

Errors in Phase 3—Check Connectivity

This phase is concerned with the directory connectivity seen in Phase 2. The meaning of Yes and No responses to **fsck** questions follows:

▰ RECONNECT?   No—Ignores the error condition. This invokes the UNREF error condition in Phase 4. A No response is only appropriate if the user intends to take other measures to fix the problem. Yes—Reconnects directory inode I to the file system in the directory for lost files. (This directory is usually called **lost+found**.) A Yes response may invoke a lost+found error condition if there are problems connecting directory inode I to **lost+found**. It will invoke a CONNECTED information message if the link is successful.

Phase 3 may generate the following error messages:

▰ UNREF DIR I=I OWNER=O MODE=M SIZE=S MTIME=T (RECONNECT?)   The directory inode I was not connected to a directory entry when the file system was traversed. The owner O, mode M, size S, and modify time T of directory inode I are printed. **fsck** forces the reconnection of a nonempty directory.

▰ SORRY. NO **lost+found** DIRECTORY   There is no **lost+found** directory in the **root** directory of the file system; **fsck** ignores the request to link a directory in **lost+found**. This invokes the UNREF error condition in Phase 4. Possible problem with access modes of **lost+found**.

▰ SORRY. NO SPACE IN **lost+found** DIRECTORY   There is no space to add another entry to the **lost+found** directory in the **root** directory of the file system; **fsck** ignores the request to link a directory in **lost+found**. This invokes the UNREF error condition in Phase 4. Clean out unnecessary entries in **lost+found** or make **lost+found** larger.

▰ DIR I=I1 CONNECTED. PARENT WAS I=I2   This is an advisory message indicating a directory inode I1 was successfully connected to the **lost+found** directory. The parent inode I2 of the directory inode I1 is replaced by the inode number of the **lost+found** directory.

Errors in Phase 4—Check Reference Counts

This phase checks the link count information seen in Phases 2 and 3. The meanings of Yes and No responses to **fsck** questions are as follows:

▟ RECONNECT? No—Ignores this error condition. This invokes a CLEAR error condition later in Phase 4. Yes—Reconnect inode I to file system in the directory for lost files (usually **lost+found**). This can cause a **lost+found** error condition in this phase if there are problems connecting inode I to **lost+found**.

▟ CLEAR? No—Ignores the error condition. A No response is only appropriate if the user intends to take other measures to fix the problem. Yes—Deallocates the inode by zeroing its contents.

▟ ADJUST? No—Ignores the error. A No response is only appropriate if the user intends to take other measures to fix the problem. Replaces the link count of file i node I with Y.

▟ FIX? No—Ignores the error. A No response is only appropriate if the user intends to take other measures to fix the problem. Yes—Replaces the count in the superblock with the actual count.

This phase may generate the following error messages:

▟ UNREF FILE I=I OWNER=O MODE=M SIZE=S MTIME=T (RECONNECT?) Inode I was not connected to a directory entry when the file system was traversed. The owner O, mode M, size S, and modify time T of inode I are printed. If the -n option is omitted and the file system is not mounted, empty files are cleared automatically. Nonempty files are not cleared.

▟ SORRY. NO **lost+found** DIRECTORY There is no **lost+found** directory in the **root** directory of the file system; **fsck** ignores the request to link a file in **lost+found**. This invokes the CLEAR error condition later in Phase 4. There may be problems with the access modes of **lost+found**.

▟ SORRY. NO SPACE IN **lost+found** DIRECTORY There is no space to add another entry to the **lost+found** directory in the **root** directory of the file system; **fsck** ignores the request to link a file in **lost+found**. This invokes the CLEAR error condition later in Phase 4. Check the size and contents of **lost+found**.

▟ (CLEAR) The inode mentioned in the immediately previous UNREF error condition cannot be reconnected.

▟ LINK COUNT FILE I=I OWNER=O MODE=M SIZE=S MTIME=T COUNT=X SHOULD BE Y (ADJUST?) The link count for inode I, which is a file, is X but should be Y. The owner O, mode M, size S, and modify time T are printed.

■ LINK COUNT DIR I=I OWNER=O MODE=M SIZE=S MTIME=T
COUNT=X SHOULD BE Y (ADJUST?)   The link count for inode I, which
is a directory, is X but should be Y. The owner O, mode M, size S, and modify
time T of directory inode I are printed.

■ LINK COUNT F I=I OWNER=O MODE=M SIZE=S MTIME=T
COUNT=X SHOULD BE Y (ADJUST?)   The link count for F inode I is X
but should be Y. The filename F, owner O, mode M, size S, and modify time T
are printed.

■ UNREF FILE I=I OWNER=O MODE=M SIZE=S MTIME=T (CLEAR?)
Inode I, which is a file, was not connected to a directory entry when the file
system was traversed. The owner O, mode M, size S, and modify time T of
inode I are printed. If the -n option is omitted and the file system is not
mounted, empty files are cleared automatically. Nonempty directories are
not cleared.

■ UNREF DIR I=I OWNER=O MODE=M SIZE=S MTIME=T (CLEAR?)
Inode I, which is a directory, was not connected to a directory entry when the
file system was traversed. The owner O, mode M, size S, and modify time T of
inode I are printed. If the -n option is omitted and the file system is not
mounted, empty directories are cleared automatically. Nonempty directories are
not cleared.

■ BAD/DUP FILE I=I OWNER=O MODE=M SIZE=S MTIME=T
(CLEAR?)   Phase 1 or Phase 1B found duplicate blocks or bad blocks
associated with file inode I. The owner O, mode M, size S, and modify time T
of inode I are printed.

■ BAD/DUP DIR I=I OWNER=O MODE=M SIZE=S MTIME=T (CLEAR?)
Phase 1 or Phase 1B found duplicate blocks or bad blocks associated with
directory inode I. The owner O, mode M, size S, and modify time T of inode I
are printed.

■ FREE INODE COUNT WRONG IN SUPERBLK (FIX?)   The actual count of
free inodes does not match the count in the superblock of the file system. If the -q
option is specified, the count will be fixed automatically in the superblock.

Errors in Phase 5—Check Free List

This phase checks the free block list. The meanings of Yes and No responses to **fsck**
questions are as follows:

■ CONTINUE?   No—Terminates the program. Ignores the rest of the free
blocks list and continues execution of **fsck**. This error condition will always
invoke the BAD BLKS IN FREE LIST error condition later in Phase 5.

▟   FIX?   No—Ignores the error condition. A No response is only appropriate if the user intends to take other measures to fix the problem. Replaces the count in the superblock with the actual count.

▟   SALVAGE?   No—Ignores the error. A No response is only appropriate if the user intends to take other measures to fix the problem. Yes—Replaces actual free block list with a new free block list. The new free block list will be ordered according to the gap and cylinder specs of the -s or -S option to reduce time spent waiting for the disk to rotate into position.

This phase may generate the following error messages:

▟   EXCESSIVE BAD BLKS IN FREE LIST (CONTINUE?)   The free block list contains too many (usually more than 10) blocks whose value is less than the first data block in the file system or greater than the last block in the file system.

▟   EXCESSIVE DUP BLKS IN FREE LIST (CONTINUE?)   The free block list contains too many (usually more than 10) blocks claimed by inodes or earlier parts of the free block list.

▟   BAD FREEBLK COUNT   The free block count in a free-list block is greater than 50 or less than 0. This error condition will always invoke the BAD FREE LIST condition later in Phase 5.

▟   X BAD BLKS IN FREE LIST   X blocks in the free block list have a block number lower than the first data block in the file system or greater than the last block in the file system. This error condition will always invoke the BAD FREE LIST condition later in Phase 5.

▟   X DUP BLKS IN FREE LIST   X blocks claimed by inodes or earlier parts of the free-list block were found in the free block list. This error condition will always invoke the BAD FREE LIST condition later in Phase 5.

▟   X BLK(S) MISSING   X blocks unused by the file system were not found in the free block list. This error condition will always invoke the BAD FREE LIST condition later in Phase 5.

▟   FREE BLK COUNT WRONG IN SUPERBLOCK (FIX?)   The actual free block count does not match the count in the superblock of the file system.

▟   BAD FREE LIST (SALVAGE?)   This message is always preceded by one or more Phase 5 information messages. If the -q option is specified, the free block list will be salvaged automatically.

Errors in Phase 6—Salvage Free Block List

This phase reconstructs the free block list. It has one possible error condition that results from bad blocks-per-cylinder and gap values. It may generate the following warning message:

■ DEFAULT FREE BLOCK LIST SPACING ASSUMED This advisory message indicates one of the following: the blocks-to-skip (gap) is greater than the blocks-per-cylinder, the blocks-to-skip is less than 1, the blocks-per-cylinder is less than 1, or the blocks-per-cylinder is greater than 500. The values of 7 blocks-to-skip and 400 blocks-per-cylinder are used.

Errors in Cleanup Phase

After checking a file system, **fsck** performs a few cleanup functions. During Cleanup Phase, advisory messages are displayed concerning the file system and its status.

■ Cleanup Phase Messages *X* files *Y* blocks *Z* free This advisory message indicates that the file system contains *X* files using *Y* blocks, leaving *Z* blocks free in the file system.

■ ***** BOOT Unix (NO SYNC!) ***** This advisory message indicates that a mounted file system or the root file system has been modified by **fsck**. If the Unix system is not rebooted immediately without **sync**, the work done by **fsck** may be undone by the in-core copies of tables that the Unix system keeps. If the -b option has been specified and the root file system has been modified, a reboot is automatically done.

■ ***** FILE SYSTEM WAS MODIFIED ***** This advisory message indicates that **fsck** has modified the current file system.

Associated Commands

When checking and repairing file systems, system administrators make extensive use of the **fsck** command. However, they should also be familiar with the **ncheck** and **fsdb** commands described next.

The ncheck Command

The **ncheck** command generates names from inode numbers. It has the following syntax:

ncheck [-i *numbers*] [-a] [-s] [*file system*]

When no argument is specified, **ncheck** generates a path name and inode number list of all files on all of the file systems specified in **/etc/mnttab**. The two characters /. are appended to directory filenames.

The fsdb Command

The **fsdb** command is the file system debugger. It has the following syntax:

fsdb *special* [-]

fsdb can be used to patch a damaged file system after a crash. It has conversions to translate block and i-numbers into their corresponding disk addresses. Also included are mnemonic offsets for accessing different parts of an inode. These greatly simplify the processes of correcting control block entries and descending the file system tree.

    fsdb contains several error-checking routines to verify inode and block addresses. You can disable these routines, if necessary, by invoking **fsdb** with the optional – argument or with the O symbol. (**fsdb** reads the *i-size* and *f-size* entries from the superblock of the file system as the basis for these checks.)

    Numbers are considered decimal by default. Octal numbers must be prefixed with a zero. During any assignment operation, numbers are checked for a possible truncation error due to a size mismatch between source and destination.

    The **fsdb** command reads a block at a time, and will therefore work with raw as well as block I/O. A buffer management routine is used to retain commonly used blocks of data. This reduces the number of read system calls. Every assignment operation results in an immediate write-through of the corresponding block.

    Consult your System V Unix manual for more information. The **fsdb** command is not available under BSD Unix.

···················

Chapter Summary

A logical disk is a useful abstraction of the physical (actual) disk. A partition is a segment of the logical disk. The file system includes several major components: data blocks, which contain programs and data; the superblock, which contains system control information; inodes, which describe files and directories; and device drivers, which are programs that control hardware devices.

Manipulating Undamaged File Systems   Creating a file system involves two basic steps. After planning your file system, you issue the **mkfs** command to make the physical file system. Then you issue the **mount** command to link the new file system to the previously existing file system. (To unlink the new file system, issue the **umount** command.) In the hands of a knowledgeable system administrator the **df**, **du**, and **find** commands reveal potential problems before they become critical. The **fsstat** command reports on the file system status. The more heavily the system is used, the more rapidly its performance will degrade. The **dcopy** command reorganizes the file system, often increasing its efficiency.

Checking and Repairing the File System   Unix offers several tools for checking and repairing the file system. The **fsck** program is the main tool. Cautious system administrators will apply this command even if the **fsstat** command reports no errors. Mastering the **fsck** command is necessary for keeping the file system, and consequently the operating system, in working order. When **fsck** denotes a problem with a given inode, you must run the **ncheck** command to determine the associated filename. Technically-oriented system administrators may apply **fsdb**, the file system debugger.

Phases of fsck   The **fsck** program consists of several phases, each performing specific actions and generating its own error messages. A given phase must complete before the next phase begins. The Initialization phase invokes the command line options, opens the special device file, and validates the superblock. Phase 1 (Check Blocks and Sizes) checks the inodes for valid size, file type, and block addresses, and for a nonzero link count. It also prepares data on block addresses and on inodes and their links to be employed in subsequent phases. Phase 2 (Check Pathnames) checks all directory entries, starting with the root for a valid inode as determined in Phase 1. It completes the link counts for each inode. Phase 3 (Check Connectivity) may create a directory entry for a directory-type inode that presently is not connected to any directory. Phase 4 (Check Reference Counts) may create directory entries for inodes whose type is not directory. The number of directory entries generated in Phase 2 must be equal to the sum of the inode link counts. The total number of inodes must be equal to the inode count appearing in the superblock. Phase 5 (Check Free List) checks the validity of the free list, making sure that no block addresses appear in the inodes. All blocks in the file system must be in the free block list, or be allocated to an inode. Phase 6 (Salvage Free Block List) reconstructs the free block list. Cleanup Phase performs a few cleanup functions after **fsck** has checked the file system.

Consider the following points with respect to using **fsck**:

Run this program on a regular basis during periods when system use is light such as nights and weekends. Run it only on unmounted file systems. Do not use the -q or -y options. Answer Y to most questions, except those relating to the **lost+found** directory and DUP TABLE overflow. Keep a record of files deleted in Phase 2 (Check Pathnames), as you may have to restore these files from backups. If **fsck** finds and corrects errors, run it again to be sure that the file system is clean.

Unix System

- Generic Unix System Startup

- One Specific Unix System Startup

- System Shutdown

- A C Language System Shutdown Program

Administration Guide

CHAPTER 9

Unix Startup and Shutdown

The system administrator is responsible for starting and shutting down the computer system on a scheduled or an emergency basis. Unlike a DOS system that can be started or shut down with the flick of a switch, initiating or terminating Unix is a complex process; doing it wrong can be dangerous to your file system. This chapter examines the principles of system startup and then looks at how a widely used microcomputer version of Unix implements startup, including system administrator installation options and error messages.

System startup is only half the issue. The chapter also examines system shutdown, including the process of restarting the system. The chapter then concludes with a C language program that provides the system administrator with a system shutdown menu.

GENERIC UNIX SYSTEM STARTUP

While the system startup process is usually automatic, the system administrator must understand the process to be able to intervene when necessary. Unix is a multi-user system, but sometimes by choice or by necessity you will run Unix in the maintenance mode, which is restricted to a single user. Of course, computer systems don't always work as expected, and sometimes don't work at all. This chapter includes an extensive discussion of possible startup errors and how to work around them. It also presents the system startup procedure including system administrator options and error messages for a widely-used Unix implementation.

Bootstrapping and System Initialization

The process by which a computer system starts working is known as *bootstrapping*, in reference to the phrase "to pull oneself up by one's bootstraps." This process involves several steps, each one providing the computer with greater powers. Once the bootstrapping process has terminated, users may log into the system. When faced with a problem during system initialization, the bootstrapping process may start the system in a maintenance mode and restrict access to the single user responsible for correcting the problem.

Loading Unix into Memory

Before the computer can perform any useful work, the Unix operating system must be loaded into memory. The exact details of this process vary from one Unix implementation to another. Turning on the hardware causes the computer to access a small startup routine located in ROM (read-only memory) that retains its contents when the computer is shut off. This ROM routine may perform elementary system verification such as assuring that the system hard disks and network server are accessible. Then ROM loads a more comprehensive program called the *boot routine* usually stored on disk or, in the case of computer networks equipped with diskless workstations, on a file server.

The boot routine may also perform more sophisticated hardware verification. It takes charge of loading the kernel (discussed in Chapter 4) into memory. Most System V Unix implementations call the kernel file **unix**, while most BSD Unix implementations call the kernel file **vmunix**. Whatever its name, the kernel file is always stored in the system's root directory.

Executing the Kernel

Once loaded into memory the kernel starts working. It sets up the information tables it needs to control the Unix environment. It tests system hardware, determining, for example, exactly how much memory is available. The kernel reserves the memory it needs for its own use, and displays memory information on the system console.

Then the kernel examines the rest of its hardware environment. It compares available hardware devices with the list of expected hardware devices, as specified by the system administrator when configuring the kernel. (See Chapter 14 for details of the kernel configuration process.) The kernel informs the system administrator of the devices encountered at system initialization. The kernel may then create the **swapper** process discussed below.

The swapper Process

The **swapper** process is identified as process 0. Its job is to monitor memory usage. Memory is usually in short supply for active Unix systems. A poorly tuned computer system spends too much time moving process segments back and forth from disk to memory and not enough time actually executing application processes. This situation calls for **swapper**.

The **swapper** process monitors memory management overhead. When the overhead is too great, **swapper** removes one or more entire processes from memory until the system performance level becomes acceptable. It also determines when these application processes may be reloaded into memory.

User Modes and Run Levels

Before continuing with the system initialization process, it is necessary to introduce several terms related to this process and to discuss the support provided to potential users. The *single-user mode* provides the system administrator or other privileged users with complete control of the Unix system. This mode is not the standard Unix operating mode; it provides minimum facilities. The single-user mode runs the Korn shell or the Bourne shell, executing as the user root. Its prompt is the number sign (#), the same prompt as the superuser account.

The usual Unix mode is the *multi-user mode,* in which several users share Unix system facilities. This mode is the standard operating mode; it provides a full range of services. Of course, the superuser password confers special privileges on whoever uses it. In a well-secured system, this password is restricted to the system administrator.

The terms single-user mode and multi-user mode apply to both BSD and System V Unix. However, System V Unix defines several additional system states or *run levels*. System administrators interested in the technical details associated with the startup and shutdown of System V Unix implementations should consult Table 9-1 for System V run levels.

The init Process

During system initialization the kernel may or may not create the **swapper** process. However, it always creates the **init** process, identified as process 1. At this point the kernel has completed its part of the initialization process, passing the baton to **init**, the parent process for all user processes. As its name indicates, **init** initiates system processes. Process names and associated information appear in the **inittab** table shown in Figure 9-1. Notice that the run level (or run levels) may appear after the first colon (:) in table entries. Because table contents may vary from one Unix implementation to another, discussion of this process appears later in this chapter under the section "One Specific Unix System Startup."

The **init** process places the system in the multi-user mode unless the single-user mode has been specified (as in the eighth line of Figure 9-1), or unless **init** is unable to create the multi-user mode. When the single-user shell terminates, **init** reads and executes the shell script or scripts contained in the **/etc/rc** (or similarly named) initialization directory. If the multi-user mode has been specified, **init** immediately reads and executes the shell script or scripts contained in this initialization directory.

TABLE 9-1

System V Run Levels

Run Level	Description
0	Power-down mode: You may turn off the system without danger.
1	Administrative mode: often equivalent to single-user mode.
s or S	Single-user mode.
2	Multi-user mode: normal mode for non-networked systems.
3	Remote File Sharing (RFS) mode: normal mode for networked systems.
4	User-definable system mode.
5	Firmware mode: used for maintenance and diagnostics.
6	Shutdown and reboot mode.

FIGURE 9-1

The **init** program
configuration table

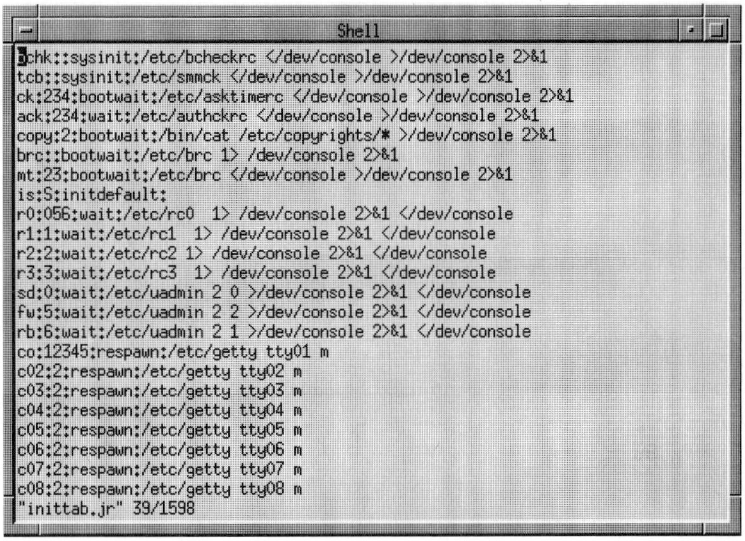

```
=                              Shell                                ▪ ▭
bchk::sysinit:/etc/bcheckrc </dev/console >/dev/console 2>&1
tcb::sysinit:/etc/smmck </dev/console >/dev/console 2>&1
ck:234:bootwait:/etc/asktimerc </dev/console >/dev/console 2>&1
ack:234:wait:/etc/authckrc </dev/console >/dev/console 2>&1
copy:2:bootwait:/bin/cat /etc/copyrights/* >/dev/console 2>&1
brc::bootwait:/etc/brc 1> /dev/console 2>&1
mt:23:bootwait:/etc/brc </dev/console >/dev/console 2>&1
is:S:initdefault:
r0:056:wait:/etc/rc0  1> /dev/console 2>&1 </dev/console
r1:1:wait:/etc/rc1  1> /dev/console 2>&1 </dev/console
r2:2:wait:/etc/rc2 1> /dev/console 2>&1 </dev/console
r3:3:wait:/etc/rc3  1> /dev/console 2>&1 </dev/console
sd:0:wait:/etc/uadmin 2 0 >/dev/console 2>&1 </dev/console
fw:5:wait:/etc/uadmin 2 2 >/dev/console 2>&1 </dev/console
rb:6:wait:/etc/uadmin 2 1 >/dev/console 2>&1 </dev/console
co:12345:respawn:/etc/getty tty01 m
c02:2:respawn:/etc/getty tty02 m
c03:2:respawn:/etc/getty tty03 m
c04:2:respawn:/etc/getty tty04 m
c05:2:respawn:/etc/getty tty05 m
c06:2:respawn:/etc/getty tty06 m
c07:2:respawn:/etc/getty tty07 m
c08:2:respawn:/etc/getty tty08 m
"inittab.jr" 39/1598
```

Initialization shell scripts perform activities such as the following:

- Set the computer name and environment variables such as PATH and HOME. System dependent activities such as setting the computer name are usually found in the directory **/etc/rc.local**. Figure 9-2 shows the part of the script that sets the system clock.

- Check the file system with the **fsck** command presented in Chapter 8. The following section discusses the relationship between this command and the user modes.

- Mount the system's disk partitions as discussed in Chapter 8.

- Delete temporary files (found in the **/tmp** directory). A well-designed shell script will recover temporary files saved by the text editor prior to a system crash. Before deletion, these files are copied to the **/usr/preserve** directory. As discussed in Chapter 2, the **vi** editor is able to recover these files.

- Initiate network services and interfaces, as discussed in Chapters 11 and 13.

- Start the **getty** process. This process must be successfully executed before users are able to log into the system.

FIGURE 9-2

The /etc/asktimerc
script

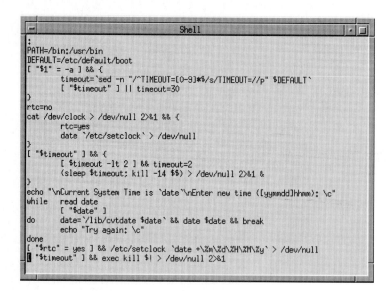

```
PATH=/bin:/usr/bin
DEFAULT=/etc/default/boot
[ "$1" = -a ] && {
        timeout=`sed -n "/^TIMEOUT=[0-9]*$/s/TIMEOUT=//p" $DEFAULT`
        [ "$timeout" ] || timeout=30
}
rtc=no
cat /dev/clock > /dev/null 2>&1 && {
        rtc=yes
        date `/etc/setclock` > /dev/null
}
[ "$timeout" ] && {
        [ $timeout -lt 2 ] && timeout=2
        (sleep $timeout; kill -14 $$) > /dev/null 2>&1 &
}
echo "\nCurrent System Time is `date`\nEnter new time ([yymmdd]hhmm): \c"
while   read date
        [ "$date" ]
do      date=`/lib/cvtdate $date` && date $date && break
        echo "Try again: \c"
done
[ "$rtc" = yes ] && /etc/setclock `date +\%m\%d\%H\%M\%y` > /dev/null
[ "$timeout" ] && exec kill $! > /dev/null 2>&1
```

> **Note**
>
> Sometimes an installation's special requirements can be met only by writing a custom initialization script. However, often the system administrator need only specify initialization options, as described in the section "One Specific Unix System Startup."

The fsck Command

The **fsck** command is the file system consistency check program. It is usually run automatically when initializing the multi-user file system. Suppressing the **fsck** command generates a quick and dirty system initialization. You will save minutes initially, but you may eventually lose hours or even days. Sooner or later you pay for such a shortcut by finding yourself with a damaged file system, probably when the system is at its busiest. The **fsck** command may be run manually but not automatically in the single-user mode. In fact, if the **init** command initializes single-user mode Unix, it's a good idea to run **fsck** to determine what went wrong and perhaps correct some errors.

The User login Process

Whenever a user attempts to initiate access to the computer system, the following activities occur:

- ◢ The **getty** process executes the **login** program employing the user's login name.

- ◢ The **login** process prompts the prospective user for a password. It validates the login name and the password against the appropriate entry in the **/etc/passwd** file and the **/etc/shadow** file.

- ◢ If the message-of-the-day file is defined, **/etc/motd** is printed.

- ◢ The user shell specified in the **passwd** file is executed. BSD Unix sets the TERM environment variable to the value appearing in the terminal configuration file.

- ◢ The Korn shell and the Bourne shell execute the **.profile** startup file. The C shell executes the **.cshrc** and then the **.login** startup files.

- ◢ The shell prints the Unix prompt, and is then ready to accept user commands.

Dealing with Bootstrapping Problems

On occasion the computer will not boot properly. If this happens, stay calm, locate your system documentation, and attempt to solve the problem. Unless you have on-site support, it usually takes hours for help to arrive. There are several things you can do yourself that may solve the problem. Every computer veteran has seen dead systems respond to actions as simple as placing a plug firmly in a socket, or turning a switch to the on position. However, don't get carried away. If you don't know what you're doing, don't dismantle your hard disks.

If your system won't work, the error is likely to be one of the following:

- ◢ Hardware errors

- ◢ Defective boot media (floppy disks or tapes)

- ◢ Initialization script errors

- ◢ Kernel errors

- ◢ File system errors

These errors and possible solutions are described below. Sometimes you'll know where to start looking. For example, if you have just changed the initialization script, there is a good chance that the error appears in the new script. Of course, you have saved a copy of the old script and so will be able to reboot and then solve the problem. In other cases you won't have any idea what caused the error. In all cases keep a logbook of system initialization errors and their solutions, whether you solved the problem yourself or required technical support. Some errors crop up time and time again. It is bad enough to pay money once to find and correct a given error, but paying money twice for a given error is unacceptable.

Console Messages and Crash Dumps

Service technicians are not magicians; they require all the help they can get. System console messages can be a big help to you and to the service technician in determining the exact state of the system prior to the crash. Many systems store these messages automatically in a system error log file, perhaps in the **/usr/adm/messages** file.

Most Unix systems generate a *crash dump,* an image of kernel memory at the time the computer stopped functioning. In the hands of a technical expert, a crash dump can be a key problem-solving tool. Even if you don't know how to read crash dumps, it's important to know how to save them for someone who can read them. Otherwise the crash dump may be overwritten when the system is rebooted, destroying valuable information.

Hardware Errors

Sometimes the system provides a clear message indicating a hardware problem. For example, it may signal a memory parity error. In this case you should call the technician and wait. In other instances the problem is not so obvious. Check the power supply and all cables. On some equipment the light panel indicates the source of the problem. If you can't find the source of the problem, try turning off the computer for at least ten seconds; then turn on the individual units. Careful verification of printouts or displayed messages generated by the kernel may help to isolate the problem. Before calling service personnel, try running any diagnostic programs supplied by the manufacturer.

Defective Boot Media

This error is usually easy to determine: for example, if the system won't boot from floppy disk A but boots from floppy disk B. Of course, you must make backup copies of your boot media before running into this problem. It's a good idea to have an emergency boot disk just in case the system won't boot from the hard disk. As you make system changes, keep this emergency disk up to date, otherwise it is almost worthless.

Initialization Script Errors

A shell script can be a fairly complex computer program. Everybody knows that computer programs are rarely written without errors (or bugs) that often seem to defy testing. Once again, it is imperative that you have a copy of the original shell script before making any changes.

Typically, initialization script (**/etc/rc**) errors prevent the system from entering the multi-user mode. Therefore you will have to fix the error from the single-user mode, which, as you recall, does not provide the full range of Unix facilities. For example, you may not be able to access the **vi** editor directly from the single-user mode.

Kernel Errors

An error in kernel configuration (see Chapter 14) can prevent you from accessing the system. Once again the advice is clear, make a backup of the kernel before you actually need it.

File System Errors

File system errors are potentially dangerous. In the worst-case scenario the system files are lost. This can happen due to hardware or software errors. System recovery requires extensive knowledge of the file system as discussed in Chapter 8.

You may have to rebuild the system from the Unix distribution tapes or disks. However, many modern Unix systems are distributed on CDs. Even if you have recent backups of the file system, this process is time-consuming and stressful, and users expect to be on-line immediately. Many installations maintain a backup of the root partition to speed the file recovery process. This necessitates well-documented procedures to boot the system from the alternate root partition. Furthermore, an alternate root partition is useful only insofar as it closely resembles the normal root partition. You must define and implement a procedure that synchronizes the two root partitions.

If you are able to boot in single-user mode, try running the **fsck** command to repair the file system, starting with the root partition. Once the root partition is clean, you may be able to apply the **mount** command to access other partitions manually.

ONE SPECIFIC UNIX SYSTEM STARTUP

Understanding the basic principles of system startup is a prerequisite for examining how Unix actually carries out this activity and the precise interaction between the system administrator and the operating system itself. This section presents an overview of the boot process, the boot options, and the **init** startup script as provided by the virtual microcomputer Unix standard, the Santa Cruz Operation (SCO) version. As you know by now, other versions may vary.

One Specific Unix boot Process

SCO employs an interactive **boot** routine to load and execute stand-alone Unix programs. This routine must be present in the root directory of the root file system to ensure successful loading of the Unix kernel. Starting the computer automatically invokes the **boot** routine. The **reboot** command may be used to restart the system without executing lengthy shutdown procedures. Value Added boot is an extension of AT&T System V provided by the Santa Cruz Operation. The **boot** process for other versions of Unix is similar. See your system documentation for the precise details.

Initiating the boot Process

The disk-based **boot** procedure has three stages:

1. ROM loads the boot block from sector 0 of the floppy, where sector 0 of the disk is the same as sector 0 of the file system.

2. The boot block loads **boot** from the floppy file system, or from cartridge tape if available.

3. boot executes and prompts the user.

The hard disk-based **boot** procedure has five stages:

1. ROM loads in the masterboot block from sector 0 on the hard disk.

2. The masterboot block then loads the partition boot block (boot0) from sector 0 of the active partition.

3. Then, assuming the Unix partition is active, boot1 is loaded from 1K into the active partition. boot1 spans 20 physically contiguous 1K blocks on the disk.

4. boot1 loads **boot** from the Unix file system.

5. boot executes and prompts the user.

Prompting the User to Load a Program

When first invoked, **boot** prompts for the location of a program to load by displaying the message:

```
Unix System V/386    (or Unix System V/486)

Boot
:
```

Specify the device name and filename, which must include the full pathname of the file containing the stand-alone program. (Type a question mark [?] to display a list of the current allowable device names.) The device and pathname format follows:

xx(*m,o*)*filename*

or

xx(*m*)*filename*

where:

xx = device name
('hd' for the hard disk or 'fd' for diskette device)

m = minor device number
(40 for the root file system on the hard disk)

o = offset in the partition (usually 0). This is optional.

filename = standard Unix pathname. Must start with a
slash if the program is not in the root directory.

All numbers are in decimal. See your manual for minor device numbers. The location of the program to be loaded must always be entered first on the command line and be present if other **boot** options are specified either on the command line or in **/etc/default/boot**.

If you enter the word **prompt** on the command line, **boot** pauses until ENTER is pressed before executing the specified program. For example, if you type **prompt** and press ENTER, **boot** prints the following message and waits for you to press the key again:

```
Loaded, press <RETURN>.
```

The prompt can be changed to another string as in the following example:

```
prompt="After inserting system diskette 1
      press the RETURN key"
```

In the above case **boot** loads **unix** from the disk, prints the above message, and waits for the ENTER key to be pressed. No other characters can appear between the word prompt, the = sign, and the prompt string, although string may contain spaces. When you press ENTER, **unix** begins execution. You may also set the prompt in the **/etc/default/boot** file. If a prompt is not specified, **boot** executes the loaded program without pausing.

If you start Unix from the distribution diskette, simply press ENTER to assign the correct default values to the **boot** routine. To load from a hard disk, enter:

```
hd(40,0)unix
```

Press ENTER when the system displays the boot prompt, and **boot** uses the values specified by DEFBOOTSTR in the **/etc/default/boot** file.

The installation process generates a custom masterboot file on the hard disk. This masterboot file contains parameters describing a non-standard disk.

Configuring the Kernel

The **boot** routine passes the *bootstring* (the characters typed at the boot prompt) to the kernel, except for the prompt string. This bootstring informs the kernel which peripherals are the root, pipe, and swap devices. Devices may be specified in the bootstring or in the **/etc/default/boot** file, otherwise the system applies the default devices compiled into the kernel. Additional arguments in the bootstring may be used to modify default values. These arguments have the following form:

dev=*xx*(*m,o*)

or

dev=*xx*(*m*)

where:

dev = the desired system device (*root[dev]*, *pipe[dev]*, or *swap[dev]*)

xx, m, o = same as for the boot device

If any combination of root, pipe, or swap is specified, then those system devices will reside on that device, otherwise the default values compiled in the kernel are used. Setting one device does not affect the default values for the other system devices.

Selecting the System Console

Select the system console either by entering the command **systty=x** at the boot prompt, or by placing the key phrase *SYSTTY=x* in the **/etc/default/boot** file. The letter *x* represents either a number or a string parameter. If you use the **systty=x** command at boot time, **boot** uses the string parameter *x* to pass the selected console device to the kernel. The values of the bootstring parameter *systty* are:

```
sio Serial port COM1
scrn Display adapter
```

For example, to assign the system console to the serial port at COM1, enter this command at the boot prompt:

```
systty=sio
```

If you do not specifically set the system console at boot time, the **boot** program follows these steps to determine the system console:

▰ boot reads the **/etc/default/boot** file and looks for the key phrase *SYSTTY=x,* where *x* specifies the system console device as follows:

> 1 indicates the serial adapter at *COM1*
> 0 indicates the display adapter

▰ If *SYSTTY* is not found or the **/etc/default/boot** file is unreadable, **boot** checks for a display adapter and assigns it as the system console.

▰ If no display adapter is found, **boot** looks for *COM1,* sets the serial port to 9600 baud, 8 data bits, 1 stop bit, and no parity, and uses it as the system console.

boot Options for One Specific Unix Version

In general it is not necessary for system administrators or their technical associates to write custom system initialization shell scripts. Most Unix implementations provide the system administrator with sufficient control of the boot process. These options can be changed via keywords in the **/etc/default/boot** file. Among the available boot options provided by SCO Unix are the following:

▰ AUTOBOOT=YES If YES, the **boot** process automatically loads Unix after a delay time specified by the *TIMEOUT* parameter. The default value is 60 seconds.

▰ SYSTTY=x If *x* is 1, the system console device is set to the serial adapter at *COM1*. If x is 0 the system console is set to the main display adapter.

▰ RONLYROOT=NO This option specifies whether or not the root file system is to be mounted read only. This should only be set to YES during installation.

▰ FSCKFIX=YES or NO This option specifies whether or not the **fsck** process automatically attempts to fix root system problems. If set to YES, then **fsck** is run on the root file system with the -rr flag.

▰ MULTIUSER=YES or NO This option specifies whether the **init** process proceeds to the multi-user mode or invokes the single-user mode.

◪ PANICBOOT=YES or NO   This option specifies whether or not the system reboots after the **panic** process is invoked. The *PANICBOOT* option is read from the **/etc/default/boot** file by **init**.

◪ TIMEOUT=*n*   *n* is the number of seconds to wait at the boot prompt before timing out and booting the kernel (if *AUTOBOOT* is set to YES).

Possible boot Error Messages

Exact error messages differ from one Unix implementation to another. In SCO Unix when the **masterboot** process detects an error, it displays an error message and locks the system. The following is a list of the most common **masterboot** error messages and their meanings:

◪ IO ERRM   An error occurred when **masterboot** tried to read in the partition boot of the active operating system.

◪ BAD TBL   The bootable partition indicator of at least one of the operating systems in the fdisk table contains an unrecognizable code.

◪ NO OS   There was an unrecoverable error that prevented the active operating system's partition boot from executing.

When the **boot** process displays error messages, it returns to the Boot prompt. The following is a list of the most common messages and their meanings:

◪ bad magic number   The given file is not an executable program.

◪ can't open *pathname*   The supplied pathname does not correspond to an existing file, or the device is unknown.

◪ boot failure, stage 1   The bootstrap loader cannot find or read the boot file. You must restart the computer and supply a file system disk with the boot file in the root directory.

◪ not a directory   The specified area on the device does not contain a valid Unix file system.

◪ zero length directory   Although an otherwise valid file system was found, it contains a directory of apparently zero length. This most often occurs when a pre-System V Unix file system (with incorrect, or incompatible word ordering) is in the specified area.

�   fload:read(*x*)=*y*   An attempted read of *x* bytes of the file returned only *y* bytes. This is probably due to a premature end-of-file. It could also be caused by a corrupted file, or incorrect word ordering in the header.

A Sample init Script

The **init** program serves as the general process dispatcher. Its most commonly invoked process is **/etc/getty** that initiates individual terminal lines. Other processes typically dispatched by **init** are daemons and the shell.

The **inittab** table is recreated automatically by **idmkinit** at boot time or whenever the kernel has been reconfigured. To construct a new **inittab** table, **idmkinit** reads the file **/etc/conf/cf.d/init.base**, which contains a base set of **inittab** entries that are required for the system, and combines these base entries with add-on entries from the device driver **init** files in the directory **/etc/conf/init.d**.

If you add an entry directly to **inittab**, the change exists only until the kernel is relinked. To add an entry permanently, you must also edit **/etc/conf/cf.d/init.base**. The **init.base** file has the same format as **inittab**. As shown previously in Figure 9-1, the **inittab** table is composed of position-dependent entries with the following format:

id:r*state*:*action*:*process*

The **inittab** table may contain unlimited entries. The entry fields are:

▪   id   This field of one to four characters uniquely identifies the entry. For example, in the second last line of Figure 9-1 the id field is c08.

▪   rstate   This field may define the entry's run level as described in Table 9-1. The system processes only entries whose rstate field contains the current run level. When **init** is requested to change run levels, all processes whose rstate field for the target run level is inappropriate are given the warning signal (SIGTERM) and allowed a 20-second grace period before being forcibly terminated by a kill signal (SIGKILL). See the SCO **init** manual (README.INIT) for a description of multiple run levels associated with the rstate field and legal values (called a, b, and c) other than run levels. The entry whose id field is c08 has a run level of 2, which means that it may be run only in multiuser mode.

▪   action   The contents of this field tell **init** how to handle processes specified in the *process* field. **init** defines the following actions:

respawn   If the process does not exist, start it, continue scanning the **inittab** table, and restart the process after it dies. If the process currently exists, do nothing and continue scanning the **inittab** table. The entry whose id field is c08 has an action field of respawn.

wait   When **init** enters the run level equal to the entry's rstate, it starts the process and waits for its termination. As long as **init** maintains the same run level, subsequent reads of the **inittab** table are ignored.

boot   Process the entry only at the boot-time read of the **inittab** table. **init** starts the process, does not wait for it to terminate, and does not restart the process when it dies. This action is meaningful if the rstate field contains the default value or is equal to **init**'s run level at boot time. This action is useful for an initialization function following a hardware reboot of the system.

bootwait   The entry is to be processed the first time **init** goes from single-user to multiuser state after the system is booted. (If *initdefault* is set to 2, the process will run right after the boot.) **init** starts the process, waits for it to terminate and does not restart the process when it dies.

powerfail   Execute the process associated with this entry only when **init** receives a power fail signal.

powerwait   Execute the process associated with this entry only when **init** receives a power fail signal (SIGPWR) and wait until it terminates before continuing any processing of **inittab**.

off   If the process associated with this entry is currently running, send the warning signal (SIGTERM) and wait 20 seconds before forcibly terminating the process via the kill signal (SIGKILL). If the process is nonexistent, ignore the entry.

ondemand   This instruction is really a synonym for the respawn action. It is used only with the a, b, or c values associated with the rstate field.

initdefault   An entry with this action is scanned only when **init** is initially invoked. The maximum run level specified in the rstate field determines the system's initial state. If the rstate field is empty, the run level is set to 6. If the **/etc/inittab** table does not contain an *initdefault* entry, **init** prompts the user for an initial run level.

sysinit   These entries are executed before **init** tries to access the console (i.e., before the Console Login: prompt). This entry should be used only to initialize those devices for which **init** might prompt for the run level. The system waits for sysinit entries to terminate before continuing.

process   This is a **sh** command to be executed. The entire process field is prefixed with exec and passed to a forked sh as **sh** -c 'exec command'. For this reason, any legal shell syntax can appear in the process field. Comments can be inserted with the ; # comment syntax. The entry whose id field is c08 has a process field of */etc/getty tty08 m,* which means keep trying (respawn) to launch the **getty** process, looking for a terminal logon.

Note

Each inittab table entry appears on a new line; however, a backslash (\) in the first column indicates continuation of the entry. Up to 512 characters per entry are permitted.

inittab Entries

Let's look at the entries in the sample **inittab** table for SCO Unix shown in Figure 9-1. The first and second entries invoke the sysinit action; they check the file system (**bcheckrc** process) and restore missing files (**smmck** process). The system waits for **sysinit** entries to terminate before continuing.

The third entry invokes the *bootwait* action; it is processed the first time **init** goes from single-user to multiuser state after the system is booted. **init** starts the **asktimerc** process starting the system clock, then waits for it to terminate and does not restart the process when it dies.

The fourth entry invokes the *wait* action; When **init** enters the run level equal to the entry's rstate of 2 (multiuser mode), 3 (Remote File Sharing mode), or 4 (user-definable system mode), it starts the **authckrc** process that checks the protected subsystem and waits for its termination.

The eighth entry invokes the *initdefault* action. It sets the default run level to S, the single-user mode. The ninth entry determines what to do in case of system shutdown. The tenth, eleventh, and twelfth refer to run level changes. As previously discussed, the final series of entries invoke the *respawn* action, continuously starting the **getty** process to accept terminal logons on the eight terminal ports available (tty01 to tty08).

Figure 9-3 illustrates the **inittab** table for the Hewlett-Packard 9000 Series 700 platform running HP-UX Release 8.07. You may wish to note the similarities and differences between this figure and Figure 9-1.

SYSTEM SHUTDOWN

Unlike MS-DOS computers where system shutdown may be as simple as pressing the power button, Unix system shutdown is a fairly complicated process. Several options are

```
┌────────────────────────────────── Shell ──────────────────────────────────┐
│init:3:initdefault:                                                          │
│stty::sysinit:stty 9600 clocal icanon echo opost onlcr isnqak ixon \         │
│                        icrnl ignpar </dev/systty                            │
│brc1::bootwait:/etc/bcheckrc </dev/console >/dev/console 2>&1 #fsck, etc      │
│slib::bootwait:/etc/recoversl </dev/console >/dev/console 2>&1 #shared libs   │
│brc2::bootwait:/etc/brc >/dev/console 2>&1 #boottime commands                │
│link::wait:/bin/sh -c "rm -f /dev/syscon: \                                  │
│                        ln /dev/systty /dev/syscon" >/dev/console 2>&1        │
│rc::wait:/etc/rc </dev/console >/dev/console 2>&1 #system initialization      │
│powf::powerwait:/etc/powerfail >/dev/console 2>&1 #power fail routines        │
│lp::off:nohup sleep 999999999 </dev/lp & stty 9600 </dev/lp                   │
│halt:6:wait:/usr/lib/X11/iiapps/haltsys.sh \                                 │
│                        # NOTE: run level 6 is reserved for system shutdown   │
│cons:012456:respawn:/etc/getty -h console console #system console            │
│vue:34:respawn:/etc/vuerc #VUE validation and invocation                     │
│^                                                                            │
└────────────────────────────────────────────────────────────────────────────┘
```

available including reverting to the single-user mode and rebooting. Only in the worst-case scenario (such as fire, flood, or earthquake) should you ever consider pulling the plug. To do so may damage the file system and may require hours of painstaking labor to restore the files.

Graceful Shutdown Steps

The exact steps involved in system shutdown depend on how much time there is, and whether you wish to work in the system maintenance mode or reboot the system. The Unix **shutdown** script includes the following steps: warning users, killing active processes, unmounting mounted file systems, entering the single-user mode, and issuing **sync** commands.

Warning Users

If possible, the first thing to do is to warn users that the system will shut down rapidly. This enables users to save their files and also to get used to the idea that the system will shortly become unavailable. It is common practice to warn users several times with increasing frequency before actually logging them off the system. Some users will hang on until the last minute, others will log off as soon as possible to avoid seeing those annoying messages more than necessary. The **shutdown** command even has a -k (for kidding) option that sends users messages to convince them to logoff even though the system will continue functioning.

Killing Active Processes

Once users have logged off, the **shutdown** script kills active processes by issuing commands such as **/usr/lib/lpshut**. The **/etc/killall** command kills all processes that have still survived.

Unmounting Mounted Files

The **unmount** command unmounts files that remain on the system by examining the contents of the **/etc/mnttab** file. In cases of error it may be necessary to issue this command from the console. Recall that the root file system cannot be unmounted.

Entering the Single-User Mode

The **shutdown** script sends a special signal to the **init** process commanding it to enter the single-user mode. If the **shutdown** script was issued with the -r flag instead of entering the single-user mode, the system reboots.

Issuing sync Commands

The **sync** command copies memory resident files to disk. For safety's sake the **shutdown** command issues several **sync** commands.

After the system issues the **sync** commands to close all accounts, it displays a message informing the system administrator that it is safe to power down the computer or to reboot. For example, on SCO Unix:

```
**    Safe to Power Off    **
         -or-
** Press Any Key to Reboot **
```

Shutting Down the System Rapidly

On occasion there is no time to shut down the system gracefully. Usually you will not have to pull the plug but will have time to apply a less dangerous solution. The **haltsys** command halts a Unix V system, the analogous BSD Unix command is **halt** (invoked by **shutdown** -h). Both these commands kill system processes, issue **sync** system calls, and halt the processor once the **sync** commands have completed writing memory contents to disk. Because these halt commands do not warn users that the system is about to shut down, you should use them only when necessary. In an emergency you can issue **sync** commands to stop the system.

A person who runs an individual Unix implementation can issue either the haltsys or the shutdown command without worrying. There are no other users to disrupt.

Rebooting the System

While many microcomputer owners are in the habit of turning off their system at least once a day, most Unix systems are left running for lengthy periods. As you have seen above, shutting down the system can be a time-consuming process. Furthermore, the bigger the system, the greater the likelihood that users will be inconvenienced by a system shutdown, even for a short time period. You will usually have to reboot the system under the following conditions:

- The system console is hung or other system devices such as the printer are unavailable due to system inconsistencies.

- You have modified files that are executed only when the system boots such as the kernel or system initialization scripts.

- You have installed new hardware, such as terminals or disk drives, and must relink, creating a new kernel.

- The system has been up and running for a while and file inconsistencies may have developed. Many installations run the **fsck** program from the maintenance mode on a weekly basis. Of course, if you have reason to suspect file system problems, you should run **fsck** more often.

- You are installing new features that require kernel modification, such as the X Window System (which is discussed in Chapter 13).

- You wish to change system parameters to meet reasonable system performance criteria or to fine-tune the system. This may involve creating a new kernel.

- You are installing a new release of Unix.

Whether or not you shut down the system gracefully, it is possible to reboot the system automatically. Recall that the Unix System V command to reboot is **init** followed by the run level. For example, to reboot the system in the maintenance mode, execute the command **init** 1. Under BSD Unix reboot by executing the **shutdown** -r command, which executes the **reboot** command.

A C LANGUAGE SYSTEM SHUTDOWN PROGRAM

The following program may be run only by the system administrator. It displays a menu providing the system administrator with several options: quitting the system, reverting to the single-user (Maintenance) mode, halting the system, or shutting down the system. This program was tested under SCO Unix. With some changes such as modifying selected #define statements, it will work on other versions of Unix, such as BSD Unix. The reader can easily extend the functionality of this program.

```c
#include <stdio.h>
#include <string.h>
#include <sgtty.h>
#include <memory.h>
#include <sys/errno.h>

#define HALTSYS "/etc/haltsys"
#define SHUTDOWN "/etc/shutdown -y -g"
#define SINGLE_MODE "/etc/init 1"
#define THREE_SYNCS "sync; sync; sync;"

void menu();

int main()
{
int sid;
char buf_1[80];
char buf_2[80];
char buf_3[80];
char buf_4[80];
int option;
int iperiod;
char aperiod;

  sid = getuid();
  if (sid != 0)
  {
    printf("\n        You are not a super-user!");
    printf("You can not run this program!\n");
    printf("\n                        Exiting ...\n");
```

```
        exit(1);
    }

    for(;;)
    {
      menu();
      printf("\n   Option? ");
      option = getchar();
      printf("\n");
      fflush(stdin);
      switch (option)
      {
        case 48: /* option 0 */
        option = 99999;
        break;
        case 49: /* option 1 */
          printf("\nSingle-user (Maintenance) Mode? [y/n]: ");
          gets(buf_1);
          if ((*buf_1 == 'y') || (*buf_1 == 'Y'))
          {
            printf("\n This program will terminate!\n");
            printf("\n System Goes to the Single-user");
            printf((Maintenance) Mode ...\n");
            printf("\n To go to the multi-user mode");
            printf(from the single-user mode: ");
            printf(" init 2 CR\n");
            sleep(15);
            system(THREE_SYNCS);
            system(SINGLE_MODE);
          }
        option = 99999;
        break;
        case 50: /* option 2 */
          printf("\nHalt System? [y/n]: ");
          gets(buf_1);
          if ((*buf_1 == 'y') || (*buf_1 == 'Y'))
          {
            printf("\n This program will terminate!\n");
            printf("\n System will halt immediately ...\n");
            system(THREE_SYNCS);
            system(HALTSYS);
```

```
      break;
   }
option = 99999;
break;
case 51: /* option 3 */
   printf("\nShut down System? [y/n]: ");
   gets(buf_1);
   if ((*buf_1 == 'y') || (*buf_1 == 'Y'))
   {
      printf("\nNumber of minutes until multi-user
               mode is stopped? ");
      gets(buf_2);
      strcpy(buf_3, SHUTDOWN);
      iperiod = atoi(buf_2);
      strcat(buf_3, buf_2);
      strcat(buf_3, " -f");
      strcat(buf_3,"\"System will shut down ...\"");
      printf("\n This program will terminate!\n");
      printf("\n Executing: %s\n",buf_3);
      system(THREE_SYNCS);
      system(buf_3);
      break;
   }
   else
   {
      printf("\nSystem maintenance mode? [y/n]: ");
      gets(buf_2);
      if ((*buf_2 == 'y') || (*buf_2 == 'Y'))
      {
         printf("\nNumber of minutes until multi-user
                  mode is stopped? ");
         gets(buf_3);
         printf("\n This program will terminate!\n");
         printf("\n System Goes to the Single-user
                  (Maintenance) Mode ...\n");
         printf("\n To go to the multi-user mode from
                  the single-user mode:");
         printf("  init 2 CR\n");
         strcpy(buf_4, SHUTDOWN);
         iperiod = atoi(buf_3);
         strcat(buf_4, buf_3);
```

```
                        strcat(buf_4, " -i1");
                        printf("\n Executing: %s\n",buf_4);
                        system(THREE_SYNCS);
                        system(buf_4);
                      break;
                  }
              }
            option = 99999;
            break;
            default:
              printf("    Wrong selection! Try again ...\n");
            break;
          }
        if (option == 99999) break;
      }
  }

void menu()
{
  printf("\n*********************************\n");
  printf("\n    Select Option and press CR  \n");
  printf("\n*********************************\n");
  printf("    0 - Quit                      \n");
  printf("    1 - Single-user (Maintenance) Mode\n");
  printf("    2 - Halt the System          \n");
  printf("    3 - Shut down the System     \n");
  printf("*********************************\n");
}
```

The MAKE file for SCO Unix associated with this shutdown program follows:

```
include INCLUDE
LIBS =
PROD = downjr

install all: $(PROD)

downjr: downjr.c
  $(CC) $(CFLAGS) -o $(TESTDIR)/downjr downjr.c $(LIBS)

clean:
  -rm -f *.o
```

```
clobber: clean
  -rm -f $(PROD)
```

where the INCLUDE file is as follows:

```
ROOT =
IROOT =
ETC = $(ROOT)etc
BIN = $(ROOT)/usr/local/bin
TESTDIR = .
SHELL = /bin/sh
REL =
INCRT = $(IROOT)/usr/include
BROOT = $(ROOT)
I = $(INCRT)
MORECPP =
CFLAGS = -O -DLAI_TCP $(MORECPP) -I$(INCRT) $(REL)
        -Di386 -DBUFFER_SIZE=8192
LDFLAGS =
SOCKETLIB = -lsocket
INS
INSDIR = $(BIN)
```

Note | The MAKE and INCLUDE files may vary in other versions of Unix.

Chapter Summary

Generic System Startup   The system administrator is responsible for starting up and shutting down the computer system on a scheduled or an emergency basis. Unlike DOS systems that may be started or shut down on the flick of a switch, initiating or terminating Unix is a complex process.

Traditionally the process by which a computer system starts working is known as bootstrapping in reference to the phrase "to pull oneself up by one's bootstraps." This process involves several steps, each one providing the computer with greater powers. These steps include loading Unix into memory, executing the kernel, creating the **swapper** process that monitors memory usage, and creating the **init** process that is the parent process for all user processes. **init** initiates system processes. Process names and associated information appear in the **inittab** table.

Modes and Run Levels   The single-user mode provides the system administrator or other privileged user with complete control of the Unix system. The "normal" Unix mode is the multi-user mode, in which several users share Unix system facilities. This mode is the standard operating mode; it provides a full range of services. The terms single-user mode and multi-user mode apply to both BSD and System V Unix. However, System V Unix defines several additional system states or run levels.

Initialization Shell Scripts   Initialization shell scripts perform activities such as the following: setting the computer name and environment variables such as PATH and HOME, checking the file system with the **fsck** command, mounting the system's disk partitions, deleting temporary files, initiating network services and interfaces, and starting the **/etc/getty** process.

The User Login Process   Whenever a user attempts to initiate access to the computer system, the following activities occur: the **getty** process executes the **login** program employing the user's login name; the **login** process prompts the prospective user for a password and validates the login name and the password; if the message-of-the-day file is defined, **/etc/motd** is printed; the user shell specified in the **passwd** file is executed; the appropriate startup files are executed; and the Unix prompt is displayed. The system is now ready to accept user commands.

Bootstrapping Problems   If your system won't work, the error is likely to be one of the following: hardware errors, defective boot media (floppy disks or tapes), initialization script errors, kernel errors, or file system errors. System console messages can be a big help to you and to the service technicians in determining the exact state of the system prior to the crash. Many systems store these messages automatically in a system error log file, perhaps in the **/usr/adm/messages** file. Most Unix systems generate a crash dump, an image of kernel memory at the time the computer stopped functioning. In the hands of a technical expert, a crash dump can be a key problem-solving tool. Even if you don't know how to read crash dumps, it's important to know how to save them for someone who can read them. Otherwise the crash dump may be overwritten when the system is rebooted, destroying valuable information.

One Specific Unix System Startup   The virtual microcomputer Unix standard is the Santa Cruz Operation (SCO) version. SCO employs an interactive **boot** routine to load and execute stand-alone Unix programs. This routine must be present in the root directory of the root file system to ensure successful loading of the Unix kernel. Starting the computer automatically invokes the **boot** routine. The **reboot** command may be used to restart the system without executing lengthy shutdown procedures. The disk-based **boot** procedure has three stages whereas the hard disk-based boot procedure has five stages.

When first invoked, **boot** prompts for the location of a program to load by displaying the message:

```
Unix System V/386    (or Unix System V/486)

Boot
:
```

The **boot** routine passes the bootstring (the characters typed at the boot prompt) to the kernel, except for the "prompt" string. This bootstring informs the kernel which peripherals are the root, pipe, and swap devices. If any combination of root, pipe, or swap is specified, then those system devices will reside on that device, otherwise the default values compiled in the kernel are used. Setting one device does not affect the default values for the other system devices. Select the system console either by entering the command **systty=x** at the boot prompt, or by placing the key phrase *SYSTTY=x* in the **/etc/default/boot** file. The letter *x* represents either a number or a string parameter. SCO provides numerous boot options enabling the system administrator to customize the startup procedure without having to write an initialization script.

The init Process and the inittab Table   The **init** program serves as the general process dispatcher. Its most commonly invoked process is **/etc/getty** that initiates individual terminal lines. Other processes typically dispatched by **init** are daemons and the shell. It dispatches processes described in the **inittab** table, which is composed of entries with the following format:

id:rstate:action:process

where:

id is a one-to-four-character field that uniquely identifies the entry.

rstate defines the entry's run level as described in Table 9-1.

action tells **init** how to handle processes specified in the *process* field. Eleven actions are defined.

System Shutdown   Unlike MS-DOS computers where system shutdown may be as simple as pressing the power button, Unix system shutdown is a fairly complicated process. Several options are available including reverting to the single-user mode and rebooting. Only in the worst-case scenario (such as fire, flood, or earthquake) should you even consider pulling the plug. To do so may damage the file system and require hours of painstaking labor to restore the files. In the case of a graceful shutdown the following steps occur: warning users, killing active processes, unmounting mounted file systems, entering the single-user mode, and issuing **sync** commands.

On occasion there is no time to shut down the system gracefully. Usually you will not have to pull the plug but will have time to apply a less dangerous solution. The **haltsys** command halts a Unix V system, the analogous BSD Unix command is **halt** (invoked by **shutdown** -h). In an emergency you can issue **sync** commands to stop the system.

Rebooting the System

While many computer owners are in the habit of turning off their system at least once a day, most Unix systems are left running for lengthy periods. It is advisable to reboot the system under the following conditions: The system console is hung; other system devices, such as the printer, are unavailable due to system inconsistencies; you have modified files that are executed only when the system boots; you have installed new hardware such as terminals or disk drives; the system has been up and running for a while and file inconsistencies may have developed; you are installing new features that require kernel modifications; you wish to change system parameters for tuning; you are installing a new release of Unix.

Whether or not you shut down the system gracefully, it is possible to reboot the system automatically. Recall that the Unix System V command to reboot is **init** followed by the run level. Under BSD Unix reboot by executing the **shutdown** -r command, which executes the **reboot** command.

Unix System

Administration Guide

CHAPTER 10

System Peripherals

A major responsibility of the system administrator is installing and maintaining printers. (Standard Unix terminology refers to line printers, independent of the actual printer technology employed.) You can gauge the importance of printers by noting what happens when a printer is unavailable. Unix provides several printer control commands, each of which offers numerous options. While tables list all available commands, the less important commands are discussed in Appendix A, rather than in this chapter.

The chapter provides shell scripts for adding and removing a line printer from the Unix system. These scripts can be run in two modes; the production mode which requires the superuser (root) password, and the test mode available to the system administrator under a regular account. This test mode enables the system administrator to gain familiarity with the printer addition and printer removal process without running the risk of disturbing the functioning print service.

The chapter concludes with a brief examination of other system peripherals, including the terminal and the mouse. While a major responsibility of system administrators is installing these devices, these peripherals require relatively little system administrator intervention once they are installed, unlike printers.

THE LINE PRINTER

It is hard to imagine a Unix computer system without one or more functioning printers. Connecting printers to the system can be fairly complex. Because of the differences among systems, this text does not describe how to make hardware connections and how to debug these connections.

This chapter examines several Unix commands associated with the line printer and their major options, summarizing key information in tables. On occasion you will have to consult your system manual for additional information. The chapter includes two documented printer shell scripts; one that adds a printer to the system, and the other that removes a printer. Before looking at individual line printer commands and their options, let's introduce some basic terminology as used by these commands.

In many cases the **lp** command does not directly send output to the printer, but sends it to a buffer known as a *spooler*, the **/usr/spool/lp** file. Unix can transfer several user print *requests* to the spooler almost simultaneously. The actual printing of the spooler contents is performed sequentially.

The **lp** command creates a print job request identified by a unique *request ID*. A *destination* is a logical printer name, constituted when the printer was added to the system. A *class* is a collection of printers. In the context of this chapter, an *interface* is a shell script or a C language program that generates the information associated with a line printer request, transforming (filtering) the output and adding additional information such as a banner page and accounting information.

The **lp** command prints requests, which may be deleted by the **cancel** command. The **lpstat** command prints information about the current status of the **lp**, including user requests, printers, or printer classes. The **lpadmin** command configures the print service. The **lpsched** command starts the print service. The **lpshut** command shuts down the print service, stopping all active printers. The **lpmove** command moves queued printer requests between destinations.

The lp Command

The **lp** command prints (via the spooling buffer) named files and associated information (collectively called a *request*). The standard input is the default filename. Files are printed in the order of appearance on the command line. The **lp** command may change a print request's (identified by the *request-id*) options. If the print request has terminated, the change command is rejected. If the print request is in process, it will be stopped and restarted from the beginning, unless the -P option has been specified.

The **lp** command associates a unique ID with each request and prints it on the standard output. This ID can be used later to cancel, change, or find the request status. Table 10-1 presents the **lp** command options. See your system manual for more information on selected options.

TABLE 10-1

The **lp** Command Options

Flag	Parameter	Description
c		Copies all files to be printed.
d	dest	Prints the request to the specified printer or printer class.
f	form-name	Prints the request on the specified form.
H	special-handling	Prints the request after special handling.
m		Sends mail after printing files.
n	number	Prints the specified number of copies.
o	option	Specifies printer-dependent or class-dependent options.
P	page-list	Prints the specified page(s).
q	priority-level	Assigns a named priority level to a queued request.
s		Suppresses lp messages.
S	character-set	Prints the request using the specified character set.
S	print-wheel	Prints the request using the specified print wheel or font cartridge.
t	title	Prints the specified title on the banner page.
T	content-type	Indicates the type of files to be printed.
w		Writes the message on the user's terminal after printing files.
y	mode-list	Prints according to locally defined printing modes; requires a filter.

Sending a Print Request

The **lp** command sends a print request to one or more printers. Its options may be specified in any order but must precede the print filenames. The following options are most important to system administrators:

- ◢ -c   When **lp** is invoked, the system immediately copies all files to be printed.

- ◢ -d *dest*   Prints the request to the specified destination (a printer or printer class). By default, the *dest* value is taken from the environment variable *LPDEST* (if set). Otherwise, a default destination (if one exists) for the computer system is used. Destination names are system dependent.

- ◢ -m   Sends mail after the files have been printed. By default, no mail is sent upon normal completion of the print request.

- ◢ -n *number*   Prints number of copies of the output, by default 1.

- ◢ -q *priority-level*   Assigns a queued request (which is a priority-level ranging from 0, the highest priority, to 39, the lowest priority). The system administrator sets the default value. One common policy is giving small print requests a high priority to ensure that they are printed rapidly.

- ◢ -w   Writes a message on the user's terminal after the files have been printed. If the user is not logged in, mail will be sent instead.

Cancelling a Print Request

The **cancel** command cancels printer requests, both scheduled and currently printing. The shell command line arguments may be request IDs or printer names as listed by the **lpstat** command. Cancelling a currently printing request frees the printer to service the next available request. The **cancel** command provides the following options:

- ◢ -R   Removes a file after sending it.

- ◢ -L   Local printing option—sends a print job to printer attached to the terminal.

Additional Considerations

The **/etc/default/lpd** file contains the variable *BANNERS*, whose value is the number of banner pages that identify each printout. This is normally set to either 1 or 2.

The variables *LPR* and *PRINTER* can each be set to *spooler* or *local* to specify the print destination. The **/usr/bin/spool** file contains the spooler setting for both variables. The **/usr/bin/local** file contains the local setting.

The "any" destination ignores printers that do not accept requests. (Use the **lpstat** -a command to see which printers are accepting requests.) On the other hand, if a request is destined for a class of printers and the class itself is accepting requests, all such printers will be considered, regardless of their acceptance status.

For printers supporting mountable print wheels or font cartridges, unless a particular print wheel or font is specified with the -S option, the system uses any mounted print wheel or font cartridge when the request prints. Use the **lpstat** -p -l command to determine print wheel and font cartridge availability.

The lpstat Command

The **lpstat** command prints information about current **lp** status, including user requests, printers, or printer classes. Arguments other than options are assumed to be request IDs (as returned by **lp**), printers, or printer classes. Options may appear in any order and may be repeated and intermixed with other arguments. Some keyletters described below are followed by an optional list appearing in one of two forms: a comma-delimited item, or a list of items enclosed in double quotes and separated from one another by a comma and/or one or more spaces. Table 10-2 presents the **lpstat** command options.

TABLE 10-2

The **lpstat**
Command Options

Flag	Parameter	Description
u	*user*	Shows the status of jobs submitted by the specified user.
a	*list*	Displays the acceptance status of request destinations.
c	*list*	Displays class names and class members.
d		Displays the system default destination for lp.
f	*list*	Displays verification that the listed forms are recognized by the print service.
r		Displays the status of the request scheduler.
s		Displays the status summary.
S	*list*	Displays verification that the character sets or print wheels are recognized.
t		Displays all status information.
u	*list*	Displays the status of output requests for the listed users.
v	*list*	Displays names and pathnames of printers and associated devices.

The following options are most important to system administrators:

☑ -a [*list*]   Prints **lp** acceptance status of request destinations—*list* intermixes printer names and class names; the default is all.

☑ -r   Prints the status of the **lp** request scheduler.

☑ -s   Prints a status summary, including the system default destination, a list of class names and their members, a list of printers and their associated devices, a list of all forms currently mounted, and a list of all recognized character sets and print wheels.

☑ -t   Prints all status information.

The lpadmin Command

The **lpadmin** command configures the print service to describe printers and devices. It is used to add and change printers, to set or change the system default destination, to define alerts for print wheels and font changes, to define printers for remote printing services, and to remove printers from the service. This command is usually reserved for system administrators. Table 10-3 shows options of the **lpadmin** command for System V Unix. Other versions may be slightly different. Because of the importance of this command to system administrators, all options are shown.

TABLE 10-3

The **lpadmin**
Command Options

Flag	Field	Description
F	*fault-recovery*	Restores print service after a printer fault.
c	*class*	Inserts the printer into the specified class.
D	*comment*	Displays a comment field.
e	*printer*	Copies the existing printer's interface program to the specified printer.
f	allow:*form-list*	Enables forms on the specified printer.
f	deny:*form-list*	Disables forms on the specified printer.
h		Indicates that the device is hardwired.

TABLE 10-3		

The **lpadmin**
Command Options (*continued*)

Flag	Field	Description
i	interface	Establishes new interface program for the specified printer.
I	*content-type-list*	Assigns the specified printer to print requests whose contents types are listed.
l		Indicates that the device associated with the specified printer is a login terminal.
M	-f *form-name*	Mounts the named form on the specified printer.
M	-S *print-wheel*	Mounts the specified print wheel or font cartridge on the specified printer.
m	*model*	Selects the model interface program for the specified printer.
o	*printing-option*	Selects a printing option, such as length or width.
R	*machine-list*	Sets up the remote machines in the specified machine list to share print services.
r	*class*	Removes the designated printer from the specified class.
S	*list*	Allows aliases for character sets or print wheels.
T	*printer-type*	Assigns the given printer type.
u	allow:*user-list*	Allows named users access to the printer.
u	deny:*user-list*	Denies named users access to the printer.
U	*dial-info*	Assigns dialing information to the printer.
v	*device*	Associates a new device with the printer.
A	*alert-type*	Sends the specified alert to the system administrator.

Adding or Changing a Printer

The **lpadmin** -p *printer option* command configures a new printer or changes an existing printer's configuration. The following section presents the **addprn** script. The **lpadmin** -p *printer option* command includes the following options, which may appear in any order.

◪   -F *fault-recovery*   Restores the print service after a printer fault according to the *fault-recovery* value: continue continues printing on the top of the page where printing stopped; beginning starts printing the request again from the beginning; and wait disables printing on the printer and waits for the administrator or a user to enable printing again. During the wait, the individual responsible for the print disable request may issue a change request that specifies where printing should resume.

- ▰ -c *class*   Inserts the printer into the specified class, which will be created if it does not already exist.

- ▰ -D *comment*   Displays but does not interpret the comment field in the printer description when requested.

- ▰ -e *printer*   Copies an existing printer's interface program to be the new interface program for the specified printer.

- ▰ -f allow:*form-list* and -f deny:*form-list*   Allows or denies printing of the listed forms on the specified printer. For each printer the print service defines an allow-list of forms that can be used with the printer and a deny-list of forms that should not be used with the printer. See your system manual for more information on this option.

- ▰ -h   Indicates that the device associated with the specified printer is hardwired. This default option may be overridden by the -l option.

- ▰ -i *interface*   Establishes a new interface program for the specified printer, in which *interface* is the pathname of the new program. This is illustrated in the **theintrsct** script that appears later in this chapter. Usually, however, the system administrator will use interface scripts appearing in the **/usr/spool/lp/model** directory.

- ▰ I *content-type-list*   Assigns the specified printer to handle print requests of the specified contents type. See your system manual for more information on this option.

- ▰ -*l*   Indicates that the device associated with the specified printer is a login terminal. The **lpsched** program automatically disables all login terminals each time that it starts. Before reenabling the printer, establish its current device using **lpadmin**.

- ▰ -M -f *form-name* [-a [-o *filebreak*]]   Mounts the named form on the specified printer. **lpadmin** warns the system administrator when the printer cannot meet the form's demands, but accepts the mount. By default, a new printer has no form mounted. See your system manual for more information on this option.

- ▰ M -S *print-wheel*   Mounts the specified print wheel or font cartridge on the specified printer. See your system manual for more information on this option.

- ▰ -m *model*   Selects a model interface program provided with the print service for the specified printer. Figure 10-1 shows the list of available printer interfaces for SCO Unix.

FIGURE 10-1

Available printer interfaces

```
                                              Shell
drwxr-xr-x   2 bin    lp          400 Apr 27 1992 .
drwxrwxrwx  10 bin    lp          192 Nov 25 18:30 ..
-----r-x---   1 bin    lp         2106 Jun 11 1990 1640
-----r-x---   1 bin    lp         3754 Jun 11 1990 5310
-----r-x---   1 bin    lp         3664 Jun 11 1990 TandyDMP
-----r-x---   1 bin    lp         1409 Jun 11 1990 crnlmap
-rwxr-xr-x   1 bin    sys       25183 Dec 14 1990 dosmodel
-----r-x---   1 bin    lp         1515 Jun 11 1990 dqp10
-----r-x---   1 bin    lp         1426 Jun 11 1990 dumb
-----r-x---   1 bin    lp         3519 Jun 11 1990 emulator
-----r-x---   1 bin    lp         2732 Jun 11 1990 epson
-----r-x---   1 bin    lp         2459 Jun 11 1990 f450
-----r-x---   1 bin    lp         2296 Jun 11 1990 hp
-----r-x---   1 bin    lp         2228 Jun 11 1990 hpjet
-----r-x---   1 bin    lp         1495 Jun 11 1990 lqp40
-----r-x---   1 bin    lp         3363 Jun 11 1990 network
-----r-x---   1 bin    lp          735 Jun 11 1990 ph.daps
-----r-x---   1 bin    lp         2736 Jun 11 1990 postscript
-----r-x---   1 bin    lp         1825 Jun 11 1990 pprx
-----r-x---   1 bin    lp         4077 Jun 11 1990 proprinter
-----r-x---   1 bin    lp         2161 Jun 11 1990 prx
-----r-x---   1 bin    lp         2117 Jun 11 1990 qume1155
-----r-x---   1 bin    lp        25144 Jun 11 1990 standard
-----r-x---   1 bin    lp         2211 Jun 11 1990 ti800
-----r-x---   1 bin    lp          531 Nov 23 17:53 xpr
JR: /usr/spool/lp/model >>
```

- **-o** *printing-option*   Each -o option, such as *length* or *width*, is the default given to an interface program if no preprinted form description exists and the user has not indicated the value explicitly. See your system manual for more information on this option.

- **-R** *machine-list*   Sets up the specified remote machines to share print services. See your system manual for more information on this option.

- **-r** *class*   Removes the designated printer from the specified class. If the designated printer is the last member of its class, then that class is removed.

- **-S** *list*   Allows the listed character sets or print-wheel aliases to be used with the designated printer. Until the list is specified, no print wheels or font cartridges are mountable on the printer, and print requests that ask for a particular print wheel or font cartridge on this printer are rejected. See your system manual for more information on this option.

- **-T** *printer-type*   Assigns the given printer type, describing the physical printer. This option must be used if the following are to work: -o *cpi=*, -o *lpi=*, -o *width=*, and -o *length=* options of the **lpadmin** and **lp** commands, and the -S and -f options of the **lpadmin** command. See your system manual for more information on this option.

- **-u** allow:*user-list* and **-u** deny:*user-list*   Allows or denies the listed users access to the specified printer. The -u allow option adds listed users to the allow-list and removes them from the deny-list. The -u deny option removes listed users from the allow-list and adds them to the deny-list. See your system manual for more information on this option.

◪ -U *dial-info* Assigns dialing information to the printer. The specified information is used with the dial routine to call the printer. See your system manual for more information on this option.

◪ -v *device* Associates a new device with the specified printer. The *device* variable indicates the pathname of the printed file.

Note | A given device can be associated with several printers.

◪ -A *alert-type* [-W *integer*] Sends the system administrator the specified alert when a printer fault is detected and periodically thereafter until the printer fault is cleared by the administrator. See your system manual for more information on the alerts listed below:

mail Sends the alert message via mail to the administrator who issues this command.

write Writes the message to the terminal on which the administrator is logged in. If the administrator is logged in on several terminals, one is chosen arbitrarily.

quiet Does not send messages for the current condition. An administrator can use this option to temporarily stop receiving further messages about a known problem.

none Does not send messages until this command is given again with a different alert; removes any existing alert definition.

shell-command The specified command executes each time the alert needs to be sent. The shell command should expect the message as standard input. Enclose the command in quotes if it contains embedded blanks.

list The alert type for the printer fault is displayed on the standard output. No change is made to the alert.

reason The **lp** print service can detect printer faults only through an adequate fast filter and only when the standard interface program or a suitable customized interface program is used. Furthermore, the level of recovery after a fault depends on the capabilities of the filter. Setting *printer-name* to all applies the specified alert to all existing printers.

If the -W option is not given or *integer1* is 0 (the default), only one message is sent per fault. In the absence of the -A option the system mails one message per fault to the printer administrator.

Printer Creation Restrictions

When creating a new printer, either the -v or the -U option must be supplied. In addition, only one of the following may be supplied: -e, -i, or -m. If none of these three options are supplied, the *model* option has the value standard. The -h (hardwired) and -l (login terminal) options are mutually exclusive. Printer and class names may be no longer than 14 characters and must consist entirely of the characters A-Z, a-z, 0-9 and _ (underscore).

Changing the System Default Destination

The -d [*dest*] option designates an existing destination as the new system default destination. If no destination is specified, there is no system default destination. No other options are allowed with -d.

Setting a Print Wheel Alert

The -S *print-wheel* -A *alert-type* [-W *integer1*] [-Q *integer2*] option sets a print wheel or font cartridge alert. The -S *print-wheel* option and the associated -A *alert-type* option send the administrator the specified alert as soon as the print-wheel or font cartridge must be mounted, and periodically thereafter. See the "Adding or Changing a Printer" section, appearing earlier in this chapter, and your system manual for more information on alerts. If the *print-wheel* value is *all*, the alerting defined in this command applies to all print wheels already defined as having an alert. Only one administrator per print wheel can be alerted.

Defining Remote Printers

The **lpadmin** command may define the remote printer, *printer-name2*, and its machine, *machine-name*, that will handle remote print requests from the local machine. The remote printer will be referred to as *printer-name1* on the local machine.

Removing a Printer Destination

The -x *dest* option removes the specified destination from the **lp** print service. If the destination is a printer and the only member of a class, the class will be deleted as well. If the destination value is *all*, all printers and classes will be removed. No other options are allowed with -x.

The lpsched, lpshut, and lpmove Commands

These commands are usually restricted to the system administrator. The **lpsched** command starts the print service; it can be issued only by the root or the **lp** command. The **lpshut** command shuts down the print service, stopping all active printers. Restarting **lpsched** causes requests that were printing when the printer was shut down to be reprinted from the beginning. The **lpmove** command moves queued printer requests between **lp** destinations, without verifying the acceptance status of the new destination. It does not change the user ID so that users can still find their requests. The **lpmove** command does not move requests whose options, such as special printer form, cannot be handled by the new destination. By default, the **/usr/spool/lp** directory holds all the files used by the **lp** print service. Figure 10-2 shows sample contents of this directory for SCO Unix. You may set the *SPOOLDIR* environment variable to another directory before running **lpsched**. In this case copy the files and directories found under **/usr/spool/lp** to the new directory. Set the *SPOOLDIR* variable before running any other **lp** print service commands.

A SHELL SCRIPT FOR ADDING A PRINTER

This Bourne shell **addprn** script allows the system administrator logged in as superuser on a root account to add a printer. A new system administrator should first run this script as a regular user, to avoid potential printer configuration errors or even system failure and the resulting disruptions. When the administrator is sufficiently familiar with the printer addition process, he or she may execute the production version of the script to add a printer to the system, as shown here:

```
#!/bin/sh
# @(#) add printer script
log_name = 'whoami'
```

FIGURE 10-2

Files used by **lp** print service

```
                                        Shell
JR: /usr/spool/lp >> l
total 20
drwxrwxrwx  10 bin     lp        192 Nov 25 18:30 .
drwxr-xr-x  13 root    bin       208 Jun 13 1990 ..
-rwxr--r--   1 lp      lp          0 Nov 25 18:30 SCHEDLOCK
drwxr-xr-x   3 bin     lp         48 Jun 13 1990 admins
drwxr-xr-x   2 bin     lp        192 Jun 13 1990 bin
-rwxr--r--   1 lp      lp          0 Jun 11 1990 default
drwxr-xr-x   4 bin     lp         80 Nov 25 18:30 fifos
drwxr-xr-x   2 bin     lp         48 Apr 06 1992 logs
drwxr-xr-x   2 bin     lp        400 Apr 27 1992 model
drwxr-xr-x   2 bin     lp         32 Jun 13 1990 requests
drwxr-xr-x   2 bin     lp         48 Apr 27 1992 system
drwxr-xr-x   2 bin     lp        160 Apr 27 1992 temp
JR: /usr/spool/lp >> █
```

The following code verifies the login name of the individual executing this script. The superuser (system administrator) runs the production script, anyone else runs the test version.

```
if [$log_name = "root"]
then
```

The following code prompts the system administrator to enter the printer name. The script displays a message confirming successful entry or displays an error message and terminates.

```
echo "\nPlease enter Printer Name: \c"
read theprinter
if [ -n "$theprinter" ]
then
  echo "Entered Printer Name -> $theprinter\n"
else
  echo "No Printer Name specified. Try again\n"
  exit 1
fi
```

```
export theprinter
```

The following code prompts the system administrator to enter the teletype printer name. The script displays a message confirming successful entry or displays an error message and terminates.

```
echo "Please enter TTY Name: \c"
read thetty
if [ -n "$thetty" ]
then
  echo "Entered TTY Name -> $thetty\n"
else
  echo "No TTY Name specified. Try again\n"
  exit 1
fi
```

The following code sets internal variables and extracts a reference number from the device name, creating the first column in the **inittab** entry.

```
export thetty
```

```
thespooler=lp
thespoolergroup=bin
thespoolerdir=/usr/spool/lp
```

```
theinittab=/etc/inittab
thettydev=/dev/$thetty
thedevnum='basename ${thettydev} | sed "s/tty//g"'

#the following case statement is for the SCO Unix V
case ${thedevnum} in
02|03|04|05|06|07|08|09|10|11|12)
thedevnum="c${thedevnum}"
;;
esac
```

If you are using a platform other than SCO Unix V, examine the **/etc/inittab** file and your system manuals to determine correct code for the above case statement. For example, if your platform's **/etc/inittab** file contains the following lines:

```
#00:2:respawn:/etc/getty tty0 9600
#01:2:respawn:/etc/getty tty1 9600
#02:2:off:/etc/getty tty2 9600
#03:2:off:/etc/getty tty3 9600
#04:2:off:/etc/getty tty4 9600
#05:2:off:/etc/getty tty5 9600
#06:2:off:/etc/getty tty6 9600
#07:2:off:/etc/getty tty7 9600
#08:2:off:/etc/getty tty8 9600
#09:2:off:/etc/getty tty9 9600
```

modify the case statement to:

```
#   case ${thedevnum} in
#     0|1|2|3|4|5|6|7|8|9)
#        thedevnum="0${thedevnum}"
#     ;;
#   esac
```

The following code checks the initial entry for the off or respawn action and informs the system administrator to change respawn to off before running the printer:

```
themode='grep "^${thedevnum}" ${theinittab} |
             awk 'BEGIN {FS=":"} {print $3}''
echo  the mode is ${theymode}

if [ "X${themode}" != "X" ];
then
  if [ "${themode}" != "off" ]
  then
```

```
      cat <<- EOH
      *****< GETTY is active on the device port $thetty >*****
      Check the file /etc/inittab and change the port $thetty:
            from the respawn to the off action
            Then you can run the printer!
      EOH
  fi
fi
```

The following code examines the **/dev/tty** file to verify that the device is a special character device. The script displays a message confirming the device type or displays an error message, indicates the commands needed to correct the situation, and terminates.

```
if [ -c ${thettydev} ]
then
  echo "\nThe device port $thettydev is a special
        character device!\n"
  echo "\nContinue ...\n\n"
else
  echo "\nThe device port $thettydev is not a special
        character device!\n"
  echo "\n        You need to execute the following
        unix commands:\n"
  echo "\n        /etc/mknod device-name c major-number
        minor-number\n"
  echo "\n                chmod 644 device-name\n"
  echo "\n                chown lp device-name\n"
  echo "\n                    Exiting ...\n\n"
  exit 1
fi
```

The following code issues the necessary Unix commands to add the printer:

```
theprintdev=/dev/$theprinter

echo "\nAdding the printer $theprinter ...\n\n\n"

rm -f ${theprintdev}

ln ${thettydev} ${theprintdev}

chown ${thespooler} ${theprintdev}

chgrp ${thespoolergroup} ${theprintdev}
```

```
chmod 660 ${theprintdev}

thelib=/usr/lib

$thelib/lpshut
$thelib/lpadmin -x$theprinterjr
$thelib/lpadmin -p$theprinter -cPostScript -h
  -i${thespoolerdir}/model/standard -v${theprintdev}
$thelib/lpsched
$thelib/accept $theprinter PostScript
$thelib/enable $theprinter
```

The following script informs the superuser that the new printer was added to the system, indicates its status, and terminates:

```
echo "***************************************************"
echo "*********<  PRINTER ADDED to the SYSTEM!  >*******"
echo "***************************************************"
$thelib/lpstat -p$theprinter -l
```

The following code executes a test script for adding a pseudo printer after determining that the system administrator has logged in as a regular user:

```
else
  echo "\nNot a Super-User(root)!
          Executing a test script ...\n\n\n"
```

The following code prompts the user to enter the pseudo printer name. The script displays a message confirming successful entry or displays an error message and terminates.

```
echo "\nPlease enter Pseudo Printer Name: \c"
read printerjr
if [ -n "$printerjr" ]
then
  echo "Entered Pseudo Printer Name -> $printerjr\n"
else
  echo "No Pseudo Printer Name specified. Try again\n"
  exit 1
fi
```

The following code prompts the user to enter the pseudo tty name for the printer. The script displays a message confirming successful entry or displays an error message and terminates.

```
echo "Please enter Pseudo TTY Name: \c"
read ttyjr
if [ -n "$ttyjr" ]
then
  echo "Entered Pseudo TTY Name -> $ttyjr\n"
else
  echo "No Pseudo TTY Name specified. Try again\n"
  exit 1
fi
```

The following code sets internal variables associated with the test directory. It creates a test directory with subordinate subdirectories similar to the subdirectories of the production version.

```
spooler=$log_name
spoolergroup=bin
testdir=/usr/$log_name/test
devtestdir=$testdir/dev
etctestdir=$testdir/etc

if test ! -d $testdir;
then
  echo "Directory $testdir not exist! Making ...\n"
  mkdir $testdir
else
  echo "Directory $testdir exists\n"
fi

if test ! -d $devtestdir;
then
  echo "Directory $devtestdir not exist! Making ...\n"
  mkdir $devtestdir
else
  echo "Directory $devtestdir exists\n"
fi
ttydevjr=$devtestdir/$ttyjr
echo "TTYDEVJR  -> $ttydevjr\n"

printdevjr=$devtestdir/$printerjr
echo "PRINTDEVJR  -> $printdevjr\n"

if test ! -d $etctestdir;
```

```
then
  echo "Directory $etctestdir not exist! Making ...\n"
  mkdir $etctestdir
  cp /etc/inittab $etctestdir/inittab.tst
  echo "File $etctestdir/inittab.tst not exist!
        Making ...\n"
else
  echo "Directory $etctestdir exists\n"
fi
inittabjr=$etctestdir/inittab.tst

devnojr='basename ${ttydevjr} | sed "s/tty//g"'
echo devnojr is ${devnojr}

case ${devnojr} in
  01|02|03|04|05|06|07|08|09|10|11|12)
    devnojr="c${devnojr}"
  ;;
esac;
echo devnojr is ${devnojr}

ttymode='grep "^${devnojr}" ${inittabjr} |
               awk 'BEGIN {FS=":"} {print $3}''
echo ttymode is ${ttymode}

if [ "X${ttymode}" != "X" ];
then
  echo entered inside
  if [ "${ttymode}" != "off" ]
  then
    cat <<- EOH
    ***< GETTY is active on the pseudo device port
        $ttydevjr >***
    Check the file $inittabjr and change the pseudo port
    $ttyjr: from respawn to the off action
    Then you can run the pseudo printer!
    EOH
  fi
fi
```

The following code examines the **/dev/tty** file to verify that the device is a special character device. The script displays a message to confirm the device type or displays an error message, indicates the commands needed to correct the situation, and terminates. If it is not a special character device, create such a device by executing the following command:

```
#   /etc/mknod device-name c major-number minor-number
```

Then set the proper access permission and device ownership by executing the following commands:

```
#   chmod 644 device-name
#   chown lp device-name
    echo "\nAdding Pseudo Printer to the system ...\n\n\n"

    rm -f ${printdevjr}

    ln ${ttydevjr} ${printdevjr}

    chown ${spooler} ${printdevjr}

    chgrp ${spoolergroup} ${printdevjr}

    chmod 660 ${printdevjr}

    echo "\nNot a real printer! The following commands
            are not executed ...\n\n\n"
    echo "lpshut\n"
    echo "lpadmin -x$printerjr\n"
    echo "lpadmin -p$printerjr -cPostScript -h
            -i${spoolerdir}/model/standard -v${printdevjr}\n"
    echo "lpsched\n"
    echo "accept $printerjr PostScript\n"
    echo "enable $printerjr\n\n"

    echo "***************************************************"
    echo "****<  PSEUDO PRINTER  ADDED to the SYSTEM!  >*****"
    echo "***************************************************"
fi
```

A SHELL SCRIPT FOR PRINTING FILES

This is an example of the basic interface script **theintrscrt**, used to print files:

```
echo "\nYou will need to execute the following
        commands as a super-user:\n"
cp theintrscrt /usr/spool/lp/model/theintrscrt\n
chmod 050 /usr/spool/lp/model/theintrscrt\n
```

```
chown bin /usr/spool/lp/model/theintrscrt\n
chgrp lp /usr/spool/lp/model/theintrscrt\n
```

Then you install a new printer by using the **addprn** script. Change the line in a script that defines the interface that should be used to the following line:

```
/usr/lib/lpadmin -p$theprinter -cPostScript -h
-i${thespoolerdir}/model/theintrscrt -v${theprintdev}\n\n"
```

The above two lines must be written on one line!

```
brk="UAGUAGUAGUAGUAGUAGUAGUAGUAGUAGUAGUAGUAGUAGUAG"
echo "\014\c"
echo "$brk\n$brk\n$brk\n"

theprinter='basename $0'
therequest=$1
theuser=$2
thebanner=$3
num_copies=$4

banner $thebanner

echo "\n                         'date'"
echo "\n***** User $theuser ** Printer
      $theprinter ** Copies $num_copies **
      Request $therequest *****\n"

echo "\014\c"

shift;shift;shift;shift;shift
thefiles="$*"

count=1
while [ $count -le $num_copies ]
do
  for file in $thefiles
  do
    cat "$file" 2>&1
    echo "\014\c"
  done
  count='expr $count + 1'
done
```

```
echo "$brk\n$brk\n$brk\n"

exit 0
```

A SHELL SCRIPT FOR REMOVING A PRINTER

This Bourne shell **rmprn** script allows the system administrator to remove a printer from the system. A new system administrator should first run this script as a regular user, to avoid potential printer configuration errors or even system failure and the resulting disruptions. When the administrator has gained sufficient familiarity with the printer removal process, he or she may execute the production script to remove a printer from the system.

Caution | Neglecting to remove a misfunctioning printer can cause system failure.

The following lines specify the Bourne shell interpreter, briefly describe the script, and define the variable *log_name*.

```
#!/bin/sh
# @(#) remove printer script
log_name = 'whoami'
```

The following code verifies the login name of the individual executing this script. The superuser (system administrator) runs the real script; anyone else runs the test version.

```
if [ $log_name = "root" ]
then
  set -u
```

The following code prompts the system administrator to enter the printer name. The script displays a message confirming successful entry or displays an error message and terminates.

```
echo "\nPlease enter Printer Name: \c"
read theprinter
if [ -n "$theprinter" ]
then
  echo "Entered Printer Name -> $theprinter\n"
else
  echo "No Printer Name specified. Try again\n"
  exit 1
fi
```

The following code removes a printer and sends a message.

```
export theprinter

printdev=/dev/$theprinter
thelib=/usr/lib

echo "\nShut down printer $theprinter ...\n\n\n"

$thelib/reject -r"Printer will be removed..." $theprinter
$thelib/disable -c -r"Removing printer..." $theprinter
$thelib/cancel $theprinter
$thelib/lpshut
$thelib/lpadmin -x$theprinter
$thelib/lpsched

rm -f ${printdev}

echo "******************************************************"
echo "********<  PRINTER REMOVED from the SYSTEM!  >******"
echo "******************************************************"
```

The following code executes a test script for removing a pseudo printer after determining that the system administrator has logged in as a regular user.

```
else
  echo "\nNot a Super-User(root)!
      Executing a test script ...\n\n\n"
```

The following code prompts the user to enter the pseudo printer name. The script displays a message confirming successful entry or displays an error message and terminates.

```
echo "\nPlease enter Pseudo Printer Name: \c"
read printerjr
if [ -n "$printerjr" ]
then
  echo "Entered Pseudo Printer Name -> $printerjr\n"
else
  echo "No Pseudo Printer Name specified. Try again\n"
  exit 1
fi
```

The following code simulates printer removal from a test directory.

```
testdir=/usr/$log_name/test
devtestdir=$testdir/dev
printdevjr=$devtestdir/$printerjr

echo "\nShut down pseudo printer ...\n\n\n"
echo "\nNot a real printer! The following commands
        are not executed ...\n\n\n"
echo "\nreject -r\"Printer will be removed...\"
$printerjr \n"
echo "\ndisable -c -r\"Removing printer...\" $printerjr \n"
echo "\ncancel $printerjr \n"
echo "\nlpshut \n"
echo "\nlpadmin -x$printerjr \n"
echo "\nlpsched \n"

rm -f ${printdevjr}

echo "********************************************************"
echo "***<   PSEUDO PRINTER   REMOVED from the SYSTEM!   >***"
echo "********************************************************"
fi
```

INSTALLING OTHER PERIPHERALS

A major responsibility for system administrators is installing hardware devices. Once you have taken care of the hardware connections (see your device manuals and follow the instructions very carefully), you execute the appropriate system script creating the necessary device files as decribed next.

The mkdev Command

The **mkdev** command calls scripts to add peripheral devices. These scripts are confidential, but you wouldn't want to see them anyway. They are often in the neighborhood of 1200 lines of ugly code. (Few sites choose to make major modifications to these scripts because of their size and complexity.) Before installing a peripheral device, read your system installation notes and make a system backup. Figure 10-3 illustrates sample contents of the **mkdev** directory for SCO Unix. In this version, the **mkdev** script appears as follows:

```
mkdev dos
mkdev fd
mkdev fs [device file]
mkdev hd [[disk] [controller|adapter]] [lun]
mkdev mouse
mkdev serial
mkdev shl
mkdev streams
mkdev tape
```

The **mkdev** command prompts the system administrator for information to create the device file or files associated with the specified peripheral device (as shown in the mouse command). Then **mkdev** calls the appropriate script found in the **/usr/lib/mkdev** directory. (This directory may also contain scripts specific to a given application or software package.) If no arguments are listed, **mkdev** prints a usage message.

The mkdev dos Command

The **mkdev** dos command initializes necessary devices and configures the system to support mounted DOS file systems.

FIGURE 10-3

The **mkdev** directory

```
                                    Shell
drwxr-xr-x    3 bin      bin         512 Apr 06 1992 .
drwxr-xr-x   49 bin      bin        2704 Jul 11 11:46 ..
-rwx------    1 bin      bin       13900 Jun 10 1990 .scsi
-rwxr--r--    2 bin      bin       36532 Jun 12 1990 bitpad
-rwx------    1 bin      bin       10898 Jun 12 1990 cdrom
-rwxr-x---    1 bin      bin       19479 Sep 20 1990 cf
-rwx------    1 bin      bin        7439 Jun 10 1990 dda
-rwx------    1 bin      bin        6002 Jun 10 1990 dos
-rwxr-x---    1 bin      bin        7810 Sep 20 1990 e3A
-rwxr-x---    1 bin      bin        8508 Sep 20 1990 e3B
-rwxr-x---    1 bin      bin        8612 Sep 20 1990 e3C
-rwxr-xr-x    1 bin      bin        9810 Jun 10 1990 fd
-rwx------    1 bin      bin        6819 Jun 10 1990 fs
-rwx------    1 bin      bin         235 Jun 10 1990 graphics
-rwx------    1 bin      bin       31032 Jun 10 1990 hd
-rwx------    1 bin      bin        5994 Jun 12 1990 high-sierra
-rwxr-xr-x    1 bin      bin         307 Jun 10 1990 lp
-rwxr-xr-x    1 bin      sys       10044 Dec 14 1990 mergestream
-rwxr--r--    2 bin      bin       36532 Jun 12 1990 mouse
drwxr-xr-x    2 bin      bin          96 Jun 13 1990 perms
-rwxr-xr-x    1 bin      bin        6877 Aug 13 1991 samples
-rwxr-x---    1 bin      bin        4668 Sep 20 1990 sendmail-init
-rwx------    1 bin      bin        6219 Jun 10 1990 serial
-rwx------    1 bin      bin       10909 Jun 10 1990 shl
-rwxr-x---    1 bin      bin        3803 Sep 20 1990 slip
-rwx------    1 bin      bin        7205 Jun 10 1990 streams
-rwx------    1 bin      bin       30429 Jun 10 1990 tape
-rwxr-x---    1 bin      bin       12275 Sep 20 1990 tcp
-rwxr-x---    1 bin      bin        8436 Sep 20 1990 token
-rwx------    1 bin      bin        6474 Jun 10 1990 vpixld
-rwxr-x---    1 bin      bin        6631 Sep 20 1990 wdn
JR: /usr/lib/mkdev >> █
```

The mkdev fd Command

The **mkdev** fd command creates bootable, root and file-system floppy disks. Several floppies can be created during a single **mkdev** fd session, but **mkdev** does not display a prompt to remove the first floppy and insert the next one. Insert the next floppy when **mkdev** prompts "Would you like to format the floppy first? (y/n)."

The mkdev fs Command

The **mkdev** fs command performs the system maintenance tasks required to add a new file system after the **mknod** process creates the device and the **mkfs** process makes the file system. It creates the **/file** and **/file/lost+found** directories, and reserves slots in the **lost+found** directory. If such a directory already exists, it is used without modification. The **mkdev** fs command modifies the **checklist**, **default/filesys**, and **default** files. It invokes the **fsck** and **mount** commands to check and mount the file system. The **mkdev** fs command is usually used in conjunction with the **mkdev** hd command when adding a second hard disk to the system or with the **mkdev** fd command when creating a mountable file system on a floppy. It can be used on any additional file system (for example, on a large internal hard disk).

The mkdev hd Command

The **mkdev** hd command creates device files for use with a peripheral (external) hard disk. The device files for an internal hard disk already exist. The **mkdev** hd command includes an extended syntax for use on multiple controllers. The **mkdev** hd must be invoked twice to install a SCSI disk. The first time, the kernel will be reconfigured to support the new disk. The second time, the disk will be initialized. Use the same **mkdev** hd arguments both times. SCSI tapes can also be installed using **mkdev** *hd.*

The mkdev mouse Command

The **mkdev** mouse command initializes necessary devices and configures the system to use any supported mouse. During the system initialization process SCO generates the following menu:

```
Invoking "mkdev mouse" command....

        Mouse Initialization Program

        1. Display current configuration
        2. Add a mouse to the system
        3. Remove a mouse from the system
```

```
4. Associate a terminal with an existing mouse
5. Disassociate a terminal from an existing mouse
6. Remove the mouse drivers from the kernel


Select an option or enter q to quit:
```

Select option 2, which displays the following menu:

```
The following mouse devices are supported:

1. Logitech Serial Mouse
2. Microsoft Serial Mouse
3. Mouse Systems PC II Serial Mouse
4. Mouse Systems PC Mouse
5. Microsoft Bus Mouse
6. Olivetti Bus Mouse
7. Logitech Bus Mouse
8. Keyboard Mouse


Select an option or enter q to return to the previous menu:
```

The system then displays additional menus that allow you to complete the mouse installation.

The mkdev serial Command

The **mkdev** serial command creates device files for use with serial cards. The device files for the first and second ports already exist. Additional device files must be created for the ports associated with the addition of expansion cards to the system.

The mkdev shl Command

The **mkdev** shl command initializes necessary devices and configures kernel parameters associated with the number of shell sessions available on the system.

The mkdev streams Command

The **mkdev** streams command configures the kernel for **streams** support.

The mkdev tape Command

The **mkdev** tape command configures the tape driver in preparation for linking a new kernel that includes tape support. It adds a standard 1/4-inch cartridge tape driver and/or a minicartridge tape driver. The current driver configurations can be displayed, and changed if necessary. A 0 in any of the fields means the driver automatically detects the type of tape device installed and uses the built-in values for that device. If the auto-configuration values are not correct for your drive, refer to your hardware manual for the correct values, configure the driver, and relink the new kernel. The **mkdev** tape command can also be used to remove a tape driver from the existing kernel.

General Comments

Once the driver is configured, you are prompted to relink the kernel. The appropriate devices in **/dev** are created. The various **init** scripts prompt for the information necessary to create the devices. The *System Administrator's Manual* has chapters devoted to the installation of most peripheral devices. Try to perform this work when few people are on the system, and make sure that your backups are up-to-date.

Terminal Configuration

Unix System V relies on the following files to describe installed terminals: the **inittab** file, described earlier in this chapter, and either **gettydefs** or **gettytab**. The exact format tends to vary from one version to another. The **gettydefs** file format follows:

label # initial flags # final flags # login prompt # next label

in which *label* is a terminal identifier, such as console or 9600, used by the **getty** process to access the appropriate table entry; *initial flags* sets flags describing the terminal state prior to login; *final flags* sets flags describing the terminal state after login; *login prompt* denotes the message displayed at login time; and *next label* identifies the following table entry to access.

BSD Unix (as of version 4.3) specifies terminal configuration in the **/etc/ttys** file whose format follows:

device program-to-run terminal-type on/off [secure]

in which *device* is the name of the device file for the given port, *program-to-run* is the process executed by **init** when the port is initialized, *terminal-type* describes the terminal, on/off indicates whether or not the **getty** (login) process is to run, and secure, when present, indicates that the terminal may be used for a root login. The System V file **/etc/gettytab** resembles this file.

The stty Command

The **stty** command sets certain terminal I/O options for the device that is the current standard input; without arguments, it reports the settings of certain options. With the -a option, **stty** reports all of the option settings. The -g option causes **stty** to output the current terminal settings as a list of twelve hexadecimal numbers separated by colons. This output may be used as a command-line argument to **stty** to restore these settings later on. It is a more compact form than **stty** -a. Among the terminal settings are parity, character size, the speed at which characters are accepted and sent, and the ability to echo characters. Figure 10-4 illustrates sample output for the **stty** command for an SCO Unix system.

FIGURE 10-4

Output of the **stty** command

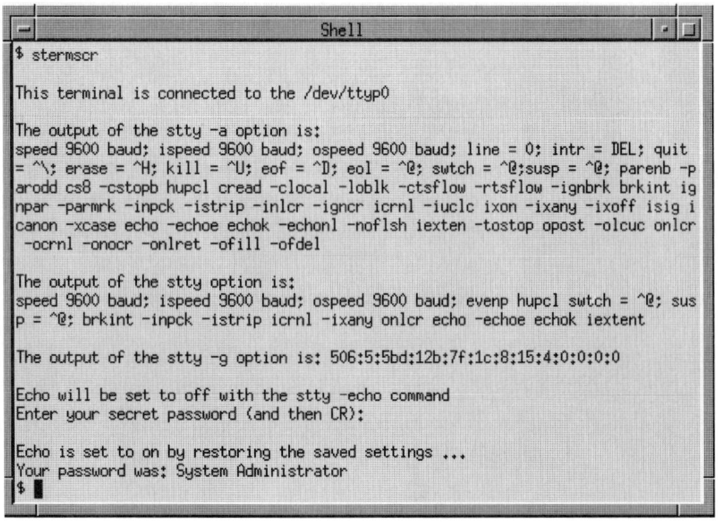

```
$ stermscr

This terminal is connected to the /dev/ttyp0

The output of the stty -a option is:
speed 9600 baud; ispeed 9600 baud; ospeed 9600 baud; line = 0; intr = DEL; quit
= ^\; erase = ^H; kill = ^U; eof = ^D; eol = ^@; swtch = ^@;susp = ^@; parenb -p
arodd cs8 -cstopb hupcl cread -clocal -loblk -ctsflow -rtsflow -ignbrk brkint ig
npar -parmrk -inpck -istrip -inlcr -igncr icrnl -iuclc ixon -ixany -ixoff isig i
canon -xcase echo -echoe echok -echonl -noflsh iexten -tostop opost -olcuc onlcr
 -ocrnl -onocr -onlret -ofill -ofdel

The output of the stty option is:
speed 9600 baud; ispeed 9600 baud; ospeed 9600 baud; evenp hupcl swtch = ^@; sus
p = ^@; brkint -inpck -istrip icrnl -ixany onlcr echo -echoe echok iextent

The output of the stty -g option is: 506:5:5bd:12b:7f:1c:8:15:4:0:0:0

Echo will be set to off with the stty -echo command
Enter your secret password (and then CR):

Echo is set to on by restoring the saved settings ...
Your password was: System Administrator
$
```

Chapter Summary

The Line Printer   The **lp** command prints, perhaps via a spooling buffer, named files and associated information (collectively called a request). The standard input is the default filename. Files are printed in the order of appearance on the command line. The **lp** command may change a print request (identified by the *request-id*) options. The **lp** command associates a unique ID with each request and prints it on the standard output. The **lpstat** command prints information about the current status of the **lp**, including user requests, printers, or printer classes. Arguments other than options are assumed to be request IDs (as returned by **lp**), printers, or printer classes.

The **lpadmin** command configures the print service to describe printers and devices. It is used to add and change printers, to set or change the system default destination, to define alerts for print wheels and font cartridges, to define printers for remote printing services, and to remove printers from the service. This command is usually reserved for system administrators as are the following commands. The **lpsched** command starts the print service; it can be issued only by the root or the **lp** command. The **lpshut** command shuts down the print service, stopping all active printers. Restarting **lpsched** causes requests that were printing when the printer was shut down to be reprinted from the beginning.

Installing Other Peripherals   A major responsibility for system administrators is installing hardware devices. The **mkdev** command calls scripts to add peripheral devices, such as the hard disk, the mouse, the serial port, and a tape backup unit. Before installing a peripheral device, read your system installation notes, and make a system backup.

Unix System V relies on the following files to describe installed terminals: the **/etc/inittab** file described earlier in this chapter, and either **/etc/gettydefs** or **/etc/gettytab**.

The **stty** command sets certain terminal I/O options for the device that is the current standard input; without arguments, it reports the settings of certain options.

Unix System

- Networking Basics
- Accessing and Managing Networks
- A C Language Program for Checking Network Communication
- A Shell Script for Adding Hosts
- A Shell Script for Removing Hosts
- A Shell Script for Adding Services
- A Shell Script for Removing Services
- Reconfiguring the Network
- The UUCP Facility

Administration Guide

CHAPTER 11

Network Administration

One reason that Unix is important is its networking facilities, which can link computing services across a campus or across the globe. As you might assume, the system administrator plays a major role in setting up, monitoring, and reorganizing computer networks. Besides presenting the theory and practice of Unix networking and its impact on the system administrator, this chapter presents a C language program for network monitoring and shell scripts for network reconfiguration.

NETWORKING BASICS

The first step in dealing with networking is learning the terminology. (While there is certainly enough networking jargon to fill a chapter, only the most important networking terms are presented here.) Computers cannot be merely connected to form a network. The system administrator or an associate must delve into the world of cables, telephone lines, and various types of connectors. As you might imagine, networks need not be isolated from each other. This section concludes by introducing the theory and practice of linking networks.

Basic Terminology

If there is one area of computing in which newcomers are easily overwhelmed, if not intimidated, by the terminology, it's networking. Not only novices complain about drowning in alphabet soup. In the interest of your sanity, this chapter introduces only the networking terminology that you, the system administrator, will need to know. Expect this list to expand over time. As you might expect, the first term to define is the term "network."

- **Network**   A computer *network* is two or more linked computers. The old-fashioned, but sometimes still useful, system composed of a mainframe computer assisted by a smaller computer dedicated to communications tasks (front-end computer) and linked to dozens or hundreds of computer terminals is an example of a computer network. So is the state-of-the-art system connecting dozens of independently functioning computer systems.

- **Host**   A *host* is a computer attached to the computer network. The host may be of any size or level of processing power. As discussed later in this chapter, the system administrator assigns the host a name, an address, and possibly one or more aliases meeting the network's naming conventions.

- **Local-Area Network (LAN)**   A *local-area network (LAN)* is a network whose components are directly linked, perhaps by private communications lines, and perhaps by the public telephone system. In general, LANs extend over a distance of a kilometer or less and do not involve signal boosting or filtering.

- **Wide-Area Network (WAN)**   A *wide-area network (WAN)* is a network whose components are linked over a large distance (perhaps across the continent or across the ocean). They usually use the services of common carriers such as the public telephone system.

- **Protocol**   A *protocol* is the set of formal rules and conventions used when processes or hosts communicate. Until protocol signals have been exchanged and verified, communication may not take place. The following section introduces communications and file-transfer protocols of interest to Unix system administrators.

▰ **Medium** A *medium* is the path over which communications flow. Common communications media are telephone lines known as twisted pair (shielded or not), coaxial cable, fiber optics cable, and air—the medium for microwave and satellite transmission.

▰ **Message** A *message* is a unit of information communicated from one location to another. Typically a message consists of three parts: a *message header* indicating the start of the message and including control information such as source, destination, date, and time; *message text*, the actual information to be transmitted; and an *end of message* indicator.

▰ **Packet Switching** *Packet switching* is a type of message transmission in which messages are broken up into segments called *packets* that are transmitted independently and then reassembled at the destination.

Protocols and Network Services

Efficient network performance requires correct selection of the network protocol. The use of an appropriate protocol increases the file transfer speed and accuracy, while reducing the inevitable security risk. Extensive discussion of protocols is beyond the scope of this text. Consider the following protocols.

TCP/IP

TCP/IP is an abbreviation for Transmission Control Protocol/Internet Protocol. As the name indicates, the Internet network, connecting hundreds of thousands of computers across the globe, relies on TCP/IP. This protocol was originally developed for the ARPA (Advanced Research Projects Agency) associated with the US Department of Defense. In spite of its age, it remains a major data transmission protocol for Unix. TCP/IP provides *reliable* data transmission; the system guarantees that every byte transmitted will reach its destination in the order that it was sent, or you will be notified. It works with the Ethernet interface associated with many local-area networks, and other interfaces.

TCP/IP provides many commands enabling users to access remote Unix hosts. These commands include logging in to remote systems and transferring files across the network. Some TCP/IP commands are discussed in the next section.

UDP/IP

UDP/IP is an abbreviation for User Datagram Protocol/Internet Protocol. It is a fast way to transmit data packets between two or more programs. However, it is *unreliable;* it does not guarantee that every byte transmitted will reach its destination in the order that it was sent. Because it performs less verification and monitoring than TCP/IP, it can generate much greater throughput. UDP/IP is often used with NFS and NIS, described next.

The Network File System

Sun Microsystems is a major manufacturer of engineering workstations running under Unix. It developed the Network File System (NFS) and the associated Network Information Services (NIS) that rely on the UDP/IP protocol, with its own method for assuring reliability. The Network File System allows users to access disks independently of their physical location. The Network Information Services aids system administrators in configuring a network-based system. These two products are available on most Unix systems and on some non-Unix systems.

TELNET

The TELNET protocol, which is part of the TCP/IP suite, enables users to log into a remote computer as if they were sitting at a directly attached terminal. Logging into a remote Internet computer via TELNET requires only that you know its name. The **telnet** command is discussed later in this text.

Hardware Components

A complete description of networking hardware requirements is beyond the scope of this text. However, as a system administrator, you should be familiar with the terms used to describe hardware components and their importance to a functioning network. This familiarity enables you to participate in networking task forces. The following material applies to Ethernet installations.

Coaxial Cable and Other Transmission Media

Most local area networks do not rely on conventional telephone lines to link computers. Telephone lines are often used in wide-area networks. A common transmission medium for LANs is the coaxial cable (somewhat similar to the cable used with CATV). The system administrator may participate in the selection of transmission media (a given network may employ more than one transmission medium). Once the decision is made to employ cable, it is necessary to pick and choose among various types of cable. Features to consider when selecting transmission media include

▰ **Length** Different types of cable have varying maximum lengths over which they can transmit a signal without loss. For example, 'Thinnet' cable has a maximum length of 185 meters, which is well under 600 feet. Cable sections may be strung together to achieve considerably greater lengths, but this procedure requires some technical expertise.

▰ **Transmission Speed** The theoretical maximum Ethernet transmission speed is 10MB/sec or 16MB/sec, a different league from modems or even serial transmission from one microcomputer to another. However, this speed may be inadequate for many LANs. In contrast the Fiber Distributed Data Interface, based on fiber optics, promises a raw speed of up to 100MB/sec.

▰ **Conformance to Fire-Code Regulations** Some types of cable such as PVC (polyvinyl chloride) emit toxic fumes when they burn. Flammable cable may not be used to connect floors within a building. Check local fire regulations carefully. Next to a fire, the last thing you want is to pull out the cable that you have so carefully strung.

▰ **Additional Hardware Requirements** The next section describes other hardware components that may be required to complete the hook-up. As when configuring any other system, network components must be chosen so that they work together meeting system objectives.

▰ **Security and Privacy Considerations** Security is discussed in detail in Chapter 12.

▰ **Cost** Cost is often the number-one selection criterion. At the time of this writing and presumably for many years to come, fiber optical cables remain considerably more expensive than coaxial cable. When evaluating media cost, don't forget to factor in the cost of installation and the cost of associated hardware, where appropriate, as discussed next.

Hardware Associated with Cable

Coaxial cable is usually purchased in standard lengths such as 23.5 meters (77 feet), 70.1 meters (230 feet), and 117 meters (384 feet). Often these lengths are not exactly what you need, and the cable must be cut and spliced. *Connectors* attach to the end of the cable and form a male or female end to which other hardware is attached. A connector may be attached to a *barrel adaptor* to link two cable sections. A connector may be attached to a *terminator*, a 50-ohm impedance inductor used to form the cable endpoint, blocking any signal reflections.

A *transceiver* is fastened to the network cable and then is attached to the Ethernet circuit board in the host computer via a *drop cable*. To reduce interference, transceivers must be at least 2.5 meters (about eight feet) apart. They draw power from the host via the drop cable. Consult your system manual for additional information. Be careful; cheating on the Ethernet specifications may cause more trouble than the dollars you might save. Connectors, adaptors, and terminators cost a few dollars each, while cable and drop cable run about fifty cents to over a dollar a foot. Transceivers cost a few hundred dollars each. Do plan your local-area or other network carefully. Don't expect it to come cheap, especially if you need to connect several LANs, as discussed next.

Internetwork Connections

Just as computer processing often outgrew single, isolated (personal) computers, organizations increasingly find they must link separate networks, including local-area networks. This requires careful planning and the specialized, relatively expensive components, discussed in the next section. The question naturally arises, why not create one large network instead of several smaller, interconnected networks? While every networking situation must be examined in detail, linking several smaller networks has potential advantages.

◢ **Location**   As a rule of thumb, a local-area network is confined to about one kilometer diameter. As a network expands geographically it runs into technological and budget problems. The longer the cable, the greater the cost and, eventually, the greater the need for special equipment and techniques to assure signal quality. Furthermore, natural or human-made barriers such as mountains and highways can restrict cable usage.

◢ **Reliability**   A single hardware or software error can disable a network, wreaking havoc until the problem is corrected. Linking several networks to each other can limit this disruption.

◢ **Performance**   LAN performance declines as cable length and the number of hosts increases, especially on busy systems. While it may be possible to improve the situation by upgrading the server or rewiring the system, separate, but connected, networks should be considered at some point.

◢ **Security**   Security costs money and is inconvenient. In general it's a good idea to separate users with normal security requirements from those with extended security requirements. The special equipment and techniques discussed in Chapter 12 may be applied to the more secure network.

Bridge

A *bridge* is a hardware device connecting local-area networks that apply the same transmission protocol. The bridge scans every packet to determine whether or not to transmit it to another LAN. It does not modify the form or the contents of the packets that it transmits. Sophisticated bridges can improve system performance by transmitting packets selectively, and can play a role in assuring system security by logging every attempt to access specified LANs.

Router

A *router* is a hardware device connecting local-area networks, sending packets to the appropriate network destination. Among the differences that a router must be able to handle are: maximum packet sizes (Ethernet has a maximum packet size of 1500 bytes), hardware and software interfaces, and addressing schemes. As they do their work, routers might have to reorganize packets.

Gateway

A *gateway* is a hardware device connecting networks that do not apply the same transmission protocol. Gateways may be used to connect LANs to LANs or LANs to mini- or mainframe computers. Because of the complexity involved in translating from one protocol to another, gateways are usually slower and handle fewer devices than do bridges.

ACCESSING AND MANAGING NETWORKS

Unix offers a wide variety of commands that enable users to access files and services on a remote machine. The system administrator will employ these commands from time to time. As well, the system administrator (or a networking assistant in the case of some large Unix networks) is responsible for network configuration. This section includes valuable information on configuring TCP/IP networks. It concludes by examining network information commands that tell the system administrator what's going on in the network, a prerequisite for the never-ending task of fine-tuning the network.

Network Use Commands

One advantage of networking is the ability for users to access files and services on a remote machine, with the aid of a few simple yet powerful additional commands. The use of remote machines can lead to important savings, for example in disk storage and personnel. Some installations choose to store all files on remote, massive hard disks instead of equipping individual hosts with their own hard disks.

The telnet Command

The **telnet** command allows users to access a remote machine on the network. The remote machine need not run Unix but must support the TELNET protocol, available on some DOS-based local-area networks. The **telnet** command supports both character-at-a-time and line-by-line data entry. Consult your system manual for the available options.

The rlogin Command

The **rlogin** command allows users to access a remote machine running BSD Unix on the network. Users must have a valid password on the remote machine. This command is relatively user-friendly; it places users in their home directory on the remote machine and passes it selected variables.

The rcp Command

The **rcp** command copies files between hosts in a network. It copies the *srchost:srcfile* to *desthost:destfile*, where *srchost:* and *desthost:* are optional system names in the network, and srcfile and destfile are file pathnames. The current system name is the default. Coding - for the *srcfile* specifies the standard input as the source. Destination directories must have write permission, and directories and files named on a remote source machine must have read permission.

The available options are:

-m   Mails and reports completion of the command, whether there is an error or not.

-u [*machine:*]*user*   Any mail goes to the named user on *machine*. The default machine is the one on which the **rcp** command is completed or on which an error was detected.

The **rcp** command is useful for transferring a few files across the network. The network consists of daemons that periodically awaken and send files from one system to another. The network must be installed using **netutil** before **rcp** can be used. To enable transfer of files from a remote system, the file **/etc/default/micnet** on the systems in the network must contain either:

rcp=/usr/bin/rcp

or

executeall
execpath=PATH=*path*

where *path* must contain **/usr/bin**.

For example, to copy the file **/tmp/abc** from the local machine **here** to the remote machine **there**, execute the following command. (The here$ serves as a prompt.)

```
here$ rcp /tmp/abc there:
```

The rsh Command

The **rsh** (remote shell) command executes a shell command on the remote Unix machine. It copies the local standard input to the remote machine before executing the command. After executing the command, it copies the remote standard output and error (if any) to the local standard output and error. The remote host name appears prior to the shell command. The following command displays the remote file **/tmp/abc** on the local machine. (The here$ serves as a prompt.)

```
here$ rsh there cat /tmp/abc
```

The **rsh** command may use pipes and redirection to mix local and remote hosts in a single command. The system administrator should master this command, for example, to offload programs from a busy computer to an idle one. Do not confuse the remote shell command **/usr/bin/rsh** with the restricted shell command **/usr/lib/rsh**.

The ftp Command

A major way in which documents and software are distributed on the Internet is called *anonymous ftp*. This procedure relies on the **ftp** utility, which applies the TCP/IP standard File Transfer Protocol and does not require a specific user password, but may require an electronic mail address.

The command line may specify a remote client host. In this case, **ftp** immediately attempts to establish a connection to an FTP server on that host. Otherwise, it displays the prompt ftp> and waits for the user to enter additional information. Table 11-1 gives an idea of the scope of this command. Consult your system manual for a more complete discussion of the **ftp** command options.

TCP/IP Networking Considerations

Networks are complicated. To put some method in this madness, the system administrator assigns names and addresses to network hosts following the Internet standard where applicable, and assigns a number to each active port. A judicious choice of aliases should make the network easier to administer. Sample Internet addresses, host names, and aliases are shown in a **/etc/hosts** file taken from an SCO Unix network. The TCP/IP network

TABLE 11-1

Options for the **ftp**
Command

Option	Parameter(s)	Meaning
$	*macro-name* [*args*]	Execute the named macro.
account	[*passwd*]	Supply a supplemental password for remote access.
append	*local-file* [*remote-file*]	Append a local file to a file on the remote machine.
ascii		Set file transfer type to network ASCII—default type.
bell		Ring a bell after each file-transfer command completes.
bye		Terminate FTP session.
cd	*remote-directory*	Change working directory on remote machine.
chmod	*mode filename*	Change permission modes of file on remote machine.
dir	[*remote-directory*] [*local-file*]	Display contents of directory or remote directory optionally places ouput in local file.
get	*remote-file* [*local-file*]	Retrieve remote file and store it on local machine.
lcd	[*directory*]	Change working directory on local machine.
mdelete	[*remote-files*]	Delete named files on remote machine.
mget	*remote-files*	Expand remote files on the remote machine and get each resultant file.
mkdir	*directory-name*	Make a directory on remote machine.
modtime	*filename*	Show last modification time of file on remote machine.
newer	*filename*	Get remote file only if its modification time is more recent than local file with the same name.
ntrans	[*inchars* [*outchars*]]	Set or unset the filename-character translation mechanism.
open	*host* [*port*]	Establish connection to host FTP server.
prompt		Toggle interactive prompting during multiple file transfers allowing user to retrieve or store files selectively.

TABLE 11-1

Options for the **ftp**
Command (*continued*)

Option	Parameter(s)	Meaning
put	*local-file* [*remote-file*]	Store local file on remote machine.
pwd		Print name of current working directory on remote machine.
size	*filename*	Return size of filename on remote machine.
user	*user-name* [*password*] [*account*]	Identify user to remote FTP server.
verbose		Toggle verbose mode; in verbose mode, all FTP server responses, as well as reports on data transfer statistics, are displayed to user.

services are supported by *daemons*, Unix processes that run in the background. The major network services are discussed below.

Host Names

Each machine on a given network must be assigned a unique name, the *host name*, which readily identifies the machine much as the user name identifies a given user. BSD Unix allows a maximum of 32 characters, while many versions of System V Unix allow a maximum of 14 characters. It is advisable to choose a short, easy-to-remember host name.

Network Addresses and Ports

The *network address* is unique for all hosts on a TCP/IP network. The Network Information Center assigns a network address to all hosts belonging to the Internet network. Other networks should employ network addresses conforming to the Internet naming standards the most common of which is described in part below.

An Internet network address, also called an IP address, consists of four bytes:

a.b.c.d

The first byte *a* determines the *address class*, which defines the meaning of the other bytes, as shown in Table 11-2.

For networks not linked to Internet, *a* is commonly set to 192 or 193. In this case *b* and *c* identify the subnetworks, and *d* identifies the individual host. Address components should not be set to 0 or 255. The network address 127.0.0.1 is assigned as a *loopback*

TABLE 11-2

Internet Network Address details

a Value	Address Class	Network Part	Host Part	Comments
1-126	Class A	a	b.c.d	Very large networks, such as Internet
128-191	Class B	a.b	c.d	Medium-sized networks
192-224	Class C	a.b.c	d	Small networks

address. Data sent to the loopback address is retransmitted to the sending host, whose host name is often defined as localhost in the **/etc/hosts** file, described next.

Each end of a TCP/IP link is attached to a *software sport*, identified by a 16-bit number. Ports whose numbers range from 0 to 1023 are known as *trusted ports*; they may be accessed only by the superuser. Trusted ports are defined by Unix; they are not part of the Internet standard.

The /etc/hosts File

The **hosts** file contains the list of the hosts on a local network. A sample file is shown here:

```
127.0.0.1     localhost     loopback
# HP 9000/750
87.0.0.21     hp_st
# SUN SPARC_station
87.0.0.22     sun_st
# DEC 5000 station
87.0.0.23     dec_st
# PC 486/Unix V
88.0.0.21     pc_unix
# MAC QUADRA/Unix
88.0.0.22     mac_aux
# Concurrent 8000
88.0.0.23     cc_rtu
# Tektronics X-Terminal 1
88.0.0.231    tecs1
# Tektronics X-Terminal 2
88.0.0.232    tecs2
# Tektronics X-Terminal 3
```

```
88.0.0.233    tecs3
# Tektronics X-Terminal 4
88.0.0.234    tecs4
# Princeton X-Terminal 1
88.0.0.235    prin1
# Princeton X-Terminal 2
88.0.0.236    prin2
```

The first line in the **/etc/hosts** file is the loopback entry. Succeeding entries occupy two lines. The first line consists of the comment symbol # followed by the host description (the full machine name). The second line begins with the Internet address, followed by the host name, and an optional alias. (This particular file did not include any entries with an alias.)

Networking Daemons

The TCP/IP network services are supported by *daemons*, Unix processes that run in the background. The major networking daemons are discussed below: first the single most important networking daemon, **inetd**, and then the others in alphabetical order:

- ▰ **inetd**   The **/etc/inetd** daemon monitors almost all network operations. It runs constantly and controls the other networking daemons according to instructions stored in the **/etc/inetd.conf** configuration file. In BSD Unix, each entry in this file includes the service name, the socket type, a protocol, the user of the server program, the server program pathname, and other information. When the **inetd** daemon receives a message, it first analyzes the message. Then it creates a copy of the required daemon that actually carries out the request.

- ▰ **comsat**   The **/etc/comsat** daemon notifies users that they have received mail. If the user is logged in and has set a flag requesting mail notification, **comsat** prints the beginning of the mail message on the user's display.

- ▰ **ftpd**   The **/etc/ftpd** daemon handles the **ftp** file transfer protocol discussed earlier in this chapter. It verifies the user password, if any. In the case of anonymous file transfer, this daemon executes a system call rendering files invisible outside the **ftp** directory, increasing system security.

- ▰ **gated**   The **/etc/gated** daemon replaces the **/etc/routed** daemon. It processes multiple routing protocols and converts routing information from one protocol to another. When run in debugging mode, its results are stored on a log file for further examination. The **/etc/gated** daemon is associated with the **/etc/gated.conf** file, which tends to get large and should be pruned by the system administrator.

◢ **named**   The **/etc/named** daemon maps host names into network addresses. The use of the **named** daemon simplifies the **/etc/hosts** file.

◢ **nntpd**   The **/etc/nntpd** (network news transfer protocol) daemon is involved in transferring Usenet news articles over the network. It handles both individuals and broadcasting of news items to multiple users.

◢ **rexecd**   The **/etc/rexecd** daemon processes commands to be executed on a remote machine. It first verifies the remote user's login name and password and then may initiate a communication channel for standard error output. The **rexecd** daemon builds the user's default environment and then forks the user shell which assumes these communications channels.

◢ **rlogind**   The **/etc/rlogind** daemon handles remote logins, received by the **rexecd** daemon. The **rlogind** daemon examines the **/etc/hosts.equiv** file and the prospective user's **~/.rhosts** file to effectuate an automatic login if possible. If an automatic login is impossible, the daemon executes a **login** process.

◢ **routed**   The **/etc/routed** daemon maintains dynamic (changeable) routing information employed in sending packets over Ethernet. It consumes extensive resources and has been replaced by the **/etc/gated** daemon.

◢ **rshd**   The **/etc/rshd** daemon handles the **rsd** remote shell and **rcmd** remote commands, as well as the **rcp** remote copy command. The **rshd** daemon verifies the user name and password, but does not prompt an unrecognized user for a password.

◢ **rwhod**   The **/etc/rwhod** daemon maintains and broadcasts a list of users logged in on the local machine and generates statistics on the load average for all network hosts. This information is recorded in the file **/usr/spool/rwho/whod.***hostname*, where *hostname* identifies the sending machine. The system administrator may examine these file contents manually or by program to help determine how and when to offload processes from one host to another.

◢ **syslogd**   The **/etc/syslogd** daemon centralizes network status information and error messages. It routes messages as directed by the appropriate entry in the **/etc/syslog.conf** file.

◢ **talkd**   The **/etc/talkd** daemon accepts connection requests issued by the **talk** program and initiates the network link where necessary.

◢ **timed**   The **/etc/timed** daemon adjusts the time of network machines according to the master machine or machines. When available **timed** uses the **adjtime** system call to adjust the time slowly, instead of creating large time changes, which can render system logs difficult to use.

Network Services

The **/etc/services** file, shown here, lists an SCO version of Internet services. Recall that these services may be initiated by the **inetd** daemon. Each entry contains an official service name, a port number, and a protocol name. Some entries contain an alias.

```
echo            7/tcp
echo            7/udp
discard         9/tcp       sink null
discard         9/udp       sink null
systat          11/tcp      users
daytime         13/tcp
daytime         13/udp
netstat         15/tcp
qotd            17/tcp      quote
chargen         19/tcp      ttytst source
chargen         19/udp      ttytst source
ftp             21/tcp
telnet          23/tcp
smtp            25/tcp      mail
time            37/tcp      timserver
time            37/udp      timserver
rlp             39/udp      resource
nameserver      42/tcp      name
whois           43/tcp      nicname
domain          53/tcp      nameserver
domain          53/udp      nameserver
mtp             57/tcp
tftp            69/udp
rje             77/tcp      netrjs
finger          79/tcp
link            87/tcp      ttylink
supdup          95/tcp
hostnames       101/tcp     hostname
pop             109/tcp     postoffice
sunrpc          111/tcp
sunrpc          111/udp
auth            113/tcp     authentication
sftp            115/tcp
uucp-path       117/tcp
nntp            119/tcp     readnews untp
ntp             123/tcp
netbios-ns      137/udp     nbns
netbios-ns      137/tcp     nbns
```

```
netbios-dgm      138/udp      nbdgm
netbios-dgm      138/tcp      nbdgm
netbios-ssn      139/tcp      nbssn
snmp             161/udp
snmp-trap        162/udp
#
# Unix specific services
#
exec             512/tcp
biff             512/udp      comsat
login            513/tcp
who              513/udp      whod
shell            514/tcp      cmd
syslog           514/udp
printer          515/tcp      spooler
talk             517/udp
ntalk            518/udp
efs              520/tcp
route            520/udp      router routed
timed            525/udp      timeserver
tempo            526/tcp      newdate
courier          530/tcp      rpc
conference       531/tcp      chat
netnews          532/tcp      readnews
netwall          533/udp
uucp             540/tcp      uucpd
remotefs         556/tcp      rfs_server rfs
listen          1025/tcp      listener RFS remote_file_sharing
nterm           1026/tcp      remote_login network_terminal
```

Network Information Commands

The system administrator's toolkit includes several commands that monitor an existing network, enabling her or him to fine-tune it. Other commands generate the list of user names, and determine whether a host is transmitting properly.

The rusers Command

The **rusers** (remote users) command lists the user names of current users on all hosts in the network. The *hostname* parameter restricts the list to a given host. The -l option generates a long listing, including the users' login ports, the time of login, and the CPU time used (in minutes).

The finger Command

The **finger** command displays the name of each logged-in user, the terminal port, the time in minutes since the user entered a command, the day and time of login, and the name of the remote host, if appropriate. A more detailed report is available for listed login names, including the day and time that the user last received and read mail. It also shows the contents of the user files **$HOME/.plan** and the first line of the user file **$HOME/.project**.

The ping Command

The **ping** command is a troubleshooting tool for tracking a single-point hardware or software failure in the Internet. It issues a message to the designated host and then informs you whether the message was successfully transmitted.

The **ping** command sends one datagram per second and prints one line of output for every ECHO_RESPONSE returned. No output is produced if there is no response. An optional *count* specifies the number of requests sent. The **ping** command displays round-trip times and packet loss statistics. If the user presses CTRL-C, it displays a brief statistical summary. Sample **ping** output is shown here:

```
PING localhost: 56 data bytes
64 bytes from 127.0.0.1: icmp_seq=0. time=16. ms
64 bytes from 127.0.0.1: icmp_seq=1. time=0. ms
64 bytes from 127.0.0.1: icmp_seq=2. time=0. ms
64 bytes from 127.0.0.1: icmp_seq=3. time=0. ms
64 bytes from 127.0.0.1: icmp_seq=4. time=0. ms
64 bytes from 127.0.0.1: icmp_seq=5. time=0. ms

----localhost PING Statistics----
6 packets transmitted, 6 packets received, 0% packet loss
round-trip (ms)  min/avg/max = 0/2/16
```

When attempting to locate a communication error, first run **ping** on the local host to verify that the local network interface is up and running. If this is unsuccessful, **ping** examines remote hosts and gateways starting with those connected to the local host.

The **ping** command is intended for use in network testing, measurement, and management. It is often used to see if a remote host is up and responding, and for manual fault isolation. The **ping** command requires extensive system resources and should not be used in normal network operations.

The netstat Command

The **netstat** command symbolically displays the contents of various network-related data structures. The Unix System V version has the following syntax:

netstat [-AainrsS] [-f *address family*] [-I *interface*]
[-p *protocol-name*] [*interval*] [*namelist*] [*corefile*]

The options have the following meanings:

-A   Shows the address of any associated protocol control blocks; used for debugging.

-a   Shows the state of all sockets; normally sockets used by server processes are not shown.

-i   Shows the state of autoconfigured interfaces. (Interfaces statically configured into a system but not located at boot time are not shown.)

-n   Shows network addresses as numbers. (Normally **netstat** interprets addresses and attempts to display them symbolically.)

-r   Shows the routing tables.

-s   Shows per-protocol statistics.

-S   Shows serial line configuration.

-f   Limits statistics and control block displays to address-family. The only address-family currently supported is inet.

-I   Shows interface state for interface only.

-p   Limits statistics and control block displays to *protocol-name*, such as tcp.

The arguments *namelist* and *corefile* allow substitutes for the defaults **/unix** and **/dev/kmem**. If an *interval* is specified, **netstat** continuously displays packet traffic information on the configured network interfaces, pausing *interval* seconds before refreshing the screen.

Several display formats are available, depending on the information presented. The default display, for active sockets, shows the local and remote addresses, send and receive queue sizes (in bytes), protocol, and, optionally, the internal state of the protocol.

Address formats are of the form *host.port* or *network.port* if a socket's address specifies a network but no specific host address. When known, the host and network addresses are displayed symbolically according to the data bases **/etc/hosts** and **/etc/networks**, respectively. If a symbolic name for an address is unknown, or if the -n option is specified, the address is printed in the Internet dot format; refer to **rhosts** for more information regarding this format. Unspecified, or wildcard, addresses and ports appear as *.

The interface display provides a table of cumulative statistics regarding transferred packets, errors, and collisions. The network address (currently Internet specific) of the interface and the maximum transmission unit (mtu) are also displayed.

The routing table display indicates available routes and their status. Each route consists of a destination host or network and a gateway to use in forwarding packets. The *flags* field shows the state of the route (U if up), and whether the route is to a gateway (G). Direct routes are created for each interface attached to the local host. The *refcnt* field gives the current number of active uses of the route. Connection-oriented protocols normally retain a single route for the duration of a connection, while connectionless protocols obtain a route then discard it. The *use* field contains the number of packets sent using that route. The *interface* entry indicates the network interface utilized for the route.

When **netstat** is invoked with an *interval* argument, it displays a running count of statistics related to network interfaces. This display consists of a column summarizing information for all interfaces and a column for the interface with the most traffic since the system was last rebooted. The first line of each information screen contains a summary since the system was last rebooted. Subsequent output lines show values accumulated over the preceding interval.

The serial line display shows the mapping of serial line units to serial devices. The baud rate and protocols in use are also shown.

A C LANGUAGE PROGRAM FOR CHECKING NETWORK COMMUNICATION

The following program uses the **ping** command to check a communication link for a specified host name or the Internet (IP) address. It redirects **ping** output, including summary communication statistics (the **kill** command replaces a manual CTRL-C keystroke) to a predefined file. Then the program parses the file and determines whether the communication was valid.

```
#include <stdio.h>
#include <string.h>
#include <sgtty.h>
#include <memory.h>
#include <fcntl.h>
#include <sys/errno.h>
#include <sys/types.h>
#include <sys/stat.h>
```

```
#define FILENAME "ping_test"

#define TOKEN0 "----"
#define TOKEN "PING Statistics----"
#define TOK "\n"
#define DIGITS "0123456789"
#define SPACE " "

extern errno;

main(argc, argv)
int argc;
char **argv;
{
FILE *hf1;
FILE *hf2;
char buf[2048];
char buf1[80];
char buf2[80];
char buf3[256];
int pid;
int fd;
int rc;
int size;
char *tstptr1;
char *tstptr2;
char *tstptr3;
char *ptr;
char result[256];
int found;
int trm_num;
int rec_num;
char host_name[16];

   trm_num = 0;
   rec_num = 0;
   found = 0;

/* sprintf loads a character string consisting      */
/* of command into a buffer, buf1                    */
/* The command in buf1 removes the FILENAME defined  */
/* as ping_test, if it exists, and then activates    */
/* the ping command with a command-line argument,    */
```

```
/* the hostname or Internet address. It redirects  */
/* this output to FILENAME.                         */
  sprintf(buf1, "rm -f ping_test; ping %s > %s",
          argv[1], FILENAME);
/* The popen function creates a pipe that activates */
/* the command stored in buf1. The r argument reads */
/* the standard output generated by this command.   */

  if ((hf1 = popen(buf1,"r")) != NULL)
  {
    printf("\npopen ok!");
  }
  else
  {
    perror("popen() failed");
  }
    sleep(5);
/* The following process is similar to the one    */
/* described above. Its final output is the PID,  */
/* after converting from ASCII to integer.        */

  sprintf(buf2, "ps -ef | grep \'ping %s\' |
          grep -v 'grep' | cut -c8-13", argv[1]);
  if ((hf2 = popen(buf2,"r")) != NULL)
  {
    printf("\npopen ok!");
    size = sizeof(buf3);
    while (fgets(buf3, size, hf2) != NULL)
    {
      pid = atoi(buf3);
    }
  }
  else
  {
    perror("popen() failed");
  }
  pclose(hf2);
  printf("\nPipe 2 Closed!");

/* The next line kills the process so that ping   */
/* generates a file containing network statistics */

  kill(pid, 2);
  printf("\nPID %d killed!",pid);
```

```
        pclose(hf1);
        printf("\nPipe 1 Closed!");

/* The following code processes the statistics      */
/* file, FILENAME, extracting the number of bytes   */
/* received and the number transmitted.             */

        fd = open(FILENAME, O_RDWR | O_NDELAY);
        if (fd == -1)
        {
          perror("open() failed");
          return(1);
        }
        else
        {printf("\nFile Opened ok!");
        }
        size = sizeof(buf);
        rc = read(fd, buf, 2048);
        if (rc == -1)
        {
          perror("read() failed");
          close(fd);
          return(2);
        }
        else
        {
          printf("\n*****************************************");
          printf("\n      File %s exists and is not empty:");
          printf("read %d bytes...", FILENAME, rc);
          printf("\n*****************************************");
          tstptr1 = strstr(buf,TOKEN0);
          ptr = tstptr1;
          tstptr1 = strstr(ptr,TOKEN);
          ptr = tstptr1;
          tstptr1 = strstr(ptr,TOKEN0);
          ptr = tstptr1;
          tstptr1 = strstr(ptr,TOK);
          ptr = tstptr1;
          ++*tstptr1;
          ++*tstptr1;
          ++*tstptr1;
          ++*tstptr1;
          strcpy(result,tstptr1);
```

```
      printf("\nResult: %s", ptr);
      found = 1;
}
if (found == 1)
{
   tstptr2 = strpbrk(result,DIGITS);
   tstptr3 = strtok(tstptr2,SPACE);
   if (tstptr3 != NULL)
   {
      trm_num = atoi(tstptr3);
      printf("\nstrtok ok!");
      printf(" TRM_NUM = %d", trm_num);
   }
   {else
   } printf("\nstrtok: not found!");
   strcpy(result,tstptr3);
   tstptr2 = strpbrk(result,DIGITS);
   tstptr3 = strtok(tstptr2,SPACE);
   if (tstptr3 != NULL)
   {
      rec_num = atoi(tstptr3);
      printf("\nstrtok ok!");
      printf(" REC_NUM = %d", rec_num);

   }
   else
   {printf("\nstrtok: not found!");
   }
}
if (rec_num > 0)
{
   printf("\n*****  HOST %s < CONNECTED and RUNNING!");
   printf("> *****\n", argv[1]);
}
else
{
   printf("\n***** HOST %s > NOT CONNECTED");
   printf("[NOT POWERED UP]! < *****\n", argv[1]);
   printf("\nCheck /etc/hosts file for the");
   printf("name[or address]: %s!\n", host_name;
   printf("\nCheck if the name[or address]");
   printf("%s powered up!\n", host_name;
   printf("\nThen run program: %s");
   printf("host name[or address]!\n", argv[0]);
```

```
    }
}
```

The MAKE file for SCO Unix associated with this network checking program follows. The MAKE file may vary when using other versions of Unix.

```
RM = rm -f
CC = cc
CFLAGS = -O
DFLAG = -DM_TERMCAP
INCLUDES = -I. -I/usr/include
#LIBS = -ltcap -ltermlib -lcurses -lsocket -lmalloc -lPW
LIBS = -lcurses -ltermlib -lsocket -lmalloc -lPW
.c.o:
$(RM) $@
$(CC) -c $(INCLUDES) $*.c
all:: netcheck
netcheck: netcheck.o
$(RM) $@
$(CC) -o $@ $(CFLAGS) netcheck.o $(LIBS)
@echo makefile for netcheck  - done!
```

A SHELL SCRIPT FOR ADDING HOSTS

The following Bourne shell script performs key steps in adding a host to a network. As in many previous scripts, only the system administrator running as superuser may execute the full script. The novice system administrator should first execute the test script using a regular password to familiarize himself or herself with the process of adding a host to the network.

Remember

Before executing the full script, it is necessary to connect the system to the network, assign the host a name and an address, and ensure that the relevant network daemons are active.

The following code specifies the Bourne shell interpreter, provides a short description of the script, and defines the variable *log_name*.

```
#!/bin/sh
# @(#) add hosts script
log_name = 'whoami'
```

The following code prompts the system administrator to enter the name of the host to be added to the system. The script displays a message confirming successful entry or displays an error message and terminates.

```
echo "\nPlease enter Host Name: \c"
read hname
if [ -n "$hname" ]
then
  echo "Entered Host Name -> $hname\n"
else
  echo "No Host Name specified. Try again\n"
  exit 1
fi
```

The following code prompts the system administrator to enter the Internet address associated with the host to be added. The script displays a message confirming successful entry or displays an error message and terminates.

```
echo "Please enter Internet Address: \c"
read iaddress
if [ -n "$iaddress" ]
then
  echo "Entered Internet Address -> $iaddress\n"
else
  echo "No Internet Address specified. Try again\n"
  exit 1
fi
```

The following code prompts the system administrator to enter an alias for the host to be added and then displays this alias. Unlike a host name and an Internet address, no alias is required.

```
echo "Please enter Alias: \c"
read aliass
if [ -n "$aliass" ]
then
  echo "Entered Alias -> $aliass\n"
else
  echo "No Alias specified.\n"
fi
```

The following code prompts the system administrator to enter a host description, which will be echoed.

```
echo "Please enter Host Description: \c"
read descr
if [ -n "$descr" ]
then
  echo "Entered Description -> $descr\n"
else
  echo "No Description specified.\n"
fi
```

The next script uses the **/etc** directory subordinate to the user directory for testing purposes. The first time this script is run it creates the test directory. Subsequent executions notify the system administrator that this directory exists.

```
thehosts=/etc/hosts
```

The following code verifies the permission level of the person running the script. Only the system administrator running in the superuser mode accesses production files; all others access test files in the test directory.

```
if [ $log_name = "root" ]
then
    echo "\nEntered as a $log_name Executing ...\n"
    echo "\nAdding New Host to the Hosts File!\n"
```

The following code updates the hosts file creating an entry for the new host and informs the superuser of the file update:

```
  if [ -n "$descr" ]
  then
    echo "#\t$descr" >> $thehosts
    echo "$iaddress\t$hname\t$aliass" >> $thehosts
  else
    echo "$iaddress\t$hname\t$aliass" >> $thehosts
  fi
  echo "\nNew Host Added to the Hosts File!\n"
else
  echo "\nEntered as a $log_name! Executing ...\n"
dirtst=/usr/$log_name/etc
hoststst=/usr/$log_name/etc/hosts
if [ -s $dirtst ]
then
  echo "Directory $dirtst exists\n"
else
  echo "Directory $dirtst not exist! Making ...\n"
```

```
     mkdir $dirtst
fi
```

The following code updates the pseudo host's file, creating an entry for the new host, and informs the user of the test file update.

```
     echo "\nAdding New Host to the Pseudo Hosts File!\n"
     if [ -n "$descr" ]
     then
       echo "#\t$descr" >> $hoststst
       echo "$iaddress\t$hname\t$aliass" >> $hoststst
     else
       echo "$iaddress\t$hname\t$aliass" >> $hoststst
     fi
     echo "\nNew Host Added to the Pseudo Hosts File!\n"
   fi
```

A SHELL SCRIPT FOR REMOVING HOSTS

The following Bourne shell script performs key steps in removing a host from the network. As in many previous scripts, only the system administrator running as superuser may execute the full script. The novice system administrator should first execute the test script using a regular password to familiarize himself or herself with the process of removing a host from the network.

```
#!/bin/sh
# @(#) remove hosts script
log_name = 'whoami'
dirtst=/usr/$log_name/etc
hoststst=/usr/$log_name/etc/hosts
thehosts=/etc/hosts
```

The following code prompts the system administrator to enter the name of the host to be removed. The script displays a message confirming successful entry or displays an error message and terminates.

```
echo "\nPlease enter Host Name: \c"
read hname
if [ -n "$hname" ]
then
  echo "Entered Host Name -> $hname\n"
else
```

```
      echo "No Host Name specified. Try again\n"
      exit 1
fi
```

The following code verifies the permission level of the person running the script. Only the system administrator running in the superuser mode accesses production files; all others access test files in the test directory. In the case of the superuser, the script updates the host's file removing the entry associated with the designated host and displays an information message. The old host's file is kept as a backup.

```
if [ log_name = "root" ]
 then
    echo "\nEntered as a $log_name! Executing ...\n"
    grep -s $hname $thehosts

    if test $? = 1
    then
      echo "\n$hname is not a valid host name! Exiting ..."
      exit 1
    fi

    echo "\nRemoving Host from the Hosts File!\n"

    cp $thehosts etc/hosts.old

    sed "/$hname/d" $thehosts > /tmp/rm$$
    mv /tmp/rm$$ $thehosts

    echo "\nHost removed from the Hosts File!\n"
  else
    echo "\nEntered as a $log_name! Executing ...\n"
```

The following code updates the pseudo host's file in the test directory /etc, removing the entry associated with the designated host, and displays an information message. The old host's test file is kept as a backup.

```
    grep -s $hname $hoststst

    if test $? = 1
    then
      echo "\n$hname is not a valid host name! Exiting ..."
      exit 1
    fi
```

```
    echo "\nRemoving Host from the Pseudo Hosts File!\n"
    cp $hoststst $dirtst/hosts.old

    sed "/$hname/d" $hoststst > $dirtst/rm$$
    mv $dirtst/rm$$ $hoststst

    echo "\nHost removed from the Pseudo Hosts File!\n"
  ;;
esac
```

A SHELL SCRIPT FOR ADDING SERVICES

The following Bourne shell script performs key steps in adding a service to a network. As in many previous scripts, only the system administrator running as superuser may execute the full script. The novice system administrator should first execute the test script using a regular password to familiarize himself or herself with the process of adding a service to the network.

The following code specifies the Bourne shell interpreter, provides a short description of the script, and defines the variable *log_name.*

```
#!/bin/sh
# @(#) add services script
log_name = 'whoami'
```

The following code prompts the system administrator to enter the name of the service to be added to the system. The script displays a message confirming successful entry or displays an error message and terminates.

```
echo "\nPlease enter Service Name: \c"
read sname
if [ -n "$sname" ]
then
  echo "Entered Service Name -> $sname\n"
else
  echo "No Service Name specified. Try again\n"
  exit 1
fi
```

The following code prompts the system administrator to enter the port number associated with the service to be added. The script displays a message confirming successful entry or it displays an error message and terminates.

```
echo "Please enter Port Number
[must be greater than 2999]:\c"read pnum
if [ -n "$pnum" ]
then
  echo "Entered Port Number -> $pnum\n"
else
  echo "No Port Number specified. Try again\n"
  exit 1
fi
```

The following code prompts the system administrator to enter the protocol name associated with the service to be added. The script displays a message confirming successful entry or displays an error message and terminates.

```
echo "Please enter Protocol Name [tcp/udp]: \c"
read pname
if [ -n "$pname" ]
then
  echo "Entered Protocol Name -> $pname\n"
else
  echo "No Protocol Name specified. Try again\n"
  exit 1
fi
```

The following code prompts the system administrator to enter the alias associated with the service to be added. Unlike a service name, a port number, and a protocol name, no alias is required.

```
echo "Please enter Alias: \c"
read aliass
if [ -n "$aliass" ]
then
  echo "Entered Alias -> $aliass\n"
else
  echo "No Alias specified.\n"
fi


theservices=/etc/services
```

The following code verifies the permission level of the person running the script. Only the system administrator running in the superuser mode accesses production files; all others access test files in the test directory.

```
if [ $log_name = "root" ]
  then
```

```
echo "\nEntered as a logname! Executing ...\n"
echo "\nAdding New Service to the Services File!\n"
```

The following code updates the services file, creating an entry for the new service, and informs the superuser of the file update.

```
echo "$sname\t$pnum/$pname\t$aliass" >> $theservices
echo "\nNew Service Added to the Services File!\n"
else
echo "\nEntered as a logname! Executing ...\n"
dirtst=/usr/$log_name/etc
servicestst=/usr/$log_name/etc/services
```

The next script uses the **/etc** directory subordinate to the user directory for testing purposes. The first time this script is run, it creates the test directory. Subsequent executions notify the system administrator that this directory exists.

```
if [ -s $dirtst ]
then
  echo "Directory $dirtst exists\n"
else
  echo "Directory $dirtst not exist! Making ...\n"
  mkdir $dirtst
fi
```

The following code updates the pseudo services file, creating an entry for the new service, and informs the superuser of the test file update.

```
echo "\nAdding New Service to the Pseudo Services File!\n"
echo "$sname\t$pnum/$pname\t$aliass" >> $servicestst
echo "\nNew Service Added to the Pseudo Services File!\n"
fi
```

A SHELL SCRIPT FOR REMOVING SERVICES

The following Bourne shell script performs key steps in removing a service from the network. As in many previous scripts, only the system administrator running as superuser may execute the full script. The novice system administrator should first execute the test script using a regular password to familiarize himself or herself with the process of removing a service from the network.

```
#!/bin/sh
# @(#) remove services shell script
log_name = 'whoami'
dirtst=/usr/$log_name/etc
servicestst=/usr/$log_name/etc/services
theservices=/etc/hosts
```

The following code prompts the system administrator to enter the name of the service to be removed. The script displays a message confirming successful entry or displays an error message and terminates.

```
echo "\nPlease enter Service Name: \c"
read sname
if [ -n "$sname" ]
then

  echo "Entered Service Name -> $sname\n"
else
  echo "No Service Name specified. Try again\n"
  exit 1
fi
```

The following code verifies the permission level of the person running the script. Only the system administrator running in the superuser mode accesses production files; all others access test files in the test directory. In the case of the superuser, the script updates the services file, removing the entry associated with the designated service, and displays an information message. The old services file is kept as a backup.

```
if [ $log_name = "root" ]
then   echo "\nEntered as a $log_name! Executing ...\n"
  grep -s $sname $theservices

  if test $? = 1
  then
    echo "\n$sname is not a valid
          service name! Exiting ..."
    exit 1
  fi
  echo "\nRemoving Service from the Services File!\n"

  cp $theservices etc/services.old

  sed "/$sname/d" $theservices > /tmp/rm$$
  mv /tmp/rm$$ $theservices
```

```
      echo "\nService removed from the Services File!\n"
   else
      echo "\nEntered as a $log_name! Executing ...\n"
```

The following code updates the pseudo services file in the test directory **etc**, removing the entry associated with the designated service, and displays an information message. The old test services file is kept as a backup.

```
   grep -s $sname $servicestst

   if test $? = 1
   then
     echo "\n$sname is not a valid service name! Exiting ..."
     exit 1
   fi
   echo "\nRemoving Service from the Pseudo Services File!\n"
   cp $servicestst $dirtst/services.old

   sed "/$sname/d" $servicestst > $dirtst/rm$$
   mv $dirtst/rm$$ $servicestst

   echo "\nService removed from the Pseudo Services File!\n"
fi
```

RECONFIGURING THE NETWORK

A network is rarely a static system. As users become convinced of the need to share resources, the network grows. As corporations downsize their computer operations, the network grows. As corporations postpone downsizing, but hook up their larger computers to micros, the network grows. As the price of microcomputers continues its virtual freefall, the network grows.

Adding a Host

As system administrator, you will often be called upon to add hosts to a network. Before invoking the **add hosts** shell script, it's important to understand the steps involved in adding a host. The following steps are required in adding a host to most Unix networks:

1. Connect the host to the network. If you are not a hardware or a cabling expert, this step could be as difficult as all the others combined.

2. Assign the host a host name and a host address. The name and address *must* be chosen in accordance with the networking naming conventions in force for your installation.

3. Add an entry describing the new host to the **/etc/hosts** file for every linked network. Create an **/etc/hosts** file for the new host. (Some Unix installations refer to this file differently; for example, **/etc/net/hosts**.) See the **add hosts** shell script presented previously.

4. Ensure that the network daemons will be executed when the system is rebooted. In System V Unix the files **/etc/rc0.d** and **/etc/rc2.d** or **/etc/rc3.d** must link to **/etc/init.d/tcp** (perhaps called **network**). In BSD Unix the network daemons must appear in the files **/etc/rc** and **/etc/rc.local**.

5. Test the network setup using the **ping** command. See the **netcheck** program presented previously.

6. Add services to the **/etc/services** file for every linked network. Create an **/etc/services** file for the new host. (Some Unix installations refer to this file differently; for example, **/etc/net/services**.) See the **add services** shell script presented previously.

7. Validate the reconfigured network applying the **client** and **server** programs (perhaps after relatively minor modifications) presented in Chapter 4. Either the **client** program or the **server** program may be run on the new host.

Note

The system administrator should master the various netstat command options and use this command liberally for checking network connectivity and activity.

Removing a Host

Networks are not static. While it is not as common to remove hosts as to add them, system administrators must be able to remove hosts on demand without destabilizing the network. Downsizing computer services often means increasing the size of the network, but sometimes it has the opposite meaning. The following steps are required in removing a host from most Unix networks:

1. Disconnect the host from the network. In many cases, the cables are not removed, as they may be required at a later date.

2. Remove the description of the designated host in the **/etc/hosts** file for every linked network. Delete the **/etc/hosts** file for this host. If there is any possibility that the host will be added again, comment it out instead of removing the entry or the file. See the **remove hosts** shell script presented previously.

3.   Test the revised network setup using the **ping** command. Running the **netcheck** program defined previously should give a negative result.

4.   You might wish to remove services. In this case run the **remove services** program defined previously.

THE UUCP FACILITY

The UUCP (Unix to Unix Copy Program) is a sophisticated, powerful facility that enables users to transfer files between Unix systems, executes commands on a remote system, and sends mail to users on a remote system. It is designed to work with the standard telephone system, and does not require specialized hardware or software or a local-area network. This chapter presents several commands associated with the UUCP facility: the **uucp** command itself, which copies files from one Unix system to another; the **uuto** command, which sends source files to a specified destination under the control of the local system; the **uupick** command, which accepts or rejects the files transmitted to the user; the **uux** command, which executes a Unix command on a specified system; and the **uustat** command, which displays the status of or cancels previously specified **uucp** commands.

The uucp Command

The **uucp** command copies files named by the *source-file* arguments to the *destination-file* argument. A file name may be a pathname for your machine or may have the following form:

system-name!*pathname*

for the Korn shell and Bourne shell or

system-name\!*pathname*

for the C shell, where *system-name* is taken from a list of system names known to **uucp** or a list of names for the Korn shell and Bourne shell, as follows:

system-name!*system-name*!....!*system-name*!*pathname*

or for the C shell:

system-name\!*system-name*\!...\!*system-name*\!*pathname* in which case an attempt is made to send the file via the specified route to the destination. Care should be taken to ensure that intermediate nodes in the route are willing to forward information.

If the result is an erroneous pathname for the remote system, the copy will fail. If the *destination-file* parameter is a directory, the last part of the *source-file* name is used.

The **uucp** command preserves execute permissions across the transmission and sets read and write permissions to the octal value 666. Among the options it provides are the following:

-c   Does not copy local file to the spool directory for transfer to the remote machine (default).

-C   Forces the copy of local files to the spool directory for transfer.

-d   Makes all necessary directories for the file copy (default).

-f   Does not make intermediate directories for the file copy.

-j   Outputs the job identification ASCII string on the standard output. This job identification can be used by **uustat** to obtain the status or terminate a job.

-m   Sends mail to the requester when the copy is completed. This option is used to send one or more files and to receive a single file. It will not receive multiple files specified by special shell characters ? * [...].

-n*user*   Notifies user on the remote system that a file was sent.

-r   Does not start the file transfer, just queues the job.

-s*file*   Reports status of the transfer to file. Note that the file must be a full pathname.

-x*debug_level*   Produces debugging output on standard output. The *debug_level* is a number between 0 and 9; higher numbers give more detailed information.

Note

For security reasons, access to remote machines should usually be severely restricted. It may not be possible to fetch files by pathname; ask a responsible person on the remote system to send them to you. Furthermore, you will probably not be able to send files to arbitrary pathnames. As distributed, remotely accessible files have names that begin /usr/spool/uucppublic (equivalent to ~/).

The **uucp** command owns all files that it receives. The forwarding of files through other systems may not be compatible with a previous **uucp** version. If forwarding is used, all systems in the route must have the same version of **uucp**.

The uucp command can send protected files and files in protected directories owned by the requester. However, if the requester is root and the directory is not searchable by "other" or the file is not readable by "other," the request will fail.

The uuto Command

The **uuto** command sends source files to a specified destination under the control of the local system. The source file name is a pathname on the local machine. The destination takes the form: *system! user* where *system* appears on a list of system names known to **uucp**. *User* is the login name of someone on the specified system.

Two options are available:

-p   Copies the source file into the spool directory before transmission.

-m   Sends mail to the sender when the copy is complete.

The files (or sub-trees if directories are specified) are sent to *PUBDIR* on *system,* where *PUBDIR* is a public directory defined in the **uucp** source. By default this directory is **/usr/spool/uucppublic**. Specifically, the files are sent to *PUBDIR*/**receive**/user /mysystem/files. The destined recipient is notified by mail of the file arrival.

The uupick Command

The **uupick** command accepts or rejects the files transmitted to the user, searching *PUBDIR* for files destined for the user. Whenever it finds a file or directory it prints the following message on the standard output:

from *system:* [file *file-name*] [dir *dirname*] ?

uupick then reads a line from the standard input to determine the file disposition:

<new-line>   Goes on to next entry.

d   Deletes the entry.

m [*dir*]   Moves the entry to the named directory. If *dir* is not specified as a complete pathname (in which case **$HOME** is legitimate), a destination relative to the current directory is assumed. The default is the current directory.

a [*dir*]   Same as m, except moves all the files sent from *system.*

p   Prints file contents.

q   Stops.

EOT (CTRL-D)   Same as q.

!*command*   Escapes to the shell to execute the command.

*   Displays a command summary.

If **uupick** is invoked with the -s*system* option, it searches only the *PUBDIR* for files sent from *system.* To send files that begin with a dot (for example, **.profile**), the files must be qualified with a dot.

The uux Command

The **uux** command collects zero or more files from various systems, executes a command on a specified system, and then sends standard output to a file on a specified system.

| **Note** | For security reasons, most installations limit the list of commands executable on behalf of an incoming request from uux, permitting only the receipt of mail. |

By default **uux** notifies the user by remote mail if the requested command for the remote system was rejected. See your system manual for additional information related to this command.

The uustat Command

The **uustat** command displays the status of, or cancels previously specified **uucp** commands. It also provides the status of **uucp** connections to other systems. The following options are mutually exclusive:

-a   Displays information about all jobs in the queue.

-m   Reports the status of accessibility of all machines.

-p   Executes a **ps** -flp command for all process IDs in the lock files.

-q   Lists the jobs queued for each machine, generating date, time, and status information if a status file exists. See your system manual to obtain more information for this command. This command may take a long time to execute even for systems with a moderate number of outstanding jobs.

-k*job-id*   Kills the specified **uucp** request. This request must belong to the individual issuing the **uustat** command or to the superuser.

-r*job-id*   Touches the files associated with the specified *job-id*, setting their modification time to the current time. This prevents the **cleanup** daemon from deleting the job until the jobs modification time reaches the limit imposed by the daemon.

Either or both of the following options can be specified with **uustat**:

-s*sys*   Reports the status of all **uucp** requests for the remote system *sys*.

-u*user*   Reports the status of all **uucp** requests issued by the specified *user*.

Output for both of these are shown in the following examples:

```
eaglen0000 4/07-11:01:03(POLL)
eagleN1bd7 4/07-11:07Seagledan522 /usr/dan/A
eagleC1bd8 4/07-11:07Seagledan59 D.3b2a1ce4924
4/07-11:07Seagledanrmail mike
```

The first field is the *job-id*. The second field is the *date/time*. The third field is either an S or an R, depending on whether the job is to send or request a file. The fourth field is the *user-id* of the user who queued the job. The fifth field contains the file size, or in the case of a remote execution the command name. The file size, if present, is followed by the file name. This file name is either the user-supplied name or an internal name (such as **D.3b2alce4924**) created for data files associated with remote executions. When no options are given, **uustat** outputs the status of all **uucp** requests issued by the current user.

Mastery of this commmand and its various options is essential for monitoring the UUCP utility to meet security goals, as discussed in Chapter 12.

Chapter Summary

Basic Networking Terminology   A computer network is two or more linked computers. A host is a computer attached to the computer network. A local-area network (LAN) is a network whose components are linked directly, usually extending over a distance of a kilometer or less. A wide-area network (WAN) is a network whose components are linked indirectly, usually over a large distance. Protocol consists of the formal rules and conventions used when two processes communicate. The medium is the path over which communications flow. A message is a unit of information communicated from one location to another. Packet switching is a type of message transmission in which messages are broken up into segments called packets that are transmitted independently and then reassembled at the destination.

Protocols and Network Services   Efficient network performance requires correct selection of the network protocol. TCP/IP is an abbreviation for Transmission Control Protocol/Internet Protocol, the major data transmission protocol for Unix. TCP/IP provides reliable data transmission; the system guarantees that every byte transmitted will reach its destination in the order that it was sent, or you will be notified. It works with the Ethernet interface associated with many local-area networks.

UDP/IP is an abbreviation for User Datagram Protocol/Internet Protocol. It serves as a fast but unreliable way to transmit data packets between two or more programs. Sun Microsystems' Network File System (NFS) allows users to access disks independently of their physical location. The associated Network Information Services (NIS) aids system administrators in configuring a network-based system. The TEL-NET protocol enables users to log in on a remote computer as if they were sitting at a directly attached terminal.

Hardware Components   The two most common transmission media for LANs are twisted pair wires used in telephone systems and coaxial cable (somewhat similar to the cable used with CATV). Among the features to consider when selecting transmission media are: length, transmission speed, conformance to fire-code regulations, the necessity for other hardware, security and privacy considerations, and cost. Other devices such as connectors are often required when using cables.

Internetwork Connections   Just as computer processing often outgrew single, isolated (personal) computers, organizations find it increasingly necessary to link separate networks, including local-area networks. To do so requires careful planning and the specialized, relatively expensive components, including bridges, hardware devices connecting local-area networks that apply the same transmission protocol;

routers, hardware devices connecting local-area networks that do not necessarily apply the same transmission protocol; and gateways, hardware devices connecting networks that do not apply the same transmission protocol. Gateways may be used to connect LANs to LANs or LANs to mini- or mainframe computers.

Accessing and Managing Networks   Unix offers a wide variety of commands that enable virtually untrained users to access files and services on a remote machine. The system administrator will employ these commands from time to time. These commands include the **rlogin** command, which allows users to access a remote machine running Unix on the network; the **telnet** command, which allows users to access a remote machine on the network; the **rcp** command, which copies files between hosts in a Micnet network; the **rsh** (remote shell) command, which executes a shell command on the remote Unix machine; and the **ftp** command, which is often used to access remote files and documents.

TCP/IP Networking Considerations   Networks are complicated. To put some method in this madness, the system administrator assigns names and addresses to network hosts following the Internet standard where applicable, and assigns a number to each active port. A judicious choice of aliases should make the network easier to administer. Each machine on a given network must be assigned a unique name, the host name, which serves to identify the machine readily much as the user name identifies a given user. The network address is unique for all hosts on a TCP/IP network. The Network Information Center assigns a network address to all hosts belonging to the Internet network. An Internet network address, also known as an IP address, consists of four bytes:

a.b.c.d

Each end of a TCP/IP link is attached to a port, identified by a 16-bit number. Ports whose number ranges from 0 to 1023 are known as trusted ports; they may be accessed only by the superuser. The **/etc/hosts** file contains the list of the hosts on a local network. The TCP/IP network services are supported by daemons. The **/etc/inetd** daemon monitors almost all network operations. It runs constantly and controls the other networking daemons according to instructions stored in the **/etc/inetd.conf** configuration file. The **/etc/services** file lists Internet services, not all of which are necessarily available under Unix.

Network Information Commands   The system administrator's toolkit includes several commands that monitor an existing network, enabling her or him to fine-tune it. Other commands generate the list of user names, and determine whether a host is transmitting properly. The **rusers** (remote users) command lists the user names of current users on all hosts in the network. The **finger** command displays the name of each logged-in user, the terminal port, the time in minutes since the user entered a command, the day and time of login, and the name of the remote host, if appropriate. The **ping** command is a troubleshooting tool for tracking a single-point hardware or software failure in the Internet. It issues a message to the designated host and then informs you whether the message was successfully transmitted. The **netstat** command symbolically displays the contents of various network-related data structures.

Reconfiguring the Network   A network is rarely a static system. As system administrator, you will often be called upon to add hosts to a network. The following steps are required in adding a host to most Unix networks: Connect the host to the network, assign the host a hostname and a host address. Add an entry describing the new host to the **/etc/hosts** file for every linked network, ensure that the network daemons will be executed when the system is rebooted, test the network setup using the **ping** command, add services, and validate the reconfigured network by applying **client** and **server** programs.

The following steps are required to remove a host from most Unix networks: Disconnect the host from the network, remove the description of the designated host in the **/etc/hosts** file for every linked network and delete the **/etc/hosts** file for this host, perhaps remove network daemons or preferably comment them out, test the revised network setup using the **ping** command, and perhaps remove services.

The UUCP Facility   The UUCP (Unix to Unix Copy Program) is a sophisticated, powerful facility that enables users to transfer files between Unix systems, execute commands on a remote system, and send mail to users on a remote system. It includes the **uucp** command itself; which copies files from one Unix system to another; the **uuto** command, which sends source files to a specified destination under the control of the local system; the **uupick** command, which accepts or rejects the files transmitted to the user; the **uux** command, which executes a Unix command on a specified system; and the **uustat** command, which displays the status of or cancels previously specified **uucp** commands.

Unix System

Administration Guide

CHAPTER 1

Security Management

Security is one of the most critical tasks of the system administrator. Proper security costs money and causes inconvience. However, security breaches cost more and cause more inconvience than does proper security. Convince your users of these truths and half the security battle is won. The system administrator's most important security task is establishing an effective security environment—convincing users of the importance of maintaining security on a 24-hour-a-day basis.

This chapter provides specific guidelines for maintaining account security, dealing with attacks on physical security including natural disasters, handling specific network security problems, and auditing the system. It contains both shell scripts and C language programs that can be run as is or modified to meet your installation's specific security requirements.

ACCOUNT SECURITY

The single most important defense of a Unix system against intruders is the password. Chapter 5 explained passwords, password selection, and the contents of the **passwd** file. It provided several methods to automate the user account creation and removal process, including shell scripts that could be used by the system administrator to manage user accounts. It also contained C language programs available to the system administrator, and her or his assistant, to manage user accounts without compromising system security. In all cases it, necessary for the system administrator and his or her assistant, if appropriate, to work through the test procedures before actually creating or removing user accounts.

This section describes methods of protecting the **passwd** file and monitoring attempts to modify user access privileges. The program that follows deals with a common cause of password leaks: failure to log off the system.

Password Security Guidelines

As system administrator you should carefully consider these guidelines for creating and managing user accounts and passwords. While some points may require modification to meet your specific installation needs, do not reject any of the following guidelines too hastily.

- ◢ Require all people who access the computer system to have their own computer accounts. Monitor account usage carefully with Unix commands such as **who** and **last**. The mere fact that the system administrator is keeping tabs on individual usage will discourage some intruders.

- ◢ Ensure that all accounts have a password. Never allow an account to exist without a password. A clever intruder could use such an account to access system resources at a later date.

- ◢ Educate users on the need to select passwords carefully and to protect their passwords. Some installations place the password selection process in the system administrator's hands. While this policy virtually eliminates easy-to-guess passwords, it usually encounters user resistance.

- ◢ Never transmit passwords by electronic mail. You never know who is reading your mail.

- ◢ Restrict your use of the root account to genuine system administrator activities. Perform all routine activities using your regular account. And never unpack or test new software while you are running under the root account.

☑   Change the password of every account supplied with the Unix system and delete any that are not needed.

☑   Disable user accounts after a predetermined period of inactivity.

☑   Require every UUCP login (see Chapter 11) to have its own, different password. Keep an eye on UUCP usage.

Data Encryption

Coding data to prevent its being read by unauthorized individuals is known as *data encryption* or simply *encryption*. Many history buffs know that during World War II, both the Allies and the Axis devoted considerable resources to devising encryption schemes and to breaking the enemy's encryption schemes. Depending on the importance of your installation, intruders may devote major resources to breaking your code.

Data is encrypted by applying a secret formula. Simple formulas such as replacing the letter A by the letter N, the letter B by the letter O, etc. are virtually useless. Some bulletin boards provide such an encryption scheme called **rot13**. Do not use this encryption scheme to protect data that is of any importance to you. Unix also provides the **crypt** program, a simple implementation of a cryptography technique employed in World War II. As you might expect, this program does not provide sufficient protection to sensitive files.

A commonly used encryption algorithm is the *Data Encryption Standard (DES)* developed in the 1970s by the United States Government and IBM. This encryption scheme is used for nonmilitary applications, but many people feel that DES is insufficiently secure for military applications.

Another commonly used encryption method relies on two special numbers called keys. The *public key* is used to encrypt the data. A *private key* is used to decrypt the data. At present there is no known method for obtaining the private key associated with a given public key.

The question is not *whether* to employ data encryption, but *when* to employ it and *how* to employ it. The system administrator might need technical assistance when answering these questions and implementing data encryption where required.

Modifying System Access

Under most circumstances only the superuser has root access privileges. Even system administrators, running under their normal accounts, may not access the root account. Restricting access to the root account increases system security. However, sometimes it is necessary to give regular users root access privileges. For example, users must access the **/etc/passwd** file to modify their own password, a privilege accorded in most Unix installations. Instead of granting the user full root access, Unix temporarily modifies the user's ID. Such a program applies a *set user ID (SUID) function*. A *set group ID (SGID) function* temporarily modifies the group ID. The **su** command grants superuser access on a temporary basis. The following section discusses the SUID and SGID file access modes and their security implications. It terminates by presenting the **su** command in detail.

SUID and SGID Programs

Executing the **passwd** command temporarily sets the user's ID to the root id (invoking a **chmod** command with the 4000 bits), modifies the user's entry in the **/etc/passwd** file, and then resets the user's ID to the original value. Because the user does not have control over the inner workings of the **passwd** command, he or she won't be able to perform mischief with the temporary root account.

The use of SUID programs, while considered necessary in most installations, presents a potential security risk. In the hands of a knowledgeable user, the root account is dynamite. Such a user could perform any operation immediately, or prepare the groundwork for later destruction. Consider the following guidelines to deal with the threat of SUID and SGID programs:

- Regularly (during off-hours only) print a complete listing of all SUID and SGID files on your system with the following command:

  ```
  find / -perm -004000 -o perm -002000 -type f -print
  ```

  and verify this list either manually or by shell script. If there is no current, valid reason for a given file to be SUID or SGID, modify the permission immediately.

- Do not use SUID or SGID shell scripts. Shell scripts allow *shell escapes,* in which the user temporarily leaves the shell to execute another program. This opens the door to executing unauthorized programs while the user has root or other temporary privileges. (You can use these shell scripts if you know how to trap signals effectively.)

- Examine the source code for all programs that accord SUID or SGID privileges. This is particularly important for public domain programs but should also be done for purchased software. Security violations have occurred with software purchased from reputable vendors.

- Accord the minimum privileges necessary. It is often possible to create a special group and write a SGID program rather than writing a SUID program. Otherwise it may be possible to create a special user and change the user ID to that user rather than to the root. Reset the modified user ID or group ID to the original value as soon as possible.

The su Command

The **su** command makes the user a superuser or another user. It has the following syntax:

su [-] [*name* [*arg...*]]

The **su** command allows authorized users to become another user without logging off. The default user name is root (i.e., superuser).

Unix allows **su** to be employed under four circumstances:

▰   Without using a password, the superuser can invoke the **su** command to become any account.

▰   Anyone with the root password can invoke the **su** command to access the superuser account.

▰   Users can invoke the **su** command to access their own accounts. (This application is useful for people with access to more than one account.)

▰   A system daemon can invoke the **su** command to access any account.

To use **su**, you must supply the appropriate password (unless you are already a superuser). If the password is valid, **su** executes a new shell whose effective user ID is set to the ID of the specified user. The **id** command links user and group IDs to processes. You may apply it to verify who is using **su**.

The file **/etc/default/su** can control several aspects of **su** utilization. Consider the following entries:

▰   *SULOG*   Designates the name of log file that records all attempts to use **su**. Usually this variable is set to **/usr/adm/sulog**. If this variable is not set, no log file is kept. (See example below.)

▰   *PATH*   Designates the *PATH* environment variable to set for non-root users. If this variable is not set, it defaults to **:/bin:/usr/bin**. The current *PATH* environment variable is ignored.

▰   *SUPATH*   Unless this variable is defined when invoked by the root, the path is set by default to **/bin:/usr/bin:/etc**. The current *PATH* is ignored.

▰   CONSOLE   All attempts to use **su** are logged to the named device, independently of the value of *SULOG*.

To log all user attempts to become root, create the file **/etc/default/su** and define a string such as:

SULOG=/usr/adm/sulog

This records all attempts to switch user IDs in the **/usr/adm/sulog** file. As shown in Figure 12-1, this **sulog** file records the date and time of the attempt, a plus sign (+) to indicate a successful attempt, a minus sign (–) to indicate an unsuccessful attempt, and the terminal ID and the user ID of the user that issued the **su** command. The **secur** shell script near the end of this chapter illustrates how the system administrator can monitor the use of the **su** command.

Monitoring System Access

The more closely the system administrator monitors system access, the lower the frequency of security violation. The system administrator has several tools available for finding out who is doing what. Unix provides log files that record system logins, logouts, and the **last** command, which displays user login information.

The Department of Defense's Trusted Computer System Evaluation Criteria defines a level of trust known as C2. This encompasses security databases including the Authentication database, the Protected Password database, the Terminal Control database, the Protected Subsystem database, and commands to process these databases. The **authck** command checks the internal consistency of the Authentication database, and the **integrity** utility examines system files against the Authentication database. Many Unix implementations provide these facilities. This chapter includes the **secur** shell script, applying some of these databases and commands.

FIGURE 12-1

Contents of the
sulog file

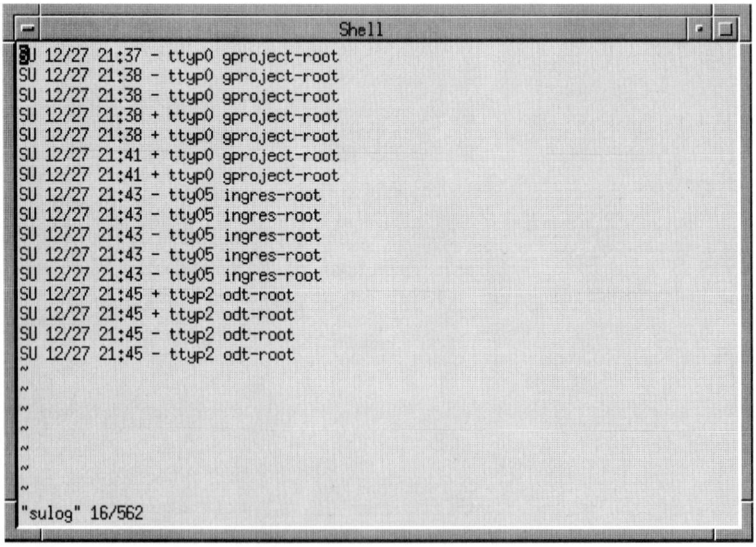

```
                                    Shell
SU 12/27 21:37 - ttyp0 gproject-root
SU 12/27 21:38 - ttyp0 gproject-root
SU 12/27 21:38 - ttyp0 gproject-root
SU 12/27 21:38 + ttyp0 gproject-root
SU 12/27 21:38 + ttyp0 gproject-root
SU 12/27 21:41 + ttyp0 gproject-root
SU 12/27 21:41 + ttyp0 gproject-root
SU 12/27 21:43 - tty05 ingres-root
SU 12/27 21:43 - tty05 ingres-root
SU 12/27 21:43 - tty05 ingres-root
SU 12/27 21:43 - tty05 ingres-root
SU 12/27 21:43 - tty05 ingres-root
SU 12/27 21:45 + ttyp2 odt-root
SU 12/27 21:45 + ttyp2 odt-root
SU 12/27 21:45 - ttyp2 odt-root
SU 12/27 21:45 - ttyp2 odt-root
~
~
~
~
~
~
"sulog" 16/562
```

Log Files

The following Unix log files can be useful in monitoring system access (the related **/usr/adm/sulog** file was presented in the discussion of the **su** command):

■ The **/usr/adm/lastlog** file records the latest login time for each user. This time is displayed whenever the user attempts to log in. Some System V versions also display the last unsuccessful login attempt. The system administrator should encourage users to examine the displayed times carefully to detect intruder activity. In case of suspicious activity, users should inform the system administrator immediately and change their password.

■ The **/etc/utmp** file contains information for users currently logged into the system. The associated **/usr/adm/wtmp** file contains information related to system logins and logouts. To keep control of your hard disk, you must purge the **/usr/adm/wtmp** file periodically. Because this file is examined by the **last** command (discussed next), you should store purged **/usr/adm/wtmp** file entries in readily available archives.

■ The **/usr/adm/acct** file contains an entry for every user command executed. Each entry includes the user name, the command name, the elapsed processor time, the clock time when the command terminated, and flags describing command use. The **lastcomm** command displays this file's contents. If you choose to use the **/usr/adm/acct** file, you will need to purge it regularly, perhaps nightly. The **/usr/etc/sa** command summarizes the **/usr/adm/acct** file, generating the **/usr/adm/savacct** file.

The last Command

The **last** command displays the most recent logins of users and terminals. It has the following syntax:

last [-h] [-n *limit*] [-t *tty*] [-w *wtmpfile*] [*name*]

The **last** command checks the **wtmp** file, which records all logins and logouts for information about a user, a serial line, or any group of users and lines. Arguments specify a user name and/or a tty. The **last** command prints the sessions of the specified users and ttys, including login name, the line used, the device name, the process ID, the login time, the elapsed time, and comments. When no argument is specified, **last** prints a record of all logins and logouts in reverse chronological order.

The options are defined as follows:

■ -h   Generates no header.

■ -n *limit*   Limits the report to the specified number of lines.

■ -t *line* Specifies the tty.

■ -w *wtmpfile* Uses the *wtmpfile* file instead of the **/etc/wtmp** file. Note that *wtmpfile* must have the same format as the **/etc/wtmp** file.

For example:

```
last -n 21
```

lists the 21 most recent entries to the **wtmp** file as shown in Figure 12-2.

The **secur** shell script near the end of this chapter illustrates an application of the **last** command.

The authck Command

The **authck** command checks the internal consistency of the Authentication database. It has the following syntax:

/tcb/bin/authck [-p] [-t] [-s] [-f] [-c] [-a] [-v]

The **authck** command checks both the overall structure and internal field consistency of all components of the Authentication database. It reports all problems it finds. The major options and tests are listed on the next page.

FIGURE 12-2

Output of the **last** command

```
┌─────────────────────────────────────── Shell ───────────────────────────────────┐
│ JR: /usr/gproject/jr_adm >> last -n 21                                            │
│ User      Line  Device    PID    Login time        Elapsed Time  Comments        │
│ gproject  c02   tty02     330    Sun Dec 27 18:15     01:14       logged in       │
│ root      co    tty01     353    Sun Dec 27 18:15     01:14       logged in       │
│ root      co    tty01     331    Sun Dec 27 17:32     00:27       shutdown        │
│ root      co    tty01     331    Sun Dec 27 17:20     00:03       shutdown        │
│ root      co    tty01     338    Sun Dec 27 17:11     00:02       shutdown        │
│ gproject  c03   tty03     2420   Sun Dec 27 01:57     02:12                       │
│ root      c02   tty02     2367   Sun Dec 27 01:41     02:46                       │
│ root      co    tty01     2366   Sun Dec 27 01:41     02:48       shutdown        │
│ root      c03   tty03     346    Sat Dec 26 23:37     02:01                       │
│ root      c02   tty02     345    Sat Dec 26 17:09     08:29                       │
│ root      co    tty01     344    Sat Dec 26 16:15     12:15       shutdown        │
│ root      co    tty01     1783   Sat Dec 26 12:47     00:07       shutdown        │
│ gproject  c02   tty02     1735   Sat Dec 26 12:47     00:04                       │
│ root      co    tty01     1768   Sat Dec 26 12:46     00:00                       │
│ root      co    tty01     1751   Sat Dec 26 12:45     00:00                       │
│ root      co    tty01     1689   Sat Dec 26 12:42     00:02                       │
│ root      co    tty01     1254   Sat Dec 26 12:10     00:44       shutdown        │
│ root      co    tty01     848    Sat Dec 26 11:50     01:03       shutdown        │
│ root      co    tty01     493    Sat Dec 26 11:48     01:06       shutdown        │
│ root      c02   tty02     330    Sat Dec 26 11:16     00:32                       │
│ root      co    tty01     329    Sat Dec 26 11:07     00:40                       │
│ JR: /usr/gproject/jr_adm >> █                                                     │
└──────────────────────────────────────────────────────────────────────────────────┘
```

- -p The Protected Password and **/etc/passwd** are checked to ensure that neither contains entries not in the other. Next, fields common to the Protected Password database and **/etc/passwd** are checked for agreement. Then, fields in the Protected Password database are checked for reasonable values. For instance, all time stamps for past events are checked to make sure they are prior to the time returned by **time**.
- -t The fields in the Terminal Control database are checked for reasonable values. For instance, all time stamps for past events are checked to make sure they are prior to the time returned by **time**.
- -s The Protected Subsystem database files are checked to ensure that they correctly reflect the subsystem authorization entries in the Protected Password database. Each name listed in each subsystem file is verified for consistent authorization against the Protected Password entry with the same name. Each Protected Password entry is scanned to ensure that all listed privileges are reflected in the Protected Subsystem database. If any inconsistencies are found, the administrator has the option of fixing the Subsystem database automatically.
- -a (all) This option is shorthand for turning on the -p, -t, and -s options.
- -v (verbose) This option provides running diagnostics as the program proceeds. It also generates warning messages for events that should not occur but otherwise do not harm the Authentication database and the routines operating on it.

The **secur** shell script near the end of this chapter illustrates how the system administrator can apply the **authchk** command.

The integrity Utility

The **integrity** utility examines system files against the Authentication database. It has the following syntax:

```
/tcb/bin/integrity [-v] [-e] [-m]
```

The **integrity** utility compares each entry in the File Control database to the corresponding file in the file system. If the owner, group, or permissions are different, it outputs an error message.

The **integrity** utility handles wildcard entries in the File Control database as follows. File names that have /* as the last entry are treated as wildcards. Any file in the directory matches the wildcard entry, except for files with an entry in the database appearing before the wildcard entry. Such files are ignored in the check because they have been located previously. If the File Control entry does not explicitly list an owner, all owners match correctly. Exactly the same rule holds for groups. Normally, (non-wildcard type) files in the File Control database that are missing from the file system are not reported. This may be overidden by the -m option described below. The **integrity** utility provides the following options:

-v   Lists all files under consideration, even those that match.

-e   Explains why discretionary checks fail and the exact nature of the discrepancy.

-m   Overrides the default and reports missing files.

The **integrity** utility returns a 0 exit status if there are no discrepancies. Otherwise, it returns a positive value equal to the number of discrepancies.

A C LANGUAGE user_out PROGRAM

Users who are too lazy or too distracted to log off a terminal might not realize it, but they are a common cause of Unix security violations. The convenience of a ready-to-run terminal without the nuisance of having to log on must be weighed against the damage caused by a security break. The answer should be clear—security must predominate. Howver, standard Unix has no built-in method for logging out users after a predetermined terminal idle time. The following C language program provides a solution to this problem. It automatically logs out users after a predetermined time period. This time delay may be defined within the program or entered from the command line, as in this example. The program warns users to save their files before logging them out. The user may press any key to prevent the automatic logout.

The system administrator should place an executable version of this program in each user's startup file (**.profile** for Bourne shell and Korn shell, and **.cshrc** for C shell) to run in the background with a very low priority. Because the user could remove this program easily, you should monitor its presence and take corrective action if necessary.

```
#include <stdio.h>
#include <pwd.h>
#include <signal.h>
#include <sys/types.h>
#include <sgtty.h>
#include <sys/stat.h>

#define BEEP '\007'
#define LOWER_LIMIT 2

void itoa();
void reverse();
```

```
main(argc, argv)
int argc;
char **argv;
{
struct passwd *pwdbuf1;
struct passwd *pwdbuf2;
char cmd[80];
struct stat statbuf;
long present, timeout;
int ppid, uid1, uid2;
char str1[9];

  if (argc != 2)
  {
    printf("\nUse: %s timeout[minutes]", argv[0]);
    printf("\nPlease, Try Again ...\n");
    exit(1);
  }
  else
  {
    timeout = 60 * atoi(argv[1]);
  }
  if (timeout < (LOWER_LIMIT + 1) * 60)
  {
    printf("\nYou must specify value for timeout >
            2! Exiting ...\n");
    printf("\nPlease, Try Again ...\n");
    exit(1);
  }
  else
  {
    nice(4);
    uid1 = getuid();
    pwdbuf1 = getpwuid(uid1);
  }
  if (!isatty(0))
  {
    printf("\n%s is not a terminal! Exiting ...", argv[0]);
    exit(1);
  }
  ppid = getppid();
```

```
      itoa(ppid, str1);
      fflush(stdout);
      if (fork())
      {
        exit(0);
      }
      while(1)
      {
        sleep(120);
/*
      The following code verifies that the original user is
      still logged in.
*/
      uid2 = getuid();
      pwdbuf2 = getpwuid(uid2);
      if (strcmp(pwdbuf2->pw_name, pwdbuf1->pw_name))
      {
        printf("\n%s and %s are not the same!");
        printf("Exiting ... pwdbuf1->pw_name, pwdbuf2->pw_name);
        exit(0);
      }
      if ((fstat(0, &statbuf)) != 0)
      {
        printf("\nCannot stat tty! Exiting ...");
        exit(1);
      }
      time(&present);
      if (present - statbuf.st_atime >= timeout)
      {
/*
        The user will be logged out within a few seconds.
*/
        strcpy(cmd, "kill -9 ");
        strcat(cmd, str1);
        printf("\nTimeout for %s Now!", pwdbuf2->pw_name);
        sleep(3);
        system(cmd);
/*
        The following system call is an alternative method for
        logging the user out.
        kill(0, SIGHUP);
*/
        exit(0);
      }
```

```
    if (present + LOWER_LIMIT * 60 -
        statbuf.st_atime >= timeout)
    {
/*

    The following code warns the user to save files because
    of the impending logout. The variable LOWER_LIMIT
    indicates the logout delay in minutes.
*/
    printf("\n%Message from System Administrator!");
    printf("\n%Timeout in %d minutes!", BEEP, LOWER_LIMIT);
    }
  }
}


void itoa(n, s)
char s[];
int n;
{
int i, sign;

  if ((sign = n) < 0)
    n = -n;
  i = 0;
  do {
    s[i++] = n % 10 + '0';
  }
    while ((n /= 10) > 0);
        if (sign < 0)
          s[i++] = '-';
        s[i] = '\0';
        reverse(s);
}

void reverse(s)
char s[];
{
int c, i, j;

  for (i = 0, j = strlen(s) - 1; i < j; i++, j--)
  {
    c = s[i];
```

```
    s[i] = s[j];
    s[j] = c;
  }
}
```

The following MAKE and INCLUDE files were used to process this program in SCO Unix. The MAKE file for other Unix versions varies.

```
include INCLUDE
LIBS =
PROD = user_out

install all: $(PROD)

user_out: user_out.c
$(CC) $(CFLAGS) -o $(TESTDIR)/user_out user_out.c $(LIBS)

clean:
-rm -f *.o

clobber: clean
-rm -f $(PROD)
```

and

```
ROOT =
IROOT =
ETC = $(ROOT)/etc
BIN = $(ROOT)/usr/local/bin
TESTDIR = .
SHELL = /bin/sh
REL =
INCRT = $(IROOT)/usr/include
BROOT = $(ROOT)
I = $(INCRT)
MORECPP =
CFLAGS = -O -DLAI_TCP $(MORECPP) -I$(INCRT) $(REL)
        -Di386 -DBUFFER_SIZE=8192
LDFLAGS =
LDLIBS =
SOCKETLIB = -lsocket
INS =
INSDIR = $(BIN)
```

PHYSICAL SECURITY

Arguably most threats to the computer system are associated with account abuse, usually via a stolen or "borrowed" password. However, many threats are more direct, consisting of individuals attempting to take over the system physically. To this must be added disasters such as earthquakes and floods, and environmental dangers such as dust and electrical noise. The system administrator has a direct role in physically protecting the system from human abuse, and equally important, in minimizing the damage caused by natural disasters and a poor environment. As always, the benefits of a more secure system must be weighed against its financial cost and the inevitable inconvenience of security.

Human Abuse

System administrators should be careful. People, even those who seem to be on your side, can compromise system security, whether by accident or by design. This section discusses concrete steps that the system administrator can take to reduce security violations due to foreign substances such as food and cigarettes, intruders, excessively open systems, unattached equipment, programmed threats, and disgruntled former employees.

Ban Foreign Substances

It is amazing the damage that a cup of coffee can cause to a computer system. One moment of inattention, and hundreds of dollars of hardware damage can occur, to say nothing of the time required to rebuild a damaged file system ("I was going to do a full system backup in ten minutes"). The system administrator should set and *enforce* a zero-tolerance policy including the following points:

No Smoking, Eating, or Drinking Near Any Computer Equipment

This policy is independent of any organizational policy related to the use of tobacco products at the workplace. Admittedly, a zero-tolerance policy is often difficult to enforce. As always, awareness is a key element. Frankly, many users (and, regrettably, computer personnel) don't realize how easy it is to damage computer equipment. A newsletter with horror stories can help to drive home the point. Install smoke detectors, and check their batteries on a regular basis. This policy also reduces the risk of fire.

Keep Individuals Under the Influence of Alcohol or Other Drugs from Accessing the System   Some people suggest applying this rule flexibly— but frankly, who wants to recompile a C language program during a Christmas party?

Ban Unauthorized Individuals

It doesn't make much sense to institute a strict password policy and then open the doors, literally or figuratively, to the computer equipment. Consider implementing the following guideline as part of your policy:

Only Authorized Individuals May Access the Computer Room or Any Computer Equipment

The very existence of computer networks makes this rule difficult to enforce absolutely. However, many systems still include nerve centers, areas in which computing resources are concentrated. Such areas must be protected against intruders. One potential policy for large computer centers is: Isolate the center on its own floor, restrict access to this floor to a single elevator, and screen all individuals attempting to gain access. Do not let the ease of network access to the computer prevent you from instituting a policy of system protection.

Don't Advertise the System

Like it or not, the days of the glass-walled computer system are over. Glass windows not only shatter under impact, they also make it easy for an individual armed with binoculars to discover passwords being typed. Many organizations have replaced the login "Welcome" message with a carefully worded message warning individuals about the penalties for computer abuse.

While you may want (or be forced) to conduct system tours for promotional or educational reasons, you need not show everybody everything. Do not point out areas of special interest. Limit the number of individuals taking the tour at any one time, and don't allow people to take notes. Finally don't refer to any security issues during the tour or make a joke of security. Repairing the damage caused by a breach of security is not funny.

Don't Make Theft Easy

The following guidelines won't eliminate theft; however, they should reduce it.

Engrave Company Identification on Valuable Equipment

Computer equipment has a salvage value. While it can be hard for a thief to dispose of a multimillion dollar mainframe (Where did you say you got it?), no one will blink an eyelash to see a laser printer advertised in the computer column of the local newspaper. Thieves will think twice about stealing equipment that has been engraved with the firm's identification. Your local police department may lend engraving kits to interested individuals and organizations.

Consider Securing Equipment with Bolts, Locks, or Other Anti-Theft Devices, Such as Alarms

Many thieves are in a hurry. If they know removal will take a long time, they might prefer to forego the opportunity. Consider installing alarm mechanisms. A sharp, piercing sound can convince the fainthearted to flee.

Shred Important Documents

Garbage cans are an important source of sensitive information such as trade secrets and computer passwords. When in doubt, shred. Of course, nonencrypted passwords should never appear on any document.

Monitor Wires for Evidence of Wiretapping

Wires transporting data across the network can be a weak point in the system. Thieves need not be present to steal sensitive information; they merely wiretap. In many cases, the organization will not even be aware of the theft. Nothing is missing; the thief has only made a copy. Shielding network cable provides a measure of protection. Because fiber optic links do not emit radiation, they provide a relatively secure system—but are also relatively expensive.

If you must transmit sensitive files across the network, encrypt them. An armored courier can be used to transmit these files. In other cases, the files can simply be relegated to the computer center and stored in secure vaults.

Don't Leave Logged-On Terminals Unattended, Even for a Short Period of Time

Thieves don't need much time to do their dirty work, stealing passwords, transferring files, or poisoning the system. Refer to the **user_out** program presented immediately prior to this section.

Prosecute Vandals

Vandalism is no joke. A disgruntled employee or an individual with a misplaced sense of humor can destroy valuable computer resources in a few seconds. Make it known that such behavior will be prosecuted to the full extent of the law.

Dealing with Programmed Threats

Computers exist for only one purpose, to run programs. Because programs are complex, it can be very difficult to determine that a given program does only what it is supposed to do and is not attacking the system. Programmed threats can be very difficult to defend against. Use software only from trusted sources. Understand what software does before using it. Run software in the root account only when necessary. The following is a partial list of programmed threats:

- **Back Door** A *back door*, also known as a *trap door*, is part of a program that provides access to system resources, bypassing the normal authorization process. Sometimes a programmer includes a back door when testing a program and forgets to remove it before putting the program into production. The SUID and SGID programs previously discussed are common ways to provide a back door.

■ **Bacteria** *Bacteria,* also known as *rabbits,* are programs that make copies of themselves until they take over, monopolizing system resources such as central memory or disk space. Set up user quotas to protect against bacteria. The system monitoring techniques discussed previously should help you determine the party responsible for the bacteria. Do not tolerate such behavior.

■ **Logic Bomb** A *logic bomb* is part of a program that lies quietly waiting for the moment to perform special, perhaps malicious behavior. Logic bombs may be set off by a date such as Friday the 13th (in this case they may be called *time bombs*), or other conditions such as the twelfth execution of the **ps** command on a given day.

■ **Trojan Horse** A *Trojan horse* is a program that seems to be doing one thing, such as a game, but actually does something else, such as deleting files. Trojan horses may be found on bulletin boards. As always, make sure that you know what software is doing before actually running it.

■ **Virus** A *virus* is computer code that can be executed only in the presence of another program. (In common language any programmed threat is called a *virus.*) Viruses mostly occur on microcomputers running DOS or Macintosh systems, but may also be found on Unix systems.

■ **Worm** A *worm* is a program that can travel across a network from one computer to another. The most famous worm attack occurred on the Internet network in November, 1988, affecting thousands of Unix-based computers. If you suspect that you are victim of a worm attack, leave the network. If you are linked to a Department of Energy network contact the Computer Incident Advisory Capability at (415) 422-8193 (business hours), or use their electronic mail address:

ciac@tiger.llnl.gov

Internet users may contact the Defense Advanced Research Projects Agency's Computer Emergency Response Team at (412) 268-7090, or use their electronic mail address:

cert@sei.cmu.edu

Handling Involuntary Separations

Let's not mince words—it is never pleasant to fire somebody. Firings or other involuntary separations can be particularly difficult when dealing with computer specialists. It can take weeks or even months to rebuild what a sufficiently mad, sufficiently competent guru can destroy in a manner of minutes (or less). Many installations refuse physical access to fired employees, *after* removing their passwords. Be sure to examine the employee's programs and files for destructive commands. These harsh measures may seem extreme in the vast majority of cases, but they can also prevent sabotage.

Protecting Against Disasters

Disasters happen. Don't hide behind their inevitability to avoid formulating and implementing a disaster recovery policy. The exact nature of the policy depends on your specific situation. An organization whose major computer resources are located within ten miles of the San Andreas fault has different priorities than one located in an area known for flooding.

Remember | Wherever you place your priorities, start planning for catastrophe now—tomorrow may be too late.

Maintain Complete, Up-to-Date, Off-Site Backup Files

This policy is key, independent of the specific measures to deal with different natural disasters such as earthquakes and floods. When a disaster destroys computer equipment, it is likely to destroy the carefully prepared backups in the accompanying drawer. As system administrator, it is your responsibility to inform users of the need to maintain their own backups and store these backups offsite. Users coming from a mainframe or a local-area network background tend to think of backups as a function automatically performed by "the system." Those coming from a microcomputer background are likely to know the importance of maintaining their own backups (a principle that they might honor in the breach), but should be reminded of the importance of off-site backups.

Many organizations choose to centralize the off-site backups, requiring users to store their backups in company vaults. This policy, while hard to enforce, has the advantage of underscoring the organizational ownership of the data. An employee who leaves the organization leaves "his or her" files behind.

Among the natural (and seminatural) disasters to defend against are: earthquakes, fire and smoke, flooding and other water damage, lightning, and war or terrorism.

Earthquakes   Earthquakes occur frequently in some regions. A few common-sense measures can help reduce earthquake damage, especially from small and medium-sized tremors. Do not place computers near windows or on high surfaces. Store heavy items such as books, magazines, and documentation so that if they fall, they will not fall on the computer (or the user!)

Fire and Smoke   Make sure that your computer installation respects the local fire code. For example, some network cable is designed with a fire-resistant jacket for safety.

This cable generates little smoke, reducing the extent of smoke damage in case of fire. Local fire regulations may require such cable in air plenums (passageways). Overloading circuits increases the likelihood of a fire, as does the presence of tobacco products.

The ready availability of a functioning fire extinguisher can reduce a fire's impact. Of course, careless handling of fire extinguishers is dangerous. Follow your local fire department guidelines on fire fighting. In addition to the danger of fire to people and property, both fire extinguishers and automatic sprinkling systems may damage your computer equipment and data.

Flooding and Other Water Damage   Water causes electrical short circuits, in effect frying electronic or electromagnetic equipment. It can also destroy documents. The most common causes of water damage are flooding and severe rainstorms, but a sprinkler system or a blocked toilet can also cause extensive damage.

Lightning   Lightning can damage the computer system in several ways. While a direct strike is unlikely, the resulting power surge will probably destroy an unprotected computer. Another source of danger is the magnetic field generated when lightning hits a building or its lightning rod. Use a high-quality surge protector and ground equipment properly.

War and Terrorism   It is debatable whether or not war and terrorism should be considered natural disasters. What is not debatable are their danger to computer installations. Just as there seems to be no magic solution to war and terrorism, there is no magic solution to their impact on computer systems.

Environmental Considerations

Environmental considerations differ from natural disasters in one important way. While it is difficult to protect a computer from an earthquake, proper precautions can reduce the likelihood of dust damage to an acceptable level. As was the case for both human damage and natural disasters, prepare adequate backups, including off-site backups. If the dust is so bad that you cannot read your files, you probably won't be able to read your on-site backups. Other environmental factors to control are electrical noise, explosions, extreme temperatures, humidity, insects, and vibration.

Dust   Given the extremely small distances between components in a computer system, a miniscule dust particle looms large. Dust particles will scratch computer circuitry beyond use, if they don't short it out first. Make sure your air filters are clean. And threaten to make smokers restore the system from low-density floppy disks if they persist in smoking within range of the computer room.

Electrical Noise   Electrical noise, such as that generated by computers, cooling equipment, and motors, can cause circuit-destroying power surges. It is amazing what plugging in even a small machine can do to a computer sharing an electrical outlet. That toaster might toast more than the Unix guru's sandwich, and a single spark emanating from the computer room carpet can send weeks of data to kingdom come. The system administrator should consider instituting the following measures:

☑   Connect each computer system on its own grounded electrical circuit.

☑   Install surge protectors to protect computer equipment and dial-up lines. Special models are available for installations located near electrical substations.

☑   Place an anti-static electricity mat at high traffic areas.

☑   Employ one or more uninterruptible power supplies (UPS) to ensure that the system keeps working, even if the power supply is cut off. Readily available models give system personnel enough time to shut down the system gracefully if necessary.

Explosions   Evaluate the contents of buildings in which computer equipment is placed. Natural gas and some chemicals can explode. Limit the extent of explosion damage by following the guidelines associated with earthquakes.

Extreme Temperatures   Computers are designed to operate at moderate temperatures. While rugged models are available, most computer systems should not operate at temperatures much below 10 degrees Celsius (50 degrees Fahrenheit) or much above 30 degrees Celsius (86 degrees Fahrenheit). You might have to invest in a proper air conditioning system and upgrade your heating system. Consider installing an alarm system that will detect when the temperature drops below or rises above a predetermined limit.

Humidity   Computers are vulnerable to both too little and too much humidity. An excessively dry environment is not only uncomfortable, it increases the possibility of static discharge. When the humidity is too great, condensation can occur, shorting out computer circuitry. The relative humidity should be maintained between 20 and 80 percent.

Insects   Students of computer history know that the first computer bug was a moth trapped inside an early computer. While most "bugs" do not literally involve insects or other creepy, crawly things, some do. Make sure that your cleaning staff removes insects and similar beings from all equipment.

Vibration   Excessive vibration can loosen circuit boards and destroy the hard disk alignment. If necessary, place the computer on a damping mat, making sure not to cover the ventilation.

NETWORK SECURITY CONSIDERATIONS

The very ease with which users can access Unix system resources across the network increases the security risk concomitantly. The system administrator must take concrete steps to increase the security of the networked system, while limiting the degradation in system performance and ease of use. This section discusses security measures related to modems, network files and programs, and the UUCP facility.

Modems

A *modem* (short for *mo*dulator/*dem*odulator) translates the digital signals found in computers and terminals into the analog signals transmitted over standard telephone lines. At the other end of the transmission another modem performs the reverse translation. Modems are found in many computer networks and other interconnected computer systems. Because they open a computer system to the outside world, modems are a potential security risk. When possible, treat the phone numbers used to access modems as you treat passwords. This reduces the probability that unauthorized users are accessing the system. The familiar techniques of passwords, data encryption, and restricting physical access should be applied to modems. Other security measures include automatic number identification, callbacks, disabling call forwarding and third-party billing, and leased lines.

Automatic Number Identification

In some locations, the phone company can supply *automatic number identification (ANI)* over digital telephone lines. This service displays the telephone number of the party making the call. It may be possible to store this phone number for future processing. Associated services block telephone calls from unauthorized parties.

Callbacks

A *callback* is a telephone service that requires the caller to provide a user name, after which the system breaks the connection. The system then employs the user name to find the caller's phone number in a stored table and finally attempts to call back the caller.

Disabling Special Features

The modem should not include special features, such as call forwarding, which could be set up to transfer calls to another computer, effectively recording passwords for future use. Disable third-party billing to avoid massive telephone bills run up by thieves or vandals.

Leased Lines

If you communicate heavily with a given location, consider leasing a private line from the telephone company. A wide variety of *leased lines*, also known as *dedicated lines*, is available. Some leased lines do not involve modems, and so they reduce the likelihood of outside intervention.

Files and Programs

Some files and programs are more dangerous than others. Over a period of time, Unix has patched security holes, replacing commands with more secure versions. This section describes programs that the system administrator should examine carefully.

Trusted Hosts and Trusted Users

Recall that a *host* is a computer attached to the computer network. A user with the same user name on two (or more) hosts can log in from the *trusted host* to another linked host without entering a password. The **/etc/hosts.equiv** file contains the list of trusted hosts for a given computer. An individual user's **.rhosts** file contains the list of additional trusted hosts for that particular user. The concept of trusted hosts and the related concept of trusted users makes it easier to go back and forth among linked machines, as there is no need to enter a second password. However, trusted hosts and trusted users open the door to security abuses. Once security has been compromised, the problem can spread at electronic speed across the network. Consider the following policies with respect to trusted hosts and trusted users:

☑ The simplest policy is to ban trusted hosts from the computer network. To do so, set the **/etc/hosts.equiv** file to blank for each computer in the network. In many installations this policy is not possible. If you do not ban trusted hosts, at least monitor the **/etc/hosts.equiv** file carefully.

☑ Many installations choose to prevent users from setting up their individual **.rhosts** file. This policy centralizes the creation of trusted hosts in the hands of the system administrator. It can be implemented by modifying the **rshd** and

rlogind programs to remove user access to the **.rhosts** file. In many installations this policy is not possible. If you do not ban individual **.rhosts** files, at least monitor them carefully on an unannounced basis.

☑ Remove any + sign from the **/etc/hosts.equiv** file as distributed. In this file, the + sign makes every host a trusted host, opening the system to abuse. You might have to make other changes to the system, such as adding remote host names to the **/etc/hosts/lpd** file for printing. The inconvenience is worth it.

Remote Execution

Users can execute commands on remote computers without first logging in by issuing the **/etc/rexecd** daemon. This daemon causes the password to be transmitted over the network and so should not be used. It is advisable to disable this daemon in the **/etc/inetd.conf** configuration file.

Electronic Mail

One major reason for networking computers is electronic mail. The very popular **sendmail** command has been responsible for many security violations. Because it runs in superuser mode, these violations are often critical. Apply the following policy when using the **sendmail** program:

☑ Use only a **sendmail** program version numbered 5.65 or greater. Previous versions include known security holes.

☑ Disable the "wizard" password (starting with the letters OW) supplied in the **sendmail.cf**. This password would allow users to start a shell without logging into the computer.

☑ Eliminate the **debug**, **kill**, and **wiz** commands from the **sendmail** program.

☑ Do not allow the **sendmail** program to deliver mail directly to a file.

☑ Remove the "decode" alias from the alias file. Inspect all aliases associated with files and programs; they might be an attempt to breach security.

Personal User Information

The **finger** command displays personal information such as the user name, full name, location, login time, and office telephone number for logged-in users. Because this command enables intruders to obtain the list of users easily, it is often considered a security risk. However, because the command is convient, it may not be possible to disable it. Use only a version of the **finger** program dated November 5, 1988 or later. (The network daemon associated with this command was responsible for the famous Internet worm that affected thousands of Unix computers.)

The UUCP Facility

Recall from Chapter 11 that the UUCP (Unix to Unix Copy Program) is a sophisticated, powerful facility that enables users to transfer files between Unix systems, executes commands on a remote system, and sends mail to users on a remote system. In spite of, or more correctly because of, its power and ease of use, the UUCP facility poses certain security risks. Consider the following security guidelines if your site provides the UUCP facility:

- As with all other accounts, assign a unique password to each UUCP account.

- Assign a unique login ID to each machine that communicates with your system. This makes it easier to determine who is doing what. It also enables you to cut off access selectively.

- Limit the scope of UUCP as much as possible. This means restricting the available commands and accessible directories.

- Set the **/usr/lib/uucp/L.sys** or **/usr/lib/uucp/Systems** file mode to 400 or 600 so that they may be read only by the UUCP facility.

- Ensure that the UUCP facility cannot read any files in the **/usr/lib/uucp** directories.

AUDITING THE SYSTEM

The system administrator should not be overwhelmed by the enormity of system security activities. When the volume warrants, security duties may be assigned to a security specialist. Furthermore, many versions of Unix provide computerized system auditing facilities. This section examines system audit personnel and introduces computerized auditing facilities for Unix. Auditing facilities may vary from one Unix implementation to another. A C language program demonstrates special auditing features available on HP-UX, the Unix version available on the widely used Hewlett-Packard computers.

The Audit Administrator

The audit administrator is responsible for system security audits, determining how the installation complies with system security objectives and monitoring potential security violations. Depending on the installation size, policy, and budget, the audit administrator may be a separate individual from the system administrator. In other cases, one person performs both system-administration and audit-administration tasks. Audit administration requires superuser privileges, since it involves complete control over events selected for audit record generation. The audit can generate a large number of audit records. The audit administrator must monitor disk space and archive the audit sessions to the backup media, removing the archived sessions when necessary. Table 12-1 presents the National Computer Security Center's model, distributing security responsibilities among various personnel, as quoted in "HP-UX System Security," for HP 9000 computers. Whether or not this particular model corresponds to your installation's specific security requirements, it forms an excellent basis for a security-task check list.

Unix Auditing Facilities

This section introduces Unix auditing facilities. It discusses **authcap**, the authentication database; **auditcmd**, the command interface for audit subsystem activation, termination, statistics retrieval, and subsystem notification; and the **chg_audit** command, which enables and disables auditing for the next session (next reboot).

The authcap Database

The **authcap** database is the authentication database. The **authcap** database contains authentication and identity information for users, kernels, and TCB files, as well as system-wide parameters. It may be used by programs to interrogate user and system values, and by authentication programs to update that information.

The complete database resides in two hierarchies: **/tcb/files/auth** and **/etc/auth**. The first hierarchy is associated with user-specific files. It contains single-letter subdirectories, each of which is the starting letter for the user name. All user names beginning with the letter x contain their authentication and identity information in a file in the directory **/tcb/files/auth/x**.

System-wide information is found in directories within **/etc/auth**. The global system settings are found in the **/etc/auth/system** directory. Subsystem authorizations associated with each *protected subsystem,* a privileged subsystem that does not require global authority to perform actions, are located in the **/etc/auth/subsystems** directory.

TABLE 12-1

Security Personnel:
Division of Labor

Personnel Classification   Responsibilities

Personnel Classification	Responsibilities
System Security Officer	Initiates and monitors auditing policy.
	Determines which users and events are audited.
	Maintains the secure password systems.
	Initiates discretionary access control of public files.
	Authorizes new user accounts.
	Checks file systems for SUID and SGID files.
System Administrator	Implements auditing procedures.
	Administers group and user accounts.
	Repairs damaged files and volumes.
	Updates system software.
	Sets system configuration parameters.
	Collects various system statistics.
	Disables and deletes accounts.
	Makes periodic system checks.
	Monitors repeated login attempts.
	Periodically scans file permissions.
	Deals with invalid superuser attempts and invalid network requests.
Operator	Installs security-relevant software.
	Performs routine maintenance, such as backups.
	Responds to user requests for routine system maintenance.
Systems Programmer	Installs system upgrades.
	Performs dump analysis.
	Writes programs that conform to security criteria.

The auditcmd Command

The **auditcmd** command is the command interface for audit subsystem activation, termination, statistic retrieval, and subsystem notification. It has the following syntax:

/tcb/bin/auditcmd [-e] [-d] [-s] [-c] [-m] [-q]

The **auditcmd** utility controls the audit subsystem. Because the audit device is used, this command may be executed only by processes that have configaudit kernel authorization. The **auditcmd** command may employ the following options:

- **-e** Enables the audit subsystem for audit record generation. This initializes subsystem parameters from the **/tcb/files/audit/audit_parms** file, established using the **auditif** command.

- **-s** Informs the audit subsystem that a system shutdown is in progress. The subsystem continues to generate audit records until disabled to a temporary directory on the root file system. This option also modifies the audit daemon so that it survives the shutdown. The subsystem will continue to generate audit records until disabled.

- **-d** Disables the audit subsystem. All audit record generation ceases, and a termination record is written to the audit trail. The subsystem ensures that the audit daemon has read all records from the audit trail before system termination.

- **-m** Informs the audit subsystem that multiuser run state has been achieved and that administrator-specified alternative audit directories using **auditif** are now mounted and available.

- **-c** Retrieves audit subsystem statistics from the audit device.

- **-q** Performs the specified option silently. Does not report errors attributable to the audit subsystem that are not being enabled at the moment.

The **secur** shell script near the end of this chapter illustrates how the system administrator can apply the **auditcmd** command.

The chg_audit Command

The **chg_audit** command enables and disables auditing for the next session (next reboot). It has the following syntax:

/tcb/lib/chg_audit [on]

The **chg_audit** command edits the **/etc/inittab** and **/etc/conf/cf.d/init.base** files to add or remove the audit startup command when the system is rebooted. The *on* parameter enables auditing. Specifying no parameter removes the audit lines from the **inittab** files.

A C LANGUAGE SELF-AUDIT PROGRAM

As explained in the discussion of audit administration, system audits tend to require voluminous disk files. To reduce file storage requirements, some Unix systems provide self-auditing programs (perhaps named otherwise). A *self-auditing program* records a single entry in the audit log for a specific process such as a **login** or **passwd**. The following C language program applies self-auditing techniques to reduce the size of audit log file output without losing valuable information. The program runs under HP-UX, applying specific features of that particular Unix version.

```
#include <stdio.h>
#include <sys/audit.h>

void writeinfo();

struct self_audit_rec sa_rec;

main()
{
char *err, *str;
int fd;

  if (audswitch(AUD_SUSPEND))
  {
    printf("\nNot a superuser! Exiting ...\n");
    exit(1);
  }
  if ((fd=creat("sedit_file",0666)) == -1)
  {
    err = "\nCannot create the sedit_file\n";
    fprintf(stderr, err);
    writeinfo(err, 3);
  }
  str = "\nStart auditing ...\n";
  if (write(fd, str, strlen(str)) == -1)
  {
    err = "\nCannot write to the sedit_file\n";
    fprintf(stderr, err);
    writeinfo(err, 3);
  }
  err = "\nCreated the sedit_file and wrote
          -> Start auditing ...\n";
  printf(err);
```

```
      writeinfo(err, 0);
}

static void writeinfo(string, err_type)
char *string;
int err_type;
{
  extern struct self_audit_rec sa_rec;

  strncpy(sa_rec.aud_body.text, string, MAX_AUD_TEXT);

  sa_rec.aud_head.ah_error = err_type;
  sa_rec.aud_head.ah_event = EN_UEVENT1;
  sa_rec.aud_head.ah_len = strlen(string);

  audswitch(AUD_RESUME);

  audwrite(&sa_rec);
  exit(err_type);
}
```

A secur SHELL SCRIPT

This shell script first invokes the system utility **authck** to check the internal consistency of the authentication database. **authck** checks both the overall structure and internal field consistency of all components of the database. It reports all problems it finds. Refer to the **authck** utility described earlier in this chapter for the precise meaning of the -p, -t, and -s options, invoked by the -a option, and the -v option. If any inconsistencies are found, the system administrator has the option of fixing the subsystem database automatically.

Then this shell script invokes the system utility **integrity** to examine system files against the authentication database. As described earlier in this chapter, the **integrity** utility traverses the File Control database and compares each entry in turn to the real file in the file system. If the owner, group, or permissions are different, an error message is returned. Finally this script records security-related events in audit form designed to meet the audit goals specified by the U.S. National Computer Security Center. Such an audit can help detect system penetration and resource misuse.

Recall that system audits are performed by the audit administrator, who may also be the system administrator. The audit administrator must have superuser privileges. The audit administrator can terminate the audit by activating the shell script **claudit**.

The **secur** script can generate user and teletype logins by activating the **last** command. The **last** command checks the **/etc/wtmp** file, which records all logins and logouts for individual users, a serial line or any group of users and lines. An additional security check monitors attempts by any users to become root. To do so, place the string

SULOG=/usr/adm/sulog

in the **/etc/default/su** file. Then all attempts to change user IDs will be recorded in the file **/usr/adm/sulog**.

> **Note**
>
> This script provides an example of security tasks performed by the audit administrator. Sites with extensive security requirements may use this script as a framework. Other sites may apply this script with minor modifications.

The following code specifies the interpreter used and the Bourne shell, provides a short description of the script, and defines the variable *log_name*.

```
#!/bin/sh
# @(#) security script
log_name = 'whoami'

if [ log_name = "root" ]
then
  echo "\nExecuting ..."
  while
    echo "\nDo you want to check Authentication
          database Consistency: [y/n] \c"
    read authent
  do
    case "$authent" in
      [yY]*)
        echo "Checking Authentication database
              Consistency ...\n"
        authck -a -v

      break
      ;;
      [nN]*)
        echo "No Authentication database Consistency
              Check! Continue ...\n"
      break
      ;;
      *)
        echo "Please enter 'y' or 'n' \n"
      ;;
```

```
        esac
    done

while
    echo "\nDo you want to check File Integrity: [y/n] \c"
    read secur
    do
      case "$secur" in
        [yY]*)
          echo "Checking File Integrity ...\n"
```

Recall that the -e option of the **integrity** utility explains why discretionary checks fail and the exact nature of the discrepancy.

```
        integrity -e

        break
        ;;
        [nN]*)
          echo "No File Integrity Check! Continue ...\n"
        break
        ;;
        *)
          echo "Please enter 'y' or 'n' \n"
        ;;
      esac
    done

while
    echo "\nDo you want to start Auditing: [y/n] \c"
    read startaudit
    do
      case "$startaudit" in
        [yY]*)
          echo "Entered Start Auditing! Continue ...\n"
```

The **auditcmd** command controls the audit subsystem. It may be executed only by processes with the configaudit kernel authorization. The -e option enables the audit subsystem for audit record generation. Refer to the desciption of the **auditcmd** command for a description of available options.

```
        auditcmd -e

        echo "\n"
        echo "Auditing Enable - done!\n"
```

```
      while
         echo "\nDo you want to retrieve
                 audit statistics: [y/n] \c"
      read stat
      do
        case "$stat" in
          [yY]*)
             echo "Displaying Audit Statistics ...\n"
```

The -c option retrieves audit subsystem statistics from the audit device.

```
            auditcmd -c

         break
         ;;
         [nN]*)
           echo "\nNo Audit Statistics
                   selected! Exiting ...\n"
         break
         ;;
         *)
           echo "Please enter 'y' or 'n' \n"
         ;;
       esac
     done
   break
   ;;
 [nN]*)
   while
      echo "\nDo you want to stop Auditing: [y/n] \c"
      read stopaudit
   do
      case "$stopaudit" in
        [yY]*)
           echo "Entered Stop Auditing ...\n"
```

The -d option of the **auditcmd** command disables the audit subsystem for audit record generation.

```
            auditcmd -d

         echo "\n"
         echo "Auditing Disable - done!\n"
      break
```

```
                      ;;
                      [nN]*)
                         echo "Disable Auditing later by
                                 activating: clraudit\n"
                      break
                      ;;
                      *)
                         echo "Please enter 'y' or 'n' \n"
                      ;;
                   esac
                done
                break
                ;;
            *)
                echo "Please enter 'y' or 'n' \n"
            ;;
      esac
done

while
   echo "\nDo you want to track User Activities: [y/n] \c"
   read track
   do
      case "$track" in
        [yY]*)
            echo "Tracking User Activities ...\n"

            while
               echo "\nDo you want to display part of
                       the report: [y/n] \c"
            read part
               do
                  case "$part" in
                     [yY]*)
                         echo "\nNumer of Lines to display:  \c"
                         read lines

                         echo "Displaying Part of
                                 User Activities ...\n"
```

The **last** command with the -n limit option, limits the report to *n* lines.

```
                   last -n $lines
```

```
                        break
                        ;;
                  [nN]*)
                     echo "Displaying All User
                               Activities ...\n"
```

The **last** command without options will print a record of all logins and logouts, in reverse
chronological order.

```
                     last | pg
# pg is a Unix System V command
# BSD Unix uses more, which is also available on
# some Unix V systems.
                     break
                     ;;
                     *)
                        echo "Please enter 'y' or 'n' \n"
                     ;;
                  esac
               done


            break
            ;;
         [nN]*)
            echo "No Track of User Activities!\n"
         break
         ;;
         *)
            echo "Please enter 'y' or 'n' \n"
         ;;
      esac
   done


sufile=/etc/default/su
sulogfile=/usr/adm/sulog
while
   echo "\nDo you want to check all attempts
         to become root: [y/n] \c"
   read attempt
   do
      case "$attempt" in
         [yY]*)
            echo "Checking all attempts to become root ...\n"
```

The **/etc/default/su** file is used to log all attempts by users to become root. This script checks if the **/etc/default/su** file exists. If it does not exist, the script creates the file, including the string SULOG=/usr/adm/sulog. All user attempts to switch user IDs will be recorded in the **/usr/adm/sulog** file.

```
                    if [ -r $sufile ]
                    then
                      :
                    else
                      echo "Making File $sufile ...\n"
                      touch $sufile
                      chmod 644 $sufile
                      chown $log_name $sufile
                      chgrp $log_name $sufile
                      echo "SULOG=/usr/adm/sulog" >> $sufile

                    fi
                    echo "\n                The $sulogfile records:\n"
                    echo "* Original User * UID of the su attempt
                          * Time of the attempt *"
                    echo "  plus sign (+) indicates successful attempt"
                    echo "  minus sign (-) indicates unsuccessful
                          attempt"
                    echo "------ Reading $sulogfile ------\n"
                    cat $sulogfile
                 break
                 ;;
                 [nN]*)
                    echo "No checking attempts to become
                          root selected!\n"
                 break
                 ;;
                 *)
                    echo "Please enter 'y' or 'n' \n"
                 ;;
              esac
           done
        else
           echo "Cannot execute -
                 not a System(audit) Administrator!\n"
           echo "Check your permissions!\n"
        fi
```

....
A clraudit SHELL SCRIPT

This Bourne shell script terminates the system audit generated by the **secur** shell script designed to meet the audit goals specified by the U.S. National Computer Security Center. This audit feature is administrated by the audit administrator, who requires superuser privileges. The audit feature can be also terminated from the general purpose **secur** shell script, provided earlier.

```sh
#!bin/sh
# @(#) clear audit script
log_name = 'whoami'

if [ log_name = "root" ]
then
  while
    echo "\nDo you want to stop Auditing: [y/n] \c"
    read answer
  do
    case "$answer" in
      [yY]*)
        echo "Entered Stop Auditing! Continue ...\n"
        auditcmd -d

        echo "\n"
        echo "Auditing Disable - done!\n"
      break
      ;;
      [nN]*)
        echo "\nExiting ...\n"
        exit 0
      ;;
      *)
        echo "Please enter 'y' or 'n' \n"
      ;;
    esac
  done
else
    echo "Cannot execute -
            not a System(audit) Administrator!\n"
    echo "Check your permissions!\n"
  fi
```

Chapter Summary

Account Security   The single most important defense of a Unix system against intruders is the password. Consider the following guidelines for the creation and management of user accounts and passwords: Ensure that all people who access the computer system have their own computer accounts. Monitor account usage carefully with Unix commands such as **ps**. Ensure that all accounts have a password. Educate users on the need to select passwords carefully and to protect their passwords. Never transmit passwords by electronic mail. Restrict your use of the root account to genuine system administrator activities. Consider offloading system administrator activities such as account creation to an assistant using programs such as those presented in Chapter 5. Perform all routine activities using your regular account. Never test new software while you are running under the root account. Change the password of every account supplied with the Unix system. Disable user accounts after a predetermined period of inactivity. Ensure that every UUCP login has its own password.

Coding data to prevent its being read by unauthorized individuals is known as data encryption or simply encryption. The question is not whether to employ data encryption but when to employ it and how to employ it. The system administrator might require technical assistance in answering these questions and implementing data encryption where required.

Under most circumstances only the superuser has root access privileges. Restricting access to the root account increases system security. Sometimes it is necessary to give regular users root access privileges, such as allowing users to modify their own password, by accessing the **/etc/passwd** file. Such a program is called a set user ID (SUID) program. A set group ID (SGID) program temporarily modifies the group ID. The use of SUID programs, while considered necessary in most installations, opens a security risk. Consider the following guidelines to deal with the threat of SUID and SGID programs: Regularly print a complete listing of all SUID and SGID files on your system. Do not use SUID or SGID shell scripts. Examine the source code for all programs that accord SUID or SGID privileges. Accord the minimum privileges necessary.

The **su** command makes the user a superuser or another user. Unix allows **su** to be used under four circumstances: The superuser can invoke the **su** command to become any account, an authorized system administrator can invoke the **su** command to access the superuser account, users can invoke the **su** command to access their own account, and a system daemon can invoke the **su** command to access any account. It is advisable to log all attempts by users to become root.

The more closely the system administrator monitors system access, the lower the frequency of security violation. The following Unix log files can be useful in monitoring system access: The **/usr/adm/lastlog** file records the latest login time for each user. The **/etc/utmp** file contains information for users currently logged into the system. The associated **/usr/adm/wtmp** file contains information related to system logins and logouts. The **/usr/adm/acct** file contains an entry for every user command.

The **last** command indicates the last logins of users and teletypes. It prints the sessions of the specified users and ttys, including login name, the line used, the device name, the process ID, the start time, and the elapsed time. When no argument is specified, **last** prints a record of all logins and logouts in reverse chronological order.

Physical Security   Arguably, most threats to the computer system are associated with account abuse, usually via a stolen or a "borrowed" password. However, many threats are more direct, consisting of individuals attempting to take over the system physically. To this must be added disasters such as earthquakes and floods, and environmental dangers such as dust and electrical noise. The system administrator has a direct role in physically protecting the system from human abuse, and equally important, in minimizing the damage caused by natural disasters and a poor environment.

To reduce the risk of human security abuse, apply the following guidelines: No smoking, eating, or drinking near any computer equipment. Individuals under the influence of alcohol or drugs should be kept from accessing the system. Unauthorized individuals should be banned from the computer room and any computer equipment. Don't advertise the system—the days of the glass-walled computer system are over. Engrave company identification on valuable equipment. Consider securing equipment with bolts, locks, or other antitheft devices such as alarms. Shred important documents. Monitor wires for evidence of wiretapping. Don't leave logged-on terminals unattended, even for a short period of time. Prosecute vandals.

Programmed threats can be very difficult to defend against. Use software only from trusted sources. Understand what software does before using it. Run software in the root account only when necessary. The following is a partial list of programmed threats: A back door, also known as a trap door, is part of a program that provides access to system resources by bypassing the normal authorization process. Bacteria, also known as rabbits, are programs that make copies of themselves until they take over, monopolizing system resources such as central memory or disk space. A logic bomb is part of a program that lies quietly waiting for the moment to perform special, perhaps malicious behavior. A Trojan horse is a program that seems to be doing one thing, such as a game, but is actually doing something else, such as deleting files. A virus is computer code that can only be executed in the presence of another program. (In common language any programmed threat is known as a virus.) A worm is a program that can travel across a network from one computer to another. The system administrator must pay particular attention to the security risk caused by involuntary separations.

Don't hide behind the inevitability of a disaster to avoid formulating and implementing a disaster recovery policy. Wherever you place your priorities, start planning for catastrophe now—tomorrow may be too late. Keep complete up-to-date backup files offsite. Among the natural (and seminatural) disasters to defend against are earthquakes, fire and smoke, flooding and other water damage, lightning, and war and terrorism.

Environmental considerations differ from natural disasters in one important way: they are easier to manage. Among the environmental factors to control are: dust, electrical noise, explosions, extreme temperatures, humidity, insects, and vibration.

Network Security Considerations

The very ease with which users can access Unix system resources across the network increases the security risk concomitantly. Treat the phone numbers used to access modems as you treat passwords; by protecting them, you reduce the frequency with which unauthorized users may access the system. The familiar techniques of passwords, data encryption, and restricting physical access should be applied to modems. Other security measures associated with modems include automatic number identification, callbacks, disabling call forwarding and third-party billing, and leased lines.

Files and Programs

Some files and programs are more dangerous than others. Over a period of time, Unix has patched security holes, replacing commands with more secure versions. A user who has the same user name on two (or more) hosts can log in from the trusted host to another linked host without entering a password. The **/etc/hosts.equiv** file contains the list of trusted hosts for a given computer. An individual user's **.rhosts** file contains the list of additional trusted hosts for that particular user. Consider the following policies with respect to trusted hosts and trusted users. The simplest policy is to ban trusted hosts from the computer network. If you do not ban trusted hosts, at least monitor the **/etc/hosts.equiv** file carefully. Many installations choose to prevent users from setting up their individual **.rhosts** file. If you do not ban individual **.rhosts** files, at least monitor them carefully on an unannounced basis. Remove any + sign from the **/etc/hosts.equiv** file as distributed.

Users can execute commands on remote computers without first logging in by issuing the **/etc/rexecd** daemon. It is advisable to disable this daemon in the **/etc/inetd.conf** configuration file. One of the major reasons that computers are networked is to provide electronic mail services. Apply the following policy when using the **sendmail** program: Carefully follow the guidelines listed in the text when applying the **sendmail** program. The **finger** command displays personal information such as the user name, full name, location, login time, and office telephone number for logged-in users. Because this command makes it easy for intruders to obtain the list of users, it is often considered a security risk.

Consider the following security guidelines if your site provides the UUCP facility: As with all other accounts, assign a unique password to each UUCP account. Assign a unique login ID to each machine with which your system communicates. Limit the scope of UUCP as much as possible by restricting the available commands and accessible directories. Set the **/usr/lib/uucp/L.sys** or **/usr/lib/uucp/Systems** file mode to 400 or 600 so that they may be read only by the UUCP facility. Ensure that the UUCP facility cannot read any files in the /usr/lib/uucp directories.

Auditing the System

The system administrator should not be overwhelmed by the enormity of system security activities. When the volume warrants, security duties may be assigned to a security specialist or the audit administrator. Furthermore, many versions of Unix provide computerized system auditing facilities.

Unix contains numerous auditing facilities, including **authcap**, the authentication database; the **authck** command, which checks the internal consistency of the authentication database; the integrity utility, which examines system files against the authentication database; the **chg_audit** command, which enables and disables auditing for the next session (next reboot); and **auditcmd**, the command interface for audit subsystem activation, termination, statistics retrieval, and subsystem notification.

Unix System

- Display Managers and Window Managers

- X Window System Clients

- A Script that Changes the Root Window Background

Administration Guide

CHAPTER 1

X Window System Administration

The X Window system provides windowing services on Unix systems. Briefly stated, appropriate use of X combines the power of Unix with the user-friendliness of the Macintosh environment (or, in the eyes of some, MS-Windows or OS/2.) In many installations, the system administrator is responsible for administering the X Window system. This relatively long chapter presents what the system administrator needs to know to manage X. The authors' earlier text, *X Window Inside & Out* (Berkeley, Osborne/McGraw-Hill, 1992) presents information that X Window system developers need to know.

This chapter introduces the hardware and software associated with X Window systems. It then presents in detail the display and window manager that the system administrator will be asked to customize. The chapter concludes by examining special X Window functions known as clients. To get an idea of X Window's look and feel, the chapter includes multiple screen dumps.

INTRODUCTION

The *X Window system* has become a standard hardware-independent windowing system for developing both monochrome and color high-resolution graphical systems. It is the standard windowing system for Unix. A schematic illustration of the X Window System is shown in Figure 13-1.

The X Window system first became available to developers with version 10.4 in 1986. Major computer vendors, including Digital Equipment Corporation (DEC), International Business Machines (IBM), American Telephone and Telegraph (AT&T), Sun Microsystems, and Hewlett-Packard, have funded the development of the X Window system on an ongoing basis. During its short life the X Window system has been upgraded several times. At the time of this writing the most recent version is X11R5 (Version 11, Release 5).

FIGURE 13-1

The X Window system

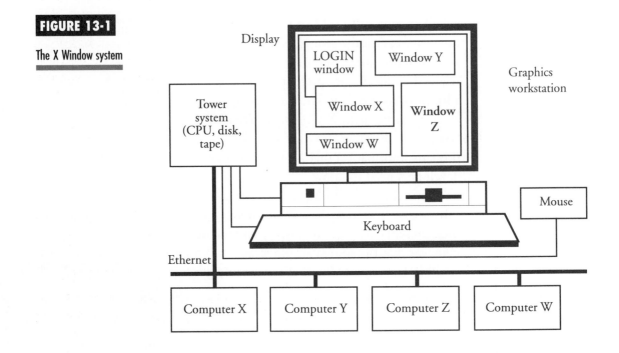

Hardware

X Window systems run on a variety of common hardware devices. The output unit is a graphics screen, usually with at least VGA (640×480) resolution. The most commonly used input devices are the keyboard and the mouse. Other input units include trackball, digitizing tablet, and touchscreen. Various processing options are described in the following sections:

Workstations

The vast majority of workstation manufacturers actively support X Window systems. The continuing decline in workstation prices and increase in individual and group computing requirements, means an ever-growing role for workstations and consequently for X Window systems.

X Terminals

An increasingly popular alternative to a full-blown workstation is an *X terminal*. X terminals are diskless graphical computer terminals that run a single program: the X Window server program introduced in the following section.

The rapid expansion of the X Window marketplace has led to the development of a wide variety of X terminals, some of which rival workstations for memory and CPU. Because X terminals do not have disks or a central processor, they are less expensive than corresponding workstations.

Other advantages of X terminals are reduced hardware and software maintenance, compared to workstations running X Window systems. X terminals offer increased control by the information systems department and protect the installation's investment in mainframe computers.

X terminals have potential disadvantages. They cannot process data when and where it is generated. The low-end models tend to be slow.

Microcomputers

X Window systems run on some powerful microcomputers. High-resolution graphics are recommended. Super VGA is certainly preferable to VGA or Hercules. Processing requirements may make the 1024×768 resolution too slow. Color is a matter of choice but if you choose color, make sure that you find the colors attractive, especially if you will be spending many hours at the screen.

The minimum processor is a 386 or equivalent (for example, a 68030). (Patient AT users may find the waiting time acceptable for simple graphics.) A large, fast hard disk is an absolute necessity. The X Window system is not a DOS system—don't even think of squeezing it into a corner of a 40-megabyte (MB) hard drive. Plan on devoting at least a 110MB drive to the X Window system and its environment, including Unix. Check your manuals to determine the necessary configuration depending on your X Window implementation and the facilities you require.

Client/Server Architecture

The heart of the X Window philosophy is the *client/server architecture.* The client/server architecture is the X Window system model by which *clients,* or application programs, communicate with *servers,* or display units over a network. The client/server architecture is shown in Figure 13-2. This section examines in detail the X Window client/server architecture components and then compares this architecture to the client/server model found in other computer systems.

FIGURE 13-2

Client/server architecture

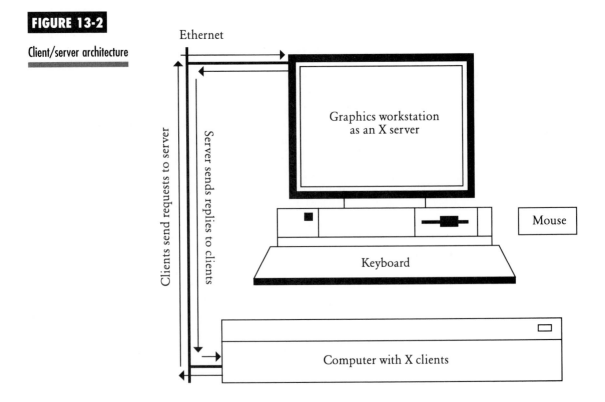

Clients

Basically, the client is the application program. Unlike traditional graphics programs, X Window clients do not directly communicate with the user. The client obtains user input such as a keypress or click of a mouse button from the server, the other half of the client/server architecture. The client executes X Window commands that request the server to draw graphics. Several clients may be attached to a single server.

The Server

An X Window server can have one or more displays, each of which may be composed of multiple physical screens. The server performs several related functions:

- ▰ It passes user input to attached clients. Common examples of user input are pressing a key, clicking a mouse button, and changing the pointer location. This input is unscheduled—any type may occur in any order.

- ▰ It decodes client messages, such as information requests and moving one or more windows. A formal X Window language expresses these requests.

- ▰ It maintains complex data structures. The server's handling of these structures reduces client storage and processing needs and diminishes the amount of data transmitted over the network.

The Client/Server Connection

An essential part of X Window systems is the physical link between the client (application program) and the server (display). *Networking protocols* describe the format and order of data and control bytes that compose a message sent from one network point to another. X Window developers and system administrators need not know the networking protocol actually used. Three commonly used networking protocols for data transfer between the server and the clients are TCP/IP, developed by the University of California; DECNet, developed by Digital Equipment Corporation; and STREAMS, developed by AT&T. X Window was written to make the use of these and other network protocols transparent to the user.

Ethernet is a widely used local-area network communications technology. It supplies the physical communications channel between the client and the server. It transmits data at a maximum theoretical rate of 10 million bits per second. Compare this speed to a typical connection between a graphics terminal and a mainframe computer at 19,200 bits per second. The X Window link can transfer more than 10 times as fast (if the collision rate, which slows data transmission, is low over the Ethernet link).

Relation to Traditional Client/Server Systems

Many people are familiar with the terms "client" and "server" as associated with other types of computer systems. For example, a local area network file server stores files and centralizes file management operations for user programs (clients). A printer server queues user printer requests. In these cases, the server is located on a remote, often heavy-duty computer, and the client is the user's program. X Window systems reverse the component locations: the server is located at the user's computer or X terminal and the client is located on a remote, often heavy-duty computer. Both traditional client/server systems and X Window systems apply the division of labor principle to centralize key graphics operations in the server, enabling the client to focus on the application at hand.

Software

Specialized software is needed to send appropriate data and control bytes from the client to the server and vice versa. The simplest X Window program that displays a hello message on the screen is almost two pages long. X Window flexibility comes at a price, but system administrators are not expected to program in X Window, only to administer it.

X Window systems include three levels of programming, ranging from coding C language calls that directly access X's network protocol, to commercially available packages whose look and feel resembles the OS/2 Presentation Manager and Microsoft Windows graphical user interfaces. These three programming levels are illustrated in Figure 13-3. These facilities are introduced here and discussed in detail in the authors' text, *X Window Inside & Out* (Berkeley, Osborne/McGraw-Hill, 1992).

Xlib Functions

X Window system client/server communication is accomplished through a network protocol, called the *X protocol.* The X protocol defines the exact bytes required to perform all X Window operations including drawing a window, moving a window, or reacting to the click of a mouse button. Programming using the X protocol is extremely arduous; this bare-bones language offers no facilities to help the programmer.

Xlib functions provide the power of X protocol with much less pain. Xlib is a library of over 300 C language functions used to generate X protocol. While it is essential for X Window system developers to master Xlib functions to know how X works, they usually prefer to program with higher-level commands, using Xt Intrinsics or proprietary toolkits.

Xt Intrinsics

X Toolkit Intrinsics, also known as *Xt Intrinsics,* enable programmers to create and use standard on-screen building blocks, called *widgets,* such as menus, scroll bars, buttons,

FIGURE 13-3

Levels of programming

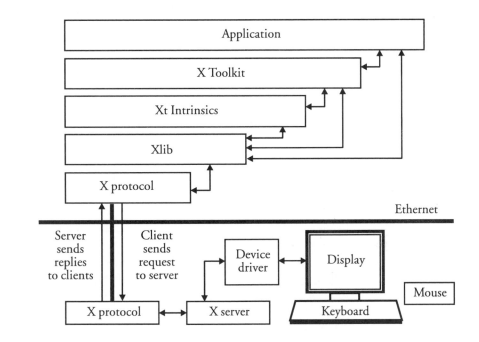

and dialog boxes. Meticulous use of widgets simplifies the X Window programming process. Perhaps more important, it gives the application a standard "look and feel" and consequently makes the application easier to use.

Proprietary Toolkits

The uppermost programming level for X Window systems is proprietary. Software houses develop their own toolkits as extensions to the Xt Intrinsics toolkit. Proprietary toolkits include custom features that promise attractive output, ease of use, and rapid application development. A *window manager* is a special client responsible for manipulating windows on the screen. Window managers associated with the X Window system include **uwm**, **wm**, and **twm**. Proprietary toolkits apply their own window manager, which may be more sophisticated.

Each proprietary toolkit produces a distinctive graphical user interface, enabling developers to create a series of applications with a standard look and feel. A warning is in order: It takes considerable skill to produce a truly user-friendly interface, even for a simple application, much less a series of applications. No matter how powerful the toolkit, sloppy programming remains sloppy programming.

The Open Software Foundation (OSF) is a consortium founded in 1988 by major hardware vendors including IBM, DEC, and Hewlett-Packard. The OSF/Motif toolkit, often called Motif, is the most widely used X Window proprietary toolkit. The Motif window manager **mwm**, presented later in this chapter, handles the details of window creation and processing. It provides an attractive interface, similar to OS/2's Presentation Manager and Microsoft Windows.

The major competitor to OSF/Motif is the Open Look graphical user interface distributed by Unix System Laboratory (USL) and Sun Microsystems. As does OSF/Motif, Open Look furnishes three-dimensional effects. Sun's version includes functions that ease conversion of previous Sun applications to the X Window system. Figure 13-4 illustrates sample windows created with the Open Look graphical user interface. Table 13-1 lists vendor and third-party support for Motif and Open Look toolkits as of mid-1991.

Quarterdeck Office Systems, the distributor of best-selling memory management programs for both MS-DOS and MS-Windows computers, has released DESQview/X. This package's purpose is to turn a high-powered microcomputer into a complete X Window client and server for network applications. Competitive microcomputer products are available.

While OSF/Motif has become the most widely used X Window proprietary toolkit, the system administrator should be familiar with competitive software. The product selection process is lengthy, and has major implications for X Window developers and possibly system administrators. Figure 13-5 illustrates sample windows created with the OSF/Motif graphical user interface.

FIGURE 13-4

A typical workspace in the Open Look graphical user interface

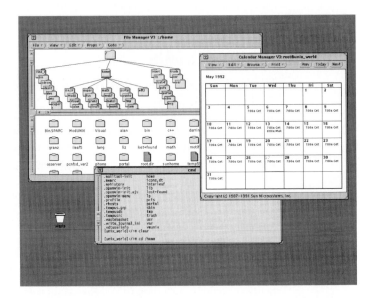

	Vendor	Motif	Open Look
TABLE 13·1 Availability of OSF/Motif and Open Look	IBM	V	T
	Digital Equipment Corp.	V	T
	Hewlett-Packard	V	T
	Unisys	V	
	Sun Microsystems	T	V
	Solbourne	V	V
	Compaq	V	
	Dell	V	
	Prime	V	
	Data General	V	
	Silicon Graphics	V	
	MIPS	V	
	NCR	V	
	AT&T	V	V
	Wang	V	
	NEC	V	
	Hitachi	V	
	Commodore		V

V - Vendor supported
T - Third-party supported
Source Sun, OSF as quoted in UnixWORLD, August, 1991 page 86.

Software Configuration Files

The X Window system under Motif uses four configuration files: **.Xdefaults**, **.x11start** (the name may vary from system to system), **.mwmrc**, and **app-defaults/***. The **.Xdefaults** file specifies default appearance and behavior characteristics for clients. The **.x11start** file specifies the clients initiated when the X Window system starts. The **.mwmrc** file specifies menus and other objects associated with the OSF/Motif Window Manager (**mwm**), discussed later in this text. The **app-defaults/*** file is optional and includes application-specific configuration resources.

FIGURE 13-5

A typical workspace
in the OSF/Motif
graphical user interface

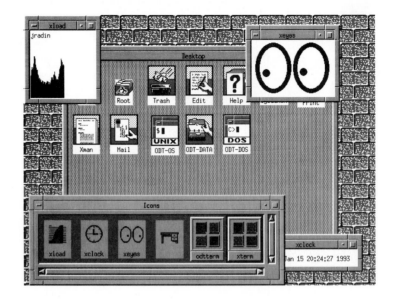

The following file presents the default system resources for SCO ODT-View. These resources may be overridden, as in the next example. Other X Window system implementations may provide somewhat different default system resources.

```
Mwm*gti*clientDecoration: -all

# SAMPLE .Xdefaults / app-defaults  RESOURCE SPECIFICATIONS
# FOR MWM
#

#
# general appearance resources that apply to Mwm (all parts)
#

Mwm*font:                      hp8.8x16b
Mwm*backgroundTile:            background
Mwm*activeForeground:          Black
Mwm*activeBackground:          Cyan
Mwm*activeTopShadowColor:      LightCyan
Mwm*activeBottomShadowColor:   Black
Mwm*makeActiveColors:          false
```

```
Mwm*menu*backgroundPixmap:        background
# Mwm*menu*fontList:              fg-20
Mwm*iconPlacement:                bottom left
Mwm*iconDecoration:               label
Mwm*resizeBorderWidth:            3

Mwm*foreground:                   Black
Mwm*background:                   Gray
Mwm*topShadowColor:               White
Mwm*bottomShadowColor:            Black
Mwm*makeColors:                   false
Mwm*buttonBindings:               DefaultButtonBindings
Mwm*rootMenu:                     DefaultRootMenu
Mwm*systemMenu:                   DefaultSystemMenu
Mwm*interactivePlacement:         true
Mwm*useIconBox:                   true

#
# general appearance resources that apply to specific parts
# of Mwm
#

Mwm*menu*background:              Gray
Mwm*menu*topShadowColor           White
Mwm*menu*bottomShadowColor        Black
Mwm*menu*makeColors:              false

#
# Mwm - specific appearance and behavior resources
#

Mwm*keyboardFocusPolicy:          pointer
Mwm*positionOnScreen:             false
# prevents xterm downsizing on ega
Mwm*moveThreshold:                10
#Mwm*transientDecoration:         title

#
# Xterm general appearance resources.
#
#xterm*borderWidth:1
#Mwm*xterm.clientDecoration: title minimize system
```

```
#
# Xhibit general appearance resources
#


#
# General appearance and behavior defaults
#

*topShadowTile:           foreground
*bottomShadowTile:        foreground
*topShadowColor:          White
*bottomShadowColor:       Black
*foreground:              Black
*background:              Gray
*selectColor:             Cyan
*invertOnSelect:          true
*borderWidth:             1
*borderColor:             Black

#

#   END OF RESOURCE SPECIFICATIONS
#
```

The following example of a user-specific resource file was taken from the authors' earlier book, *X Window Inside & Out* (Berkeley, Osborne/McGraw-Hill, 1992).

```
*fontList:*times-bold*180*iso8859-1
*borderWidth:2
*XmRowColumn.XmPushButton.background: lightgray
*XmRowColumn.XmPushButton.foreground: white
*XmRowColumn.XmPushButton.borderColor: black
#   BEGINING OF RESOURCE SPECIFICATIONS FOR EXAMPLE5_1
*hellow.width:445
*hellow.height:50
*hellow.alignment:XmALIGNMENT_END
*hellow.background: lightgray
*hellow.foreground:black
*hellow.labelString: Levi Reiss and Joseph Radin \
  - X Window Inside and Out!
#   END OF RESOURCE SPECIFICATIONS FOR EXAMPLE5_1
```

```
#
#
#   BEGINNING OF RESOURCE SPECIFICATIONS FOR EXAMPLE5_2
*ghellow.width:445
*ghellow.height:100
*ghellow.alignment:XmALIGNMENT_END
*ghellow.background: gray
*ghellow.foreground: black
*ghellow.labelString: Levi Reiss and Joseph Radin \
 - To Exit Click Here Once!
#   END OF RESOURCE SPECIFICATIONS FOR EXAMPLE5_2
#
#
#   BEGINNING OF RESOURCE SPECIFICATIONS FOR EXAMPLE5_3
#*rc.packing: XmPACK_TIGHT
*rc.background: gray
*rc.foreground: white
*rc.borderColor: black
*rc.orientation: XmHORIZONTAL
*fbutton.labelString: Levi Reiss
*sbutton.labelString: Joseph Radin
*tbutton.labelString: To Exit Click Here Once!!!
#   END OF RESOURCE SPECIFICATIONS FOR EXAMPLE5_3
#
#
#   BEGINNING OF RESOURCE SPECIFICATIONS FOR EXAMPLE5_4
*thewindow.width: 500
*thewindow.scrollingPolicy: XmAUTOMATIC
*thewindow.background: gray
*thewindow.foreground: lightgray
*thebar.background: gray
*thebar.foreground: black
*theframe.width: 700
*theframe.height: 700
*theframe.background: lightgray
*theframe.foreground: gray
*theframe.borderColor: white
*themenu.background: white
*themenu.foreground: gray
*thebutton.background: gray
*thebutton.foreground: black
*thebutton.borderColor: white
*thebutton.labelString: Press Here and See ...
*quitbutton.labelString: Press Here and Quit!
```

```
*quitbutton.background: gray
*quitbutton.foreground: black
*quitbutton.borderColor: white
#  END OF RESOURCE SPECIFICATIONS FOR EXAMPLE5_4
#
#
#  BEGINNING OF RESOURCE SPECIFICATIONS FOR EXAMPLE5_5
*thehelp.width: 200
*thehelp.scrollingPolicy: XmAUTOMATIC
*thehelp.background: lightgray
*thehelp.foreground: black
*thehelp.borderColor: white
*thehelp.labelString: Press Here for Help!
*thehelpbox.background: gray
*thehelpbox.foreground: black
*thehelpbox.width: 300
*thehelpbox.height: 400
*thehelpbox.messageString:This example creates
                          a basic popup menu:\n\n\
 basic popup menu:\n\n\
button - Press Here and See:\n\
- while pressing you get popup button:\n\
    button - Press Here and Quit:\n\
     - while pressing - program terminates!
*thehelpbox.dialogTitle: Help
#  END OF RESOURCE SPECIFICATIONS FOR EXAMPLE5_5
```

DISPLAY MANAGERS AND WINDOW MANAGERS

A *display manager* manages one or more output displays. The **xdm** manages a collection of X displays, both local and remote. The X Display Manager should be invoked for users who wish to run X permanently on their display. (Others should start via the **xinit** client, described later in this chapter.)

Window managers are special clients that are responsible for manipulating windows on the screen. Several window managers are available on X Window systems, Motif provides the **mwm** (Motif Window Manager). Another widely used window manager is the **olwm** (Open Look Window Manager). Refer to Table 13-1 for vendor support. Note that some sites may run multiple proprietary toolkits and consequently multiple window managers.

The X Display Manager

The **xdm** (X Display Manager) program manages both local and remote X displays. The emergence of X terminals guided the design of several parts of this system. The **xdm** is designed to provide services similar to those provided by **init**, **getty**, and **login** on character terminals. These services include prompting for logins and passwords, authenticating users, and running a session.

A *session* is defined by the lifetime of a particular Unix process. For traditional character-based terminals, a session is the user's login shell process. The **xdm** handles sessions by a session manager or if one is not available, by a terminal emulator or a window manager with an exit option. When the session terminates, **xdm** resets the X server and may restart the entire process.

The **xdm** provides the initial user interface, and so it has been designed for simplicity and ease of customization, with many options, described below.

The xdm Options

Except for -config, all **xdm** options can be replaced by resources in the configuration file.

- ▨ -config *configurationfile* Specifies a resource file containing the remaining configuration parameters.

- ▨ -daemon   Specifies TRUE as the DisplayManager.daemonMode resource value. This makes **xdm** close all file descriptors, disassociate the controlling terminal, and put itself in the background at initial startup (as many other daemons do). The default value is TRUE.

- ▨ -debug *debuglevel* Specifies a numeric value for the DisplayManager.debugLevel resource. A nonzero value prints multiple debugging statements at the terminal and disables the DisplayManager.daemonMode resource, which makes **xdm** run synchronously.

- ▨ -error *errorlogfile* Specifies the value for the DisplayManager.errorLogFile resource. This file contains **xdm** errors and other output written to **stderr** by any scripts and programs run during the session.

- ▨ -nodaemon   Sets the DisplayManager.daemonMode resource value to FALSE.

- ▨ -resources *resourcefile* Specifies the DisplayManager*resources resource value. This file is loaded using **xrdb** to specify the authentication widget configuration parameters. (The **xrdb** and the authentication widget are discussed later in this chapter.)

- ▨ -server *serverentry* Specifies the value for the DisplayManager.servers resource. See the next section for an in-depth description of this resource.

- ▨ -xrm *resourcespecification* Allows you to specify an arbitrary resource.

Resources

The configuration file, in the Xresource format, provides extensive control of **xdm**. Some resources modify the behavior of **xdm** on all displays, while others modify its behavior on a single display. Where actions relate to a specific display, the display name is inserted into the resource name between DisplayManager and the final resource name segment. For example, **DisplayManager.expo.0.startup** names the resource defining the startup shell file on the expo:0 display, where :0 indicates the first display on the expo system. Because the resource manager uses colons to separate the resource name from the resource value, **xdm** substitutes dots for the colons when generating the resource name.

DisplayManager.servers lists servers local to this host on separate lines. A resource value that begins with a slash (/) is assumed to name the Unix file containing the list. Each entry consists of three parts: a display name, a display type, and a type-dependent entry. A typical entry for local display number 0 is:

```
:0 local /usr/bin/X11/X :0
```

DisplayManager.errorLogFile Error output is normally directed at the system console, but can be redirected, for example to **syslog**. This file also contains any output directed to **stderr** by **Xstartup**, **Xsession**, and **Xreset**.

Table 13-2 describes the DisplayManager Display files. For simplicity, the initial two segments of the filename are omitted; they are DisplayManager.DISPLAY. in all entries.

Table 13-3 describes the DisplayManager Display resources. For simplicity, the initial two segments of the resource name are omitted; they are DisplayManager.DIS-PLAY. in all entries.

TABLE 13-2

DisplayManager
Display Files

Filename	Description	Default Name	Conventional Name
resources	Name of file loaded by xrdb as resource database.	None	Xresources
xrdb	Program used to load resources.	/usr/bin/X11/xrdb	
startup	Program run as root after successful authentication.	None	Xstartup
session	Session to be executed.	/usr/bin/X11/xterm	Xsession
reset	Program run as root after session terminates.	No program	Xreset

TABLE 13-3

DisplayManager
Display Resources

Resource Name	Description	Default Value
grabtimeout	Maximum waiting time for server and keyboard grab.	3 seconds
terminateServer	Terminates (TRUE) server or resets it when session terminates.	FALSE
userpath	Sets PATH environment variable for the session.	Specified in system config. file with DefUserPath*
systempath	Sets PATH environment variable for startup session and resets scripts to value of this resource.	Specified in system config. file with DefSystemPath†
systemshell	Sets SHELL environment variable for startup and resets scripts to value of this resource.	/bin/sh
failsafeclient	If default session fails to execute, this program is executed.	/usr/bin/X11/xterm

*Often set to :/bin:/usr/bin:/usr/bin/X11:/usr/ucb.
†Often set to /etc:/bin:/usr/bin:/usr/bin/X11:/usr/ucb.

Controlling the Server

The **xdm** program controls local servers by using Unix signals. The SIGHUP signal attempts to reset the server, closing all client connections and performing other cleanup duties. The SIGTERM signal attempts to terminate the server. If these signals do not perform the expected actions, an error condition occurs.

To control remote servers, **xdm** searches the window hierarchy on the display. It uses the protocol request **KillClient** to try to clean up the terminal for the next session. This may not kill all clients, since only those that have created windows are noticed.

Controlling xdm

The **xdm** program responds to two signals: SIGHUP and SIGTERM. When sent a SIGHUP signal, **xdm** rereads the file specified by the DisplayManager.servers resource, and notices if entries have been added or deleted. If a new entry was added, **xdm** starts a session on the associated display. Deleted entries are disabled immediately, any session in progress is terminated without notice, and no new session starts.

When sent a SIGTERM, **xdm** terminates all sessions in progress and exits. This can be used when shutting down the system.

Authentication Widget

The *authentication widget* application reads the user name and password from the keyboard. Resources for this widget belong in the filenamed by DisplayManager.DISPLAY.resources. In many cases the default values will meet your needs. A few examples are shown here (consult the system manual for the complete list):

- xlogin.Login.*foreground* Specifies the color for displaying the typed-in user name.

- xlogin.Login.*greeting* Specifies a string identifying this window. The default is "Welcome to the X Window System."

- xlogin.Login.*greetFont* Specifies the font for displaying the greeting.

- xlogin.Login.*greetColor* Specifies the color for displaying the greeting.

- xlogin.Login.*Passwdprompt* Specifies the string to prompt for a password. The default is "Password: ".

- xlogin.Login.*fail* Specifies the message displayed when the authentication fails. The default is "Login Failed."

The Xstartup File

This file is typically a shell script. You should run it as root and take adequate security precautions. Use this file to store commands that make fake entries in **/etc/utmp**, mount users' home directories from file servers, display the message of the day, or abort the session if logins are not allowed. Set the following environmental variables:

- DISPLAY the associated display name
- HOME the user's home directory
- USER the user name
- PATH the value of DisplayManager.DISPLAY.systempath
- SHELL the value of DisplayManager.DISPLAY.systemShell

No arguments are passed to the script. The **xdm** waits for the script to exit before starting the user session. If the **Xstartup** exit value is not 0, **xdm** discontinues the session immediately and starts another authentication cycle.

The Xsession Program

The **Xsession** command runs as the user's session. It runs with the permissions of the authorized user and employs the following environment variables:

▰   DISPLAY   the associated display name

▰   HOME   the user's home directory

▰   USER   the user name

▰   PATH   the value of DisplayManager.DISPLAY.userPath

▰   SHELL   the user's default shell (from **/etc/passwd**)

In most installations, **Xsession** looks in $HOME for the **.xsession** file, which contains the user-specific session commands, overriding the system default session. **Xsession** should implement the system default session if no user-specified session exists. See the section describing system startup below.

Use set-session-argument to pass an argument to the **Xsession** program from the authentication widget, selecting different session styles. This allows users to escape from the ordinary session when it fails, enabling them to repair their own **.xsession** file. The section on typical usage demonstrates this feature.

The Xreset Script

The **Xreset** script runs after the user session has terminated. Run as root, it should contain commands that undo the effects of commands in **Xstartup**—removing fake entries from **/etc/utmp** or unmounting directories from file servers. Environment variables passed to **Xstartup** are supplied to **Xreset** as well.

Starting a Session

First set up the **xdm** configuration file. Make a directory such as **/usr/lib/X11/xdm** to contain all relevant files. A sample configuration file, perhaps named **xdm-Config** follows:

```
DisplayManager.servers: /usr/lib/X11/xdm/Xservers
DisplayManager.errorLogFile: /usr/lib/X11/xdm/xdm-errors
DisplayManager*resources: /usr/lib/X11/xdm/Xresources
DisplayManager*startup: /usr/lib/X11/xdm/Xstartup
DisplayManager*session: /usr/lib/X11/xdm/Xsession
DisplayManager*reset: /usr/lib/X11/xdm/Xreset
```

This file is composed of references to other files. Some resource names include an asterisk (*) separating the components. You can make a resource unique for each different display by replacing the asterisk with the display name. This specification is usually not very useful. See the previous section on resources for more information.

The first file, **/usr/lib/X11/xdm/Xservers**, contains the list of displays to manage. Most workstations have only one display, numbered 0, so this file looks like this:

```
:0 local /usr/bin/X11/X :0
```

This keeps **/usr/bin/X11/X** running on this display and manages a continuous cycle of sessions.

The most interesting script is **Xsession**. This version recognizes the special *failsafe* mode, specified in the preceding translations in the **Xresources** file, to provide an escape from the ordinary session:

```
#!/bin/sh
# @(#) X session version recognizing failsafe mode


case $# in
1)
  if ($1=failsafe) in
    exec xterm -geometry 80x24+50+50
  fi
esac

startup=$HOME/.xsession
resources=$HOME/.Xresources
if [ -f $startup ]; then
  if [ -x $startup ]; then
    exec $startup
  else
    exec /bin/sh $startup
  fi
  else
    if [ -f $resources ]; then
      xrdb -load $resources
  fi
  mwm &
  exec xterm -geometry 80x24+10+10 -ls
fi
```

The mwm Window Manager

The **mwm** command is an X11 client providing window management and some session management services. It facilitates user and programmer control of elements of window states such as placement, size, icon/normal display, and input focus ownership. Among its session management functions are stopping a client.

The **mwm** includes two options:

- -display *display*   Specifies the display to use.
- -xrm *resourcestring*   Specifies the resourcestring to use.

The following sections describe the basic default behavior of windows, icons, the icon box, input focus, and window stacking. The window manager's appearance and behavior can be modified by changing the configuration of specific resources.

Window Default Behavior

Default **mwm** window frames have distinct components with associated functions, as shown in Figure 13-6.

The Title Area   This object displays the client's title and is also used to move the window. To do so, place the pointer over the title area, press the left button and drag the window to a new location. A wire frame is moved during the drag to indicate the new location. Release the button and the window is moved.

FIGURE 13-6

The default window menu

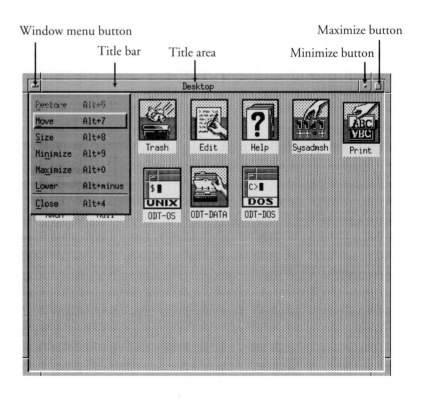

The Title Bar The title bar includes the title area, the minimize button, the maximize button, and the window menu button.

The Minimize Button To reduce the window to its icon, click the left button on the minimize button (the small square in the frame box).

The Maximize Button To make the window fill the screen (or enlarge it to the largest size allowed by the configuration files), click the left button on the maximize button (the large square in the frame box).

The Window Menu Button The window menu button is the horizontal bar in the frame box. To pop up the window menu, press the left button. While pressing, drag the pointer to the menu selection, and release the button when the selection is highlighted. Alternatively, click the left button to pop up the menu and keep it posted; then position the pointer and select.

The Default Window Menu The elements of the default window menu are described in Table 13-4 and displayed in Figure 13-6, where the menu is superimposed on the SCO ODT.

Default Icon Behavior

Icons are small graphical representations of windows. To minimize (iconify) a window, press the minimize button on the window frame. When properly used, icons reduce the clutter on the screen.

TABLE 13-4

The Default Window Menu

Selection	Accelerator Key	Description
Restore	ALT-F5	Inactive (not an option for windows).
Move	ALT-F7	Allows the window to be moved with keys or mouse.
Size	ALT-F8	Allows the window to be resized.
Minimize	ALT-F9	Shrinks the window into an icon.
Maximize	ALT-F10	Expands the window to fill the screen.
Lower	ALT-F11	Moves the window to the bottom of the window stack.
Close	ALT-F4	Removes client from mwm management.

Pressing the left mouse button when the pointer is over an icon pops up the associated icon's window menu. Releasing the button (press + release without moving mouse = click) causes the menu to stay posted. Table 13-5 explains the options on the icon window menu.

Double-clicking the left button on an icon transforms the icon into its associated window. Double-clicking (clicking the button twice in rapid succession without moving the mouse) the left button on an icon in the icon box opens that icon box, allowing access to the contained icons. (In general, double-clicking a mouse button offers a quick way to perform a function.)

Icon Boxes   If you find that icons are cluttering the screen, pack them into an *icon box,* an object that holds client icons. (To use an icon box, **mwm** must be started with the icon box configuration already set.) Icons in the icon box can be manipulated with the mouse.

Other Default Behavior

Other default behavior includes the input focus and window stacking. The *input focus,* also called the *keyboard focus,* is the window associated with the keyboard. *Window stacking* describes relationships among windows; for example, if Window A covers (obscures) Window B, Window A is said to be higher on the stacking order.

Input Focus   By default **mwm** supports a keyboard input focus policy of explicit selection. A window selected for keyboard input continues to get keyboard input until it is withdrawn from window management, another window is explicitly selected for keyboard input, or the window is iconified. Numerous resources control the input focus. The client window with the keyboard input focus has a distinct (highlighted) window frame.

TABLE 13-5

The Icon Window Menu

Selection	Accelerator Key	Description
Restore	ALT-F5	Opens the associated window.
Move	ALT-F7	Allows the icon to be moved with keys.
Size	ALT-F8	Inactive (not an option for icons).
Minimize	ALT-F9	Inactive (not an option for icons).
Maximize	ALT-F10	Opens the associated window and expands it to fill the screen.
Lower	ALT-F11	Moves the icon to the bottom of the icon stack.
Close	ALT-F4	Removes client from mwm management.

Window Stacking The window stacking order may be changed by setting the keyboard input focus, iconifying a window, or executing a window manager window stacking function. When a window is iconified, its icon is placed on the bottom of the stack.

The Resource Database

The **mwm** resource database provides three basic types of resources: component-appearance resources, specific appearance and behavior resources, and client-appearance resources. Before examining each of these categories, consider how **mwm** builds this resource database.

The following four sources may be used to build the resource database. They are listed in order of increasing priority; the command-line options override all the others.

- ◪ app-defaults/Mwm
- ◪ RESOURCEMANAGER root window property or $HOME/.Xdefaults
- ◪ XENVIRONMENT variable or $HOME/.Xdefaults-host
- ◪ mwm command line-options

Mwm is the resource class name of the **mwm** window manager and mwm is the resource name used by the window manager to look up resources. In the following discussion of resource specification, Mwm and mwm may be used interchangeably.

Component appearance resources control the appearance of window manager menus, feedback windows, client window frames, and icons. Component appearance resources associated with window manager icons, menus, and client window frames may be coded as follows:

```
Mwm*resourceid
```

For example, Mwm*foreground specifies the foreground color for mwm menus, icons, and client window frames.

Specific appearance and behavior resources designate **mwm** features such as window management policies. Specific appearance and behavior resources may be coded as follows:

```
Mwm*resourceid
```

For example, **Mwm*keyboardFocusPolicy** specifies the window manager policy for setting the keyboard focus to a particular client window.

Client-specific resources designate the icon and window frame appearance and behavior for individual clients or groups of clients. Client-specific resources may be coded as follows:

```
Mwm*clientnameorclass*resourceid
```

For example, Mwm*mterm*windowMenu specifies the window menu to be used with mterm clients.

X WINDOW SYSTEM CLIENTS

X Window furnishes dozens of clients, application programs that perform many useful tasks. It is useful to regroup these clients into functional categories. The *Using the X Window System* manual published by Hewlett-Packard discusses six categories of X clients: initialization and configuration, window management, graphics functions, cut and paste, viewable services, and font management. Table 13-6 presents X Window clients, organized according to the above categories, as interpreted by the authors. Clients of particular interest to system administrators are described in the text.

Initialization and Configuration Clients

Initialization and configuration clients start the X Window system and provide the tools to set it up to meet system default or individual needs. The following clients are described next: **xinit**, which starts X server and clients; **xset**, which sets user preference options; and **xrdb**, which loads the resource database.

The xinit Command

The **xinit** command initializes the X Window system. It has the following syntax:

xinit [[*client*] *options*] [-- [*server*] [*display*] *options*]

The **xinit** program starts the X Window System server and an initial client program (usually a terminal emulator) on systems that cannot start the server directly from **/etc/init** or in multiple window system environments. When this initial client exits, **xinit** kills the server and terminates.

The **xinit** program first looks for the client program in the command line, and if none exists, it accesses the **.xinitrc** shell script in your home directory. If neither is found, **xinit** uses the following default:

```
xterm -geometry +1+1 -n login -display :0
```

Client Name	Description	Type
TABLE 13-6 X Window System Clients		

Client Name	Description	Type
bitmap	Creates bitmap files	Viewable Sv
xbiff	Displays mailbox informs user of mail	Viewable Sv
xcal	Calendar	Viewable Sv
xcalc	Mouse-based calculator	Viewable Sv
xclipboard	Clipboard to cut and paste	Cut/Paste
xclock	Displays clock	Viewable Sv
xev	Displays contents of events	Viewable Sv
xeyes	Displays eyes following pointer	Viewable Sv
xfd	Displays fonts	Font Mgmt
xhost	Manages list of available hosts	Init/Config
xinit	Starts X server and clients	Init/Config
xload	Displays system load average	Viewable Sv
xlock	Locks screen	Window Mgmt
xlogo	Displays X Window system logo	Viewable Sv
xlsfonts	List names of available fonts	Font Mgmt
xlswins	Displays server window list	Window Mgmt
xmail	Reads and creates mail	Viewable Sv
xman	Displays manual	Viewable Sv
xmodmap	Loads keyboard map	Init/Config
xpr	Prints window dump	Graphics Fn
xrdb	Loads resource database	Init/Config
xrefresh	Redraws screen	Window Mgmt
xset	Sets user preference options	Init/Config
xsetroot	Changes background display	Viewable Sv
xterm	Terminal emulator for DEC VT100 or Tektronix graphics terminal	Viewable Sv
xwd	Dumps window bitmap to a file	Graphics Fn
xwininfo	Displays window information	Window Mgmt
xwud	Displays dump generated by xwd	Graphics Fn

The **xinit** program first looks for the server program in the command line and if none exists, accesses the **.xserverrc** shell script in your home directory. If neither is found, **xinit** uses X :0 by default.

This default value assumes that the current search path contains a program named **X**. However, servers are usually named X*displaytype*, where *displaytype* is the type of graphics display driven by this server. The system administrator should make a link to the appropriate type of server or create a shell script that runs **xinit** with the appropriate server.

It is important that programs launched by **.xinitrc** and **.xserverrc** run in the background if they do not exit right away, so that other programs may start. However, the last long-lived program to be launched (usually a window manager or terminal emulator) should run in the foreground so that the script won't exit (which causes **xinit** to exit).

You may specify an alternative client and server on the **xinit** command line. If you do, first specify the desired client program and its arguments. Then append a double hyphen (- -) followed by the server command.

Both the client and server program name must begin with a slash (/), a period (.), or a letter of the alphabet. Otherwise, these names are treated as arguments to be appended to their respective startup lines. This syntax enables you to add options, such as foreground and background colors, without retyping the entire command line.

In the absence of a server name, when the first argument following the double hyphen (- -) is a colon followed by a digit, this digit replaces 0. All remaining arguments are appended to the server command line.

The following examples illustrate the use of **xinit** command-line arguments.

```
xinit
```

starts up a server named X and runs your existing **.xinitrc** file, or starts an **xterm** session. This example also runs your existing **.Xserverrc** file or starts the default: X:0.

```
xinit -- /usr/bin/X11/Xqds:1
```

starts a specific type of server on an alternative display.

```
xinit -geometry =80x65+10+10 -fn 8x13 -j -fg white -bg navy
```

starts a server named X and appends the given arguments to the default **xterm** command.

```
xinit -e widgets -- ./Xsun -l -c
```

executes the command **./Xsun -l -c** to start the server, appending the -e widgets option to the default **xterm** command.

```
xinit /usr/ucb/rsh fasthost cpupig -display
      ws:1 -- :1 - a 2 -t 5
```

starts the **X** server on display 1 with the options -a 2 -t 5. It then starts a remote shell on the machine **fasthost**, which executes the **cpupig** command with the argument -display ws:1. The **cpupig** command will display output on the local workstation.

The following **.xinitrc** shell script starts a clock and several terminals, and leaves the window manager running as the *last* application. If the window manager has been configured properly, you can choose the Exit menu item to shut down the server.

```
xsetroot -solid gray &
xclock -g 50x50-0+0 -bw 0 &
xload -g 50x50-50+0 -bw 0 &
xterm -g 80x24+0+0 &
xterm -g 80x24+0-0 &
mwm
```

The following code invokes **xinit** with a specific shell script, usually named **x11**, **xstart**, or **startx**. This method provides a simple interface for novice users:

```
xinit /usr/local/bin/startx -- /usr/bin/X11/Xhp :1
```

The xset Command

The **xset** command is a user-preference utility for X. It has the following syntax:

> xset *options*

This program sets various parameters for the display. It includes the following options:

- -display *display*   Specifies the server.

- b [-b] [b on/off] [b [*volume*] [*pitch*] [*duration*]]   Controls bell volume, pitch, and duration. This option accepts up to three numerical parameters, a preceding hyphen (-), or an on/off flag. If you specify no parameters or the on flag, **xset** uses the system defaults. If you specify the dash or the off flag, the bell turns off. A numerical parameter (0-100) sets the bell volume to that percentage of the maximum. The second numerical parameter specifies the bell pitch, in hertz, and the third numerical parameter specifies the duration in milliseconds. Some servers do not support volume control.

- c [-c] [c on/off] [c [*volume*]]   Controls key click. If you specify no parameter or the on flag, **xset** uses the system defaults. Specify the dash or the off flag to disable the key click. A numerical parameter (0-100) sets the key click volume to that percentage of the maximum. Not all servers support key click. Those that do will set the volume to the nearest value supported by the hardware.

◪   fp= [[-+]fp[-+=] path[,*path*[,..]]] [fp default]   Sets the font path to directories specified in the path argument. The directories are interpreted by the server, not by the client, and are server-dependent. The server ignores directories that do not contain font databases created by **mkfontdir**.

   fp default   Resets the font path to the server's default.

   fp rehash   Causes the server to reread the font databases in the current font path. Generally you use this option when adding new fonts to a font directory (after running **mkfontdir** to recreate the font database).

   -fp or fp-   The -fp and fp- options remove elements from the current font path. They must be followed by a comma-separated list of directories.

   +fp or fp+   The +fp and fp+ options add elements to the current font path. They must be followed by a comma-separated list of directories.

◪   led [[-]led [*integer*]] [led on/off]   Controls the keyboard LEDs. To turn on the LEDs, specify no parameter or the on flag. To turn them off, specify a preceding dash or the off flag. A value between 1 and 32 turns on (no dash) or turns off (preceding dash) the designated LED. For example, depending on the specific hardware, to turn LED #3 (Caps Lock) on, type: **xset led 3**. To turn it off, type: **xset -led 3**.

◪   m [m[ouse] [*acceleration* [*threshold*]]] [m[ouse] default]   Controls the mouse acceleration and threshold. The mouse, or alternative pointing device, will go *acceleration* times as fast as normal when it travels more than *threshold* pixels in a short time. This way, you can move the mouse slowly when you need precise alignment, and you increase its speed with a flick of the wrist. A single parameter is interpreted as the acceleration. Some servers do not support threshold control.

◪   p [p *pixel color*]   Controls pixel color values. The parameters are the color map entry number pixel (in decimal), and a color specification. You can change the root background colors on some servers by altering the entries for BlackPixel (often 0) and WhitePixel (often 1). Errors occur if the server attempts to allocate those colors privately or the map entry is a read-only color.

◪   r [[-]r] [r on/off]   Controls automatic repeat. The preceding dash or the off flag disables the autorepeat, while no parameters or the on flag enables it. Not all servers support this option.

◪   s [s [*length* [*period*]]] [s blank/noblank] [s expose/noexpose] [s on/off] [s default]   Sets the screen saver parameters. This option accepts up to two numerical parameters, and several flags. To set the default screen saver characteristics, use no parameters or the default flag. The on/off flags turn the screen saver functions on or off.

blank   Sets the preference to blank out the video (if the hardware can do so) rather than display a background pattern; noblank sets the opposite preference.

expose   Sets the preference to allow window exposures. The server can freely discard window contents.

noexpose   Disables screen saver unless the server can regenerate the screens without causing exposure events.

length   Determines how long the server must be inactive to activate screen saving. The *period* parameter determines how often to change the background pattern to avoid burn-in. Specify these arguments in seconds. A single parameter is interpreted as the length.

▰   q   Provides information on the current settings. After logging out, these settings return to their default values. Not all X implementations are guaranteed to honor all of these options.

The xrdb Command

The **xrdb** utility gets or sets the contents of the RESOURCEMANAGER property on the root window of screen 0. It has the following syntax:

xrdb -*options filename*

You normally run **xrdb** from your X startup file. The resource manager (used by the Xlib routine **XGetDefault** and the X Toolkit) uses the RESOURCEMANAGER property to get user preferences about color, fonts, and so on, for applications. Because this information is in the server, it is available to all clients, and so default files are not required for each machine. It also allows for dynamic changing of defaults without editing files.

To maintain compatibility with previous versions of X, if no RESOURCEMAN-AGER property is defined (because **xrdb** was not run or this property was removed), the resource manager looks for the **.Xdefaults** file in your home directory.

Based on your server's capabilities, **xrdb** passes the filename (or the standard input if you specify – or no input file) through the C preprocessor. The C preprocessor ignores lines beginning with an exclamation mark (!), so you can use these lines for comments. The following parameters are defined:

▰   HOST=*hostname*   The *hostname* variable is the host name portion of the display to which you are connected.

▰   WIDTH=*num*   The *num* variable is the width of the screen in pixels.

▚ HEIGHT=*num*   The *num* variable is the height of the screen in pixels.

▚ XRESOLUTION=*num*   The *num* variable is the X resolution of the screen in pixels per meter.

▚ YRESOLUTION=*num*   The *num* variable is the Y resolution of the screen in pixels per meter.

▚ PLANES=*num*   The *num* variable is the number of bit planes for the default visual.

▚ BITSPERRGB=*num*   The *num* variable is the number of significant bits in an RGB color specification. This is the log base 2 of the number of distinct shades of each primary color that the hardware can generate. This value is independent of the number of planes, which is the log base 2 of the size of the color map.

▚ CLASS=*visualclass*   The *visualclass* variable is one of the following:

   StaticGray
   GrayScale
   StaticColor
   PseudoColor
   TrueColor
   DirectColor

▚ COLOR   Defined only if the default visual's type is one of the color options.

Window Management Clients

Window management clients provide useful information about windows. The following clients are described below: **xwininfo** that displays information about windows and **xlswins** that displays the window list.

The xwininfo Command

The **xwininfo** utility displays window information. It has the following syntax:

    xwininfo [-*options*]

The **xwininfo** command is important for the system administrator, who should become familiar with the various options. Sample command output is shown in Figure 13-7.
    If you choose no options, **xwininfo** assumes -stats. For the meaning of such technical terms as "parent window" and "bit gravity" consult the authors' text, *X Window Inside & Out* (Berkeley, Osborne/McGraw-Hill, 1992).

FIGURE 13-7

Sample **xwininfo**
client output

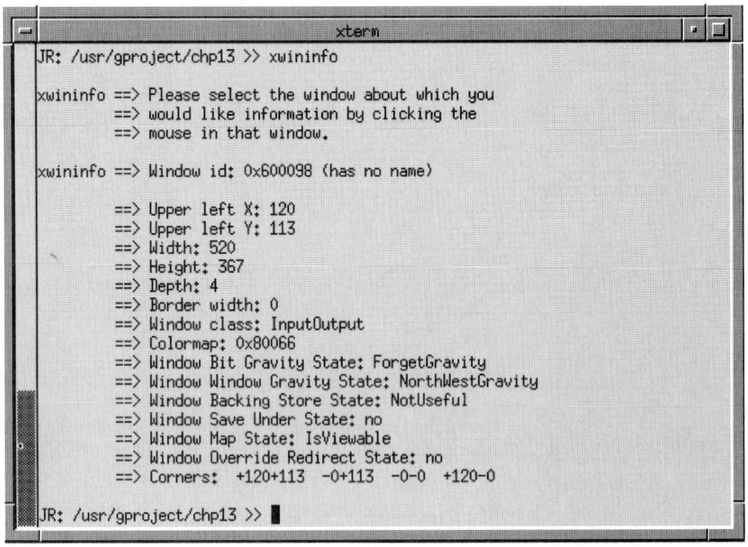

```
┌─                              xterm                           ┌·┐□
  JR: /usr/gproject/chp13 >> xwininfo

  xwininfo ==> Please select the window about which you
           ==> would like information by clicking the
           ==> mouse in that window.

  xwininfo ==> Window id: 0x600098 (has no name)

           ==> Upper left X: 120
           ==> Upper left Y: 113
           ==> Width: 520
           ==> Height: 367
           ==> Depth: 4
           ==> Border width: 0
           ==> Window class: InputOutput
           ==> Colormap: 0x80066
           ==> Window Bit Gravity State: ForgetGravity
           ==> Window Window Gravity State: NorthWestGravity
           ==> Window Backing Store State: NotUseful
           ==> Window Save Under State: no
           ==> Window Map State: IsViewable
           ==> Window Override Redirect State: no
           ==> Corners:  +120+113  -0+113  -0-0  +120-0

  JR: /usr/gproject/chp13 >> █
```

You can select the target window with the mouse (by clicking any mouse button in the desired window) or on the command line by specifying the window ID with the -id option. You can also use the -name option to specify the desired window.

The **xwininfo** command options are as follows:

▰ -help   Prints out the command syntax summary.

▰ -id *id*   Specifies a target window ID on the command line. This is very useful in debugging X applications where the target window is not mapped to the screen or when you cannot use the mouse.

▰ -name *name*   Specifies the window name as the target window.

▰ -root   Specifies the root window as the target window. This option is useful when the root window is completely obscured.

▰ -int   Displays all X window IDs as integer values. The default displays them as hexadecimal values.

▰ -tree   Displays the root, parent, and children window IDs, as well as the name of the selected window.

▰ -stats   Displays various attributes of the selected window. Information displayed includes the location of the window, its width and height, its depth, border width, class, colormap ID if any, map state, backing-store hint, and location of the corners.

- ◪ -bits   Displays information on the target window's bit gravity, window gravity, backing-store hint, backing-planes value, backing pixel, and whether or not the window has save-under set.

- ◪ -events   Displays the selected window's event masks. This option displays both the event mask of events selected by a client and the event mask of events not to propagate.

- ◪ -size   Displays sizing hints for the selected window. The information is displayed for both normal size and zoom size hints and includes where applicable: the user-supplied location, the program-supplied location, the user-supplied size, the program-supplied size, the minimum size, the maximum size, the resize increments, and the minimum and maximum aspect ratios.

- ◪ -wm   Displays the hints for the selected window manager. Information displayed may include whether or not the application accepts input, the window's icon window number and name, the desired location of the window's icon, and the window's initial state.

- ◪ -metric   Displays all individual height, width, and X and Y positions in millimeters, as well as number of pixels, based on what the server thinks the resolution is. Geometry specifications in the +x+y form are not changed.

- ◪ -english   Displays all individual height, width, and X and Y positions in inches (and feet and yards if necessary), as well as number of pixels. You can specify both -metric and -english at the same time.

- ◪ -all   Displays all available information.

- ◪ -display *display*   Specifies the server.

Graphics Functions Clients

Graphics functions clients provide graphical services to the system administrator (and to all users). The following clients are described below: **xpr** for printing window dumps, **xwd** for dumping a window bitmap to a file, and **xwud** for displaying dumps generated by **xwd**.

The xpr Command

The **xpr** utility prints an X window dump. It has the following syntax:

    xpr -*options filename*

Input to the **xpr** utility is a window dump file produced by **xwd**, described below. **xpr** formats this file for output on the LN03, LA100, PostScript printers, or IBM PP3812 page printer. If you do not specify a file argument, **xpr** uses the standard input. To print **xwd** files, you must use the -xy option to the **xwd** program.

By default, **xpr** prints the largest possible representation of the window. Given the importance of printed output, the system administrator should be familiar with this command's options, explained below:

- -scale *scale* Affects the size of the window on the page. The LN03 and PostScript printers can translate each bit in a window pixel map into any specified size grid. For example, to translate each bit into a 5×5 grid, code -scale 5. By default, **xpr** prints a window with the largest scale that can fit onto the page for the specified orientation.

- -height *inches* Specifies the maximum height of the window.

- -width *inches* Specifies the maximum width of the window.

- -left *inches* Specifies the left margin in inches. Fractions are allowed. By default, the window is centered in the page.

- -top *inches* Specifies the top margin for the picture in inches. Fractions are allowed.

- -header *header* Specifies a header string printed above the window.

- -trailer *trailer* Specifies a trailer string printed below the window.

- -landscape Prints the window in landscape mode. By default the window prints so that its longest side follows the long side of the paper.

- -portrait Prints the window in portrait mode. By default, the window prints so that its longest side follows the long side of the paper.

- -rv Prints the window in reverse video.

- -compact Specifies a simple run-length encoding for compact representation of windows containing many white pixels. This option is only supported for PostScript output. It compresses white space but not black space, so it is not useful for reverse-video windows.

- -output *filename* Specifies an output filename. The default is standard output.

- -append *filename* Appends a window to a designated file previously generated by **xpr**.

- -noff When specified in conjunction with -append, the window appears on the same page as the previous window.

- -split *n* Splits a window onto several pages. This might be necessary to generate clear output for very large windows.

▧   -device *device*   Specifies the device on which the file prints. The LN03 (-device ln03), LA100 (-device la100), PostScript printers (-device ps), and IBM PP3812 (-device pp) are supported. As of Release 4, HP LaserJet and compatible printers (-device ljet), the HP PaintJet (color mode) printer (-device pjet), and HP PaintJet XL Color Graphics (color mode) printer (-device pjetxl) are supported. The -device lw (LaserWriter) setting is equivalent to -device ps and is provided only for backward compatibility.

Note

To print files generated by xwd, you must use the -xy option to the xwd program. In this case, the LN03 printer is usually limited to printing X windows no larger than two-thirds of the screen. For example, xpr can print a large Emacs window, but usually fails to print the entire screen. The LN03 has memory limitations that can cause problems when printing very large or complex windows. The xpr program provides limited support for the LA100 printer. The picture always prints in portrait mode; there is no scaling, and the aspect ratio is slightly off. Currently, PostScript printers cannot apply the -append, -noff, or -split options. The xpr program prints color images in black and white.

The xwd Utility

The **xwd** program dumps an X window image. It has the following format:

xwd *-options*

The **xwd** utility lets you store window images in a specially formatted dump file. This file can then be read by various other X programs for redisplaying, printing, editing, formatting, archiving, image processing, and so on.

You select the target window by clicking the mouse in the desired window. The program beeps once at the beginning of the dump and twice when the dump is completed. The following options are available:

▧   -display *display*   Specifies the server.

▧   -help   Prints the command syntax summary on your screen.

▧   -nobdrs   Specifies that the window dump should not include pixels that compose the X window border. This is useful if you want to include the window contents in a document as an illustration.

▧   -out *file*   Specifies the output file on the command line. The default is standard output.

▧   -xy   Specifies xy format dumping, instead of the default z format.

▧   -add *value*   Specifies a signed value to add to every pixel.

The xwud Command

The **xwud** program is an image displayer for X. It has the following syntax:

xwud -*options*

The **xwud** window image undumping utility allows you to display window images that were saved by **xwd** in a specially formatted dump file. The window image appears at the coordinates of the original window from which the dump was taken. This utility displays monochrome dump files on a color monitor in the default foreground and background colors. The following options are defined:

- -help Prints out a short description of the allowable options.
- -in *file* Specifies the input file on the command line. The default is the standard input.
- -inverse Undumps the window in reverse video. This is mainly needed because the display is "write white," whereas dump files intended to be written to a printer are generally "write black." This option applies to monochrome window dump files only.
- -display *display* Specifies the server.

The **xwud** utility does not do color translation when the destination screen does not have a colormap exactly matching that of the original window.

Viewable Services Clients

Viewable services clients provide system administrators and users with X emulation on selected terminals and other desktop facilities. The following clients are described next: **xman**, which displays manual pages; **xterm**, which is a terminal emulator for DEC or Tektronix terminals; **xload**, which displays the system load average; **xclock**, which displays a digital or analog clock; **xbiff**, which informs users whether they have mail; and **xsetroot**, which sets the color and appearance of the root window. A shell script illustrates the use of the **xsetroot** client.

The xman Command

The **xman** command displays manual pages in the X Window environment. Figure 13-8 shows the **xman** output for the **integrity** command, discussed in Chapter 12. The **xman** has the following syntax:

xman -*options*

FIGURE 13-8

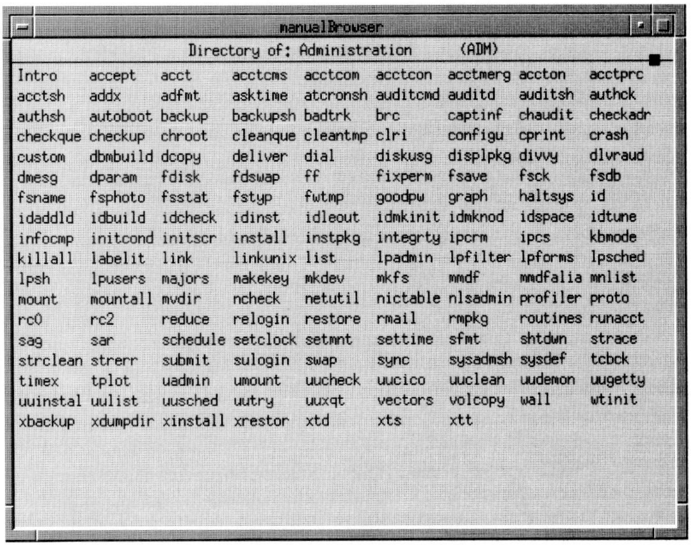

Sample **xman** client output

```
                               manualBrowser
                      Directory of: Administration       (ADM)
Intro    accept   acct      acctcms  acctcom  acctcon  acctmerg acctcon  acctprc
acctsh   addx     adfmt     asktime  atcronsh auditcmd auditd   auditsh  authck
authsh   autoboot backup    backupsh badtrk   brc      captinf  chaudit  checkadr
checkque checkup  chroot    cleanque cleantmp clri     configu  cprint   crash
custom   dbmbuild dcopy     deliver  dial     diskusg  displpkg divvy    dlvraud
dmesg    dparam   fdisk     fdswap   ff       fixperm  fsave    fsck     fsdb
fsname   fsphoto  fsstat    fstyp    fwtmp    goodpw   graph    haltsys  id
idaddld  idbuild  idcheck   idinst   idleout  idmkinit idmknod  idspace  idtune
infocmp  initcond initscr   install  instpkg  integrty ipcrm    ipcs     kbmode
killall  labelit  link      linkunix list     lpadmin  lpfilter lpforms  lpsched
lpsh     lpusers  majors    makekey  mkdev    mkfs     mmdf     mmdfalia mnlist
mount    mountall mvdir     ncheck   netutil  nictable nlsadmin profiler proto
rc0      rc2      reduce    relogin  restore  rmail    rmpkg    routines runacct
sag      sar      schedule  setclock setmnt   settime  sfmt     shtdwn   strace
strclean strerr   submit    sulogin  swap     sync     sysadmsh sysdef   tcbck
timex    tplot    uadmin    umount   uucheck  uucico   uuclean  uudemon  uugetty
uuinstal uulist   uusched   uutry    uuxqt    vectors  volcopy  wall     wtinit
xbackup  xdumpdir xinstall  xrestor  xtd      xts      xtt
```

The **xman** client is a manual page-browser. The default size of the initial **xman** window is small so that you can leave it running throughout your entire login session.

The initial window contains three options:

▰ Help Pops up a window with on-line help.

▰ Quit Exits.

▰ Manual Page Pops up a window containing a manual page-browser.

You can pop up more than one manual page-browser window with a single execution of **xman**.

The **xman** program allows customization of both the search directories for manual pages and the name that each directory maps to in the Manual Sections menu. It determines the search directories by reading the MANPATH environment variable. Directory list entries are separated by colons.

The **xman** utility creates temporary files in **/tmp** for all unformatted manual pages. Major command options include the following:

▰ -helpfile *filename* Specifies a nondefault help file.

▰ -bothshown Allows both the manual page and manual directory to be on the screen at the same time.

▰ -notopbox Starts without the top menu with the three buttons in it.

▰ -geometry $W \times H + X + Y$ Sets the size and location of the top menu with the three buttons in it. W represents the width, H is the height, X is the horizontal position, and Y is the vertical position.

▰ -pagesize $W \times H + X + Y$ Sets the size and location of all the manual pages. (The variables are defined as for -geometry above.)

▰ -bw *pixels* or -borderwidth *pixels* Specifies the border width for all **xman** windows.

▰ -bd *color* or -bordercolor *color* Specifies border colors of all **xman** windows.

▰ -fg *color* or -foreground *color* Specifies the foreground color to be used.

▰ -bg *color* or -background *color* Specifies the background color to be used.

▰ -fn *font* or -font *font* Specifies the font to use for all buttons and labels.

▰ -display *host:display*[.*screen*] Specifies a display other than the default specified by the DISPLAY environment variable.

▰ -xrm *resources* Allows a resource to be specified on the command line.

The xterm Command

The **xterm** utility is the terminal emulator for X. It has the following syntax:

> xterm *-toolkitoption -option*

The **xterm** client provides DEC VT102 (character terminal) and Tektronix 4014 (graphics terminal)-compatible terminal emulation to execute programs unable to use the window system directly. If the underlying operating system supports terminal resizing capabilities, **xterm** uses these capabilities to notify programs running in the window whenever it is resized.

The VT102 and Tektronix 4014 terminals operate separate windows to enable simultaneous text editing and graphics display. The **xterm** restricts Tektronix graphics to the largest box that fits in the window while maintaining the correct aspect ratio (height:width) for a 4014. This box is located in the upper-left area of the window.

One of the displayed windows is considered active; it receives keyboard input and terminal output. The active window contains the text cursor, and its border is highlighted whenever the pointer is in a window. You can choose the active window through escape sequences, the Modes menu in the VT102 window, and the Tektronix menu in the 4014 window.

The **term** terminal emulator accepts all standard X Toolkit command-line options and additional options, the most important of which are listed below. To restore an option to its default value, type + instead of –. Available options are described here:

▰ -help   Prints message describing **xterm** options.

▰ -ah   Highlights the text cursor and borders. By default, **xterm** displays a hollow text cursor whenever the focus is lost or the pointer leaves the window.

▰ -b*number*   Specifies the size in pixels of the inner border (the distance between the outer edge of the characters and the window border). The default is 2.

▰ -cr *color*   Specifies the text cursor color. The default uses the same foreground color used for text.

▰ -cu   Fixes a bug in the cursor-motion package. This bug occurs when you use **more** on a file containing a line exactly the width of the window followed by another line beginning with a tab. Without this option, the leading tabs disappear.

▰ -e *program* [*arguments* ...]   Specifies the program (and its command-line arguments) to be run in the **xterm** window. It also sets the window title and icon name to be the basename of the program being executed if neither -T nor -n are given on the command line. This must be the last option on the command line.

▰ -j   Indicates that **xterm** should do jump scrolling. Instead of scrolling text one line at a time; text scrolls multiple lines at a time, and so, **xterm** doesn't fall as far behind. This option is particularly important when scanning large amounts of text. The VT100 escape sequences for enabling and disabling smooth scrolling, as well as the Modes menu, can be used to turn this feature on or off.

▰ -l   Sends all terminal output to a log file, as well as to the screen. You can enable or disable this option with the X11 menu.

▰ -lf *filename*   Specifies the log filename associated with the -l option. The default filename is **XtermLog.*XX*** (where *XX* is the **xterm** process ID. *XX* is created in the directory that launched **xterm** or the user's home directory in the case of a login window).

▰ -rw   Permits reverse wraparound, allowing the cursor to back up from the leftmost column of one line to the rightmost column of the previous line. This feature is very useful for editing long shell command lines. You can turn this option on and off from the Modes menu.

▰ -s   Permits *asynchronous scrolling*, which means that the screen need not be kept completely up-to-date while scrolling. This option increases **xterm** speed when network traffic is very high. The default is synchronous scrolling.

▰ -sb   Saves a number of lines (specified by the -sl option) as they scroll off the top of the window and displays a scroll bar for viewing those lines. You can turn this option on and off from the Modes menu.

▰ -sl *number*   Specifies the number of scrolled lines to save. The default is 64.

▰ -tn *name* Specifies the terminal type to be set in the TERM environment variable. This terminal type must exist in the **termcap** database and should have li# and co# entries.

▰ -ut Suppresses writing a record into the system log file **/etc/utmp**.

The following standard X Toolkit command-line arguments are commonly used with **xterm**:

▰ -bg *color* Specifies the window background color. The default is white.

▰ -bd *color* Specifies the window border color. The default is black.

▰ -bw *number* Specifies the width of the window border in pixels.

▰ -fg *color* Specifies the color for displaying text. The default is black.

▰ -fn *font* Specifies the font for displaying normal text. The default is fixed.

▰ -name *name* Specifies the application name under which resources are to be obtained, rather than the default executable filename. The name should not contain a period (.) or an asterisk (*).

▰ -title *string* Specifies the window title string, which the window manager can display at your choosing. The default title is the command line specified after the -e option, if any; otherwise, it's the application name.

▰ -rv Simulates reverse video by swapping the foreground and background colors.

▰ -geometry *geometry* Specifies the preferred size and position of the VT102 window in characters.

▰ -display *display* Specifies the X server to contact.

▰ -xrm *resourcestring* Specifies a resource string. This is especially useful for setting resources that do not have separate command-line options.

▰ -iconic Starts **xterm** as an icon, rather than as the normal window.

The xload Command

The **xload** client displays a periodically updating histogram of the system load average. Sample **xload** client output for an HP system appears in the center of Figure 13-9.

It enables the system administrator to examine system performance at any time. Therefore, the system administrator should master the **xload** command options. This command has the following syntax:

xload [-*options* ...]

FIGURE 13-9

Sample **xload** client output

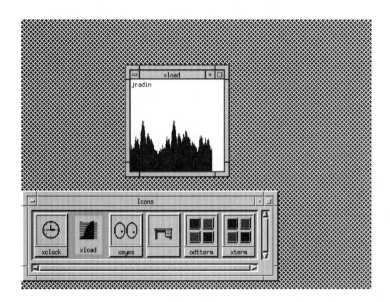

The **xload** program accepts all standard X Toolkit command-line options, along with the additional options listed here:

- -decay *number*   Specifies a number between 1 and 0 that determines how quickly **xload** responds to system load changes. Low values cause **xload** to respond quickly. Values near 1 provide a smoother curve. The default is 0.85.

- -scale *integer*   Specifies the minimum number of tick marks in the histogram, where one division represents one load average point. If the load exceeds this number, **xload** creates more divisions. The default is 1.

- -update *seconds*   Specifies the display update frequency in seconds. If you uncover the load average window (by moving windows with a window manager or by using the **xrefresh** program), the graph is also updated. The minimum time allowed between updates is 5 seconds, the default value.

- -hl *color*   Specifies the color for the label and scale lines.

The **xload** program commonly applies the following standard X Toolkit options:

- -bd *color*   Specifies the border color. The default is black.

- -bg *color*   Specifies the background color. The default is white.

- -bw *pixels*   Specifies the window border width in pixels. The default is 2.

- ▰ -fg *color*   Specifies the graph color. The default is black.

- ▰ -fn *fontname*   Specifies the font for displaying the name of the host whose load is being monitored. The default is the 6×10 pixel, fixed-width font.

- ▰ -rv   Simulates reverse video by swapping the foreground and background colors.

- ▰ -geometry *geometry*   Specifies the preferred window size and position.

- ▰ -display *display*   Specifies the X server to contact.

- ▰ -xrm *resourcestring*   Specifies a resource string. This option is especially useful for setting resources that do not have separate command-line options.

This program uses the Load widget in the X Toolkit. It understands all of the core resource names and classes, as well as the following:

- ▰ *width* (class *Width*)   Specifies the load average graph width.

- ▰ *height* (class *Height*)   Specifies the load average graph height.

- ▰ *decay* (class *Decay*)   Specifies how quickly **xload** responds to system load changes.

- ▰ *update* (class *Interval*)   Specifies the frequency in seconds of the load display refresh.

- ▰ *scale* (class *Scale*)   Specifies the initial number of ticks on the graph. The default is 1.

- ▰ *minScale* (class *Scale*)   Specifies the minimum number of ticks displayed. The default is 1.

- ▰ *foreground* (class *Foreground*)   Specifies the graph color. The default is black because the core background default is white.

- ▰ *highlight* (class *Foreground*)   Specifies the text and scale lines color. The default is the same as for the foreground resource.

- ▰ *label* (class *Label*)   Specifies the graph label. The default is the host name.

- ▰ *font* (class *Font*)   Specifies the label font. The default is fixed.

- ▰ *reverseVideo* (class *ReverseVideo*)   Specifies that the foreground and background should be reversed.

Note

This program requires the permission to open and read the special system file /dev/kmem. Sites that do not allow general access to this file should put xload in the same group as /dev/kmem and turn on the set-group-id-permission flag. When using reverse video, you must explicitly specify the border color.

The xclock Utility

The **xclock** client is an analog and digital clock for X. It has the following syntax:

xclock -*options*

The **xclock** program displays the time in analog or digital form. A sample analog clock for a SCO system appears in Figure 13-10. (The **xsetroot** client, which sets the background display pattern, is discussed later in this chapter.)

You can specify how often the time is updated. It accepts all of the standard X Toolkit command-line options, along with several additional options. The major options of interest to system administrators are listed below:

▧   -help   Prints a brief summary of options on the standard error.

▧   -analog   Specifies a conventional 12-hour clock face with tick marks and hands. This is the default.

▧   -digital   Specifies a 24-hour digital clock.

▧   -update *seconds*   Specifies the frequency (in seconds) of the clock display update. After being obscured, a clock is updated immediately upon exposure. A value of less than 30 seconds enables a second hand on the analog clock. The default is 60 seconds.

Consult a system manual for standard X Toolkit command-line options commonly used with **xclock**. The **Xdefaults** program uses the Clock widget in the X Toolkit. It understands all of the core resource names and classes, as well as several options described in the system manual.

The xbiff Command

The **xbiff** program informs users whether they have mail. It has the following syntax:

xbiff -*options*

The **xbiff** program displays a little image of a mailbox, as shown in Figure 13-11. When the mailbox is empty, the flag on the mailbox is down. When mail arrives, the flag goes up and the mailbox beeps.

The **xbiff** utility accepts all standard X Toolkit command-line options, along with the following options:

▧   -help   Prints a brief summary of the allowed options on the standard error.

▧   -update *seconds*   Specifies how frequently in seconds **xbiff** updates its display. If the mailbox is obscured and then exposed, it is updated immediately. The default is 30 seconds.

FIGURE 13-10

Sample **xclock** client output

FIGURE 13-11

Sample **xbiff** client output

◪   -file *filename* Specifies the file to be monitored. By default, **xbiff** watches **/usr/spool/mail/***username*, where *username* is your login name.

◪   -volume *percentage* Specifies how loud the bell should ring, as a percentage of the default, when new mail comes in.

Many standard X Toolkit command-line arguments are commonly used with **xbiff** including the following:

◪   -display *display* Specifies the X server to contact.

◪   -geometry *W×H+X+Y* Specifies the preferred size and position of the mailbox window. By default, the mailbox is 48 pixels wide, 48 pixels high and centered in the window.

◪   -bg *color* Specifies the color for the window background. The default is white.

See your system manual for other **xbiff** options and **.Xdefaults** file values.

The xsetroot Command

The **xsetroot** command sets root window parameters. It has the following syntax:

    xsetroot -*options*

The **xsetroot** command enables you to tailor the appearance of the background ("root") window. Spend some time trying out the **xsetroot** options, and then place your favorite selection in the X startup file. Figure 13-12 shows a standard X Window background pattern, while Figure 13-13 shows a proprietary Hewlett-Packard background pattern.

Specifying no options, or -def, resets the window to its default state. Specifying the -def option with other options, resets only the non-specified characteristics to the default state.

Only one of the background color or tile changing options (-solid, -gray, -bitmap, and -mod) can be specified at a given time. The following options are available:

◪   -help Prints a brief description of the allowable options.

◪   -def Resets unspecified attributes to the default values. (Restores the background to the familiar gray mesh and the cursor to the hollow X shape.)

◪   -cursor *cursorfile maskfile* Lets you change the pointer to any desired shape, provided that it is outside of any window. Cursor and mask files are bitmaps (little pictures) created with the **bitmap** program. If you are unfamiliar with masks, consider setting the mask file to all black.

FIGURE 13-12

A Standard X Window
background pattern

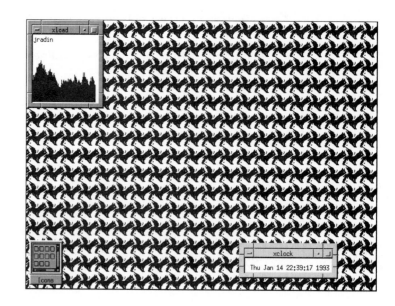

FIGURE 13-13

A Proprietary
(Hewlett-Packard) pattern

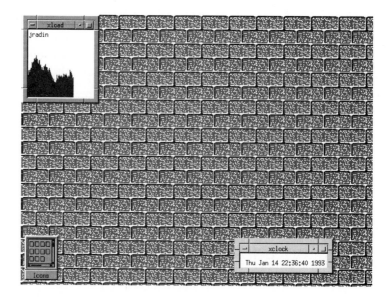

▰ *-cursorname* Lets you specify one of the built-in cursor fonts contained in the file **usr/include/x11/cursorfont.h.**

▰ -bitmap *filename* Specifies the **bitmap** in the designated file to set the window pattern. The background is composed of "tiles" defined by the **bitmap.**

▰ -mod *x y* Makes a plaid-like grid pattern on your screen. *x* and *y* are integers ranging from 1 to 16; 0 and negative numbers are taken as 1.

▰ -gray Makes the entire background gray, which some people feel is easier on the eyes.

▰ -fg *color* Sets the foreground to the designated color. Foreground and background colors are meaningful only when the -cursor, -bitmap, or -mod options are used.

▰ -bg *color* Sets the background to the designated color.

▰ -rv Exchanges the foreground and background colors. Normally the foreground color is black and the background color is white.

▰ -solid *color* Sets the window color to the specified value.

▰ -name *string* Sets the root window name to the designated string. There is no default value. This root window name enables the window manager to use a text representation when the window is iconified. You cannot iconify the root window.

▰ -display *display* Specifies the server.

A SCRIPT THAT CHANGES THE ROOT WINDOW BACKGROUND

The following script generates a different root window background for each day of the week. For example, on Saturday, the **wingdogs** image is displayed. The **setroot** command has been broken here to fit on the page, but must be coded to appear on a single line in programs and shell scripts.

```
#!/bin/csh
# @(#) set root window background script

if ( $TERM == xterm ) then
  set DAY = 'date | cut -c -3'
  echo "Today $DAY ..."
  switch ($DAY)
    case Sat:
      xsetroot -bitmap /usr/include/X11/bitmaps/wingdogs
      -fg black - bg white
```

```
          breaksw
          case Sun:
            xsetroot -bitmap /usr/include/X11/bitmaps/woman
            -fg black - bg white
          breaksw
          case Mon:
            xsetroot -bitmap /usr/include/X11/bitmaps/mensetmanus
            -fg black - bg white
          breaksw
          case Tue:
            xsetroot -bitmap /usr/include/X11/bitmaps/calculator
           -fg black - bg white
          breaksw
          case Wed:
            xsetroot -bitmap /usr/include/X11/bitmaps/xlogo64
            -fg black - bg white
          breaksw
          case Thu:
            xsetroot -bitmap /usr/include/X11/bitmaps/letters
            -fg black - bg white
          breaksw
          case Fri:
            xsetroot -bitmap /usr/include/X11/bitmaps/wide_weave
            -fg black - bg white
          breaksw
            default:
            echo wrong selection, check day abbreviation!
          breaksw
        endsw
        else
          echo this terminal is $TERM, not an xterm!
        endif
```

Font Management Clients

Font management clients provide various font services. The **xlsfonts** client, which lists the fonts matching a given pattern, is described next.

The xlsfonts Command

The **xlsfonts** command displays the server font list. It has the following syntax:

xlsfonts [-*options* ...] -fn *pattern*

The **xlsfonts** program lists the fonts that match the given pattern. The wildcard character "*" matches any sequence of characters (including none), and "?" matches any single character. If you do not specify a pattern, **xlsfonts** uses the "*" character. Quotes must surround the "*" and "?" characters to prevent them from being expanded by the shell.

This command includes the following options:

■   -fn *pattern*   Specifies the font name pattern.

■   -display *host*:dpy   Specifies the X server to contact.

■   -l   Generates a long listing for each font. This list can immobilize a single-threaded, non-preemptible server for a very long time.

■   -m   Indicates that long listings should include the minimum and maximum bounds of each font.

■   -C   Specifies multiple-column listings. This is the same as -n 0.

■   -1   Specifies single-column listings. This is the same as -n 1.

■   -w *width*   Specifies the width (in characters) that determines how many columns to print. The default is 79.

■   -n *columns*   Specifies the number of columns in the display output. By default, it attempts to fit as many columns of font names into the number of characters specified by -w width.

Many new font names in X11, Release 3 contain embedded spaces. You must surround these names with quotes. Some font names are long and difficult to type. These names may be shortened, but must be unique. For example, the following font name:

-adobe-helvetica-medium-r-normal—8-80-75-75-p-46-1508859-1

could be shortened as follows:

"*helvetica-medium-r-normal—8-80-75-75-p-46*"

as long as this shortened name would still be unique.

The wildcard character, "*" delineates the common portion of the font name.

The xlswins Command

The **xlswins** command displays the server window list. It has the following syntax:

xlswins [-*options* ...] [*windowid* ...]

This command lists the window tree. By default, it uses the root window as the starting point. Specify a given window or windows by coding the ID on the command line. To find out a window's ID, use the **xwininfo** client, presented previously.

This **xlswins** command allows the following options:

- ▉ -display *displayname*   Specifies the X server to contact.

- ▉ -l   Generates a long listing for each window. This listing includes the window's depth, its geometry relative to the parent window, and its location relative to the root window.

- ▉ -format *radix*   Specifies the radix to use when printing out window IDs. Allowable values are: hex, octal, and decimal. The default is hex. Hexadecimal numbers begin with 0x, octal numbers begin with 0, and decimal numbers print as is.

- ▉ -indent *number*   Specifies the number of spaces indented for each level in the window tree. The default is 2.

Chapter Summary

The X Window system has become a standard hardware-independent and netware-independent windowing system for developing both monochrome and color high-resolution graphical systems. It is the standard windowing system for Unix. At the time of this writing the most recent version is X11R5 (Version 11 Release 5). X Window systems run on a variety of common hardware devices. The output unit is a graphics screen, usually with at least VGA resolution. The most commonly used input devices are the keyboard and the mouse. The vast majority of workstation manufacturers actively support X Window systems. An increasingly popular alternative to a full-blown workstation is an X Terminal, a diskless graphical computer terminal that runs a single program, the X Window server program. X Window systems run on some large microcomputers.

The heart of the X Window philosophy is the client/server architecture. The client/server architecture is the X Window system model by which clients, or application programs, communicate with servers, or display units over a network. Networking protocols describe the format and order of data and control bytes that compose a message sent from one network point to another. X Window developers and system administrators need not know the networking protocol actually used.

Specialized software is needed to send appropriate data and control bytes from the client to the server and vice versa. Xlib functions provide the power of X protocol with much less pain. X Toolkit Intrinsics, also known as Xt Intrinsics, enable programmers to create and use standard on-screen building blocks called widgets, such as menus, scroll bars, buttons, and dialogue boxes. The uppermost programming level for X Window systems is proprietary. Each proprietary toolkit produces a trademark graphical user interface, enabling developers to create a series of applications with a standard look and feel. The OSF/Motif toolkit, often called Motif, is the most widely used X Window proprietary toolkit. Its major competitor is the Open Look graphical user interface.

The X Window system under Motif uses four configuration files: **.Xdefaults**, **.x11start** (the name may vary from system to system), **.mwmrc**, and **app-defaults/***. The **.Xdefaults** file specifies default appearance and behavior characteristics for clients. The **.x11start** file specifies the clients initiated when the X Window system starts. The **.mwmrc** file specifies menus and other objects associated with the OSF/Motif Window Manager (**mwm**). The **app-defaults/*** file is optional and includes application-specific configuration resources.

The X Display Manager   The **xdm** (X Display Manager) program manages both local and remote X displays. It should be invoked for users who wish to run X permanently on their display. The **xdm** provides services similar to **init**, **getty**, and **login** services on character terminals. These include prompting for logins and passwords, authenticating users, and running a session.

The **xdm** provides the initial user interface, and so has been designed for simplicity and ease of customization, with many options. The configuration file, in the *Xresource* format, provides extensive control of **xdm**. Some resources modify the behavior of **xdm** on all displays, while others modify its behavior on a single display.

The **Xstartup** file is typically a shell script. You should run it as root and be very careful about security. Use this file to store commands that make fake entries in **/etc/utmp**, mount users' home directories from file servers, display the message of the day, or abort the session if logins are not allowed. The **Xsession** command runs as the user's session. It runs with the permissions of the authorized user and employs several environment variables. The **Xreset** runs after the user session has terminated.

The mwm Window Manager   The **mwm** is an X11 client providing window management and some session management services. It includes functions facilitating user and programmer control of elements of window states such as placement, size, icon/normal display, and input focus ownership. Among its session management functions are stopping a client.

Default **mwm** window frames have distinct components with associated functions: title area, title bar, minimize button, maximize button, window menu button, and default window menu.

Icons are small graphic representations of windows. When properly used, icons reduce the clutter on the screen.

Other default behavior includes the input focus and window stacking. The input focus, also called the keyboard focus, is the window associated with the keyboard. Window stacking describes relationships among windows.

The following four sources may be used to build the mwm resource database, starting from the lowest: app-defaults/Mwm, RESOURCEMANAGER root window property or $HOME/.Xdefaults, XENVIRONMENT variable or $HOME/.X defaults-host, and mwm command-line options. This resource database provides three basic types of resources. Component appearance resources can control the appearance of window manager menus, feedback windows, client window frames, and icons. Specific appearance and behavior resources designate **mwm** features such as window management policies. Client-specific resources designate the icon and window frame appearance and behavior for individual clients or groups of clients.

X Window System Clients   X Window furnishes dozens of clients, application programs that perform many useful tasks. It is useful to regroup these clients into functional categories: initialization and configuration, window management, graphics functions, cut and paste, viewable services, and font management. Initialization and configuration clients start the X Window system and provide the tools to set it up to meet system default or individual needs. They include **xinit**, **xset**, and **xrdb**. Window management clients provide useful information about windows. Such clients include **xwininfo** and **xlswins**. Graphics functions clients provide graphical services to the system administrator and to users in general. They include **xpr**, **xwd**, and **xwud**. Viewable services clients provide system administrators and users with X emulation on selected terminals and other desktop facilities. They include **xman**, **xterm**, **xload**, **xclock**, **xbiff**, and **xsetroot**. This text does not include examples of cut and paste clients.

Unix System

- System Tuning

- A stat Script

- A sar Script

- A tune Script

- Troubleshooting

Administration Guide

CHAPTER 14

Tuning and Troubleshooting

As system administrator, you are responsible for running the Unix system. Among other duties, you must ensure that the system runs, and doesn't crawl, stumble, or sputter. This chapter presents system report commands that provide specific information on what the system is doing. You can then apply this information to tune the system, increasing productivity and user satisfaction. Perhaps the best news is that system administrators usually won't have to do much system tuning. However, they must be familiar with the process. The chapter includes two scripts for determining what the system is doing and another script for tuning the system. It concludes with an examination of several common system errors and how to deal with them.

SYSTEM TUNING

The system tuning process consists of two basic steps. First you determine exactly what is happening in the system by running special commands such as **pstat** and then you change the appropriate system parameters. It is essential that you be familiar with the system tuning process for the times that you will need to do so.

The Need for System Tuning

Upscale products such as high-performance cars must be tuned from time to time to obtain maximum performance. Unix does too. However, because system administrators have so many duties, and because the system tuning process takes the system out of use for a period of time, in general system administrators will not tune the system often. While it is a bit of an exaggeration, the familiar phrase "If it ain't broke, don't fix it" applies. Consider tuning the system in the following circumstances:

- ▟ **When you set up the initial system** As it comes out of the box, Unix is configured to meet general needs. Sites with special needs should change parameters to increase system efficiency. For example, sites with very large databases may increase the default number of file locks. On the other hand, sites that definitely do not require facilities such as UUCP might increase performance slightly by disabling them.

- ▟ **When you add system resources** Whenever you add a disk drive or a line printer, you must reconfigure the system to recognize the new unit. When you add memory, you should reconfigure the system to optimize its use.

- ▟ **If the system "always" runs slowly** Be careful before making changes; according to most users, the system is always running slowly.

- ▟ **If the system generates numerous errors** The final section of this chapter discusses system problems (including slow response time) and how to deal with them.

System Report Commands

The Unix system report commands are summarized in Table 14-1.

Command	Description
df	Reports the number of free disk blocks.
du	Summarizes disk usage.
nice	Changes scheduling priority for a specified command.
ps	Reports selective active process status.
pstat	Reports system information, such as inode table or process table.
sar	Reports on system activity, such as CPU utilization and buffer activity.
time	Prints elapsed time, system time, and command execution time.
timex	Reports process data and system activity, such as command execution time and accounting data.
uptime	Reports system activity, such as the time of day and the length of time that the system has been up.
vmstat	Reports paging and system statistics, such as the number of forks issued.
w	Displays information indicating who is on the system and what they are doing (BSD Unix only).
who	Lists who is on the system and other information, such as login time.

The ps Command

The **ps** command reports process status. It has the following syntax:

ps [*options*]

The **ps** command prints selected information about active processes. Entering **ps** without options describes processes associated with the current terminal. The default is a short listing containing process ID, terminal (tty) identifier, cumulative execution time, and the command name. The following major options may be used:

- ■   -e   Prints information about all processes.

- ■   -a   Prints information about all processes, except process group leaders and processes not associated with a terminal.

- ■   -f   Generates a full listing; **ps** tries to determine and print the process's original command name and arguments. If it cannot, it prints the short listing version of the command name within square brackets. A full listing contains more than a dozen column headings.

■ -l   Generates a long listing, including status, priority, location, and memory usage information for each process.

■ -t *tlist*   Restricts the listing to data describing processes associated with the terminals designated in *tlist*. The *tlist* is either a comma-delimited list of terminal identifiers or a list of terminal identifiers enclosed in double quotes and delimited by a comma and/or one or more spaces.

■ -p *plist*   Restricts the listing to data describing processes whose process ID numbers appear in *plist*, where *plist* has the same format as *tlist*.

■ -u *ulist*   Restricts the listing to data describing processes whose user ID numbers or login names appear in *ulist*, where *ulist* has the same format as *tlist*. The listing contains the numerical user ID unless the -f option is used, in which case the login name is printed.

■ -g *glist*   Restricts the listing to data describing processes whose process groups appear in *glist*, where *glist* has the same format as *tlist*.

■ -s swapdev   Uses the file **swapdev** in place of **/dev/swap**. This option is useful when examining a core file.

■ -n *namelist*   Specifies an alternate file *namelist* to **/unix**.

Display Columns   The headings and meanings of columns in a **ps** listing are given below. The letters f and l indicate the option (full or long) that causes the corresponding heading to appear; *all* means that the heading always appears. These options only determine the information provided for a process; they do not determine which processes will be listed. See the **man** utility (detailed in Appendix A) or your system manual for a description of column headings.

Note

The situation can change while ps is running; the picture it gives is only a close approximation of reality. Some data printed for defunct processes are irrelevant.

The pstat Command

The **pstat** command reports system information. It has the following syntax:

pstat [-aipf] [-u *ubase1 ubase2*] [-n *namelist*] [*file*]

The **pstat** command generates more detailed information than does the **ps** command. This information is found in system tables, by default contained in **/dev/mem** and **/dev/kmem**. However, the source file may be specified file. The required *namelist* is taken from **/unix**. Options are as follows:

◪   -a   Similar to -p, but describes all process slots.

◪   -i   Prints the inode table with these headings: LOC, the core location of this
     table entry; FLAGS, miscellaneous state variables encoded thus:

> L   Locked.
>
> U   Update time file system(F) must be corrected.
>
> A   Access time must be corrected.
>
> M   File system is mounted here.
>
> W   Wanted by another process (only if L flag is on).
>
> T   Contains a text file.
>
> C   Changed time must be corrected.
>
> CNT   Number of open file table entries for this inode.
>
> DEV   Major and minor device numbers of the file system in which this
> inode resides.
>
> INO   I-number within the device.
>
> MODE   Mode bits.
>
> NLK   Number of links to this inode.
>
> UID   User ID of owner.
>
> SIZ/DEV   Number of bytes in an ordinary file, or major and minor device
> of special file.

◪   -p   Prints process table for active processes. See the **man** utility or your system
     manual for a description of the column headings.

◪   -u *ubase1 ubase2*   Prints user process information. *ubase1* and *ubase2* are the
     physical page frame numbers of the process u-area. They may be obtained by
     using the long listing (-l option) of the **ps** command.

◪   -n *namelist*   Specifies an alternative file *namelist* to **/unix**.

◪   -f   Prints the open file table with these headings:

> LOC   The core location of this table entry.
>
> FLG   Miscellaneous state variables.
>
> R   Open for reading, W open for writing, and P pipe.
>
> CNT   Number of processes that know this open file.
>
> INO   The location of the inode table entry for this file.
>
> OFFS   The file offset; see **lseek**.

The sar Command

The **sar** command generates system activity reports. It has the following syntax:

sar [-ubdycwaqvmnprDSAC] [-o *file*] t [*n*]
sar [-ubdycwaqvmnprDSAC] [-s *time*]
  [-e *time*] [-i *sec*] [-f *file*]

The **sar** command samples cumulative activity counters in the operating system at *n* intervals of *t* seconds, where *t* should be 5 or greater. The -o option directs **sar** to save the samples in a binary format file. The default value of *n* is 1.

The **sar** command provides the following options to print data subsets:

▰   -u Reports CPU utilization (the default):

%usr Portion of time running in user mode; when used with -D, %sys is split into percent of time servicing requests from remote machines (%sys remote) and all other system time (%sys local).

%sys Portion of time running in system mode.

%wio Portion of time idle with some process waiting for block I/O.

%idle Portion of time otherwise idle.

▰   -b Reports buffer activity:

bread/s, bwrit/s Transfers per second of data between system buffers and disk or other block devices.

lread/s, lwrit/s Accesses of system buffers.

%rcache, %wcache Cache hit ratios (that is, 1-bread/lread) as a percentage.

pread/s, pwrit/s Transfers via raw (physical) device mechanism; when used with -D, buffer caching is reported for locally mounted remote resources.

▰   -d Reports activity for each block device, for example, disk or tape drive. The device specification *dsk* generally represents a disk drive. The device specification representing a tape drive is machine dependent. The activity data reported is as follows:

%busy, avque Portion of time the device was busy servicing a transfer request, average number of requests outstanding during that time.

r+w/s, blks/s Number of data transfers from or to device, number of bytes transferred in 512-byte units.

avwait, avserv Average time in milliseconds that transfer requests wait idly on queue and average time to be serviced (which, for disks, includes seek, rotational latency, and data transfer times).

◪ -n   Reports name cache statistics:

    c_hits, cmisses   Number of name cache hits and misses.

    hit%   The hit ratio as a percentage figure indicating the caching efficiency.

◪ -y   Reports TTY device activity:

    rawch/s, canch/s, outch/s   Input character rate, input character rate processed by canon, and output character rate.

    rcvin/s, xmtin/s, mdmin/s   Receive, transmit, and modem interrupt rates.

◪ -c   Reports system calls:

    scall/s   System calls of all types.

    sread/s, swrit/s, fork/s, exec/s   Specific system calls.

    rchar/s, wchar/s   Characters transferred by read and write system calls; when used with -D, the system calls are split into incoming, outgoing, and strictly local calls.

◪ -w   Reports system swapping and switching activity:

    swpin/s, swpot/s, bswin/s, bswot/s   Number of transfers and number of 512-byte units transferred for swapins and swapouts (including initial loading of some programs).

    pswch/s   Process switches.

◪ -a   Reports use of file access system routines.

    iget/s

    namei/s

    dirblk/s

    These figures monitor the frequency (per second) of Unix file system access.

◪ -q   Reports average queue length while occupied and percentage of time occupied:

    runq-sz, %runocc   Run queue of processes in memory and runnable.

    swpq-sz, %swpocc   Swap queue of processes swapped out but ready to run.

◪ -v   Reports status of process, inode, file tables:

    text-sz, proc-sz, inod-sz, file-sz, lock-sz   Entries/size for each table, evaluated once at sampling point.

    ov   Overflows that occur between sampling points for each table.

■ -m Reports message and semaphore activities: msg/s, sema/s, in primitives per second.

■ -p Reports paging activities:

> vflt/s Address translation page faults (valid page not in memory).
>
> pflt/s Page faults from protection errors (illegal access to page) or "copy-on-writes."
>
> pgfil/s vflt/s satisfied by page-in from file system.
>
> rclm/s Valid pages reclaimed for free list.

■ -r Reports unused memory pages and disk blocks:

> freemem Average pages available to user processes.
>
> freeswap Disk blocks available for process swapping.

■ -D Reports remote file sharing activity; when used in combination with -u, -b, or -c, it causes **sar** to produce the remote file-sharing version of the corresponding report. -Du is assumed when only -D is specified.

■ -S Reports server and request queue status:

> serv/lo-hi Average number of remote file-sharing servers on the system.
>
> request %busy Percentage of time receive descriptors are on the request queue, average number of receive descriptors waiting for service when queue is occupied (request avg lgth).
>
> server %avail Percentage of time there are idle servers.
>
> server avg avail Average number of idle servers when idle ones exist.

■ -A Reports all data.

■ -C Reports remote file-sharing buffer caching overhead:

> snd-inv/s Number of invalidation messages per second sent by your machine as a server.
>
> snd-msg/s Total outgoing RFS messages sent per second.
>
> rcv-inv/s Number of invalidation messages received from the remote server.
>
> rcv-msg/s Total number of incoming RFS messages received per second.
>
> dis-bread/s Number of buffer reads that would be eligible for caching if caching were not turned off; indicates the penalty of running uncached.
>
> blk-inv/s Number of buffers removed from the client cache.

The time Command

The **time** command generates clock times for a specified command. It has the following syntax:

time *command*

After the given command is executed, **time** prints the elapsed time, the system time, and the execution time. All times are reported in seconds.

The timex Command

The **timex** command reports process data and system activity. It has the following syntax:

timex [*options*] *command*

The **timex** command prints (in seconds) the elapsed time, user time, and system time spent in executing the specified command. In addition, process accounting data for the command and all its children can be listed or summarized, and total system activity during the execution interval can be reported.

Options are as follows:

- ■ -p Lists process-accounting records for the command and all its children. This option requires installed process-accounting software. The following suboptions are available:

- ■ -f Prints the fork/exec flag and system exit status columns.

- ■ -h Prints the fraction of total available CPU time consumed during process execution, instead of the mean memory size. This hog factor is computed as (total CPU time)/(elapsed time).

- ■ -k Prints total kcore-minutes, instead of memory size.

- ■ -m Prints mean core size (the default).

- ■ -r Prints the CPU factor defined as (user time/(system time + user time).

- ■ -t Prints separate system and user CPU times. The number of blocks read or written and the number of characters transferred are always reported.

- ■ -o Prints the total number of blocks read or written and total characters transferred by command and all its children. This option requires installed process accounting software.

- ■ -s Prints total system activity (not just that due to command) that occurred during command execution. All data items listed in **sar** are reported.

Process records associated with the command are selected from the accounting file **/usr/adm/pacct** by inference, since process genealogy is not available. Background processes having the same user ID, terminal ID, and execution time window will be spuriously included.

Here is a **timex** example:

```
timex -ops sleep 60
```

A terminal session of arbitrary complexity can be measured by timing a sub-shell:

```
timex -opskmt sh
```

The uptime Command

The **uptime** command displays information about system activity. It has the following syntax:

```
uptime
```

The **uptime** command prints the current time of day, the length of time the system has been up, and the number of users logged onto the system. On systems that maintain the necessary data, load averages are also shown. These load averages are the number of processes in the run queue averaged over 1, 5, and 15 minutes. All this information is also contained in the first line of the **w** command.

The df Command

The **df** command reports the number of free disk blocks. It has the following syntax:

```
df [-t] [-f] [-v -i] [file systems]
```

The **df** command examines the counts in the superblocks and then prints the number of free blocks and free inodes available for on-line file systems. The file systems parameter may be specified by device name (for example, **/dev/root**). If this parameter is not specified, the standard output provides statistics for all mounted file systems. The list of mounted file systems appears in **/etc/mnttab**.

Options include:

 -t Prints total allocated blocks and total free blocks.

 -f Prints only the actual count of blocks in the free list and not free inodes. With this option, **df** reports on raw devices.

▰ -v Prints the percent of blocks used, the number of blocks used, and the number of free 512-byte blocks.

▰ -i Prints the percent of inodes used, the number of inodes used, and the number of free inodes. The -v and -i options may be used together but may not be used with other **df** options. (-v and -i are SCO only.)

The **df** utility reports sizes in 512-byte blocks. It will report two blocks less free space, rather than one block, since the file uses one system block of 1024 bytes. The directory **/etc/fscmd.d/TYPE** contains programs for each file system type; **df** invokes the appropriate binary.

The du Command

The **du** command summarizes disk usage. It has the following syntax:

du [-afrsu] [*names*]

The **du** command gives the number of blocks contained in all files and directories recursively within each directory and file specified by the *names* argument. The block count includes indirect file blocks. If *names* is missing, the current directory is used. The **du** command is normally silent about directories that cannot be read, files that cannot be opened, and so on. The options are defined as follows:

▰ -s Generates only the grand total (for each specified *name*).

▰ -a Generates an entry for each file. If neither -s nor -a is coded, **du** generates an entry for each directory only.

▰ -f Displays file usage in the current file system only. It ignores directories containing mounted file systems.

▰ -u Ignores files with more than one link.

▰ -r Generates messages for directories that cannot be read and files that cannot be opened. A file with two or more links is only counted once.

Note

Unless the -a option is used, nondirectories given as arguments will not be listed. If there are too many distinct linked files, du will count the excess files more than once. Files with holes will cause an incorrect block count. This utility reports sizes in 512-byte blocks. The du command interprets one block from a 1024-byte block system as two of its own 512-byte blocks. Thus a 500-byte file will be interpreted as two blocks rather than one.

The vmstat Command

The **vmstat** command provides report paging and system statistics. It has the following syntax:

vmstat [-fs] [-n *namelist*] [-l *lines*] [*interval* [*count*]]

The **vmstat** command generates selected system statistics for processes, demand paging, and cpu and trap activity, as shown in Figure 14-1. Three report types are available:

- default A summary of the number of processes in various states, paging activity, system activity, and cpu cycle consumption.

- -f The Number of **fork**s done.

- -s A verbose listing of paging and trap activity. If no interval or count is specified, the totals since system bootup are displayed. If an interval is given, the number of events that occurred in the last *interval* seconds is shown. If no count is specified, this display is repeated every *interval* seconds. When a count is also specified, the information is displayed *count* times.

FIGURE 14-1

Output of the **vmstat**
command

```
 ┌─                              odtterm                              ▪ □
 │ JR: /usr/gproject/chp14 >> vmstat 3 19
 │
 │ PROCS      PAGING                                        SYSTEM  CPU
 │  r  b  w  frs dmd sw cch fil pft frp pos pif pis rso rsi  sy  cs  us su id
 │
 │  0 41  0 9368   0   0   0   0   0   0   0   0   0   0   0 505  10   1  3 96
 │  0 41  0 9368   1   1   1   0   0   0   0   0   0   0   0 766  28   5  8 87
 │  0 41  0 9352   1   0   0   3   5   2   0   0   0   0   0 487  26   3  8 89
 │  0 41  0 9352   1   0   2   1   5   0   0   0   0   0   0 549  16   2  6 92
 │  0 41  0 9352   1   0   2   1   5   0   0   0   0   0   0 549  15   0  5 95
 │  0 41  0 9352   0   0   0   0   0   0   0   0   0   0   0 517  10   1  3 96
 │  0 42  0 9352   1   0   0   2   3   0   0   0   0   0   0 514  18   1  7 92
 │  0 46  0 9250   3   0   0   8  15  14   1   0   0   3   0 633  64   8 26 66
 │  0 46  0 9250   0   0   0   0   0   0   0   0   0   0   0 574  12   2  4 94
 │  0 46  0 9250   0   0   0   0   0   0   0   0   0   0   0 459   9   1  3 96
 │  0 46  0 9250   0   0   0   0   0   0   0   0   0   0   0 581  11   0  4 96
 │  0 46  0 9250   0   0   0   0   0   0   0   0   0   0   0 487  10   1  5 94
 │  0 46  0 9250   0   0   0   0   0   0   0   0   0   0   0 517  10   1  3 96
 │  0 41  0 9250   0   0   0   0   2   0   0   0   0   0   0 481  14   4  5 91
 │  0 41  0 9250   1   0   0   3   5   0   0   0   0   0   0 547  16   2  6 92
 │  0 41  0 9250   0   0   0   0   0   0   0   0   0   0   0 580  10   0  4 96
 │  0 41  0 9250   0   0   0   0   0   0   0   0   0   0   0 453   9   0  3 97
 │  0 41  0 9250   1   0   2   1   5   0   0   0   0   0   0 548  14   2  4 94
 │  0 41  0 9250   0   0   0   0   0   0   0   0   0   0   0 451   9   1  3 96
 │ JR: /usr/gproject/chp14 >> ▮
 └─
```

The -f and -s reports are a series of lines of the form: number description, which means that number of the items described by description happened (either since boot or in the last interval seconds, as appropriate). These reports should be self-explanatory.

Other flags that may be specified include the following:

- ◪ -n *namelist* Specifies an alternative symbol table to **/unix**.

- ◪ -l *lines* For the default display, repeat the header every *lines* reports. (The default is 20.)

The fields in the default report are as follows:

- ◪ procs The number of processes, which are r, in the run queue; b, blocked waiting for resources; and w, swapped out. These values always reflect the current situation, even if the totals since boot are being displayed.

- ◪ paging Reports on the demand paging system performance. Unless the totals since boot are displayed, this information is averaged over the proceeding interval seconds.

    frs Free swap space.

    dmd Demand zero and demand fill pages.

    sw Pages on swap.

    cch Pages in cache.

    fil Pages on file.

    pft Protection faults.

    frp Pages freed.

    pos Processes swapped out successfully.

    pif Processes swapped out unsuccessfully.

    rso Regions swapped out.

    rsi Regions swapped in.

- ◪ system Reports on the general system activity. Unless the totals since boot are shown, these figures are averaged over the last *interval* seconds:

    sy Number of system calls.

    cs Number of context switches.

    cpu Percentage of cpu cycles spent in various operating modes.

    us User, su System, and id Idle This information is not available on some systems.

The nice Command

The **nice** command changes the scheduling priority for a specified command. It has the following syntax:

nice [-*increment*] *command* [*arguments*]

The **nice** command causes a specified command to execute at a different scheduling priority than usual. Each process has a **nice** value used in calculating its priority, ranging from 0 to 39; the higher the number, the lower the priority. The default **nice** value is 20. The **nice** command sets the **nice** value to 20 plus the *increment*. The default *increment* is 10.

The superuser may increase command priority by using a double negative increment. For example, an argument of --8 decrements the default value and generates a **nice** value of 12. Users cannot give their jobs a higher priority.

The **nice** command returns the *command* exit status. A calculated **nice** value greater than 39 is set to 39. A calculated **nice** value less than 0 is set to 0.

Note

This description of nice applies only to programs run under the Bourne Shell. The C Shell has its own nice command, documented in Appendix C.

The who Command

The **who** command lists who is on the system. It has the following syntax:

who [-uATHldtasqbrp] [*file*]

The **who** can list the user's name, terminal line, login time, and the elapsed time since activity occurred on the line. It also lists the process ID of the command interpreter (shell) for each current user. The **/etc/inittab** file provides information for the Comments column, and the **/etc/utmp** provides the other information. The specified file is usually **/etc/wtmp**, which contains a history of all logins since the file was last created. This command with option -a (all) is shown in Figure 14-2.

Except for the default -s option, the general format for output entries is shown here:

name [*state*] *line time activity pid* [*comment*] [*exit*]

The major options are as follows:

- -u Lists only currently logged-in users. The *name* is the user's login name. The *line* is the name of the line as found in the directory **/dev**. The *time* is the time that the user logged in. The *activity* is the number of hours and minutes since activity last occurred on that particular line. A dot (.) indicates that the terminal has seen activity in the last minute and is therefore current. If more than twenty-four hours have elapsed or the line has not been used since boot time, the entry is marked old. This field helps determine whether a person is working

FIGURE 14-2

Output of the **who** -a command

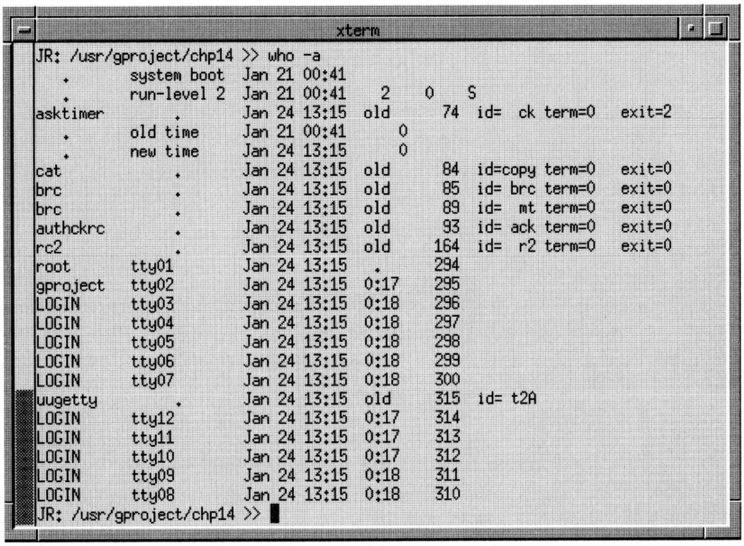

```
                                              xterm
JR: /usr/gproject/chp14 >> who -a
           .      system boot  Jan 21 00:41
           .      run-level 2  Jan 21 00:41     2    0    S
asktimer          .            Jan 24 13:15  old       74  id= ck term=0  exit=2
           .      old time     Jan 21 00:41        0
           .      new time     Jan 24 13:15        0
cat               .            Jan 24 13:15  old       84  id=copy term=0  exit=0
brc               .            Jan 24 13:15  old       85  id= brc term=0  exit=0
brc               .            Jan 24 13:15  old       89  id= mt term=0  exit=0
authckrc          .            Jan 24 13:15  old       93  id= ack term=0  exit=0
rc2               .            Jan 24 13:15  old      164  id= r2 term=0  exit=0
root       tty01              Jan 24 13:15    .      294
gproject   tty02              Jan 24 13:15   0:17   295
LOGIN      tty03              Jan 24 13:15   0:18   296
LOGIN      tty04              Jan 24 13:15   0:18   297
LOGIN      tty05              Jan 24 13:15   0:18   298
LOGIN      tty06              Jan 24 13:15   0:18   299
LOGIN      tty07              Jan 24 13:15   0:18   300
uugetty           .            Jan 24 13:15  old      315  id= t2A
LOGIN      tty12              Jan 24 13:15   0:17   314
LOGIN      tty11              Jan 24 13:15   0:17   313
LOGIN      tty10              Jan 24 13:15   0:17   312
LOGIN      tty09              Jan 24 13:15   0:18   311
LOGIN      tty08              Jan 24 13:15   0:18   310
JR: /usr/gproject/chp14 >>
```

at the terminal. The *pid* is the user's shell process ID. The *comment* is the comment field, containing information such as the terminal location, the telephone number, the terminal type (hard-wired, for example).

- -A Displays Unix accounting information.

- -T The same as the -u option, but also prints the terminal line state. A plus (+) indicates that the terminal is writable by anyone; a minus (-) indicates the contrary. Root can write to all lines with a plus or a minus in the *state* field. A question mark (?) indicates a bad line.

- -q (quick) Displays only the names and the number of users currently logged on. When this option is used, all other options are ignored.

- -d Displays all expired processes that have not been respawned by **init**. The *exit* field appears for dead processes and contains the termination and exit values (as returned by **wait**) of the dead process. This can be useful in determining why a process terminated.

- -t Indicates the last change to the system clock by root (via the **date** command).

- -a Processes the **/etc/utmp** file or the named file with all options turned on.

- -s This default option lists only the *name, line,* and *time* fields.

- -p Lists any other currently active process that has been previously spawned by **init**. The *name* field specifies the program executed by **init** as found in

/etc/inittab. The *state, line,* and *idle* fields have no meaning. The *comment* field shows the *id* field of the line from /etc/inittab, which spawned this process.

  -b   Indicates the time and date of the last reboot.

  -r   Indicates the current run level of the **init** process. It also generates the process termination status, process id, and process exit status (see **utmp**) with the idle, pid, and comment headings, respectively.

The w Command

The **w** command (BSD Unix) displays information about who is on the system and their activities. It has the following syntax:

   w [-hlqtw] [-n *namelist*] [-s swapdev] [-u utmpfile] [*users...*]

The **w** command prints a summary of current system activity, including what each user is doing. The heading line shows the current time of day, how long the system has been up, and the number of users logged onto the system. It also shows load averages, when available. Recall that load averages are the number of processes in the run queue averaged over 1, 5, and 15 minutes.

The options are:

  -h   Don't print the heading or title lines.

  -l   Long format (default): The **w** command outputs each user's login name, the terminal or pseudo terminal in use, the time that the user logged onto the system, the number of minutes the user has been idle (how much time has expired since the user last typed anything), the CPU time used by all processes and their children attached to the terminal, the CPU time used by the currently active process, and the name and arguments of the currently active process.

  -q   Quick format: The **w** command outputs each user's login name, the terminal or pseudo terminal currently in use, the number of minutes the user has been idle, and the name of the currently active process.

  -t   Prints only the heading line (equivalent to **uptime**).

  -w   Prints both the heading line and the summary of users.

  -n*namelist*   Specifies an alternative file *namelist* to /unix.

  -swapdev   Uses the file **swapdev** in place of /dev/swap. This is useful when examining a core file.

  -utmpfile   The file **utmpfile** is used instead of /etc/utmp as a record of who is currently logged in. If any users are given, the user summary is limited to those users.

System Parameters

Unix enables technically proficient system administrators to increase system performance by modifying special values known as *system parameters*. Sometimes, such as when you add a disk drive to the system, one or more parameters must be changed. In most cases, however, the system administrator need not change system parameters.

The optimal settings for system parameters are hardware dependent and a function of the installation's specific processing activity and goals. Parameter settings for top-security systems differ from those for systems that value speed of response. System parameters are interdependent. Sometimes the dependency is explicit; parameter X must be greater than parameter Y. In many cases the relationship is implicit, and may not even be documented. Testing the effect of parameter changes requires time, and a representative job mix. Benchmarking software is available for many Unix implementations, but must be used with care.

If you decide to go ahead with parameter modifications, and sometimes you must, two principles are key:

1. Make backups, using the **cp** command and not the **mv** command.

2. Keep a log book of parameter changes and their effects.

A properly designed and maintained log book is useful for the system administrator, trainees, technical personnel, and installation management ("I made all these changes and system performance is still inadequate, we really need another hard disk").

The specific tunable parameters available, and the file that contains them, differ from one Unix implementation to another. For example, SCO Unix offers 14 categories of tunable system parameters, including disks and buffers; files, inodes, and file systems; processes, memory management, and swapping; clock; shared data; STREAMS data; and event queues and devices. Consult your system manual for a discussion of the specific tunable system parameters available on your Unix implementation. Remember, you may be required to modify some parameters when modifying the system configuration.

The exact steps required to change a kernel parameter may vary from one version of Unix to another. Some implementations, such as SCO Unix, provide a menu-driven utility to smooth the process. The following section introduces representative Unix system parameters; the categories and names may differ from implementation to implementation. Consult your system manuals.

Disks and Buffers

The NDISK parameter indicates the number of disk drives attached to the system. This parameter must be reset when the number of disk drives is modified.

The NBUF parameter specifies the number of system buffers allocated at boot time. These buffers form a cache. This parameter is usually set to a value between 100 and 600. The **sar** -b command reports on buffer activity. The cache hit ratios %rcache and %wcache indicate the system buffering effectiveness.

Files, Inodes, and File Systems

Recall from Chapter 1 that an inode (short for information node) for a given file indicates the file owner, size, type, permissions (who is allowed to access the file and restrictions on this file access), and the list of the physical disk blocks that compose the file. The NINODE parameter specifies the number of inode table entries to allocate. The default value is 300, and values usually range from 100 to 400.

Processes, Memory Management, and Swapping

Swapping is the procedure by which Unix "makes room" in central memory for a given process by removing another process from memory. Inefficient swapping degrades system performance. The MAXSC parameter specifies the maximum number of pages swapped out in a single operation. Its default value is 1.

Clock

The TIMEZONE parameter is referred to in the **ctime** system call. Remember, Unix is a worldwide system.

Shared Data

These parameters are associated with interprocess communication shared memory. The SHMSEG parameter specifies the number of attached shared-memory segments per process. The default value is 6, and the maximum value is 15.

STREAMS Data

STREAMS is a network protocol developed by AT&T. This protocol may be used for the X Window System. The NQUEUE parameter is the number of STREAMS queues to be configured. Because queues are always allocated in pairs, this parameter value should be even.

Event Queues and Devices

Event queues are used in the X Window System. The EVQUEUES parameter specifies the maximum number of open event queues in the system.

A stat SCRIPT

This Bourne shell script applies the **pstat** and **vmstat** commands to monitor the system, prior to any tuning. This script does not require root permission; it does not write any system files, and cannot damage the system. However, for both security and performance reasons, its use should be restricted to those who need the information it generates. The **vmstat** results may be redirected to a file. The first three lines specify the Bourne shell interpreter, generate a short description of the script, and set the *log_ name* variable.

```
#!/bin/sh
# @(#) system status script
logname = 'whoami'
```

The following five lines define locations for your system administration scripts, menus, and log files. If necessary, change these definitions.

```
VMMENU=/usr/$log_name/scripts/vmstat_menu
PMENU=/usr/$log_name/scripts/pstat_menu
STATMENU=/usr/$log_name/scripts/stat_menu
VMSTATFILE=/usr/$log_name/scripts/vmstat.sav
PSTATFILE=/usr/$log_name/scripts/pstat.sav
```

The following code prompts the user to enter the desired **stat** name option. If no option is entered, the script terminates with an error message.

```
cat $STATMENU | more
# on System V you may use pg instead of more
# See menu at end of script
while
  echo "Please enter Stat Name (vV)mstat/(pP)stat: \c"
  read answer
do
  case $answer in
    [vV]*)
        echo "\nExecuting VMSTAT Case ...\n"
        def=0
```

The following code prompts the user to enter the desired option. If no option is entered, the script terminates with an error message.

```
        cat $VMMENU | more
# On system V, you may use pg instead of more
# See menu at end of script
        while
          echo "Please enter Option: \c"
          read option
          do
            case "$option" in
              [f]*)
                sflag=f
              break
              ;;
              [s]*)
                sflag=s
              break
              ;;
              [n]*)
                flag=n
                space=" "
                echo "Enter file as an alternative symbol table
                      (CR for /unix)?  \c"
                read namelist
                if [ -n "$namelist" ]
                then
                  echo "File Specified: $namelist"
                else
                  namelist=/unix
                  echo "No File Specified, using default:
                        $namelist"
                fi
                sflag=$flag$space$namelist
              break
              ;;
              [l]*)
                flag=l
                space=" "
                echo "Number of lines reports to repeat
                      the header (CR for 20)?  \c"
                read lines
                if [ -n "$lines" ]
                then
```

```
            echo "Lines Specified: $lines"
          else
            lines=20
            echo "No Lines Specified, using default:
                  $lines"
          fi
          sflag=$flag$space$lines
        break
        ;;
        [a]*)
          def=1
          break
        ;;
        [q]*)
          sflag=q
          break
        ;;
        *)
          echo "No Valid Option specied ...\n"
          echo "Please, try again!"
        ;;
    esac
done
if [ "$sflag" = "q" ]
then
  echo "\nQUIT Option - Exiting ..."
  exit 0
fi

echo "OK to report paging and
      system statistics? (y/n) \c"
read vmans
case $vmans in
  [yY]*)
    echo "Report Paging and
          System Statistics ..."
    echo "Please enter interval in seconds  \c"
    read nsec
    if [ -n "$nsec" ]
    then
      echo "Interval Specified: $nsec second(s)"
    else
      nsec=1
      echo "No Interval Specified, using default:
```

```
                    $nsec second"
        fi
        echo "Please enter count [time(s) to display]
                ?   \c"
        read count
        if [ -n "$count" ]
        then
          echo "Count Specified: $count time(s)"
        else
          count=10
          echo "No Count Specified, using default:
                $count times"
        fi
        echo "VMSTAT: option $sflag interval
        $nsec count $count ... "
        echo "Is it OK to save data to file
                $VMSTATFILE? (y/n) \c"
        read res
        case $res in
          [yY]*)
            if [ "$def" = "0" ]
            then
              vmstat -$sflag $nsec $count > $VMSTATFILE
            else
              vmstat $nsec $count > $VMSTATFILE
            fi
          break
          ;;
          [nN]*)
            if [ "$def" = "0" ]
            then
              vmstat -$sflag $nsec $count
            else
              vmstat $nsec $count
            fi
          break
          ;;
          *)
            echo "Please enter 'y' or 'n' \n"
          break
          ;;
        esac
break
;;
```

```
        [nN]*)
          echo "No Report Paging and System
                  Statistics Selected ..."
          echo "Removing $VMSTATFILE ...\n"
          rm -f $VMSTATFILE
        break
        ;;
        *)
          echo "Please enter 'y' or 'n' \n"
        ;;
      esac
      ;;
      [pP]*)
        echo "\nExecuting PSTAT Case ...\n"

        cat $PMENU | more
# On System V you may use pg instead of more
# See menu at end of script
```

The following code prompts the user to enter an option. If no option is entered, the user will be asked to try again.

```
      while
        echo "Please enter Option: \c"
        read option
      do
        case "$option" in
          [a]*)
            lflag=a
          break
          ;;
          [i]*)
            lflag=i
          break
          ;;
          [p]*)
            lflag=p
            break
          ;;
          [n]*)
            flag=n
            space=" "
            echo "Enter file as an alternative symbol
                    table (CR for /unix)?  \c"
```

```
          read namelist
          if [ -n "$namelist" ]
          then
            echo "File Specified: $namelist"
          else
            namelist=/unix
            echo "No File Specified, using default:
                  $namelist"
          fi
          lflag=$flag$space$namelist
        break
        ;;
        [f]*)
          lflag=f
          break
        ;;
        [q]*)
          lflag=q
          break
        ;;
        *)
          echo "No Valid Option specified ...\n"
          echo "Please, try again!"
        ;;
    esac
done

if [ "$lflag" = "q" ]
then
  echo "\nQUIT Option - Exiting ..."
  exit 0
fi

echo "OK to report system information? (y/n) \c"
read pans
case $pans in
  [yY]*)
    echo "Report System Information ..."
    echo "PSTAT: option $lflag ... "
    echo "Is it OK to save data to file
          $PSTATFILE? (y/n) \c"
    read res
    case $res in
      [yY]*)
```

```
                pstat -$lflag  > $PSTATFILE
            break
            ;;
            [nN]*)
                pstat -$lflag
            break
            ;;
            *)
                echo "Please enter 'y' or 'n' \n"
            break
            ;;
        esac
        break
        ;;
    [nN]*)
        echo "No Report System
                Information Selected ..."
        echo "Removing $PSTATFILE ...\n"
        rm -f $PSTATFILE
    break
    ;;
    *)
        echo "Please enter 'y' or 'n' \n"
    ;;

esac
;;
[qQ]*)
    echo "Exiting ...\n"
    exit 0
;;
*)
    echo "No Valid Option specified ...\n"
    echo "Please, try again!"
;;
esac
done
```

The **stat** menu is shown here:

q	Quit Menu
v	vmstat (paging/system statistics)
p	pstat (system information)

The **vmstat** menu appears below:

q	Quit Menu (no report)
a	Processes, Paging, System and CPU Activity
f	Number of Forks
s	Paging (listing) and Trap Activity
n	Namelist
l	Lines (default 20)

The **pstat** menu appears below:

q	Quit Menu
a	Process Slots Description
i	Inode Table Printing
p	Process Table Printing
n	Namelist

A sar SCRIPT

This **sar** Bourne shell script allows the system administrator using root permission to generate a system activity report using the **sar** command. Other users may generate a local activity report. The generated binary output files may be analyzed by technical specialists to find out in detail what is happening prior to tuning the system. Among the available information is buffer activity (-b), CPU utilization (-u), process throughput (-q), system tables (-v), and swapping activity (-w).

The first three lines specify the Bourne shell interpreter, generate a short description of the script, and set the *log_ name* variable.

```
#!/bin/sh
# @(#) system activity report script
log_name = 'whoami'
```

The following two lines define locations for your system administration scripts, menus, and log file. If necessary, change these definitions.

```
OSAR=/usr/$log_name/scripts/sar_menu
SFILE=/usr/$log_name/scripts/sar.sav
```

The following code checks that the person who runs this script has superuser permission. If not, the script reporting on local files is executed.

```
if [ $log_name = "root" ]
then
  DSAR=/usr/adm/sa
  echo "\nSuperuser(root)! Executing a system script ...\n"
  while
    echo "Do you want to see SAR available
          daily data files [y/n]: \c"
    read answer
    do
      case "$answer" in
        [yY]*)
          echo "Displaying ..."
          ls -al $DSAR | more
        break
        ;;
        [nN]*)
          echo "Continue ...\n"
        break
        ;;
      *)
        echo "Please enter 'y' or 'n' \n"
      ;;
    esac
  done
```

The following code prompts the system administrator to enter the filename. If no name is entered, the script terminates with an error message. The following files require root permission (system administrator), as shown in Figure 14-3. The filenames in the **/usr/adm/sa** directory indicate the day of the month, but do not indicate the month. These files do not appear in the test version of the script.

```
while
  echo "Please enter Filename [sa]01-30: \c"
  read saname
  do
    case "$saname" in
      [sa]*)
      break
      ;;
      [01-30]*)
        pre=sa
        saname=$pre$saname
```

```
        break
        ;;
        *)
          echo "No Valid Option specified ...\n"
          echo "Please, try again!"
        ;;

    esac
done

if file='find $DSAR -name $saname 2>/dev/null'
then
  echo "Name $saname Found in the directory: $DSAR\n"
  echo "Continue ...\n"
else
  echo "Name $saname Not Found in the directory: $DSAR\n"
  echo "Please, Try Again. Exiting ...\n"
  exit 2
fi

cat $OSAR | more
# on System V you may use pg instead of more
```

FIGURE 14-3

Files generated by
sar commands

```
ROOT: /usr/adm/sa >> l
total 174
drwxr-xr-x   2 adm      bin        448 Jan 31 18:52 .
drwxr-xr-x   5 bin      bin        176 Dec 16 19:17 ..
-rw-------   1 root     sys        612 Jan 12 00:00 sa12
-rw-------   1 root     sys       3592 Jan 13 23:00 sa13
-rw-------   1 root     sys       2996 Jan 14 22:00 sa14
-rw-------   1 root     sys       3592 Jan 15 23:00 sa15
-rw-------   1 root     sys       1208 Jan 16 01:00 sa16
-rw-------   1 root     sys       2400 Jan 17 11:00 sa17
-rw-------   1 root     sys       5976 Jan 18 23:00 sa18
-rw-------   1 root     sys       1804 Dec 19 15:00 sa19
-rw-------   1 root     sys       3592 Jan 20 23:32 sa20
-rw-------   1 root     sys        612 Jan 21 00:00 sa21
-rw-------   1 root     sys       3592 Dec 23 23:00 sa23
-rw-------   1 root     sys       5380 Jan 24 23:04 sa24
-rw-------   1 root     sys       2996 Jan 25 23:00 sa25
-rw-------   1 root     sys       3592 Jan 26 23:31 sa26
-rw-------   1 root     sys      11936 Dec 27 22:00 sa27
-rw-------   1 root     sys      13724 Dec 28 23:00 sa28
-rw-------   1 root     sys       3592 Dec 29 23:40 sa29
-rw-------   1 root     sys       5976 Jan 30 23:00 sa30
ROOT: /usr/adm/sa >>
```

The following code prompts the system administrator to enter the option. If no option is entered, the script terminates with an error message.

```
while
   echo "Please enter Option: \c"
   read option
do
   case "$option" in
     [u]*)
        sflag=u
     break
     ;;
     [b]*)
        sflag=b
     break
     ;;
     [d]*)
        sflag=d
     break
     ;;
     [n]*)
        sflag=n
     break
     ;;
     [y]*)
        sflag=y
     break
     ;;
     [c]*)
        sflag=c
     break
     ;;
     [w]*)
        sflag=w
     break
     ;;
     [a]*)
        sflag=a
     break
     ;;
     [q]*)
        sflag=q
     break
     ;;
```

```
      [v]*)
        sflag=v
      break
      ;;
      [m]*)
        sflag=m
      break
      ;;
      [p]*)
        sflag=p
      break
      ;;
      [r]*)
        sflag=r
      break
      ;;
      [D]*)
        sflag=D
      break
      ;;
      [S]*)
        sflag=S
      break
      ;;
      [C]*)
        sflag=C
      break
      ;;
      [A]*)
        sflag=A
      break
      ;;
      [Q]*)
        sflag=Q
      break
      ;;
      *)
          echo "No Valid Option specified ...\n"
          echo "Please, try again!"
      ;;
    esac
done
if [ "$sflag" = "Q" ]
then
```

```
      echo "\nQUIT Option - Exiting ..."
      exit 0
fi

echo "OK to review System Activities from the
        System file $saname?(y/n) \c"
read ans
case $ans in
   [yY]*)
      echo "Review SAR from the System file $saname"
      echo "with option set to $sflag"
      sar -$sflag -f $DSAR/$saname
   break
   ;;
   [nN]*)
      echo "\nOption for SAR  is now set to $sflag"
      echo "OK to review System Activity from the
            local file $SFILE?(y/n) \c"
      read local
      case $local in
         [yY]*)
           if file='ls $SFILE'
           then
             echo "Review SAR from the local file $SFILE"
             echo "with option set to $sflag"
             sar -$sflag -f $SFILE
           else
             echo "File $SFILE Not Found\n"
           fi
           break
             ;;
         [nN]*)
           echo "No file selected ...\n"
         break
         ;;
         *)
           echo "Please enter 'y' or 'n' \n"
         ;;
      esac
      break
      ;;
      *)
        echo "Please enter 'y' or 'n' \n"
      ;;
```

```
esac

nsec30=30
echo "OK to generate System Activity Report(SAR)?(y/n) \c"
read anse
case $anse in
  [yY]*)
    echo "Generating
          System Activity Report(SAR) ...\n"
    echo "For how many minutes?  \c"
    read nmin
    if [ -n "$nmin" ]
    then
      echo "Period Specified: $nmin minute(s)"
    else
      nmin=1
      echo "No Period Specified, using default: $nmin minute"
    fi
    echo "Is it OK to save data to file $SFILE? (y/n) \c"
    read res
    case $res in
      [yY]*)
        sar -o $SFILE $nsec30 $nmin
        break
        ;;
      [nN]*)
        sar $nsec30 $nmin
        break
        ;;
      *)
        echo "Please enter 'y' or 'n' \n"
        break
        ;;
    esac
    break
    ;;
  [nN]*)
    echo "Removing $SFILE, Exiting ...\n"
    rm -f $SFILE
    exit 0
    ;;
  *)
    echo "Please enter 'y' or 'n' \n"
    ;;
```

```
      esac
else
  echo "\nNot a Superuser(root), but $log_name! Reporting on
  local files ...\n"

  echo "SAR Options:"
  cat $OSAR | more
# on System V you may use pg instead of more
  while
    echo "Please enter Option: \c"
    read option
    do
      case "$option" in
        [u]*)
          lflag=u
        break
        ;;
        [b]*)
        lflag=b
      break
      ;;
      [d]*)
        lflag=d
      break
      ;;
      [n]*)
        lflag=n
      break
      ;;
      [y]*)
        lflag=y
      break
      ;;
      [c]*)
        lflag=c
      break
      ;;
      [w]*)
        lflag=w
      break
      ;;
      [a]*)
        lflag=a
      break
```

```
;;
[q]*)
  lflag=q
break
;;
[v]*)
  lflag=v
break
;;
[m]*)
  lflag=m
break
;;
[p]*)
  lflag=p
break
;;
[r]*)
  lflag=r
break
;;
[D]*)
  lflag=D
break
;;
[S]*)
  lflag=S
break
;;
[C]*)
  lflag=C
break
;;
[A]*)
  lflag=A
break
;;
[Q]*)
  lflag=Q
break
;;
*)
    echo "No Valid Option specified ...\n"
    echo "Please, try again!"
```

```
      ;;
   esac
done

if [ "$1flag" = "Q" ]
then
   echo "\nQUIT Option - Exiting ..."
   exit 0
fi

echo "OK to review System Activity from the
      local file $SFILE?(y/n) \c"
read local
case $local in
   [yY]*)
     if file='ls $SFILE'
     then
       echo "Review SAR from the local file $SFILE"
       echo "with option set to $1flag"
       sar -$1flag -f $SFILE
     else
       echo "File $SFILE Not Found\n"
     fi
   break
   ;;
   [nN]*)
     echo "No file selected ...\n"
   break
   ;;
   *)
     echo "Please enter 'y' or 'n' \n"
   ;;
esac

nsec30=30
echo "OK to generate System Activity Report(SAR)?(y/n) \c"
read anse
case $anse in
   [yY]*)
     echo "Generating
           System Activity Report(SAR) ...\n"
     echo "For how many minutes? \c"
     read nmin
     if [ -n "$nmin" ]
```

```
        then
          echo "Period Specified: $nmin minute(s)"
        else
          nmin=1
          echo "No Period Specified,
                using default: $nmin minute"
        fi
          echo "Is it OK to save data to file $SFILE? (y/n) \c"
          read res
          case $res in
            [yY]*)
              sar -o $SFILE $nsec30 $nmin
            break
            ;;
            [nN]*)
              sar $nsec30 $nmin
            break
            ;;
            *)
              echo "Please enter 'y' or 'n' \n"
            break
            ;;
          esac
        break
        ;;
        [nN]*)
          echo "Removing $SFILE, Exiting ...\n"
          rm -f $SFILE
          exit 0
        ;;
        *)
          echo "Please enter 'y' or 'n' \n"
        ;;
      esac
    fi
```

A tune SCRIPT

The following **tune** Bourne shell script sets system tuning parameters, saving the previous tuning parameters. This script, based on SCO Unix, can change a single parameter, several parameters, or sets of parameters prior to rebuilding the kernel. Because the kernel rebuilding process is totally system dependent, and in most cases proprietary, the script does not show the precise code for rebuilding the kernel.

This script includes a production version available only to root (system administrator) and a test script. The system administrator who is not completely familiar with system tuning should run the test version and carefully examine its output before running the root version. Remember that rebuilding the kernel may take about five minutes, and the actual time required for the entire system tuning process is considerably longer, especially with irate users breathing down your neck. If possible, rebuild the kernel at night, or on the weekend. Both test and root script output may be directed to local or external technical personnel for examination. The first three lines specify the Bourne shell interpreter, generate a short description of the script, and set the *log_ name* variable.

```
#!/bin/sh
# @(#) system tuning script
log_name = 'whoami'
```

The following code checks whether the person who runs this script has superuser permission. If not, the test version of the script is executed.

```
if [ $log_name = "root" ]
then
  STUNE=/etc/conf/cf.d/stune
  STUNESAVE=/etc/conf/cf.d/stune.save

echo "\n$log_name executing a system script ...\n\n\n"

while
  echo "Do you want to see current settings: [y/n] \c"
  read answer
  do
    case "$answer" in
      [yY]*)
        echo "Displaying ..."
        cat $STUNE | more
      break
      ;;
      [nN]*)
        echo "Continue ...\n"
      break
      ;;
      *)
        echo "Please enter 'y' or 'n' \n"
      ;;
    esac
  done
```

The following code requests that the superuser enter a name. If no name is entered, the script terminates with an error message.

```
echo "Please enter Name: \c"
read name
if [ -n "$name" ]
then
  echo "Entered Name -> $name\n"
else
  echo "No Name specified ...\n"
  echo "Please, try again!"
  exit 1
fi
```

The following code tries to find the name entered in the configuration file. If it is not found, the script terminates with an error message.

```
if line='grep "^$name[     ]" $STUNE 2>/dev/null'
then
  echo "Name $name Found in the file: $STUNE!\n"
  echo "Continue ...\n"
else
  echo "Name $name Not Found in the file: $STUNE!\n"
  echo "Please, Try Again. Exiting ...\n"
  exit 2
fi
```

The following code prompts the superuser to enter a value. If no value is entered, the script terminates with an error message. If a value is entered, the superuser is required to confirm the entry, and the dialog continues.

```
echo "Please enter Value: \c"
read new_value
if [ -n "$new_value" ]
then
  echo "Entered Value -> $new_value\n"
else
  echo "No Value specified ...\n"
  echo "Please, try again!"
  exit 1
fi

while
  echo "Confirm the changes: [y/n] \c"
  read answ
```

```
do
  case "$answ" in
    [yY]*)
      conf=1
    break
    ;;
    [nN]*)
      conf=0
      break
    ;;
    *)
      echo "Please enter 'y' or 'n' \n"
    ;;
  esac
done

if [ ! -f $STUNE ]
then
  echo "$name\t$new_value" >$STUNE
  cp $STUNE $STUNESAVE
  exit $?
fi

set - $line
old_value=$2
if [ "$old_value" = "$new_value" ]
then
  exit 0
fi

if [ "$conf" ]
then
  echo "\nTuneable Parameter \"$name\" is currently set
        to ${old_value}."
  echo "Is it OK to change it to $new_value? (y/n) \c"
  read ans
  case $ans in
    [yY]*)
      echo "Changing $name to $new_value ...\n"
      cp $STUNE $STUNESAVE
    break
    ;;
    [nN]*)
      echo "\n\"$name\" left at ${old_value}.\n"
```

```
        exit 0
    ;;
    *)
      echo "Please enter 'y' or 'n' \n"
    ;;
  esac
  echo
fi

ed - $STUNE >/dev/null 2>&1 <<-!
/^$name/c
$name $new_value
.
w
!

while
  echo "Rebuild KERNEL: [y/n] \c"
  read config
  do
    case "$config" in
      [yY]*)
        echo "\n******** Rebuild Kernel Here ********"
        echo "Activate script that rebuilds the kernel"
        echo "*** For SCO Unix
              /etc/conf/cf.d/link_unix ***"
        echo "After rebuilding - boot the new kernel
              with /etc/shutdown ...\n"
      break
      ;;
      [nN]*)
        echo "After changing parameters -
              rebuild new kernel.\n"
      break
      ;;
      *)
        echo "Please enter 'y' or 'n' \n"
      ;;
    esac
  done

else
```

```
TSTTUNEFILE=/usr/$log_name/test/stune.test
SAVTUNEFILE=/usr/$log_name/test/stune.save

echo "\nNot Superuser(root), but $log_name!
      Executing a test script ...\n"

while
  echo "Do you want to see current settings: [y/n] \c"
  read answer
  do
    case "$answer" in
      [yY]*)
        echo "Displaying ..."
        cat $TSTTUNEFILE | more
      break
      ;;
      [nN]*)
        echo "Continue ...\n"
      break
      ;;
      *)
        echo "Please enter 'y' or 'n' \n"
      ;;
    esac
  done
```

The following code requests that the user enter a pseudo (test) name. If no pseudo name is entered, the script terminates with an error message.

```
echo "Please enter Pseudo name: \c"
read name
if [ -n "$name" ]
then
  echo "Entered Pseudo name -> $name\n"
else
  echo "No Pseudo name specified ...\n"
  echo "Please, try again!"
  exit 1
fi
```

The following code tries to find the pseudo name entered in the configuration file. If it is not found, the script terminates with an error message.

```
if result='grep "^$name" $TSTTUNEFILE 2>/dev/null'
then
  echo "Pseudo Name $name Found in the file: $TSTTUNEFILE!\n"
  echo "Continue ...\n"
else
  echo "Pseudo name $name Not Found
        in the file: $TSTTUNEFILE!\n"
  echo "Please, Try Again. Exiting ...\n"
  exit 2
fi
```

The following code prompts the user to enter a pseudo value. If no pseudo value is entered, the script terminates with an error message. If a pseudo value is entered, the user is required to confirm the entry, and the dialog continues.

```
echo "Please enter Pseudo value: \c"
read new_value
if [ -n "$new_value" ]
then
  echo "Entered Pseudo value -> $new_value\n"
else
  echo "No Pseudo value specified ...\n"
  echo "Please, try again!"
  exit 1
fi

while
  echo "Confirm the changes: [y/n] \c"
  read answ
  do
    case "$answ" in
      [yY]*)
        conf=1
      break
      ;;
      [nN]*)
        conf=0
      break
      ;;
      *)
        echo "Please enter 'y' or 'n' \n"
      ;;
    esac
  done
```

```
if [ ! -f $TSTTUNEFILE ]
then
  echo "Changing $name to $new_value ...\n"
  echo "$name\t$new_value" >$TSTTUNEFILE
  cp $TSTTUNEFILE $SAVTUNEFILE
  exit $?
fi

set - $result
old_value=$2
if [ "$old_value" = "$new_value" ]
then
  echo "No Change! Exiting ...\n"
  exit 0
fi

if [ "$conf" ]
then
  echo "\nPseudo Name \"$name\" is currently
        set to ${old_value}."
  echo "OK to change to $new_value? (y/n) \c"
  read ans
  case $ans in
    [yY]*)
      echo "Changing $name to $new_value ...\n"
      cp $TSTTUNEFILE $SAVTUNEFILE
    break
    ;;
    [nN]*)
      echo "\n\"$name\" left at ${old_value}.\n"
      exit 0
    ;;
    *)
      echo "Please enter 'y' or 'n' \n"
    ;;
  esac
  echo
fi
ed - $TSTTUNEFILE >/dev/null 2>&1 <<-!
/^$name/c
$name $new_value
.
w
```

```
        !

    while
       echo "Rebuild KERNEL: [y/n] \c"
       read config
       do
       case "$config" in
         [yY]*)
            echo "Simulating Kernel!\n"
            echo "After rebuilding -
                  boot the new kernel with /etc/shutdown ...\n"
         break
         ;;
         [nN]*)
            echo "After changing parameters -
                  rebuild new kernel.\n"
         break
         ;;
         *)
            echo "Please enter 'y' or 'n' \n"
         ;;
       esac
    done
fi
```

TROUBLESHOOTING

All this system tuning, tricky and painstaking as it can be, has its benefits. Keeping the system properly tuned can help avoid certain problems. For example, if you keep an eye on your system, you can reduce the likelihood of system slowdown or a full disk. As always, prevention is the best medecine.

Of course, no matter how carefully you monitor your system, problems arise sooner or later. This chapter concludes with a discussion of common problems and potential solutions. Before looking at specific problems, consider the following general troubleshooting guidelines:

■ Make a list of symptoms. Be quantitative where possible.

■ Try the listed solutions (if any). Record the solution in your log book and continue to monitor the situation.

■ If you are unable to solve the problem, record the problem and your attempted solutions. Attempt to reproduce the problem. Call your customer service representative or technical support.

Slow System

The bane of both system administrators and users alike is a slow system. Users expect systems that are not only always available, but that also respond quickly. Possible causes for slow systems include the following:

- ◪ Too many files in a given directory. Use **dir** to determine the number of files, and either delete some files or reorganize your directories.

- ◪ Too few free disk blocks. Use **df** to determine the number of free blocks and either delete files or acquire more disk space.

- ◪ Too few free inodes. Use **df** -i to determine the number of free inodes and either clean up the file system or remake it.

- ◪ Excessively demanding process. Use **ps** -ef or **ps** -ev to examine current processes, and reschedule those taking excessive resources, if possible.

Full Disk

If you have been using the **df** command on a regular basis, you won't be caught with the following dreaded message:

```
System full, cannot write
```

If you do get caught short of disk space, log in as root and do the following:

- ◪ Examine the contents (file fragments) of the **/lost+found** directory in each file system. Delete these file fragments or move them to the appropriate directory. Do not delete the **/lost+found** directory.

- ◪ Remove any unneeded system log files, mail files, and files in the **/tmp** and **/usr/tmp** directories.

- ◪ Convince users to archive files that they are not presently using. This is easier said than done. Some users may be convinced by viewing selected system statistics. Others may require a week of system downtime.

System Hangs

The following procedure has been known to get systems to respond to the keyboard. If it doesn't work, the problem may be a runaway program, discussed in the next section.

- ☑ Check the keyboard connection.

- ☑ Press CTRL-Q (to resume output). On some systems, this annuls a CTRL-S (suspend output).

- ☑ Press CTRL-C.

- ☑ Type **stty** sane followed by CTRL-J.

- ☑ Turn the monitor off and turn it back on.

- ☑ Check your terminal documentation for a keystroke sequence to unlock the keyboard. Log in at another terminal and send these commands to the hung terminal.

Runaway Programs

Programs that cannot be stopped from the terminal that started them are known as *runaway programs.* The most common example is a program containing an infinite loop. A single command, improperly coded, can generate an infinite loop. For obvious reasons, no example appears here. Try the following to regain control of the terminal:

- ☑ Log into another terminal as root. Use **ps** -al to examine current processes. Note the process identification numbers (PID) of possible culprits. Use **kill** -9 PID to remove these processes until the system responds.

- ☑ If nothing else works, reboot the system. Sometimes a killed process takes awhile to disappear. Don't jump the gun.

Blank Screen

A blank screen is likely to be a hardware problem. Try the following before calling service personnel:

- ☑ Check all connections, including the monitor on switch, and the mouse.

- ☑ Check for burnt fuses.

- ☑ Swap cables with a monitor that is working.

- ☑ Determine if the system is in console mode. If it is, but the terminal is not designated as the console terminal, no display appears. Either designate the terminal as console terminal or reboot to multi-user mode and log in at the terminal.

Other Terminal Problems

Sometimes terminal output is visible but displayed incorrectly. After checking all connections as in the previous section, verify that the terminal name was set correctly. The terminal name is found in the **/usr/lib/terminal** file for System V Unix, and in the **/etc/termcap** file for BSD Unix, and is then placed in the TERM environment variable.

System Doesn't Boot

Refer to Chapter 9 for a thorough discussion of bootstrapping problems.

Chapter Summary

System Tuning   The system tuning process consists of two basic steps. First you determine exactly what is happening in the system and then you change the appropriate system parameters. Most system administrators will not tune Unix on a regular basis. However, consider tuning the system in the following circumstances: setting up the initial system, adding system resources (in this case parameter changes may be required), the system "always" runs slowly, or the system generates numerous errors.

System Tuning Commands   System tuning commands include **df**, which reports number of free disk blocks; **du**, which summarizes disk usage; **nice**, which changes scheduling priority for a specified command; **ps**, which reports selective active process status; **pstat**, which reports system information such as inode table or process table; **sar**, which reports on system activity such as CPU utilization and buffer activity; **time**, which reports times associated with a specified command; **timex**, which reports process data and system activity such as command execution time and accounting data, **uptime**; which reports system activity such as time of day and time system has been up; **vmstat**, which reports paging and system statistics such as number of forks issued; **w**, which displays information indicating who is on system and what they are doing; and **who**, which lists who is on system and other information such as login time.

System Parameters   Unix enables technically proficient system administrators to increase system performance by modifying special values known as system parameters. The optimal settings for system parameters are hardware dependent and a function of the installation's specific processing activity and goals. System parameters may be explicity or implicitly interdependent. Testing the effect of parameter changes requires time and a representative job mix.

When making parameter modifications, follow two principles: make backups, and keep a log book of parameter changes and their effects. A properly designed and maintained log book is useful for the system administrator, trainees, technical personnel, and installation management.

The specific tunable parameters available and the file that contains them differ from one Unix implementation to another. The exact steps required to change a kernel parameter may vary from one version of Unix to another. Some implementations, such as SCO Unix, provide a menu-driven utility to smooth the process.

Troubleshooting   Keeping the system properly tuned can help avoid certain problems. For example, if you keep an eye on your system, you can reduce the likelihood of system slowdown and a full disk. Possible causes for slow systems include: too many files in a given directory, too few free disk blocks, too few free inodes, and excessively demanding processes. If you get caught with a shortage of disk space, log in as root and do the following (in order): eliminate ordinary files from the **/dev** directory; examine the contents (file fragments) of the **/lost+found** directory in each file system; remove any unneeded system log files, mail files, and files in the **/tmp** and **/usr/tmp** directories; and convince users to archive files that they are not presently using.

The following procedure has been known to get systems to respond to the keyboard: check the keyboard connection, press CTRL-C, type **stty** sane followed by CTRL-J, turn the monitor off and turn it back on, log into another terminal as root, and if nothing else works, reboot the system, after waiting awhile.

A blank screen is likely to be a hardware problem. Try the following before calling service personnel: check all connections, including the monitor on-switch and the mouse; check for burnt fuses; and swap cables with a monitor that is working. There may also be a problem if the system is in console mode, but the terminal is not designated as the console terminal. Bootstrapping problems were discussed in Chapter 9.

PARTTHREE

A Fundamental
Application

Unix System

- The main Script

- The Menu Options

Administration Guide

CHAPTER 15

A User-Friendly Interface

This final chapter consists of a user-friendly interface to Unix, providing menu-driven access to system administration shell scripts and C language programs. Except for the Testing option, C language programs that add or remove a pseudo user, all menu options must be executed by the system administrator with the root password. The shell scripts and programs have all been written using the SCO Open Desktop, but were written with compatibility in mind. Most shell scripts in this chapter are written in the Korn shell and could easily be modified to run under the Bourne shell. Use this interface as the starting point, adding or modifying options as required.

One very important point, already addressed in Chapter 12, is the question of a possible security breach via the LOGNAME environment variable, which could be used to ensure that the user is logged in as superuser (root). On many systems, it is possible to fool such a script merely by redefining the LOGNAME variable before running the script. For example, a mischievous or malicious user could type

echo $LOGNAME

to which the system responds with a user name. Then the user could type in the Korn shell or the Bourne shell

LOGNAME=root

while in the C shell the user could type

setenv LOGNAME root

After this, if the user again types

echo $LOGNAME

the system responds with the root as user name. A script applying an **if** statement to test the LOGNAME would erroneously accept this user as the root user, effectively destroying system security.

Let's discuss two solutions to this problem. One solution is setting the ownership of all system administration scripts to root, and restricting permission to the owner (root). Exceptions should be accorded only when it is necessary to offload routine system administration work to a trusted assistant. Ownership is transferred to the assistant. However, the superuser should closely monitor use of these programs.

Caution Adopting this solution makes it impossible to activate the test mode for scripts.

An alternative solution is available for scripts that include a test mode, as well as the root mode. In such instances, you may use the **whoami** command (BSD Unix and some versions of System V) or the equivalent **whoami** C language progam as given below. The **whoami** program prints your current user name, even if you have used the **su** command, which changes your login name. In contrast, the command **who** *am i* will report your initial login name because it employs **/etc/utmp**.

The system administrator, running as "regular" user (not root), or a trusted assistant can activate the script's test version. After testing, this individual may execute the **su** root command with the proper password and access the script's final version with the help of **whoami**, invoked by the script. When this solution is used, script ownership is not verified. The **whoami** C language program is shown here:

```
#include <stdio.h>
#include <pwd.h>

main()
{
struct passwd *pwd;
unsigned short euid;
char *log_name;

  pwd = getpwuid(geteuid());
  log_name = pwd->pw_name;
  if (log_name != NULL)
    printf("%s\n", log_name);
  return (log_name);
}
```

If **whoami** is not available, this program should be compiled using the following MAKE file. The INCLUDE file appears after the program removing a pseudo user toward the end of this chapter. Make this program available to all users. The MAKE file is shown here:

```
include INCLUDE
LIBS =
PROD = whoami

install all: $(PROD)

whoami: whoami.c
$(CC) $(CFLAGS) -o $(TESTDIR)/whoami whoami.c $(LIBS)

clean:
-rm -f *.o

clobber: clean
-rm -f $(PROD)
```

Both the MAKE file and the INCLUDE file have been written for SCO Unix; they may require some modification to run under other versions of Unix.

THE main SCRIPT

The following Korn shell script displays the main menu of the user-friendly interface to Unix. This menu includes ten options, in addition to the option of quitting the interface. Some options are executed immediately, for example, the Time option, which allows the system administrator to set the system date and time. Other options, such as the Files option, display a menu with a new set of choices. The source code for these menus appears here. To save space, rather than repeat the source code for an option appearing in a previous chapter, a chapter reference and summary description are provided. The menu hierarchy does not necessarily correspond to the chapter hierarchy.

```ksh
#!/bin/ksh
# @(#) main script

log_name='whoami'
dir=/usr/$log_name/scripts
#The above line (dir...) defines a location for your
#system administration scripts. If necessary, change the
#dir definition.

PS3="Press Enter and Select by Number: "
select i in Disks Files Maintain Network Printer
            Security Time User System Testing Quit
  do case $REPLY in
     [a-z]*)
       i=$REPLY
     ;;
     esac
     case $i in
     q|Q|Quit)
       print "done!"
       exit 0
     ;;
     m|M|Maintain)
       $dir/down
     ;;
     u|U|User)
       $dir/usersk
     ;;
     t|T|Time)
       $dir/st
     ;;
     f|F|Files)
```

```
        $dir/filesk
    ;;
    d|D|Disks)
        $dir/frk
    ;;
    s|S|Security)
        $dir/sck
    ;;
    p|P|Printer)
        $dir/prk
    ;;
    n|N|Network)
        $dir/ntk
    ;;
    y|Y|System)
        $dir/jb
    ;;
    t|T|Testing)
        $dir/testsk
    ;;
    *)
        print -r - "Undefined menu selection! Try again..."
    ;;
    esac
done
```

THE MENU OPTIONS

Figure 15-1 shows how the menu options can be activated. Starting from the top of the screen, the main menu options are displayed. The first selection is 2, to activate the Files menu, displaying available options. The second selection is 3, to activate the Check program, which displays a message concerning file system integrity. In this case the user has entered **n**, so the initial menu remains on the screen.

The Maintain Option (Shutting Down the System)

This option invokes the C language shutdown program presented in Chapter 9. It displays a menu providing the system administrator with several options: quitting the system, reverting to the single-user (Maintenance) mode, halting the system, or shutting down the system.

```
$ menukshjr
 1) Disks
 2) Files
 3) Maintain
 4) Network
 5) Printer
 6) Security
 7) Time
 8) User
 9) System
10) Testing
11) Quit
Press Enter and Select by Number: 2
1) Backup
2) Clean
3) Check
4) Restor
5) Quit
Press Enter and Select by Number: 3

Do you want to check Filesystem Integrity: [y/n] n

Exiting ...

Press Enter and Select by Number: █
```

The User Option

The User option of the main menu provides three level-3 options: adding a user, removing
a user, and disabling a terminal if the user has not pressed a key within a predetermined
time period. The User option script (Korn shell) appears next, after which the level 3
options are discussed.

```
#!/bin/ksh
# @(#) user option script

log_name='whoami'
dir=/usr/$log_name/scripts
#The above line (dir...) defines a location for your
#system administration scripts. If necessary, change the
#dir definition.

PS3="Press Enter and Select by Number: "
select i in  Add Remove Timeout Quit
  do case $REPLY in
    [a-z]*)
      i=$REPLY
    ;;
    esac
```

```
    case $i in
      q|Q|Quit)
        print "done!"
        exit 0
      ;;
      a|A|Add)
#  See Chapter 5, "Users and Accounts"
        $dir/add
      ;;
      r|R|Remove)
#  See Chapter 5, "Users and Accounts"
        $dir/rm
      ;;
      t|T|Timeout)
#  See Chapter 12, "Security Management"
        $dir/user_out
      ;;
      *)
        print -r - "Undefined menu selection! Try again..."
      ;;
    esac
  done
```

Adding a User

Chapter 5 presented both a test shell script and a production shell script for adding users to the system. The test version adds pseudo users to a test directory. After successfully executing the test version, you may apply the production version.

Removing a User

Chapter 5 presented both a test shell script and a production shell script for removing users from the system. The test version removes pseudo users from a test directory. After successfully executing the test version, you may apply the production version.

Timing Out a User

Users who are too lazy or too distracted to log off of a terminal may not realize it, but they are a common cause of Unix security violations. The convenience of a ready-to-run terminal without the nuisance of having to log in must be weighed against the damage caused by a security break. The answer should be clear; security must predominate.

However, standard Unix has no built-in method for logging out users after a predetermined terminal idle time. The C language program **user_out**, presented in Chapter 12, automatically logs out users after a predetermined time period.

The Time Option

The following Bourne shell script allows the system administrator, running under the root password, to set the system date and time:

```
#!/bin/sh
# @(#) time option script
log_name='whoami'

while
  echo "\nDo you want to set new date/time: [y/n/q] \c"
  read answer
  do
    case "$answer" in
      [yY]*)
        echo "Entered yes! Continue ...\n"
        break
      ;;
      [nN]*)
        echo "Entered no updates ... "
# The two lines that follow must be coded on a single line.
        date '+Current Date is: %m/%d/%y%n
              Current Time is: %H:%M:%S'
        echo "\nExiting ...\n"
        exit 1
      ;;
      [qQ]*)
        echo "Entered quit! Exiting ...\n"
        exit 0
      ;;
      *)
        echo "Please enter 'y' or 'n' or 'q' \n"
      ;;
    esac
  done
  if [ $log_name = "root" ]
  then
    echo "\nSetting Time ...\n"
```

```
        rtc=no
# If we have a real-time clock, synchronize system clock to it.
      cat /dev/clock > /dev/null 2>&1 && {
        rtc=yes
        date '/etc/setclock' > /dev/null
      }
      echo "\nSystem Time is 'date'"
      echo "\nEnter new time ([YearMonthDay]HourMin): \c"
      while
        read date
        [ "$date" ]
        do
          echo "\nNew Date and Time is -> \c"
          date='/lib/cvtdate $date' && date $date && break
          echo "\nTry again ([YearMonthDay]HourMin): \c"
        done
        [ "$rtc" = yes ] && /etc/setclock
                    'date +\%m\%d\%H\%M\%y' > /dev/null
        echo "\n"
        echo "Setting Time - done!\n"
    else
      echo "Cannot execute - not a root user!\n"
    fi
```

The Files Option

The Files option of the main menu provides four level-3 options: backing up a file, cleaning a file, checking a file, and restoring a file. The File option source code (Korn shell) appears here, after which the level 3 options are discussed.

```
#!/bin/ksh
# @(#) files option script

log_name='whoami'
dir=/usr/$log_name/scripts
#The above line (dir...) defines a location for your
#system administration scripts. If necessary, change the
#dir definition.


PS3="Press Enter and Select by Number: "
select i in Backup Clean Check Restor Quit
```

```
      do case $REPLY in
        [a-z]*)
          i=$REPLY
        ;;
      esac
      case $i in
        q|Q|Quit)
          print "done!"
          exit 0
        ;;
        b|B|Backup)
#     See Chapter 7, "File System Backup and Restoration"
          $dir/bkpk
        ;;
        c|C|Clean)
#     See Chapter 8, "Unix File Systems"
          $dir/cn
        ;;
        h|H|Check)
#     See Chapter 8, "Unix File Systems"
          $dir/fk
        ;;
        r|R|Restor)
#     See Chapter 7, "File System Backup and Restoration"
          $dir/resk
        ;;
        *)
          print -r - "Undefined menu selection! Try again..."
        ;;
      esac
done
```

Backing Up a File

Chapter 7 offers two backup shell scripts, one employing the **tar** command and one employing the **cpio** command. See that chapter for a comparison of these two commands.

Cleaning Up the File System

The following Bourne shell script may be used to clean up the file system. It is available only to the system administrator using the root account.

```
#!/bin/sh
# @(#) cleaning up the file system script

log_name='whoami'
clnsys=/dev/root

/bin/df
while
  echo "\nDo you want to clean File system: [y/n] \c"
  read answer
  do
    case "$answer" in
      [yY]*)
        echo "\007Entered yes! Continue ...\n"
        break
      ;;
      [nN]*)
        echo "\nExiting ...\n"
        exit 0
      ;;
      *)
        echo "Please enter 'y' or 'n' \n"
      ;;
    esac
  done
  if [ $log_name = "root" ]
  then
    echo "Start Cleanup! Please Wait ...\n"
    /etc/cleanup
    echo "\n"
    echo "\007Cleanup - done!\n"
    /bin/df
  else
    echo "Cannot execute - not a root user!\n"
  fi
```

Checking the File System

Chapter 8 presented a shell script that checks for file system integrity. This shell script is available only to system administrators using the root password.

Restoring a File

Chapter 7 offered two C shell restore scripts, one employing the **tar** command and one employing the **cpio** command. See that chapter for a comparison of these two commands. The following shell script was written for the Korn shell, but also runs under the Bourne shell. By comparing the following shell script with the **tar** version presented in Chapter 7, you can get a good idea what's required to convert a shell script from Korn to C (or vice versa).

```
#!/bin/ksh
# @(#) restoring a file script

typeset devcase med file files ok
scr=backup_menu

log_name='whoami'
dir=/usr/$log_name/scripts
#The above line (dir...) defines a location for your
#system administration scripts. If necessary, change the
#dir definition.

while true
do
  devcase=1
  cat $dir/$scr
  read reply?"Select by number? "
  case $reply in
    0)
      print "   Exiting ..."
      exit 0
    ;;
    1)
      med=/dev/rfd0135ds18
#      1440K floppy/3 1/2"/drive 0
    ;;
    2)
      med=/dev/rfd096ds15
#      1200K floppy/5 1/4"/drive 0
    ;;
    3)
      med=/dev/rfd0135ds9
#      720K floppy/3 1/2"/drive 0
    ;;
    4)
```

```
            med=/dev/rfd096ds9
#           720K floppy/5 1/4"/drive 0
        ;;
        5)
            med=/dev/rfd1135ds18
#           1440K floppy/3 1/2"/drive 1
        ;;
        6)
            med=/dev/rfd196ds15
#           1200K floppy/5 1/4"/drive 1
        ;;
        7)
            med=/dev/rfd1135ds9
#           720K floppy/3 1/2"/drive 1
        ;;
        8)
            med=/dev/rfd196ds9
#           720K floppy/5 1/4"/drive 1
        ;;
        9)
            med=/dev/rct0
#           QIC Cartridge tape
        ;;
        10)
            med=/dev/rctmini
#           Mini-Cartridge tape
        ;;
        *)
            devcase=0
            print -r - "Wrong selection! Try again ..."
        ;;
    esac
    if (($devcase))
    then
      read rep?"Are you sure? [y/n]: "
      case $rep in
        y|Y)
            read resp?"List of contents(before restoring) [y/n]? "
            case $resp in
              y|Y)
                  print -r - "List of contents ..."

# tar options are:
# t names of specified files listed as they occur on archive
```

```
# v (verbose) displays names of files treated
# f next argument ($med) is archive name

        tar tvf $med | pg -cnsp "RETURN for next ..."
        print "Executing: tar tvf $med | pg -cnsp
                RETURN for next ..."
        ;;
    n|N)
        print -r - "No list of contents selected! ..."
        ;;
    *)
        print -r - "Please enter 'y' or 'n'"
        ;;
esac
files=""
ok=1
print -r - "List file(s) to be restored, when done
            press Enter key twice:"
while (($ok))
do
    read -r file
    if test "$file" != ""
    then
        files="$files $file"
    else
        ok=0
    fi
done
if test "$files" != ""
then
    print "Files to restore: $files"
else
    exit 0
fi
print "   Restoring ..."
cd /

# tar options are:
# x extracts named files from the archive
# v (verbose) displays names of files treated
# f next argument ($med) is archive name

    tar xvf $med $files
;;
```

```
      n|N)
        print -r - "   Exiting ..."
        exit 1
      ;;
      *)
        print -r - "Wrong selection! Please enter 'y' or 'n'"
      ;;
    esac
  fi
done
```

The Disk Option

The following Korn shell script formats a floppy disk for use with either the Unix (SCO) or the DOS (MS-DOS) operating system. First you specify the operating system, and then you specify the disk type and drive.

```
#!/bin/ksh
# @(#) disk option script

typeset mod odtos dcase dir dosmed scr devcase med good done ok
dosmed=/dev/fd0
scr=floppy_menu

log_name='whoami'
dir=/usr/$log_name/scripts
#The above line (dir...) defines a location for your
#system administration scripts. If necessary, change the
#dir definition.

odtos=1
while true
do
  while (($odtos))
  do
    read reply?"Format floppy under Operating System
                [uU]nix/[dD]os? "
    case $reply in
      u|U)
        mod=1
        dcase=1
        odtos=0
```

```
          ;;
      d|D)
        mod=0
        dcase=0
        odtos=0
      ;;
      *)
        print -r - "Wrong selection! Please enter 'u' or 'd'"
      ;;
    esac
  done
  devcase=1
  if (($dcase))
  then
    while (($devcase))
    do
      devcase=0
      cat $dir/$scr
      read reply?"Select by number? "
      case $reply in
        0)
          print "   Exiting ..."
          exit 0
        ;;
        1)
          med=/dev/rfd0135ds18
#         1440K floppy/3 1/2"/drive 0
          ;;
        2)
          med=/dev/rfd096ds15
#         1200K floppy/5 1/4"/drive 0
        ;;
        3)
          med=/dev/rfd0135ds9
#         720K floppy/3 1/2"/drive 0
        ;;
        4)
          med=/dev/rfd096ds9
#         720K floppy/5 1/4"/drive 0
        ;;
        5)
          med=/dev/rfd1135ds18
#         1440K floppy/3 1/2"/drive 1
        ;;
```

```
        6)
          med=/dev/rfd196ds15
#         1200K floppy/5 1/4"/drive 1
        ;;
        7)
          med=/dev/rfd1135ds9
#         720K floppy/3 1/2"/drive 1
        ;;
        8)
          med=/dev/rfd196ds9
#         720K floppy/5 1/4"/drive 1
        ;;
        *)
          devcase=1
          print -r - "Wrong selection! Try again..."
        ;;
      esac
    done
  fi
  good=1
  while (($good))
  do
    read reply?"Are you sure? [y/n]: "
    case $reply in
      y|Y)
        print "   Continue ..."
        done=1
        ok=1
        while (($done))
        do
          if (($ok))
          then
            if (($mod))
            then
              /bin/format -v $med
              print formating $med
            else
              /usr/bin/dosformat $dosmed
              print formating $dosmed
            fi
          fi
          # read
          read res?"Another floppy?
                   [cC]ontinue/[aA]bort/[eE]xit: "
```

```
            case $res in
              c|C)
                ok=1
              ;;
              a|A)
                done=0
                good=0
                odtos=1
              ;;
              e|E)
                print "   Exiting ..."
                exit 1
              ;;
              *)
                ok=0
                print -r - "Wrong selection!
                          Please enter 'c' or 'a' or 'e'"
              ;;
            esac
          done
        ;;
        n|N)
          print -r - "   Exiting ..."
          exit 1
        ;;
        *)
          print -r - "Wrong selection! Please enter 'y' or 'n'"
        ;;
    esac
  done
done
```

The Security Option

The following Korn shell script provides auditing services to the system administrator, as
discussed in Chapter 12. This script only works if your Unix version supports auditing.

```
#!/bin/ksh
# @(#) security option script

typeset ok
scr=secur_menu
```

```
log_name='whoami'
dir=/usr/$log_name/scripts
#The above line (dir...) defines a location for your
#system administration scripts. If necessary, change the
#dir definition.

sulogfile=/usr/adm/sulog

ok=1
while (($ok))
do
   cat $dir/$scr
   read reply?"Select by number? "
   case $reply in
     0)
        print "Exiting ..."
        exit 0
      ;;
     1)
        auditcmd -c
#  Audit Statistics
        ok=0
      ;;
     2)
        authck -a -v
#  Authentication Database Consistency
        ok=0
      ;;
     3)
        integrity -e
#  File Integrity
        ok=0
      ;;
     4)
        auditcmd -e
#  Start Auditing
        ok=0
      ;;
     5)
        auditcmd -d
#  Stop Auditing
        ok=0
      ;;
```

```
      6)
        last | more
#  User Activities
        ok=0
      ;;
      7)
        cat $sulogfile | more
#  Monitor Entries
        ok=0
      ;;
      *)
        ok=1
        print -r - "Wrong selection! Try again..."
      ;;
    esac
done
```

The Printer Option

The Printer option of the main menu provides two level-3 options: adding a printer and removing a printer. The Printer option script (Korn shell) appears here, after which the level-3 options are discussed. The corresponding programs appeared in Chapter 10.

```
#!/bin/ksh
# @(#) printer option script

log_name='whoami'
dir=/usr/$log_name/scripts
#The above line (dir...) defines a location for your
#system administration scripts. If necessary, change the
#dir definition.

PS3="Press Enter and Select by Number: "
select i in  Add Remove Quit
  do case $REPLY in
    [a-z]*)
      i=$REPLY
    ;;
    esac
    case $i in
      q|Q|Quit)
        print "done!"
```

```
        exit 0
      ;;
      a|A|Add)
#  See Chapter 10, "System Peripherals"
        $dir/addprn
      ;;
      r|R|Remove)
#  See Chapter 10, "System Peripherals"
        $dir/rmprn
      ;;
      *)
        print -r - "Undefined menu selection! Try again..."
      ;;
    esac
  done
```

Adding a Printer

Chapter 10 presented a Bourne shell script that allows the system administrator, logged in as superuser on a root account, to add a printer. A new system administrator should first run this script as a regular user, to avoid potential printer configuration errors or even system failure and the resulting disruptions. When the administrator is sufficiently familiar with the printer addition process, he or she may execute the production version of the script to add a printer to the system.

Removing a Printer

Chapter 10 presented a Bourne shell script that allows the system administrator to remove a printer from the system. A new system administrator should first run this script as a regular user, to avoid potential printer configuration errors or even system failure and the resulting disruptions. When the administrator has gained sufficient familiarity with the printer removal process, he or she may execute the production script to remove a printer from the system.

The Network Option

The Network option of the main menu provides five level-3 options: adding a service, removing a service, checking network statistics, adding a host, and removing a host. The Network option source code (Korn shell) and the resulting services and hosts menus appear here, after which the options are discussed. (The actual source code for all networking options appeared in Chapter 11.)

```
#!/bin/ksh
# @(#) network option script

log_name='whoami'
dir=/usr/$log_name/scripts
#The above line (dir...) defines a location for your
#system administration scripts. If necessary, change the
#dir definition.

PS3="Press Enter and Select by Number: "
select i in Connectivity Hosts Services Quit
  do case $REPLY in
    [a-z]*)
      i=$REPLY
    ;;
  esac
  case $i in
    q|Q|Quit)
      print "done!"
      exit 0
    ;;
    s|S|Services)
      $dir/services
    ;;
    c|C|Connectivity)
      $dir/netstat
    ;;
    h|H|Hosts)
      $dir/hosts
    ;;
    *)
      print -r - "Undefined menu selection! Try again..."
    ;;
  esac
done
```

Selecting Services from the Network option activates the following source code, displaying the options for adding and removing services:

```
#!/bin/ksh
# @(#) selecting services script

log_name='whoami'
dir=/usr/$log_name/scripts
```

```
#The above line (dir...) defines a location for your
#system administration scripts. If necessary, change the
#dir definition.

PS3="Press Enter and Select by Number: "
select i in  Add Remove Quit
  do case $REPLY in
    [a-z]*)
      i=$REPLY
    ;;
    esac
    case $i in
    q|Q|Quit)
      print "done!"
    exit 0
    ;;
    a|A|Add)
      $dir/addservices
    ;;
    r|R|Remove)
      $dir/rmservices
    ;;
    *)
      print -r - "Undefined menu selection! Try again..."
    ;;
  esac
done
```

Selecting hosts from the Network option activates the following script, displaying the options for adding and removing hosts.

```
#!/bin/ksh
# @(#) selecting hosts script

log_name='whoami'
dir=/usr/$log_name/scripts
#The above line (dir...) defines a location for your
#system administration scripts. If necessary, change the
#dir definition.

PS3="Press Enter and Select by Number: "
select i in  Add Remove Quit
  do case $REPLY in
    [a-z]*)
```

```
          i=$REPLY
    ;;
  esac
  case $i in
    q|Q|Quit)
      print "done!"
      exit 0
    ;;
    a|A|Add)
      $dir/addhosts
    ;;
    r|R|Remove)
      $dir/rmhosts
    ;;
    *)
      print -r - "Undefined menu selection! Try again..."
    ;;
  esac
done
```

Adding a Service

Chapter 11 presented a shell script that guides the system administrator through the key steps in adding a service to a network. As in many previous scripts, only the system administrator running as superuser may execute the full script. The novice system administrator should first execute the test script using a regular password to familiarize himself or herself with the process of adding a service to the network.

Removing a Service

Chapter 11 presented a shell script that guides the system administrator through the key steps in removing a service from the network. As in the add services script, only the system administrator running as superuser may execute the full script.

Checking Network Statistics

Chapter 11 presented a program that uses the **ping** command to check a communication link for a specified host name or Internet address. It redirects **ping** output, including summary communication statistics to a predefined file. Then the program parses the file and determines whether the communication was valid.

Adding a Host

Chapter 11 presented a shell script that guides the system administrator through the key steps in adding a host to a network. Only the system administrator running as superuser may execute the production script. Remember, before executing the production script, it is necessary to connect the system to the network, assign the host a name and an address, and ensure that the relevant network daemons are active.

Removing a Host

Chapter 11 presented a shell script that guides the system administrator through the key steps in removing a host from a network. Only the system administrator running as superuser may execute the production script.

The Testing Option

The following Korn shell script provides a menu of available test procedures. Presently it includes two entries: one for adding a pseudo user, and another for removing a pseudo user, discussed in the next section. The system administrator may modify the present script to add new test scripts.

```ksh
#!/bin/ksh
# @(#) testing option script

log_name='whoami'
dir=/usr/$log_name/scripts
#The above line (dir...) defines a location for your
#system administration scripts. If necessary, change the
#dir definition.

PS3="Press Enter and Select by Number: "
select i in  User Printer Quit
  do case $REPLY in
    [a-z]*)
      i=$REPLY
    ;;
    esac
    case $i in
      q|Q|Quit)
        print "done!"
        exit 0
```

```
          ;;
      u|U|User)
        PS3="Press Enter and Select by Number: "
        select i in  Add Remove Quit
        do case $REPLY in
           [a-z]*)
             i=$REPLY
           ;;
        esac
        case $i in
           q|Q|Quit)
             print "done!"
             exit 0
           ;;
           a|A|Add)
             $dir/addtc
           ;;
           r|R|Remove)
             $dir/rmtc
           ;;
           *)
             print -r - "Undefined menu selection!
                          Try again..."
           ;;
        esac
      done
      ;;
      p|P|Printer)
        PS3="Press Enter and Select by Number: "
             select i in  Add Remove Quit
        do case $REPLY in
           [a-z]*)
             i=$REPLY
           ;;
        esac
        case $i in
           q|Q|Quit)
             print "done!"
             exit 0
           ;;
           a|A|Add)
             $dir/addprn.test
           ;;
           r|R|Remove)
```

```
                $dir/rmprn.test
       ;;
       *)
         print -r - "Undefined menu selection!
                     Try again..."
       ;;
     esac
   done
   ;;
   *)
     print -r - "Undefined menu selection! Try again..."
   ;;
  esac
done
```

A Program for Adding a Pseudo User

As discussed in Chapter 5, a C language program requires a password, but it does not require the root password. The system administrator can issue his or her assistant a password for user account maintenance, a time-consuming, but not particularly sophisticated, activity. Furthermore, the assistant need not have access to the C language program (source) code, but may run the binary file. This provides an additional level of security because the binary file is composed of 0s and 1s and is thus illegible, rendering tampering virtually impossible. Chapter 5 discusses the necessary steps in detail. The following code adds pseudo users to a test directory. Execute this program before executing the corresponding program that adds real users to the production directory.

```
/* This program was written in the SCO environment  */
/* and creates a test directory under /usr . Other  */
/* Unix implementations may require different        */
/* directories, for example, /users .                */

#include <stdio.h>
#include <string.h>
#include <sgtty.h>
#include <memory.h>
#include <sys/errno.h>

#define TSTDIR "/usr/ctest"
#define TSTDIR1 "/usr/ctest/"
#define TSTDIRM "/usr/ctest/mail"
#define TSTDIRM1 "/usr/ctest/mail/"
#define TSTPASSWD "/usr/test/passwd.tst"
```

```
#define DEFAULT_USER_ID "999"
#define DEFAULT_GROUP_ID "10"

/* The following statement sets the default shell   */
/* to the Bourne shell, because not all Unix        */
/* implementations provide the Korn shell. Replace  */
/* sh with ksh if you wish a default Korn shell.    */
/*All #define statements must be coded on one line  */

#define DEFAULT_SHELL "sh"
#define REALUSER "gproject"
#define PROFILET "profile.tst"
#define LOGINT "login.tst"
#define LOGOUTT "logout.tst"
#define CSHRCT "cshrc.tst"

#define PRFSTR1 "SHELL=/bin/sh"
#define PRFSTR2 "HOME="
#define PRFSTR3 "MAIL="
#define PRFSTR4 "PATH=/bin:/usr/bin:/usr/hosts:
                        /usr/local:/etc:."
#define PRFSTR5 "TERM="
#define PRFSTR6 "export TERM PATH SHELL HOME MAIL"

#define LINSTR1 "stty dec"
#define LINSTR2 "umask 0"
#define LINSTR3 "set ignoreeof mail=(0 $user)"
#define LINSTR4 "tset -s -Q -m
                        'unknown:?wy75' > /tmp/tset\$\$"
#define LINSTR5 "source /tmp/tset\$\$"
#define LINSTR6 "alias cmdx chmod +x"
#define LINSTR7 "set path=(. /bin /usr/bin /usr/hosts
                                /usr/local /etc)"
#define LINSTR8 "set history=150"

#define CSHSTR1 "set path=(. /bin /usr/bin /usr/hosts
                                /usr/local /etc)"
#define CSHSTR2 "set history=150"
#define CSHSTR3 "alias h history"

#define LOTSTR1 "clear"

char keep_user[16];
char str[512];
```

```
int size;

void prepare_profile();
void prepare_login();
void prepare_cshrc();
void prepare_logout();

int main()
{
char buf_1[256];
char tstbuf_1[80];
char tstbuf_2[80];
char keep_gid[16];
char keep_uid[16];
FILE *fd;

  printf("\nEnter new Pseudo User :");
  gets(keep_user);
  if (strlen(keep_user) < 1)
  {
    printf("ERROR: NO PSEUDO USER ENTERED! Exiting ...\n");
    exit(1);
  }
  printf("\n");
  strcpy(tstbuf_1,keep_user);
  printf("\nEnter pseudo user ID :");
  gets(keep_uid);
  if (strlen(keep_uid) < 2)
  {
    printf("WARNING: NO PSEUDO USER ID ENTERED!");
    printf("Using default value ...\n");
    strcpy(keep_uid,DEFAULT_USER_ID);
  }
  printf("\n");
  strcat(tstbuf_1,"::");
  strcat(tstbuf_1,keep_uid);
  printf("\nEnter Group ID :");
  gets(keep_gid);
  if (strlen(keep_gid) < 2)
  {
    printf("WARNING: NO PSEUDO USER GROUP ENTERED!");
    printf("Using default value ...\n");
    strcpy(keep_gid,DEFAULT_GROUP_ID);
  }
```

```
printf("\n");
strcat(tstbuf_1,":");
strcat(tstbuf_1,keep_gid);
printf("\nEnter Real User Name :");
gets(tstbuf_2);
printf("\n");
strcat(tstbuf_1,":");
strcat(tstbuf_1,tstbuf_2);
strcat(tstbuf_1,":");
strcat(tstbuf_1,"/usr/");
strcat(tstbuf_1,keep_user);
printf("\nShell? [ksh/csh] :");
gets(tstbuf_2);
if (strlen(tstbuf_2) < 2)
{
  printf("WARNING: NO SHELL ENTERED!");
  printf("Using default shell  Bourne shell ...\n");
  strcpy(tstbuf_2,DEFAULT_SHELL);
}
printf("\n");
strcat(tstbuf_1,":");
strcat(tstbuf_1,"/bin/");
strcat(tstbuf_1,tstbuf_2);
strcat(tstbuf_1,"\n");
size = strlen(tstbuf_1);
fd = fopen(TSTPASSWD,"a");
if (!fd)
{
  printf("\nCannot open file %s! Exiting ...\n",TSTPASSWD);
  exit(1);
}
else
{
  if(!fwrite(tstbuf_1,size,1,fd))
  {
    fclose(fd);
    printf("\nCannot write to the file");
    printf("%s! Exiting ...\n",TSTPASSWD);
    exit(1);
  }
  else
  {
    printf("New pseudo user in the
    printf("%s file: %s\n",TSTPASSWD,tstbuf_1);
```

```
    }
}
fclose(fd);
strcpy(tstbuf_1,"mkdir ");
strcat(tstbuf_1,TSTDIR);
printf("Executing:  %s\n", tstbuf_1);
system(tstbuf_1);
strcpy(tstbuf_1,"mkdir ");
strcat(tstbuf_1,TSTDIRM);
printf("Executing:  %s\n", tstbuf_1);
system(tstbuf_1);
strcpy(tstbuf_1,"mkdir ");
strcat(tstbuf_1,TSTDIR1);
strcat(tstbuf_1,keep_user);
printf("Executing:  %s\n", tstbuf_1);
system(tstbuf_1);
strcpy(tstbuf_1,"chown ");
strcat(tstbuf_1,REALUSER);
strcat(tstbuf_1," ");
strcat(tstbuf_1,TSTDIR1);
strcat(tstbuf_1,keep_user);
printf("Executing:  %s\n", tstbuf_1);
system(tstbuf_1);
strcpy(tstbuf_1,"chgrp ");
strcat(tstbuf_1,keep_gid);
strcat(tstbuf_1," ");
strcat(tstbuf_1,TSTDIR1);
strcat(tstbuf_1,keep_user);
printf("Executing:  %s\n", tstbuf_1);
system(tstbuf_1);
strcpy(tstbuf_1,TSTDIR1);
strcat(tstbuf_1,keep_user);
strcat(tstbuf_1,"/");
strcat(tstbuf_1,PROFILET);
fd = fopen(tstbuf_1, "w");
if (!fd)
  printf("\nCannot open file %s\n",tstbuf_1);
else
{
  prepare_profile();
  if(!fwrite(str,size,1,fd))
  {
    fclose(fd);
    printf("\nCannot write to the file %s\n",tstbuf_1);
```

```
      }
      fclose(fd);
   }
   strcpy(tstbuf_1,TSTDIR1);
   strcat(tstbuf_1,keep_user);
   strcat(tstbuf_1,"/");
   strcat(tstbuf_1,LOGINT);
   fd = fopen(tstbuf_1, "w");
   if (!fd)
      printf("\nCannot open file %s\n",tstbuf_1);
   else
   {
      prepare_login();
      if(!fwrite(str,size,1,fd))
      {
         fclose(fd);
         printf("\nCannot write to the file %s\n",tstbuf_1);
      }
      fclose(fd);
   }
   strcpy(tstbuf_1,TSTDIR1);
   strcat(tstbuf_1,keep_user);
   strcat(tstbuf_1,"/");
   strcat(tstbuf_1,LOGOUTT);
   fd = fopen(tstbuf_1, "w");
   if (!fd)
   {
      printf("\nCannot open file %s\n",tstbuf_1);
   }
   else
   {
      prepare_logout();
      if(!fwrite(str,size,1,fd))
      {
         fclose(fd);
         printf("\nCannot write to the file %s\n",tstbuf_1);
      }
      fclose(fd);
   }
   strcpy(tstbuf_1,TSTDIR1);
   strcat(tstbuf_1,keep_user);
   strcat(tstbuf_1,"/");
   strcat(tstbuf_1,CSHRCT);
   fd = fopen(tstbuf_1, "w");
```

```
if (!fd)
{
  printf("\nCannot open file %s\n",tstbuf_1);
}
else
{
  prepare_cshrc();
  if(!fwrite(str,size,1,fd))
  {
    fclose(fd);
    printf("\nCannot write to the file %s\n",tstbuf_1);
  }
  fclose(fd);
}
strcpy(tstbuf_1,"touch ");
strcat(tstbuf_1,TSTDIRM1);
strcat(tstbuf_1,keep_user);
printf("Executing:  %s\n", tstbuf_1);
system(tstbuf_1);
strcpy(tstbuf_1,"chmod 660 ");
strcat(tstbuf_1,TSTDIRM1);
strcat(tstbuf_1,keep_user);
printf("Executing:  %s\n", tstbuf_1);
system(tstbuf_1);
strcpy(buf_1,"chown ");
strcat(buf_1,REALUSER);
strcat(buf_1," ");
strcat(buf_1,TSTDIR1);
strcat(buf_1,keep_user);
strcat(buf_1,"/");
strcat(buf_1,PROFILET);
strcat(buf_1," ");
strcat(buf_1,TSTDIR1);
strcat(buf_1,keep_user);
strcat(buf_1,"/");
strcat(buf_1,LOGINT);
strcat(buf_1," ");
strcat(buf_1,TSTDIR1);
strcat(buf_1,keep_user);
strcat(buf_1,"/");
strcat(buf_1,CSHRCT);
strcat(buf_1," ");
strcat(buf_1,TSTDIR1);
strcat(buf_1,keep_user);
```

```
                strcat(buf_1,"/");
                strcat(buf_1,LOGOUTT);
                strcat(buf_1," ");
                strcat(buf_1,TSTDIRM1);
                strcat(buf_1,keep_user);
                printf("Executing:  %s\n", buf_1);
                system(buf_1);
                strcpy(buf_1,"chgrp ");
                strcat(buf_1,keep_gid);
                strcat(buf_1," ");
                strcat(buf_1,TSTDIR1);
                strcat(buf_1,keep_user);
                strcat(buf_1,"/");
                strcat(buf_1,PROFILET);
                strcat(buf_1," ");
                strcat(buf_1,TSTDIR1);
                strcat(buf_1,keep_user);
                strcat(buf_1,"/");
                strcat(buf_1,LOGINT);
                strcat(buf_1," ");
                strcat(buf_1,TSTDIR1);
                strcat(buf_1,keep_user);
                strcat(buf_1,"/");
                strcat(buf_1,CSHRCT);
                strcat(buf_1," ");
                strcat(buf_1,TSTDIR1);
                strcat(buf_1,keep_user);
                strcat(buf_1,"/");
                strcat(buf_1,LOGOUTT);
                printf("Executing:  %s\n", buf_1);
                system(buf_1);
                strcpy(buf_1,"chgrp ");
                strcat(buf_1,"mail");
                strcat(buf_1," ");
                strcat(buf_1,TSTDIRM1);
                strcat(buf_1,keep_user);
                printf("Executing:  %s\n", buf_1);
                system(buf_1);
                printf("\n*******************************************\n");
                printf("\n   New Pseudo User < %s > entered",keep_user;
                printf("\n   to the Unix system!\n"
                printf("\n*******************************************\n");
        }
```

```
void prepare_profile()
{

  strcpy(str,":");
  strcat(str,"\n");
  strcat(str,PRFSTR1);
  strcat(str,"\n");
  strcat(str,PRFSTR2);
  strcat(str,TSTDIR1);
  strcat(str,keep_user);
  strcat(str,"\n");
  strcat(str,PRFSTR3);
  strcat(str,TSTDIRM1);
  strcat(str,keep_user);
  strcat(str,"\n");
  strcat(str,PRFSTR4);
  strcat(str,"\n");
  strcat(str,PRFSTR5);
  strcat(str,"\n");
  strcat(str,PRFSTR6);
  strcat(str,"\n");
  size = strlen(str);
}

void prepare_login()
{

  strcpy(str,LINSTR1);
  strcat(str,"\n");
  strcat(str,LINSTR2);
  strcat(str,"\n");
  strcat(str,LINSTR3);
  strcat(str,"\n");
  strcat(str,LINSTR4);
  strcat(str,"\n");
  strcat(str,LINSTR5);
  strcat(str,"\n");
  strcat(str,LINSTR6);
  strcat(str,"\n");
  strcat(str,LINSTR7);
  strcat(str,"\n");
  strcat(str,LINSTR8);
  strcat(str,"\n");
  size = strlen(str);
```

```
}
void prepare_cshrc()
{

  strcpy(str,CSHSTR1);
  strcat(str,"\n");
  strcat(str,CSHSTR2);
  strcat(str,"\n");
  strcat(str,CSHSTR3);
  strcat(str,"\n");
  size = strlen(str);
}
void prepare_logout()
{

  strcpy(str,LOTSTR1);
  strcat(str,"\n");
  size = strlen(str);
}
```

A Program for Removing a Pseudo User

The following C language program removes a pseudo user from the test directory. See the comments prior to the preceding program for an explanation of how to use this program.

```
#include <stdio.h>
#include <string.h>
#include <sgtty.h>
#include <memory.h>
#include <sys/errno.h>

#define TSTDIR1 "/usr/test/"
#define TSTDIRM1 "/usr/test/mail/"
#define TSTPASSWD "/usr/test/passwd.tst"
#define TSTPASSWDOLD "/usr/passwd.old"
#define TSTPASSWDNEW "/usr/passwd.new"
#define REALUSER "gproject"
#define PROFILET "profile.tst"
#define LOGINT "login.tst"
#define LOGOUTT "logout.tst"
#define CSHRCT "cshrc.tst"
```

```
int main()
{
char tstbuf_1[80];
char tstbuf_2[80];
char keep_user[16];
char user[16];
int size;
FILE *fd;
FILE *fdd;
char chr;
int i, found, first;

  printf("\nEnter Pseudo User to remove :");
  gets(user);
  if (strlen(user) < 1)
  {
    printf("ERROR: NO PSEUDO USER ENTERED! Exiting ...\n");
    exit(1);
  }
  printf("\n");
  fd = fopen(TSTPASSWD,"r");
  if (!fd)
  {
    printf("\nCannot open the file");
    printf("%s! Exiting ...\n", TSTPASSWD);
    exit(1);
  }
  fdd = fopen(TSTPASSWDNEW,"w");
  if (!fdd)
  {
    printf("\nCannot open the file");
    printf("%s! Exiting ...\n", TSTPASSWDNEW);
    exit(1);
  }
  i = 0;
  first = 0;
  found = 0;
  do
  {
    chr = getc(fd);
    tstbuf_1[i] = chr;
    if (!first)
    {
      if (i < 16)
```

```
      {
        keep_user[i] = chr;
      }
      else
      {
        printf("\n buffer overflow\n");
      }
    }
    ++i;
    if ((chr == '::') && (!first))
    {
      --i;
      keep_user[i] = '\0';
      if (strcmp(user,keep_user) == 0)
      {
        printf("\nPseudo User found in the file");
        printf("%s\n", TSTPASSWD);
        found = 1;
      }
      first = 1;
      ++i;
    }
    if (chr == '\n')
    {
      i = 0;
      first = 0;
      if (!found)
      {
        if (!fwrite(tstbuf_1,strlen(tstbuf_1),1,fdd))
        {
          printf("\nCannot write to the file");
          printf("%s\n", TSTPASSWDNEW);
          fclose(fdd);
        }
        else
        {
          printf("\nUpdated the file %s\n",TSTPASSWDNEW);
        }
      }
    }
} while (!feof(fd));
fclose(fd);
fclose(fdd);
printf("\ntstbuf_1 is %s\n", tstbuf_1);
```

```
if (!found)
{
  printf("ERROR: NO PSEUDO USER FOUND TO REMOVE!
          Exiting ...\n");
  exit(1);
}
printf("\n Removing Pseudo User %s ...\n",user);
strcpy(tstbuf_1,"cp ");
strcat(tstbuf_1,TSTPASSWD);
strcat(tstbuf_1," ");
strcat(tstbuf_1,TSTPASSWDOLD);
printf("Executing:  %s\n", tstbuf_1);
system(tstbuf_1);
strcpy(tstbuf_1,"mv ");
strcat(tstbuf_1,TSTPASSWDNEW);
strcat(tstbuf_1," ");
strcat(tstbuf_1,TSTPASSWD);
printf("Executing:  %s\n", tstbuf_1);
system(tstbuf_1);
strcpy(tstbuf_1,"rm -rf ");
strcat(tstbuf_1,TSTDIR1);
strcat(tstbuf_1,user);
printf("Executing:  %s\n", tstbuf_1);
system(tstbuf_1);
strcpy(tstbuf_1,"rm -f ");
strcat(tstbuf_1,TSTDIRM1);
strcat(tstbuf_1,user);
printf("Executing:  %s\n", tstbuf_1);
system(tstbuf_1);
strcpy(tstbuf_1,"rmdir ");
strcat(tstbuf_1,TSTDIRM1);
strcat(tstbuf_1,user);
printf("Executing:  %s\n", tstbuf_1);
system(tstbuf_1);
strcpy(tstbuf_1,"rm -f ");
strcat(tstbuf_1,TSTDIR1);
strcat(tstbuf_1,user);
strcat(tstbuf_1,"/");
strcat(tstbuf_1,PROFILET);
printf("Executing:  %s\n", tstbuf_1);
system(tstbuf_1);
strcpy(tstbuf_1,"rm -f ");
strcat(tstbuf_1,TSTDIR1);
strcat(tstbuf_1,user);
```

```
                strcat(tstbuf_1,"/");
                strcat(tstbuf_1,LOGINT);
                printf("Executing:  %s\n", tstbuf_1);
                system(tstbuf_1);
                strcpy(tstbuf_1,"rm -f ");
                strcat(tstbuf_1,TSTDIR1);
                strcat(tstbuf_1,user);
                strcat(tstbuf_1,"/");
                strcat(tstbuf_1,LOGOUTT);
                printf("Executing:  %s\n", tstbuf_1);
                system(tstbuf_1);
                strcpy(tstbuf_1,"rm -f ");
                strcat(tstbuf_1,TSTDIR1);
                strcat(tstbuf_1,user);
                strcat(tstbuf_1,"/");
                strcat(tstbuf_1,CSHRCT);
                printf("Executing:  %s\n", tstbuf_1);
                system(tstbuf_1);
                strcpy(tstbuf_1,"rmdir ");
                strcat(tstbuf_1,TSTDIR1);
                strcat(tstbuf_1,user);
                printf("Executing:  %s\n", tstbuf_1);
                system(tstbuf_1);
                printf("\n********************************************\n");
                printf("\n   Pseudo User < %s >",user);
                printf("\n    removed from the Unix system\n);
                printf("\n********************************************\n");
        }
```

The MAKE file for the test programs as run under SCO appears here. The MAKE file for other implementations may vary.

```
include INCLUDE
LIBS =
PROD = addtc rmtc

install all: $(PROD)

addtc: addtc.c
$(CC) $(CFLAGS) -o $(TESTDIR)/addtc addtc.c $(LIBS)

rmtc: rmtc.c
$(CC) $(CFLAGS) -o $(TESTDIR)/rmtc rmtc.c $(LIBS)

clean:
```

```
-rm -f *.o

clobber: clean
-rm -f $(PROD)
```

The INCLUDE file for the test programs as run under SCO appears here. The INCLUDE file for other implementations may vary.

```
ROOT =
IROOT =
ETC = $(ROOT)/etc
BIN = $(ROOT)/usr/local/bin
TESTDIR = .
SHELL = /bin/sh
REL =
INCRT = $(IROOT)/usr/include
BROOT = $(ROOT)
I = $(INCRT)
MORECPP =
CFLAGS = -O -DLAI_TCP $(MORECPP)
        -I$(INCRT) $(REL) -Di386 -DBUFFER_SIZE=8192
LDFLAGS =
LDLIBS =
SOCKETLIB = -lsocket
INS =
INSDIR = $(BIN)
```

▪▪▪▪▪▪▪▪▪▪▪▪▪▪▪▪▪▪▪▪▪▪
Chapter Summary

A User-Friendly Interface   This final chapter consists of a user-friendly interface to Unix, providing menu-driven access to system administration shell scripts and C language programs. Except for the Testing option and C language programs that add or remove a pseudo user, all menu options must be executed by the system administrator with the root password. The menu options are for shutting down the system; adding, removing, and timing out users; setting the system time and date; backing up, restoring, cleaning, and checking the file system; formatting floppy disks for Unix or DOS; providing auditing services; adding and removing printers; adding and removing services and hosts, and checking network connectivity; tuning the system; and running test programs that add and remove pseudo users. To save space, rather than repeat the source code for an option appearing in a previous chapter, a chapter reference and summary description are provided. The menu hierarchy does not necessarily correspond to the chapter hierarchy.

The shell scripts and programs have all been written using the SCO Open Desktop, but were written with compatibility in mind. Most shell scripts in this chapter are written in the Korn shell and could easily be modified to run under the Bourne shell. Use this interface as the starting point, adding or modifying options as required.

PART FOUR

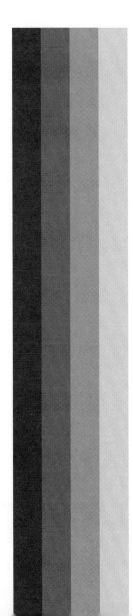

Appendixes

Unix System

Administration Guide

APPENDIX A

Major Unix Commands

This appendix contains commands of interest to Unix system administrators. In many cases it refers back to the chapter in which the command was introduced. Every attempt was made to be generic, but because Unix is not 100 percent compatible across platforms (what is?), the command descriptions occasionally refer to Unix V. Several BSD commands are discussed. Use the **man** command described in this appendix to access on-line documentation for your Unix implementation.

at

The **at** command accepts one or more commands from the standard input to be executed at a later time. **at** has the following syntax:

at *time* [*date*] [*increment*]
at *option* [*job-id* ...]
at -l[job-id ...]

The **at** command allows you to specify the job execution time. After a job is queued with the **at** command, the program writes to standard error a job identifier (a number and a letter) and the time when the job will execute.

The **at** command uses the following optional arguments:

▱ *time* One-digit and two-digit numbers denote hours; four digits denote hours and minutes. Alternatively *time* may be specified in the form *hour.minute.*

▱ *date* One format is a month name followed by a day number (and possibly year number preceded by an optional comma). Another is day of the week either complete or three-character abbreviation. Both *today* and *tomorrow* are recognized.

▱ *increment* Modifies time and date arguments. Takes the form "+*n units*", where *n* is an integer and *units* is one of the following: minutes, hours, days, weeks, months, or years.

▱ -r *job-id* Removes job or jobs previously scheduled by the **at** command. *job-id* is a job identifier supplied by **at**.

▱ -l [*job-id* ...] Lists schedule times of specified jobs. If none, lists all jobs currently scheduled for the invoking user.

▱ -q*letter* Places the specified job in a queue denoted by *letter,* any lowercase letter from a to z. The queue letter is appended to the job identifier.

awk

The **awk** command is used for pattern processing. It has the following syntax:

awk [*f filename*] [*program*] [*parameters*] [*files*]

The **awk** command scans input files for lines that match any of a specified set of patterns. Among its many uses are verifying that contents conform to a specified layout, and removing unwanted lines. See your system manual for information about **awk**.

backup

The **backup** command performs Unix backup functions. The **backup** utility is a front end for **cpio**. Use **restore** to restore backups made with this utility. The **backup** command has the following syntax:

backup [-t] [-p | -c | -f *files* | -u "*user1* [*user2*]"]
    -d *device*
backup -h

This command is further described in Chapter 7, starting on page 172.

basename

The **basename** command removes directory names from pathnames. It has the following syntax:

basename *string* [*suffix*]

The **basename** command deletes any prefix ending in / and the *suffix,* if present, from *string* and prints the result on the standard output. The result is the file "base" name–that is, the filename without any preceding directory path and without an extension. The **basename** command is used inside substitution marks (") in shell procedures to construct new filenames.

batch

The **batch** command accepts one or more commands from the standard input to be executed at a later time. The **batch** command has the following syntax:

batch

The batch command prompts the user to enter commands to be executed when the system permits. CTRL-D specifies the end.

calendar

The **calendar** command invokes a reminder service. It has the following syntax:

calendar [-]

The **calendar** command accesses the file calendar in the user's current directory and mails her or him lines containing today's or tomorrow's date. When an argument is present, **calendar** applies to every user whose login directory contains a file calendar and sends the result to the standard output.

cancel

The **cancel** command cancels requests to a line printer. It has the following syntax:

cancel [*ids*] [*printer*]

The **lpstat** command may be used to determine the *ids* or *printer* to cancel.

cat

The **cat** command concatenates and displays files. It has the following syntax:

cat [-u] [-s] [-v] [-t] [-e] [*file* ...]

The **cat** command reads each file in sequence and writes it on the standard output. If no input file is given, or if a single dash (-) is given, **cat** reads from the standard input, terminated by CTRL-D. Except for special files, no input file may have the same name as the output file.
The options are

- -s Suppresses warnings about nonexistent files.
- -u Causes the output to be unbuffered.
- -v Displays non-printing characters (except for tabs, newlines, and form feeds).
- -t Causes tabs to be printed as "^I" and form feeds as "^L".
- -e Causes a $ character to be printed at the end of each line (prior to the newline).

cd

The **cd** command changes your working directory. The specified directory, if any, becomes the new working directory; otherwise the value of the shell parameter $HOME is used. It has the following syntax:

cd [*directory*]

This command is further described in Chapter 3, starting on page 46.

chgrp

The **chgrp** command changes the group ownership of files, directories, and devices. It has the following syntax:

chgrp *groupid filenames*

This command is further described in Chapter 5, starting on page 104.

chmod

The **chmod** command and the corresponding **chmod** systems call, changes the access mode for specified files. It has the following syntax:

chmod *permission files*

This command is further described in Chapter 5, starting on page 104.

chown

The **chown** command is used to change ownership of a file or a directory. It has the following syntax:

chown *logname filenames*

This command is further described in Chapter 5, starting on page 103.

cmp

The **cmp** command compares two files. It has the following syntax:

cmp [-l] [-s] *file1 file2*

The **cmp** command compares two files and displays the byte and line number of the differences, if any. If *file1* is -, the standard input is used. This command should be used to compare binary files. The options are

▧   -l   Prints the byte number (decimal) and the differing bytes (octal) for each difference.

▧   -s   Returns an exit code only. 0 denotes identical files, 1 denotes different files, and 2 denotes an inaccessible or missing file.

conv

The **conv** command is the common object file converter. It has the following syntax:

conv [-a] [-o] [-p] -t *target* [- | *files*]

The **conv** command converts object files in the common object file format from their current byte-ordering to the byte-ordering of the target machine. It writes the converted file to **file.v**. The **conv** command can be used on either the source (sending) or target (receiving) machine.
    Command line options are

▧   –   Indicates that filenames should be read from the standard input.

▧   -a   If the input file is an archive, produces the output file in the System V Release 2.0 portable archive format.

▧   -o   If the input file is an archive, produces the output file in the old (pre-System V) archive format.

▧   -p   If the input file is an archive, produces the output file in the System V Release 1.0 random access archive format.

▧   -t *target*   Converts the object file to the byte ordering of the target machine, another host or a target machine. Legal values for *target* are pdp, vax, ibm, x86, b16, n3b, mc68, and m32.

compress

The **compress**, **uncompress**, **zcat** commands compress data for storage, uncompress, and display compressed files. They have the following syntaxes:

> compress [-dfFqc] [-b *bits*] *file*
> uncompress [-fqc] *file*
> zcat *file*

The **compress** command reduces a file as much as possible, creates a compressed output file, and removes the original file unless the -c option is present. The **uncompress** command restores a compressed file to its initial state and removes the compressed file. The **zcat** command decompresses a file and displays it on standard output. See also **pack**.

If the command line specifies no *file,* standard input and standard output are used. The default output filename is the input filename with the suffix ".Z". The output files have the same permissions and ownership as the corresponding input files or the user's standard permissions if output is directed through the standard output.

The following options are available from the command line:

- -d Decompresses a compressed file.

- -c Writes output on the standard output and does not remove original file.

- -b *bits* Specifies the maximum number of bits to use in encoding.

- -f Overwrites previous output file.

- -F Writes an output file even if compression does not save space.

- -q Generates no output (except for any error messages).

cp

The **cp** command copies files. It has the following syntax:

> cp *file1 file2*
> cp *files directory*

The command **cp** *file1 file2* copies *file1* to *file2*; *file1* and *file2* may not be identical. In the second form of the **cp** command, *directory* is the location of a directory into which one or more files are copied. This directory must exist prior to the execution of the **cp** command. Copying to an existing file overwrites the file.

cpio

The **cpio** command (Unix V) copies file archives in and out. It has the following syntax:

cpio -o[acBvV] [-C *bufsize*] [[-O *file*] [-K *volumesize*]
    [-M *message*]]

cpio -i[BcdmrtTuvVfsSb6k] [-C *bufsize*] [[-I *file*]
    [-K *volumesize*] [-M *message*]] [*pattern* ...]

cpio -p[adlmuvV] *directory*

This command is further described in Chapter 7, starting on page 169.

crontab

The **crontab** command schedules commands to be executed at regular intervals. It has the following syntax:

crontab [*file*]
crontab -r
crontab -l

The **crontab** command schedules commands stored in the user's **crontab** file, **/usr/spool/cron/crontabs/***username*. Command output including errors are mailed to the user.

   The **crontab** command without options copies the specified file, or standard input if no file is specified, into the **crontabs** directory, replacing any previous **crontab** file.

   -r Removes the user's **crontab** file from the **crontab** directory.

   -l Lists the contents of the user's **crontab** file.

crypt

The **crypt** command encodes and decodes files. It has the following syntax:

crypt [*password*]
crypt [-k]

The **crypt** command reads from the standard input and writes to the standard output. The *password* is a key that selects a particular transformation. The **crypt** command without an argument demands a key from the terminal and turns off printing while the key is being typed in. The -k option denotes the use of the key assigned to the environment variable CRYPTKEY.

ct

The **ct** command spawns **getty** to a remote terminal. It has the following syntax:

ct [-w*n*] [-x*n*] [-h] [-v] [-s *speed*] *telno*

The **ct** command dials the telephone number of a modem attached to the terminal and spawns a **getty** process to that terminal. The *telno* is a telephone number, with equal signs for secondary dial tones and minus signs for delays at appropriate places. The *telno* is a maximum of 58 characters, which may be 0 through 9, −, =, *, and #. If several telephone numbers are specified, **ct** dials each in succession until one answers; this is useful for specifying alternative dialing paths. Normally, **ct** will hang up the current line, so the line can answer the incoming call. (See option -h.) The command recognizes the following arguments:

- ▰ -x*n* Generates detailed program execution output for debugging purposes on **stderr**. The debugging level, *n*, is a single digit; the higher the *n*, the more detailed the output.

- ▰ -v Sends a running narrative to the standard error output stream.

- ▰ -h Does not hang up the current line. It waits for the specified **ct** process to terminate before returning control to the user's terminal.

- ▰ -s *speed* Sets the data rate, where *speed* is expressed in baud.

cu

The **cu** command calls another Unix system. It has the following syntax:

cu [-s *speed*] [-l*line*] [-h] [-t] [-x*n*] [-o | -e | -oe] [-n] *telno*
cu [-s *speed*] [-h] [-xn] [[-o | -e | -oe] -l *line* [*dir*]
cu [-h] [-x*n*] [-o | -e | -oe] *systemname*

The **cu** command calls up another Unix system, a terminal, or possibly a non-Unix system. It manages an interactive conversation and can transfer ASCII files. By default, **cu** expects and sends eight-bit characters without parity.

The **cu** command accepts the following options and arguments:

- -s *speed*   Specifies the transmission speed (150, 300, 600, 1200, 2400, 4800, 9600, 19200, or 38400).

- -l*line*   Specifies a device name to use as the communication line.

- -h   Emulates local echo, supporting calls to other computer systems employing terminals set to half-duplex mode.

- -t   Dials an ASCII terminal set to auto answer. It sets appropriate mapping of carriage-return to carriage-return-line-feed.

- -x*n*   Generates detailed program execution output on **stderr**. The debugging level, *n*, is a single digit; the higher the *n*, the more detailed the output.

- -n   Prompts the user for the telephone number. This may be more secure than extracting the telephone number from the command line.

- *telno*   When using an automatic dialer, the argument is the telephone number with equal signs for secondary dial tone or minus signs placed appropriately for delays of four seconds.

- *systemname*   Uses a UUCP system name instead of a telephone number.

- *dir*   Used with **cu** -l*line* to talk directly to a modem on that *line,* instead of talking to another system via that modem. This can be useful when debugging or checking modem operation.

Note
| The cu -l*line dir* command is restricted to users with write access to the Devices file.

The **cu** command employs the following options to determine communications settings:

- -o   The remote system expects or sends seven-bit with odd parity.

- -e   The remote system expects or sends seven-bit with even parity.

- -oe   The remote system expects or sends seven-bit, ignoring parity and sends seven-bit with either parity.

cut

The **cut** command removes selected fields of each line of a file. It has the following syntax:

cut -c*list* [*file* ...]
cut -f*list* [-d *char*] [-s] [*file...*]

The **cut** command removes columns from a table or fields from each line of a file. The fields specified by *list* may be fixed length, or may vary from line to line, being marked with a field delimiter character like tab. The options follow.

- ◪   *list*   Specifies a comma-separated list of integers (in increasing order).

- ◪   -c*list*   Specifies character positions, for example c1-60 keeps the first 60 characters of each line.

- ◪   -f*list*   Designates the fields to be separated in the file by a delimiter character (see -d). For example, -f4,8 copies the fourth and eighth fields only. Lines without field delimiters remain unchanged (useful for table subheadings), unless -s is specified.

- ◪   -d*char*   Is the field delimiter (used with -f option only). Default is tab. Space or other characters with special meaning to the shell must be quoted.

- ◪   -s   If the -f option is used, -s suppresses lines with no delimiter characters.

date

The **date** command displays and sets the date. It has the following syntax:

date [*mmddhhmm*[*yy*]] [+*format*]

This command is further described in Chapter 3, starting on page 51.

dcopy

The **dcopy** command copies Unix file systems for optimal access time. It has the following syntax:

dcopy [-s*X*] [-a*n*] [-d] [-v]
           [-f*size*[:*isize*]] *inputfs outputfs*

This command is further described in Chapter 8, starting on page 202.

dd

The **dd** command converts and copies a file. It has the following syntax:

dd [*options*]

This command is further described in Chapter 7, starting on page 171.

df

The **df** command reports the number of free disk blocks. It has the following syntax:

df [-t] [-f] [-v -i] [*file systems*]

This command is further described in Chapter 14, starting on page 430.

diff

The **diff** command compares two text files, listing their differences. It has the following syntax:

diff [-befh] *file1 file2*

This command is further described in Chapter 3, starting on page 50. See your system manual for more information.

dircmp

The **dircmp** command compares directories. It has the following syntax:

dircmp [-d] [-s] [-w*n*] *dir1 dir2*

The **dircmp** command examines *dir1* and *dir2* and generates tabulated information about their contents. It outputs a list of files unique to each directory and a list indicating whether the files common to both directories have the same contents. It provides the following options:

   -d   Performs a full **diff** on each pair of similarly named files if the contents of the files are not identical.

■ -s Suppresses output of identical filenames.

■ -w*n* Changes the width of the output line to *n* characters. The default width is 72.

dirname

The **dirname** command delivers the directory part of pathname. It has the following syntax:

> dirname *string*

The **dirname** command delivers all but the last component of the pathname in *string* and prints the result on the standard output. If the pathname contains a single component, only a dot is printed. **dirname** is usually employed inside substitution marks (") within shell procedures.

disable

The **disable** command turns off printers. It has the following syntax:

> disable [-c][-r[*reason*]] *printers*

disable stops print requests from being sent to the named printer or printers. The following options are available:

■ -c Cancels any currently printing requests.

■ -r[*reason*] Designates the *reason* for disabling the printer. The *reason* applies to all printers until another -r option is issued. A default *reason* may be set.

du

The **du** command summarizes disk usage, giving the number of 512-byte blocks contained in all files and subdirectories for each directory and file specified by the *names* argument. It has the following syntax:

> du [-afrsu] [*names*]

This command is further described in Chapter 3, starting on page 52.

dump

The **dump** command generates an incremental file system dump for BSD Unix. It has the following syntax:

dump [*key* [*argument...*]] [*file system*]

This command is further described in Chapter 7, starting on page 175.

enable

The **enable** command turns on terminals and line printers. It has the following syntax:

enable *terminals ...*
enable *printers*

For terminals, **enable** signals **init** to allow logins on a particular terminal. See your system manual for affected files. For line printers, **enable** activates the named printers and enables them to print requests.

env

The **env** command sets an environment for command execution. It has the following syntax:

env [-] [*options*] [*command* [*args*]]

This command is further described in Chapter 3, starting on page 52.

find

The **find** command locates files matching specified selection criteria. It has the following syntax:

find *pathname-list expression*

This command is further described in Chapter 8, starting on page 201. See your system manual for more information.

finger

The **finger** command finds information about users. The **finger** command originated with BSD Unix. Its syntax varies widely; the SCO Unix implementation is discussed here:

finger [-bfilpqsw] [*login1_name* ...]]

By default **finger** lists the login name, full name, terminal name and write status (as a * before the terminal name if write permission is denied), idle time, login time, office location, and phone number (if known) for each current user. (Idle time is minutes if it is a single integer, hours and minutes if a colon (:) is present, or days and hours if a d is present.)

The **finger** command uses a longer format whenever a list of names is given. (It accepts both account names and user first and last names.) This is a multiline format; it includes all the information described above, as well as the user's home directory and login shell, any plan which the person has placed in the file **.plan** in their home directory, and the project on which they are working from the file **.project**, which is also in the home directory.

The **finger** options are:

- -b   Designates a briefer output format of users.
- -f   Suppresses the printing of the header line (short format).
- -i   Generates a quick list of users with idle times.
- -l   Forces a long output format.
- -p   Suppresses printing of **.plan** files.
- -q   Generates a quick list of users.
- -s   Forces a short output format.
- -w   Forces a narrow format list of specified users.

fsck

The **fsck** command audits and interactively repairs inconsistent conditions for all supported file systems. If the file system is consistent, it reports the number of files, number of blocks used, and number of free blocks. If the file system is inconsistent, the operator is prompted for permission attempting each correction. It has the following syntax:

fsck [*options*] [*file system*]

This command is further described in Chapter 8, starting on page 205.

fsdb

The **fsdb** command is the file system debugger. It can be used to patch a damaged file system after a crash. It has the following syntax:

fsdb *special* [-]

This command is further described in Chapter 8, starting on page 216.

fsstat

The **fsstat** command reports the file system status. It has the following syntax:

fsstat special_file

This command is further described in Chapter 8, starting on page 201.

ftp

The **ftp** command is the Internet file-transfer program. It allows a user to transfer files to and from a remote network site. It has the following syntax:

ftp [-v] [-d] [-i] [-n] [-g] [*host*]

This command is further described in Chapter 11, starting on page 289. See your system manual for additional information.

getopt

The **getopt** command parses command options. It has the following syntax:

set - - ‘getopt *optstring* $*‘

The **getopt** command checks and breaks up command line options for parsing by shell procedures. The *optstring* is a string of recognized option letters. If a letter is followed by a colon, the option is expected to have an argument, which may or may not be separated from it by white space.

getopts

Both **getopts** and **getoptcvt** parse command options. They have the following syntaxes:

getopts *optstring name* [*arg* ...]
/usr/lib/getoptcvt [-b] *file*

The **getopts** command is used by shell procedures to parse positional parameters and to check for legal options. It should be used in place of **getopt**. It is only available in the Bourne shell and the Korn shell. The **getopts** and **getoptcvt** commands recognize the following arguments:

- *optstring* Must contain the option letters recognized by the parsed command. A letter followed by a colon is expected to have one or more arguments, separated from the command by white space. Each time it is invoked, **getopts** places the next option in the shell variable name and the index of the next argument to be processed in the shell variable OPTIND. This variable is initialized to 1 whenever the shell or a shell procedure is invoked. When an option requires an option argument, **getopts** places it in the shell variable OPTARG. If an illegal option is encountered, ? is placed in *name.* When it encounters the end of options, **getopts** exits with a nonzero exit status. The special option "--" may delimit the end of options. By default, **getopts** parses the positional parameters. It parses any extra command line arguments (*arg* ...).
- -b Ports the results of running **/usr/lib/getoptcvt** to earlier Unix releases. The **/usr/lib/getoptcvt** modifies the shell script in file so that when the resulting shell script is executed, it determines at run time whether to invoke **getopts** or **getoptcvt**.

See your system manual for more information, including examples.

grep

The **grep**, **egrep**, **fgrep** commands search a file for a pattern. They have the following syntaxes:

grep [-bchilnsvy] [-e *expression*] [*files*]
egrep [-bchlnv] [-e *expression*] [*files*]
fgrep [-bclnvxy] [-f *expfile*] [*files*]

The **grep** family commands search standard input or specified input files for lines matching a pattern. Normally, each matching line is copied to the standard output.

If more than one file is being searched, the name of the file in which each match occurs is also written to the standard output (unless the -h option is used). The major difference among these commands lies in their ability to process expressions: **grep** processes some regular expressions, **fgrep** processes only fixed strings, and **egrep** processes arbitrary regular expressions. The following options are recognized:

- ▰   -v   Displays all unmatching lines.

- ▰   -x   Displays only exact matches of an entire line (**fgrep** only).

- ▰   -c   Displays only a count of matching lines.

- ▰   -l   Displays only the names of files with matching lines, separated by newlines.

- ▰   -h   Prevents the name of the file containing the matching line from being prepended to that line—used when searching multiple files (**grep** and **egrep** only).

- ▰   -n   Precedes each line by its relative line number in the file.

- ▰   -b   Precedes each line by the block number on which it was found. This is sometimes useful in locating disk block numbers by context.

- ▰   -s   Suppresses error messages produced for nonexistent or unreadable files (**grep** only).

- ▰   -y   Turns on matching of letters of either case in the input so that case is insignificant. Conversion between uppercase and lowercase letters is dependent on the locale setting.

- ▰   -e *expression or strings*   Same as a simple expression argument, but useful when the expression begins with a dash (-).

- ▰   -f *expfile*   The regular expression for **grep** or **egrep**, or strings list for **fgrep** is taken from the *expfile*.

id

The **id** command prints user and group IDs and names. It has the following syntax:

    id

The **id** command writes a message on the standard output, giving the user and group IDs and the corresponding names of the invoking process. If the effective and real IDs do not match, both are printed. The **id** command was introduced in Chapter 3, starting on page 55.

init

The **init** and **telinit** commands process control initialization. They have the following syntaxes:

```
/etc/init [0123456SsQqabc]
/bin/telinit [0123456SsQqabc]
```

The **init** command is a general process spawner. Its primary role is to create processes from information stored in the file **/etc/inittab**.

At any given time, the system is in one of eight possible run levels. A *run level* is a software configuration of the system under which only a selected group of processes exist. The processes spawned by **init** for each of these run levels is defined in **/etc/inittab**. The **init** command can be in one of eight run levels, 0-6 and S or s (run levels S and s are identical). The run level changes when a privileged user runs **/etc/init**. This user-spawned **init** sends appropriate signals to the original **init** spawned by the operating system when the system was booted, telling it which run level to become.

The **init** command employs the following arguments:

- 0   Shuts down the machine, making it safe to remove the power.

- 1   Puts the system in single-user mode.

- 2   Puts the system in multi-user mode.

- 3   Starts the remote file-sharing processes and daemons.

- 4   Is available to be defined as an alternative multi-user environment configuration.

- 5   Stops the Unix system and goes to the firmware monitor.

- 6   Stops the Unix system and reboots to the state defined by the initdefault entry in **/etc/inittab**.

- a,b,c   Processes only those **/etc/inittab** entries having the a, b, or c run level set.

- Q,q   Reexamines **/etc/inittab**.

- S,s   Enters single-user mode.

kill

The **kill** command terminates a process. It sends signal 15 (terminate) to the specified process(es). This will normally kill processes that do not catch or ignore the signal. It has the following syntax:

kill [-*signo*] *processid*

This command is further described in Chapter 3, starting on page 52.

last

The **last** command displays the most recent logins of users and terminals. It checks the **wtmp** file, which records all logins and logouts for information about a user, a serial line, or any group of users and lines. It has the following syntax:

last [-h] [-n *limit*] [-t *tty*] [-w wtmpfile] [*name*]

This command is further described in Chapter 12, starting on page 331.

logname

The **logname** command gets the login name. It has the following syntax:

logname

The **logname** command returns the user's login name as found in **/etc/utmp**. If no login name is found, **logname** returns the user's user ID number.

lp

The **lp** command sends requests to the line printer. It has the following syntax:

lp [*options*] *files*
lp -i *options*

This command (System V) is further described in Chapter 10, starting on page 252.

lpadmin

The **lpadmin** command configures the print service to describe printers and devices. It has the following syntax:

/usr/lib/lpadmin -p *printer options*
/usr/lib/lpadmin -x *dest*
/usr/lib/lpadmin -d [*dest*]
/usr/lib/lpadmin -S *print-wheel*
        -A *alert-type* [-W *integer1*]
        [-Q *integer2*]

This Unix V command is further described in Chapter 10, starting on page 256.

lpc

The **lpc** command is the Unix BSD line printer control program. It has the following syntax:

/etc/lpc [*command* [*argument* ...]]

The **lpc** command is used by the system administrator to enable or disable a printer or a printer's spooling queue; change the order of jobs in a spooling queue; and display printer, printer queue, and printer daemon status.

The **lpc** command without parameters prompts for commands from standard input. Using redirection, **lpc** may read commands from a file instead of standard input. The following commands are recognized:

▰ help [*command* ...]   Prints a short description of each specified *command*. If no *command* is coded, prints the list of *commands*.

▰ abort {all | *printer*}   Terminates a spooling daemon on the local host and then disables specified printers.

▰ clean {all | *printer*}   Removes all control files, data files, and temporary files that cannot be printed from the specified printer queue or queues on the local machine.

▰ disable {all | *printer*}   Turns off the spooling queues for the specified printers.

▰ down {all | *printer*} *message*...   Turns off the spooling queue for the specified printers, disables printing, and puts *message* in the printer status file. Then **lpq** prints the status message.

▰ enable {all | *printer*}   Enables spooling on the local queue for the specified printers. Then **lpr** can place new print jobs in the queue.

▰ exit   Leaves **lpc**.

▰ quit   Leaves **lpc**.

restart {all | *printer*} Attempts to start a new printer daemon. Use this option when the printer daemon has died and left jobs in the queue.

 start {all | *printer*} Enables printing and starts a spooling daemon for the listed printers.

 status {all | *printer*} Displays the status of daemons and queues on the local printer.

 stop {all | *printer*} Stops a spooling daemon and disables printing after the current job terminates.

 topq {all | *printer*} [*jobnum* ...] [*user* ...] Places the specified job or jobs at the top of the print queue (in the order listed).

 up {all | *printer*} Turns on the spooling queue, enables printing, and starts a new printer daemon. This option cancels the effect of the down option.

lpmove

The **lpmove** command moves requests queued by **lp** between LP destinations. It has the following syntax:

/usr/lib/lpmove *requests dest*
/usr/lib/lpmove *dest1 dest2*

This command is further described in Chapter 10, starting on page 262.

lpq

The **lpq** command is a BSD Unix command that examines the spool queue. It has the following syntax:

lpq [+[*n*]] [-l] [-P*printer*] [-] [*jobno*...] [*user*...]

The **lpq** command reports the status of all specified jobs for the designated user. For each job, it reports the user's name, rank in the queue, names of files, a job identifier, and its size in bytes. It provides the following options:

 -P*printer* Specifies the queue associated with the designated printer.

 +*n* Displays the spool queue until it empties. *n* specifies the number of seconds to sleep between scans of the queue.

 -l Prints information about each file comprising the job.

lpr

The **lpr** command is a BSD command that prints files when a printer is available. It has the following syntax:

    lpr [-Pprinter] [-#num] [-C class] [-Jjob]
        [-T title] [-i [numcols]] [-1234 font]
        [-wnum] [-pltndgvcfrmhs] [name ...]

The **lpr** command uses a spooling daemon to print named files or, if none are named, standard input. The following options are available.

- ▧ -r Removes the file after spooling or printing terminates.

- ▧ -m Sends mail after printing terminates.

- ▧ -h Suppresses printing of the burst page.

- ▧ -s Uses symbolic links. Usually copies files to the spool directory.

- ▧ -C *class* Takes *class* as the job classification for use on the burst page.

- ▧ -J *job* Takes *job* as the job name for use on the burst page. Usually the first file's name is used.

- ▧ -T *title* Specifies the *title*.

- ▧ -#*num* Specifies the number of copies to print.

- ▧ -i Indents the output.

- ▧ -w Specifies the page width.

- ▧ -s Uses **symlink** to link data files rather than attempting to copy them. This enables large files to be printed. Do not modify or remove files until printed.

- ▧ -1234 Specifies a font to be mounted on font position i.

lprm

The **lprm** command is a BSD Unix command that removes jobs from the line printer spooling queue. It has the following syntax:

    lprm [-Pprinter] [-] [jobno...] [user...]

The **lprm** command is the command by which users may stop a job from printing. The **lprm** command without arguments deletes the current job if owned by the person who invoked it. The superuser may issue **lprm** with one or more user names to delete all jobs associated with the specified user or users. The following options are available:

- -P*printer* Specifies the queue associated with the designated printer.
- – Removes all jobs owned by the user invoking the command. If the superuser invokes this command, all jobs in the queue are removed.

lpsched

The **lpsched** command starts the LP print service; this can be done only by root or **lp**. It has the following syntax:

/usr/lib/lpsched [-apqs] *integer*

This command is further described in Chapter 10, starting on page 262.

lpshut

The **lpshut** command shuts down the print service, stopping all active printers. It has the following syntax:

/usr/lib/lpshut

This command is further described in Chapter 10, starting on page 262.

lpstat

The **lpstat** command prints information about the current status of the LP print service. It has the following syntax:

lpstat [*options*]

This command is further described in Chapter 10, starting on page 255.

ls

The **ls** command gives information about contents of directories. For each directory named, **ls** lists the contents of that directory; for each filenamed, **ls** repeats its name and any other information requested. It has the following syntax:

ls [-ACFRabcdfgilmnopqrstux] [*names*]

This command is further described in Chapter 3, starting on page 46. See your system manual for additional information.

mail

The **mail** command sends and receives mail. The **mail** command provides commands to facilitate saving, deleting, and responding to messages that are read. For sending mail, **mail** allows editing, reviewing, and other modification of the message as it is entered. It has the following syntax:

mail [*options*] [*name...*]

The **mail** command is discussed in detail in Chapter 6 starting on page 146. See your system manual for additional information.

mailx

The **mailx** command is a more sophisticated mail processing command than **mail**, enabling you, for example, to invoke an editor to process your messages. It has the following syntax:

mail [*options*] [*name...*]

The **mailx** command provides the following options:

- ◪ -e Exits with 0 if there is mail; exits with 1 if no mail.
- ◪ -f*file* Reads designated file for mail.
- ◪ -F Places a copy of mail in a special filenamed for the first person to receive the mail.
- ◪ -h*n* Specifies number of network hops so far as *n*.

- -H   Prints header information.

- -i   Ignores interrupts.

- -n   Does not read **mail.rc** file.

- -N   Does not print header information.

- -r *address*   Uses *address* as network destination.

- -s *subject*   Designates *subject*.

- -u *user*   Reads mail for *user*.

- -U   Uses internet and not **uucp** addresses.

man

The **man** command prints references in on-line Unix manual. It has the following syntax:

man [-afbcw] [-t*proc*] [-p*pager*] [-d*dir*]
    [-T*term*] [*section*] [*title*]

The **man** command locates and prints the named title from the designated reference section. For historical reasons, "page" is often used as a synonym for "entry." The **man** command recognizes the following arguments:

- *title*   Is always entered in lowercase. If no *section* is specified, **man** searches the entire guide for *title* and prints its first occurrence. To search multiple sections, separate section names with colons (:) on the command line.

- -a   "All" mode. Displays all matching titles; -a is incompatible with the -f option.

- -f   "First" (default) mode. Displays only the first matching title; incompatible with the -a option.

- -b   Leaves blank lines in output. The **nroff** command pads entries with blank lines for printing. By default, **man** filters out excess blank lines, displaying at most two of them.

- -c   Causes **man** to invoke **col**. The **man** command automatically invokes **col** unless *term* is one of the following: 300, 300s, 450, 37, 4000a, 382, 4014, tek, 1620, or X.

- -w   Prints on the standard output only the entry pathnames.

- -t*proc*   Indicates an unprocessed manual page is passed to *proc* for formatting. The *proc* can be any command script in **/usr/man/bin** or an absolute filename of a text processing program elsewhere on the system, such as **/bin/nroff**. See your system manual for more information.

▧   -p*pager* Selects paging program *pager* to display the entry. Paging systems such as **more**, **pg** (default), **cat**, or any available custom pagers are valid arguments for this flag. See your system manual for more information.

▧   -T*term* Formats the entry, passes the *term* value to the processing program, and then prints it on the standard output (usually, the terminal).

See your system manual for additional information.

mesg

The **mesg** command permits or denies messages sent to a terminal. It has the following syntax:

    mesg [n] [y]

The **mesg** command with the argument n forbids messages via **write** by revoking nonuser write permission on the user's terminal. The **mesg** command with the argument y reinstates permission. Without options, **mesg** reports the current state, but does not change it.

mkdev

The **mkdev** command calls scripts to add peripheral devices. It has the following syntax:

    mkdev dos
    mkdev fd
    mkdev fs [*device file*]
    mkdev hd [[*disk*] [*controller* | *adapter*]] [*lun*]
    mkdev mouse
    mkdev serial
    mkdev shl
    mkdev streams
    mkdev tape

This command is further described in Chapter 10, starting on page 273. See your system manual for additional information.

mkdir

The **mkdir** command makes a directory, providing that you have the proper permissions. It has the following syntax:

mkdir [-m *mode*] [-p] *dirname*

This command is further described in Chapter 3, starting on page 48. See your system manual for additional information.

mkfs

The **mkfs** command constructs a file system. It has the following syntax:

mkfs [-y | -n] [-f *fstype*]
    special blocks [: *inodes*] [*gap inblocks*]

This command is further described in Chapter 8, starting on page 198.

mknod

The **mknod** command builds special files. It has the following syntax:

mknod *name* [c | b] *major minor*
mknod *name* p
mknod *name* s
mknod *name* m

The **mknod** command makes a directory entry and corresponding inode for a special file. The first argument is the name of the entry. *b* denotes that the special file is block-type (disks, tape), and *c* denotes that it is character-type (other devices). The *major* and *minor* are numbers specifying the major device type and the minor device (for example, unit, drive, or line number), which may be either decimal or octal. The assignment of major device numbers is specific to each system.

The **mknod** command creates named pipes with the *p* option, semaphores with the *s* option, and shared data (memory) with the *m* option.

more

The **more** command displays on a terminal, one screen at a time. It has the following syntax:

> more [-cdflsie] [-n] [+ *linenumber*] [+/*pattern*] [name]

The **more** command originated with BSD Unix, but is available on some other implementations. See your system manual for further details.

mount

The **mount** command mounts a file structure and announces to the system that a removable file structure is present on *special-device*. It has the following syntax:

> mount [-v] [-r] [-f *fstyp*] *special device*

This command is further described in Chapter 8, starting on page 199.

mv

The **mv** command moves or renames files and renames directories. It has the following syntax:

> mv [-f] *file1 file2*
> mv [-f] *directory1 directory2*
> mv [-f] *file directory*

The **mv** command moves (changes the name of) *file1* to *file2* (or renames *directory1* to *directory2*). If *file2* already exists, it is removed before *file1* is moved. If *file2* has a mode that forbids writing, **mv** prints the mode and reads the standard input to obtain a line. If the line begins with y, the move takes place; if not, **mv** exits. In the third form, one or more files are moved to the directory with their original filenames.

No questions are asked when the -f option is given. The **mv** command refuses to move a file onto itself.

mwm

The **mwm** command, Motif window manager, is an X Window system (X11) client providing the system administrator and programmers with window-management functionality and session-management functionality. It has the following syntax:

mwm [*options*]

This command is further described in Chapter 13, starting on page 386.

ncheck

The **ncheck** command generates names from inode numbers. It has the following syntax:

ncheck [-i *numbers*] [-a] [-s] [*file system*]

This command is further described in Chapter 8, starting on page 216.

netstat

The **netstat** command symbolically displays the contents of various network-related data structures. The Unix System V version has the following syntax:

netstat [-AainrsS] [-f *address family*] [-I *interface*]
[-p *protocol name*] [*interval*] [*namelist*]
[*corefile*]

This command is further described in Chapter 11, starting on page 298.

newgrp

The **newgrp** command logs the user into a new group. It has the following syntax:

newgrp [-] [*group*]

The **newgrp** command changes the group identification of the user invoking it. This user continues to be logged in with the same current directory, but has access permissions based on the new group ID.

The **newgrp** command without an argument changes the group identification to the group defined in the **password** file, in effect resetting the group identification back to its original value.

news

The command **news** prints news items. It has the following syntax:

news [-a] [-n] [-s] [*items*]

The **news** command informs the user of current events. By convention, these events are described by files in the directory **/usr/news**.

When invoked without arguments, **news** prints the contents of all current files in **/usr/news**, most recent first, preceding each with an appropriate header. The **news** command recognizes the following arguments:

- -a   Prints all items, no matter how current, without changing the stored time.

- -n   Prints the names of the current items without printing their contents. It does not change the stored time.

- -s   Prints the number of current items, without printing their names or contents. It does not change the stored time.

nice

The **nice** command changes the scheduling priority for a specified command. It has the following syntax:

nice [-*increment*] *command* [*arguments*]

This command is further described in Chapter 14, starting on page 434.

nm

The **nm** command prints a name list of common object files. It has the following syntax:

nm [-oxhvnefurpVT] [*filenames*]

This command is further described in Chapter 3, starting on page 55. See your system manual for additional information.

nohup

The **nohup** command continues to run a command after the user logs out. It has the following syntax:

nohup *command* [*arguments*]

The **nohup** command executes commands with hangups and quits ignored.

nroff

The **nroff** command formats one or more files for printing. It has the following syntax:

nroff [*options*] [*files*]

The **nroff** command formats output for line and letter-quality printers. It employs codes to specify formatting. See your system manual for details of the similar **troff** command which formats output for typesetters. The **nroff** command recognizes the following arguments:

- -c*name* Prepends **/usr/lib/macros/cmp.[nt].[dt].***name* to files.

- -e Spaces words equally.

- -h Uses tabs for large spaces.

- -i Reads standard input after processing files.

- -k*name* Compacts macros and output to **[dt].***name*.

- -m*name* Prepends **/usr/lib/tmac/tmac.***name* to files.

- -n*n* Numbers first page *n*.

- -o*list* Prints only pages in the specified *list*; *n-m* specifies a page range.

- -q Invokes simultaneous input-output of .rd requests (reading input and printing prompts).

- -r*an* Sets register *a* to the value *n*.

- -s*n* Stops every *n* pages.

- -T*name* Places output on the device *name*.

- -u*n* Overstrikes *n* times.

- -z Suppresses printing of standard output.

od

The **od** command displays files in octal format. It has the following syntax:

>   od [-bcdox] [*file*] [[+]*offset*[.][b]]

This command is further described in Chapter 3, starting on page 56. See your system manual for additional information.

pack

The **pack**, **pcat**, **unpack** commands compress and expand files. They have the following syntaxes:

>   pack [-][-f] *names*
>   pcat *names*
>   unpack *names*

The **pack** command attempts to store the specified files in a compressed form. Wherever possible, each input filename is replaced by a packed file **name.z** with the same access modes, access and modified dates, and owner of *name*. If **pack** is successful, *name* will be removed. Restore packed files to their original form using **unpack** or **pcat**.

The space saved depends on the input file size and character frequency distribution. It is usually not worthwhile to pack files smaller than three blocks, unless the character frequency distribution is very scattered, such as for printer plots or pictures. See also **compress**.

passwd

The **passwd** command creates or modifies a user password. It has the following syntax:

>   passwd *user*

The **passwd** command creates or modifies the password of the designated user. Only the owner or the superuser may change a password.

pg

The **pg** command displays files on a terminal, one screen at a time. It has the following syntax:

pg [- *number*] [-p *string*] [-cefns] [+ *linenumber*]
[+/ *pattern* /] [*files* ...]

The **pg** command displays files one screen at a time on a soft-copy terminal and then prompts the user. Press RETURN to display another screen. The **pg** command enables the user to display previous pages.
    The command line options are:

- -*number* Specifies the size (in lines) of the display.

- -p *string* Uses the designated string as the prompt.

- -c Clears the screen and places the cursor at the home position before displaying each screen.

- -e Disables the pause after each file.

- -f Inhibits **pg** from splitting lines.

- -n Normally, commands must be terminated by pressing RETURN.

- -s Displays all messages and prompts in standout mode (usually inverse video).

- +*linenumber* Starts display at *linenumber*.

- +/*pattern*/ Starts display at the first line containing the regular expression *pattern*.

ping

The **ping** command is a troubleshooting tool for tracking a single-point hardware or software failure in the Internet. It is also used to determine whether a given *host* is alive. It has the following syntax:

ping [-r] [-v] *host* [*packetsize*] [*pcount*]

This command is further described in Chapter 11, starting on page 297.

pr

The **pr** command formats files for printing on the standard output. It has the following syntax:

pr [*options*] [*files*]

The **pr** command prints the named files on the standard output. Standard input is assumed if *file* is − or is not specified. The default listing is separated into pages, each headed by the page number, the date and time, and the name of the file. The options may appear singly or combined in any order. The command recognizes the following arguments:

- ▰ +k Begins printing with page k. (The default is 1.)

- ▰ -k Produces k-column output. (The default is 1.) The options -e and -i are assumed for multicolumn output.

- ▰ -a Prints multicolumn output across the page.

- ▰ -m Merges and prints all files simultaneously, one per column. (Overrides the -k and -a options.)

- ▰ -d Double-spaces the output.

- ▰ -eck Expands input tabs to designated character positions.

- ▰ -ick In output, replaces white space wherever possible by inserting tabs to designated character positions.

- ▰ -nck Provides k-digit line numbering. (The default is 5.)

- ▰ -wk Sets the width of a line to k character positions. (The default is 72 for equal-width multicolumn output; no limit otherwise.)

- ▰ -ok Offsets each line by k character positions. (The default is 0.)

- ▰ -lk Sets the page length to k lines. (The default is 66.)

- ▰ -h Prints the next argument as the header.

- ▰ -p Pauses before beginning each page for terminal output.

- ▰ -f Uses form feed character for new pages. (The default is a sequence of line feeds.)

- ▰ -r Prints no diagnostics if it cannot open files.

◢ -t Suppresses printing the usual five-line identifying header and the five-line trailer normally supplied for each page.

◢ -s*c* Separates columns by the character *c* instead of by the appropriate number of spaces. (The default for *c* is a tab.)

ps

The **ps** command reports process status. It has the following syntax:

ps [*options*]

This command is further described in Chapter 14, starting on page 423.

pstat

The **pstat** command reports more detailed system information than the **ps** command. It has the following syntax:

pstat [-aipf] [-u *ubase1 ubase2*] [-n *namelist*] [*file*]

This command is further described in Chapter 14, starting on page 424.

pwd

The **pwd** command prints working directory name. It has the following syntax:

pwd

The **pwd** command prints the pathname of the working (current) directory.

rcp

The **rcp** command copies files between systems in a Micnet network. It has the following syntax:

rcp [*options*] [*srcmachine*:]*srcfile* [*destmachine*:]*destfile*

This command is further described in Chapter 11, starting on page 288.

restor

The **restor** command performs an incremental file system restore for BSD Unix. It reads magnetic tapes containing the output of the **dump** command. It has the following syntax:

> restor *key* [*argument ...*] [*file system*]

This command is further described in Chapter 7, starting on page 176.

restore

The **restore** command performs an incremental file system restore of a previous backup. This utility acts as a front end to **cpio**, and thus reads **cpio** format tapes or floppies. It has the following syntax:

> restore [-c] [-i] [-o] [-t] [-d *device*]
> [*pattern ...*]

This command is further described in Chapter 7, starting on page 173.

rm

The **rm** command removes files or directories. It has the following syntax:

> rm [-fri] *files*

The **rm** command removes the entries for one or more files from a directory. If an entry was the last link to the file, the file is destroyed. Removal of a file requires write permission in its directory, but does not require read or write permission on the file itself.

The **rm** command does not delete directories unless the -r option is used. The following options are recognized:

- ◪   -f   Does not prompt the user to confirm removing files for which the user does not have write permission. The files are simply removed.

- ◪   -r   Deletes recursively the entire contents of the specified directories and the directories themselves.

- ◪   -i (interactive)   Asks whether to delete each file and, if the -r option is in effect, whether to examine each directory.

rmdir

The **rmdir** command removes directories. It has the following syntax:

rmdir [-p] [-s] *dirnames*

The **rmdir** command removes the entries for one or more subdirectories from a directory. A directory must be empty before it can be removed. The **rmdir** command will not remove the root directory of a mounted file system. The command recognizes the following arguments:

◪   -p Allows users to remove the *dirname* and its parent directories, which become empty. A message is printed on standard output indicating whether the entire path was removed or part of the path remains for some reason.

◪   -s Suppresses the message printed on standard error when -p is in effect.

sag

The **sag** command generates the system activity graph. It has the following syntax:

sag [*options*]

The **sag** command graphically displays the system activity data stored in a binary data file by a previous **sar** run. Any **sar** data items may be plotted singly, or in combination; as cross plots, or versus time. Simple arithmetic combinations of data may be specified. **sag** invokes **sar** and finds the desired data by string-matching the data column header. See your system manual for options.

sar

The **sar** command generates system activity reports. It has the following syntax:

sar [-ubdycwaqvmnprDSAC] [-o *file*] t [n]
sar [-ubdycwaqvmnprDSAC] [-s *time*]
      [-e *time*] [-i *sec*] [-f *file*]

This command is further described in Chapter 14, starting on page 426.

sed

The **sed** command invokes the stream editor, which combines some of the best features of **vi** and **grep**. It has the following syntax:

sed [*options*] [*files*]

See your system manual for information about **sed**.

shl

The **shl** command is the shell layer manager. It has the following syntax:

shl

The **shl** command allows a user to interact with more than one shell from a single terminal. The user controls these shells, known as layers, using the commands described next.

The current layer is the one that can receive input from the keyboard. Other layers attempting to read from the keyboard are blocked. A layer is a shell that has been bound to a virtual tty device. Each layer has its own process group ID.

The following commands may be issued from the **shl** prompt level:

- create [*name*]   Creates a layer called *name* and makes it the current layer.
- block name [*name* ...]   Blocks the output of the corresponding layer for each *name* when it is not the current layer.
- delete name [*name* ...]   Deletes the corresponding layer for each *name*.
- help (or ?)   Prints the syntax of the **shl** commands.
- layers [-l] [*name* ...]   Lists the layer name and process group for each *name*.
- resume [*name*]   Makes the layer referenced by *name* the current layer.
- toggle   Resumes the layer that was current before the last current layer.
- unblock name [*name* ...]   For each *name*, does not block the output of the corresponding layer when it is not the current layer.
- quit   Exits **shl**.
- *name*   Makes the layer referenced by *name* the current layer.

shutdown

The **shutdown** command terminates all processing. It has the following syntax:

        shutdown [-y] [-g[*hh*:]*mm*]
                     [-i[0156sS]] [-f"*mesg*"] [-f*FILE*] [su]

The **shutdown** command terminates all currently running processes in an orderly and cautious manner. The options follow:

■   -y   Runs the command silently. If this option is not specified, **shutdown** demands confirmation before shutting down the system.

■   -g[*hh*:]*mm*   Specifies the number of hours and minutes before shutdown (maximum: 72 hours). 60 seconds is the default.

■   -i[0156sS]   Specifies the init level to bring the system to. By default, the system is brought to level 0.

■   -f*mesg mesg*   The message enclosed in double quotes ("") is sent to all terminals warning of the imminent shutdown.

■   -f*FILE*   Similar to -f*mesg*, except that *FILE* is the pathname for a file containing the message.

size

The **size** command prints section sizes of common object files in bytes. It has the following syntax:

        size [-n] [-f] [-o] [-x] [-V] *files*

The **size** command produces section size information in bytes for each loaded section in the common object files. By default, numbers are printed in decimal. The command recognizes the following arguments:

■   -n   Includes NOLOAD sections in the size.

■   -f   Produces full output, namely, the size of every loaded section, followed by the section name in parentheses.

■   -o   Prints numbers in octal format.

■   -V   Supplies the version information on the **size** command.

■   -x   Prints numbers in hexadecimal format.

sleep

The **sleep** command suspends execution for an interval. It has the following syntax:

> sleep *time*

The **sleep** command suspends execution for *time* seconds. Use it to execute a command after a certain amount of time, or to execute a command every so often.

sort

The **sort** command sorts and merges files. It has the following syntax:

> sort [-cmu] [-o*output*] [-y*kmem*] [-z*recsz*]
> [-d*fiMnr*] [-b*tx*] [+*pos1*] [-*pos2*] [*files*]

The **sort** command sorts lines of all named *files* together and writes the result on the standard output. The standard input is read if - is used as a filename or if no input files are named.

    Comparisons are based on one or more sort keys extracted from each line of input. By default, there is one sort key, the entire input line, and ordering is determined by the collating sequence defined by the locale. The following options are available:

- ◪   -bt -b Ignores leading spaces when determining starting and ending positions of the sort key. -t *char* uses *char* as the field separator character.

- ◪   -c Checks that the input file is sorted according to the ordering rules; generates output only when the file is out of sort.

- ◪   -m Merges only; the input files are already sorted.

- ◪   -u Unique: Suppresses all but one in each set of lines having equal keys.

- ◪   -o*output* Specifies the *output* file to use instead of the standard output.

- ◪   -y*kmem* Starts the sort with the specified kilobytes of memory, if possible.

- ◪   -z*recsz* Specifies the buffer size in bytes for the merge phase.

stty

The **stty** command sets certain terminal I/O options for the current standard input device, or reports the settings of certain options. It has the following syntax:

stty [-a] [-g] [*options*]

This command is further described in Chapter 10, starting on page 278.

su

The **su** command allows an authorized user to become a superuser or another user without logging off. It has the following syntax:

su [-] [*name*][*arg ...*]

This command is further described in Chapter 12, starting on page 329.

sum

The **sum** command calculates checksum and counts blocks in a file. It has the following syntax:

sum [-r] *file*

The **sum** command calculates and prints a 16-bit checksum for the named file and prints the number of 512-byte blocks in the file. It is commonly used to validate file communication and to verify bad spots. The -r option invokes an alternative algorithm to compute the checksum.

sync

The **sync** command updates the superblock. It has the following syntax:

sync

The **sync** command executes the **sync** system primitive. Invoke **sync** to ensure file system integrity before shutting down the system.

tail

The **tail** command displays the last part of a file. It has the following syntax:

tail [+/-[*number* [*lbc*] [-f]]] [*file*]

The **tail** command copies the named file to the standard output beginning at a designated place. If no file is named, the standard input is used.

If you use the -f ("follow") option and the input file is not a pipe, the program does not terminate after copying the input file line. Instead it enters an endless loop, sleeps for a second, and then attempts to read and copy further records from the input file. Use this option to monitor the growth of a file written by another process.

talk

The **talk** command talks to another user. It has the following syntax:

talk *person* [*ttyname*]

The **talk** command is a visual communication program that copies lines from your terminal to that of another user. If that user is connected to your own machine, then *person* is her or his login name. If you wish to talk to a user on another host, then *person* is of the form:

host!*user* or
host.*user* or
host:*user* or
user@*host*

where *user*@*host* is preferred. See your system manual for more information.

tar

The **tar** command saves and restores files to and from an archive medium, typically a floppy disk or tape. It has the following syntax:

tar [*key*] [*files*]

This command is further described in Chapter 7, starting on page 167.

telnet

The **telnet** command is the used to connect to a remote host, using the TELNET protocol. It has the following syntax:

telnet [*host* [*port*]]

This command is further described in Chapter 11, starting on page 288. See your system manual for additional information.

time

The **time** command generates clock times for a specified command. It has the following syntax:

time *command*

This command is further described in Chapter 14, starting on page 429.

timex

The **timex** command prints (in seconds) the elapsed time, user time, and system time spent in executing the specified command. It has the following syntax:

timex [*options*] *command*

This command is further described in Chapter 14, starting on page 429.

touch

The **touch** command updates access and modification times of a file. It has the following syntax:

touch [-a*mc*] [*mmddhhmm*[*yy*]] *files*

The **touch** command causes the access and modification times of each argument to be updated. If no time is specified, the current time is used. When **touch** creates a file, its modification and access times can be set to any time. However, the creation time is automatically set to the current time at the time of creation, and cannot be changed. The first *mm* denotes the month, *dd* denotes the day, *hh* denotes the hour, the second *mm* denotes the minute, and *yy* denotes the year. The default option is -am. The command recognizes the following arguments:

- ▰ -a   Updates only the access time.
- ▰ -m   Updates only the modification time.
- ▰ -c   Silently prevents **touch** from creating the file if it did not previously exist.

tty

The **tty** command gets the terminal's name. It has the following syntax:

>   tty [-s] [-1]

The **tty** command prints the pathname of the user's terminal on the standard output. The -s option inhibits printing, allowing you to test just the exit code. The -1 option displays the synchronous line number.

umount

The **umount** command dismounts a file structure. It announces to the system that the removable file structure previously mounted on device *special-device* is to be removed. It has the following syntax:

>   umount *special device*

This command is further described in Chapter 8, starting on page 200.

uname

The **uname** command prints the current system name of the Unix system on the standard output file. It has the following syntax:

>   uname [-s*nrvma*]
>   uname [-S *system name*]

The **uname** command is mainly useful to determine which system one is using. The following options are available:

- ▣ -s Prints the system name. (This is the default option.)
- ▣ -n Prints nodename, the name by which the system is known to a communications network.
- ▣ -r Prints the operating system release.
- ▣ -v Prints the operating system version.
- ▣ -m Prints the machine hardware name.
- ▣ -a Prints all of the above information.

uptime

The **uptime** command prints the current time of day, the length of time the system has been up, and the number of users logged into the system. It has the following syntax:

    uptime

This command is further described in Chapter 14, starting on page 430.

uucp

The **uucp** command is the Unix-to-Unix system copy utility that copies files on your machine or on a remote system recognized by **uucp**. It has the following syntax:

    uucp [*options*] *source-files destination-file*

This command is further described in Chapter 11, starting on page 315.

uulog

The **uulog** command is associated with **uucp**, the Unix-to-Unix system copy. It has the following syntax:

    uulog [*options*] [-s | f] *system*
    uulog [*options*] -f*system*

The **uulog** command queries a log file of **uucp** or **uuxqt** transactions in a file **/usr/spool/uucp/.Log/uucico/system**, or **/usr/spool/uucp/.Log/uuxqt/system**.

uuname

The **uuname** command is associated with **uucp**, the Unix-to-Unix system copy. It has the following syntax:

    uuname [-l] [-c]

The **uuname** command lists the names of systems known to **uucp**. The command recognizes the following arguments:

- -c   Returns the names of systems known to **cu**.
- -l   Returns the local system name.

uupick

The **uupick** command accepts or rejects the files transmitted to the user. It has the following syntax:

    uupick [-s *system*]

This command is further described in Chapter 11, starting on page 317.

uustat

The **uustat** command is the **uucp** status inquiry and job control utility. It displays the status of, or cancels, previously specified **uucp** commands, or provides general status on **uucp** connections to other systems. It has the following syntax:

    uustat [-a I m I p I q]
    uustat [-h I r*jobid*]
    uustat [-s*system*] [-u*user*]

This command is further described in Chapter 11, starting on page 318.

uuto

The **uuto** command is the public Unix-to-Unix system file copy that uses the **uucp** facility to send files, while it allows the local system to control the file access. It has the following syntax:

uuto [*options*] *source-files destination*

This command is further described in Chapter 11, starting on page 317.

uux

The **uux** command is the Unix-to-Unix system command execution utility. It gathers zero or more files from various systems, executes a command on a specified system, and then sends standard output to a file on a specified system. It has the following syntax:

uux [*options*] *command-string*

This command is further described in Chapter 11, starting on page 318. See your system manual for additional information.

vi

The **vi** command activates a commonly used screen-oriented text editor. It has the following syntax:

vi [*options*] [*files*]

This command is the main focus of Chapter 2.

vmstat

The **vmstat** command provides report paging and system statistics. It has the following syntax:

vmstat [-fs] [-n *namelist*] [-l *lines*]
        [*interval* [*count*]]

This command is further described in Chapter 14, starting on page 432.

volcopy

The **volcopy** command makes a literal copy of the file system using a block size matched to the device. It has the following syntax:

> volcopy [*options*] *fsname srcdevice volname1 destdevice*
> *volname2*

This command is further described in Chapter 7, starting on page 174.

w

The **w** command (BSD) displays information about who is on the system and their activities. It has the following syntax:

> w [-hlqtw] [-n *namelist*] [-s swapdev]
> [-u utmpfile] [*users...*]

This command is further described in Chapter 14, starting on page 436.

wait

The **wait** command awaits completion of background processes. It has the following syntax:

> wait

The **wait** command pauses until all background processes started with an ampersand (&) have finished and reports on abnormal terminations.

wall

The **wall** command writes to all users. It has the following syntax:

> wall

The **wall** command reads a message from the standard input until an end-of-file. It then sends this message to all users currently logged in.

what

The **what** command identifies files. It has the following syntax:

what *files*

The **what** command searches the given files for all occurrences of the pattern @(#) and prints out what follows until the first tilde (~), greater-than sign (>), newline, backslash (\), or null character.

who

The **who** command lists system users. It has the following syntax:

who [-uATHldtasqbrp] [*file*]
who am i

This command is further described in Chapter 14, starting on page 434.

write

The **write** command writes to another user. It has the following syntax:

write *user* [*terminal*]

The **write** command copies lines from your terminal to that of another user. The recipient of the message should write back at this point. Communication continues until an end-of-file is read from the terminal or an interrupt is sent.

xbiff

The **xbiff** command displays a little image of a mailbox to inform users whether they have mail. It has the following syntax:

xbiff [*options*]

This command is further described in Chapter 13, starting on page 409.

xclock

The **xclock** command is an analog and digital clock for the X Window system. It has the following syntax:

> xclock [*options*]

This command is further described in Chapter 13, starting on page 409.

xdm

The **xdm** command manages a collection of X displays, both local and possibly remote. It has the following syntax:

> xdm [*options*]

This command is further described in Chapter 13, starting on page 381.

xinit

xinit initializes the X Window system. It has the following syntax:

> xinit [[*client*] *options*] [-- [*server*] [*display*] *options*]

This command is further described in Chapter 13, starting on page 391.

xload

The **xload** command displays a periodically updating histogram of the system load average as an indication of system performance. It has the following syntax:

> xload [*options*]

This command is further described in Chapter 13, starting on page 406.

xlsfonts

The **xlsfonts** command displays the list of server fonts that match a supplied pattern. It has the following syntax:

xlsfonts [*options*] -f*n pattern*

This command is further described in Chapter 13, starting on page 414.

xlswins

The **xlswins** command displays the server window list in tree form. It has the following syntax:

xlswins [*options*] [*windowid* ...]

This command is further described in Chapter 13, starting on page 415.

xman

The **xman** command displays manual pages in the X Window environment. It has the following syntax:

xman [*options*]

This command is further described in Chapter 13, starting on page 402.

xpr

The **xpr** command prints an X Window dump. It has the following syntax:

xpr [*options*] *filename*

This command is further described in Chapter 13, starting on page 399.

xrdb

The **xrdb** command gets or sets the contents of the RESOURCEMANAGER property on the root window of screen 0. It has the following syntax:

xrdb [options] [*filename*]

This command is further described in Chapter 13, starting on page 396.

xset

The **xset** command is a user-preference utility for X Window systems. It has the following syntax:

xset [*options*]

This command is further described in Chapter 13, starting on page 394.

xsetroot

The **xsetroot** command sets root window parameters. It has the following syntax:

xsetroot [*options*]

This command is further described in Chapter 13, starting on page 411.

xterm

The **xterm** command provides DEC VT102 (character terminal) and Tektronix 4014 (graphics terminal) compatible terminal emulation. It has the following syntax:

xterm [-*toolkitoption*] [*option*]

This command is further described in Chapter 13, starting on page 404.

xwd

The **xwd** command dumps an X Window image. It has the following syntax:

xwd [*options*]

This command is further described in Chapter 13, starting on page 401.

xwininfo

The **xwininfo** command displays window information. It has the following syntax:

xwininfo [*options*]

This command is further described in Chapter 13, starting on page 397.

xwud

The **xwud** command displays window images saved by **xwd** in a specially formatted dump file. It has the following syntax:

xwud [*options*]

This command is further described in Chapter 13, starting on page 402.

Unix System

Administration Guide

APPENDIX

Korn Shell and Bourne Shell Commands

This appendix describes the major Korn shell and Bourne shell commands. All of the listed commands are available in the Korn shell; most are also available in the Bourne shell.

alias

The **alias** command has the following syntax:

alias [-tx] [*word*[*=command*] ...]

The **alias** command defines *word* to signify *command*. When *word* is used, *command* is executed, for example, to shorten lengthy command sequences. The **alias** command is not available in the Bourne shell.

bg

The **bg** command has the following syntax:

bg [%*n*...]

The **bg** command places the job *n* in the background. If *n* is not specified, the current job is placed in the background. This command is not available in the Bourne shell.

break

The **break** command has the following syntax:

break [*n*]

The **break** command exits loops created by any of the keywords **for**, **select**, **until**, or **while**. The optional parameter *n* specifies the number of nested loops exited.

case

The **case** control structure has the following syntax:

case *word* in
pattern1)
  command-list1
;;
pattern2)
  command-list2

> ;;
> esac

If the character string *word* matches *pattern1*, the script executes the commands denoted by *command-list1*. If the character string *word* matches *pattern2*, the script executes the commands denoted by *command-list2*. Note the use of the double semicolon (;;) to terminate each command list. The **esac** operator terminates the **case** control structure.

cd

The **cd** command has the following syntax:

> cd [*newdir*]

The **cd** command changes the directory from your current directory to your new directory.

continue

The **continue** command has the following syntax:

> continue [*n*]

The **continue** command skips any lines that follow in a **for**, **select**, **until**, or **while** loop, restarting at the top of the loop. The optional parameter *n* denotes that execution resumes at the *n*th enclosing loop.

echo

The **echo** command has the following syntax:

> echo [*message*]

The **echo** command writes to standard output specified arguments separated by blanks. If no arguments are specified, it outputs a blank line. A \c causes the echo to complete without printing a newline. A \n in the *message* causes a newline to be printed. See your system manual for other \ options or escape characters.

eval

The **eval** command has the following syntax:

    eval [arg ...]

The **eval** command makes it possible to execute command lines after evaluation of their contents.

exec

The **exec** command has the following syntax:

    exec [arg ...]

The **exec** command replaces the current shell with the new shell or program designated by *arg*. It does not spawn a new process or a subshell.

exit

The **exit** command has the following syntax:

    exit [n]

The **exit** command leaves the shell with the exit status *n*, if specified, or the status of the most recently executed command.

export

The **export** command has the following syntax:

    export [name ...]

The **export** command marks *name* parameters to be passed to the environment for other commands and subshells. When name is not specified, the command lists all currently exported values.

fc

The **fc** command has the following syntax:

> fc [-e *editor*] [-nlr] [*first*] [*last*]
> fc -e - [*old=new*] [*command*]

The **fc** command lists and edits command lines, which may be in the **history** file. This command is not available in the Bourne shell.

fg

The **fg** command has the following syntax:

> fg [%*n*]

The **fg** command places the job *n* in the foreground. If *n* is not specified, the current job is placed in the foreground. This command is not available in the Bourne shell.

for

The **for** control structure has the following syntax:

> for *name* [in *word* ...]
> do
>   *command list*
> done

When the shell encounters the **for** control structure, it sets the variable *name* to the first value in the word list and executes all commands between **do** and **done**. It then sets the variable *name* to the next value in the word list and executes all commands between **do** and **done**. Execution ends when there are no more *words* in the list.

hash

The **hash** command has the following syntax:

> hash [-r] [*commands*]

The **hash** command searches for the designated commands and notes their location. If no command is specified, **hash** lists currently hashed commands. The -r flag removes the specified command from the hash list.

if

The **if** control structure has the following syntax:

    if *expression* then
      command-list
    fi

The **if** control structure allows conditional command execution. If the *expression* is TRUE, all commands between the **then** and the **fi** (**if** spelled backward) are executed. If the *expression* is FALSE, commands between the **then** and the **fi** are skipped. Indentation is often used to show that the *command list* "belongs to" the **if fi** control structure.

    if *expression* then
      command-list1
    else
      command-list2
    fi

If the *expression* is TRUE, the commands in *command-list1* are executed. If the *expression* is FALSE, the commands in *command-list2* are executed. Notice the use of indentation as in the first version of the **if** command.

jobs

The **jobs** command has the following syntax:

    jobs [-l]

The **jobs** command lists all jobs currently running in your shell. Output includes job number and status. Coding the -l parameter outputs the process ID. This command is not available in the Bourne shell.

let

The **let** command has the following syntax:

> let *vars*

The **let** command modifies the value of designated variables. This command is not available in the Bourne shell.

login

The **login** command has the following syntax:

> login [*user*]

The **login** command enables a currently active user to log in with a different user name.

newgrp

The **newgrp** command has the following syntax:

> newgrp [*group*]

The **newgrp** command changes the group ID of the invoking user.

print

The **print** command has the following syntax:

> print [-Rnprsu[*n*]] [*arg...*]

The **print** command writes to standard output specified arguments separated by blanks. If no arguments are specified, it outputs a blank line. It provides the following options:

- ✓ -R Ignores all **echo** escape sequences except -n.
- ✓ -n Prevents a newline from being added to output.
- ✓ -p Writes output to the process spawned by |& instead of to standard output.

☑   -r   Ignores all **echo** escape sequences.

☑   -s   Writes *args* to the history file.

☑   -u*n*   Writes to file descriptor *n*.

This command is not available in the Bourne shell.

pwd

The **pwd** command has the following syntax:

pwd

The **pwd** command displays the name of the current working directory.

read

The **read** command has the following syntax:

read [-prsu[*n*]] [*name?prompt*] [*name...*]

The **read** command reads a line from standard input and places each word into the parameter *name,* parsing according to the separator specified by the IFS shell parameter. If no *name* is specified, the line is read into the REPLY variable. It provides the following options:

☑   -p   Reads from the output of the spawned process.

☑   -r   Prevents the \ at the end of a line from being interpreted as a line continuation.

☑   -s   Puts the input line into the history file.

☑   -u*n*   Reads the input from file descriptor *n*.

readonly

The **readonly** command has the following syntax:

readonly [*name...*]

The **readonly** command marks the listed parameters so that they cannot be assigned values.

return

The **return** command has the following syntax:

return [*n*]

The **return** command ceases function execution and returns to the calling script with the exit status *n,* if specified, or the status of the most recently executed command.

select

The **select** command has the following syntax:

select *parameter* in *words*
do
   command_lines
done

The **select** control structure prints on the screen a series of *words* each preceded by a sequence number. The PS3 prompt is printed and the line typed by the user is read into the REPLY variable. If this response is a number corresponding to one of the listed *words, parameter* is set to that *word;* otherwise it is set to null. This command is not available in the Bourne shell.

set

The **set** control structure has the following syntax:

set [-aefhkmnostuvx][-o *option...*][*arg...*]

The **set** command sets shell options and resets the values of positional parameters. When the − is replaced by a +, the specified option is turned off. The following options are defined:

- ▟ -a All subsequent parameters defined are automatically exported; the option name is allexport.

- ▟ -e If the shell is non-interactive, execute the ERR trap when a command fails, and exit immediately. Does not apply while reading **.profile**; the option name is errexit.

▰ -f Disables file name generation; the option name is noglob.

▰ -h Each command whose name is an *identifier* becomes a tracked alias when first encountered; the option name is trackall.

▰ -k All parameter assignment arguments are placed in the environment for a command to use; the option name is keyword.

▰ -m Runs background jobs in a separate process group, and prints a line including exit status upon completion; the option name is monitor.

▰ -n Reads commands but does not execute them; the option name is noexec.

▰ -o Turns on the specified option.

▰ -s Sorts the positional parameters.

▰ -t Exits after reading and executing one command.

▰ -u Treats unset parameters as an error when substituting; the option name is nounset.

▰ -v Prints shell input lines as they are read; the option name is verbose.

▰ -x Prints commands and their arguments as they are executed; the option name is xtrace.

▰ − Turns off -x and -v flags and stops examining arguments for flags.

▰ -- Does not change any of the flags.

▰ + Causes specified flag to be turned off.

shift

The **shift** command has the following syntax:

    shift [*n*]

The **shift** command moves the contents of the positional parameters ($1, $2, etc.) one position to the left. After execution, $1 contains the previous contents of $2, and $2 contains the previous contents of $3, etc.

test

The **test** command has the following syntax:

test *expr*

or

[*expr*]

The **test** command evaluates the named expression. It returns a zero exit status if the expression is TRUE, and returns a nonzero exit status if the expression is FALSE. The following primitives are used to construct *expr*:

- -r *file*   TRUE if *file* exists and is readable.
- -w *file*   TRUE if *file* exists and is writable.
- -x *file*   TRUE if *file* exists and is executable.
- -f *file*   TRUE if *file* exists and is a regular file.
- -d *file*   TRUE if *file* exists and is a directory.
- -c *file*   TRUE if *file* exists and is a character special file.
- -b *file*   TRUE if *file* exists and is a block special file.
- -u *file*   TRUE if *file* exists and its set-user-ID bit is set.
- -g *file*   TRUE if *file* exists and its set-group-ID bit is set.
- -k *file*   TRUE if *file* exists and its sticky bit is set.
- -s *file*   TRUE if *file* exists and has a size greater than 0.
- -t [*fildes*]   TRUE if the open file whose file descriptor number is *fildes* (1 by default) is associated with a terminal device.
- -z *s1*   TRUE if the length of string *s1* is 0.
- -n *s1*   TRUE if the length of string *s1* is nonzero.
- *s1*=*s2*   TRUE if strings *s1* and *s2* are identical.
- *s1*!=*s2*   TRUE if strings *s1* and *s2* are not identical.
- *s1*   TRUE if *s1* is not the null string.
- *n1* -eq*n2*   TRUE if the integers *n1* and *n2* are algebraically equal. Any of the comparisons -ne, -gt, -ge, -lt, and -le may be used in place of -eq.

time

The **time** command has the following syntax:

time *command_line*

The **time** command executes the command line and displays the execution time of the user, the system, and *command_line*. This command is not available in the Bourne shell.

times

The **times** command has the following syntax:

times

The **times** command prints the accumulated user and system times for the shell and for processes run from the shell.

trap

The **trap** command has the following syntax:

trap [*arg*] [*signal...*]

The **trap** command waits for the designated *signal* and then executes the command line specified by *arg*. The following signals are defined:

- 0   Exit from shell
- 1   Hangup
- 2   Interrupt
- 3   Quit
- 4   Illegal instruction
- 5   Trace trap
- 6   IOT instruction
- 7   EMT instruction
- 8   Floating-point exception
- 10 Bus error
- 12 Bad argument to a system call
- 13 Write to a pipe without a process to read output

▟   14 Alarm timeout

▟   15 Software termination

type

The **type** command has the following syntax:

> type *commands*

The **type** command prints information about the specified *commands*.

typeset

The **typeset** command has the following syntax:

> typeset [-HLRZfilprtux[*n*][*name*][=*value*]]...]

The **typeset** command sets the shell variable name to the *value* whose type depends on the options used. When the − is replaced by a +, the type is turned off. The following options are defined:

▟   -H Provides Unix to host-file name mapping on non-Unix machines.

▟   -L Left-justifies and removes leading blanks from the value.

▟   -R Right-justifies and fills the value with leading blanks.

▟   -Z Right-justifies and fills with leading zeros if the first non-blank character is a digit and the -L flag has not been set.

▟   -e Tags the parameter as having an error; currently unused by the shell.

▟   -f The names refer to function names rather than parameter names.

▟   -i The name is an integer, speeding arithmetic operations.

▟   -l Converts uppercase letters to lowercase.

▟   -p Writes the output onto the two-way pipe.

▟   -r Sets given names to readonly.

▟   -t Tags the *name* for user processing.

▟   -u Converts lowercase letters to uppercase.

- ▰ -x Marks given *names* for automatic export to the environment of subsequently executed commands.
- ▰ + Causes specified flag to be turned off.

ulimit

The **ulimit** command has the following syntax:

    ulimit [*option*] [*n*]

The **ulimit** command sets the maximum size of files or pipes to *n* blocks. Options include f for file size and p for pipe size.

umask

The **umask** command has the following syntax:

    umask [*value*]

The **umask** command sets the user's file creation permission mask to the specified octal value.

unalias

The **unalias** command has the following syntax:

    unalias *names*

The **unalias** command reverses the effect of the **alias** command. This command is not available in the Bourne shell.

unset

The **unset** command has the following syntax:

    unset *names*

unset removes the specified *name* set by the shell.

until

The **until** control structure has the following syntax:

> until *condition*
> do
>   *commands*
> done

The **until** control structure repeats a series of commands as long as the designated condition is not TRUE.

wait

The **wait** command has the following syntax:

> wait [*n*]

The **wait** command suspends the shell until the spawned process *n* terminates, and then reports the process termination status.

whence

The **whence** command has the following syntax:

> whence [-v] *names*

The **whence** command indicates for each *name* how it would be interpreted if used as a command name. This command is not available in the Bourne shell.

while

The **while** control structure has the following syntax:

```
while expression
do
  command-list
done
```

The **while** control structure repeats a series of commands while (as long as) a given condition is TRUE. First the *expression* is evaluated. If it is TRUE, the *command-list* is executed and then *expression* is evaluated again. If the *expression* is FALSE, control passes to the command following the **done** statement. Sooner or later the *expression* must be FALSE; if not, an *infinite loop* occurs, and execution stops, perhaps necessitating that the system be rebooted.

Unix System

Administration Guide

APPENDIX C

C Shell Commands

This appendix describes the major C shell commands.

alias

The **alias** command has the following syntax:

alias *[name [wordlist]]*

The **alias** command provides another name, often shorter, as an alias for a given command. The first form prints all aliases. The second form prints the alias for *name*. The final form assigns the specified wordlist as the alias of *name*; *wordlist* is one or more commands and filename substitution is applied to *wordlist*. The *name* is not allowed to be alias or unalias.

bg

The **bg** command has the following syntax:

bg [%*job*...]

The **bg** command places the current job or the specified job in the background.

break

The **break** command has the following syntax:

break

The **break** command causes execution to resume after the end of the nearest enclosing **foreach** or **while** statement. The remaining commands on the current line are executed. Multilevel breaks are thus possible by writing them all on one line.

breaksw

The **breaksw** statement has the following syntax:

breaksw

The **breaksw** statement causes a break from a switch in a **case** control structure, resuming after the **endsw**.

case

The **case** control structure has the following syntax:

```
switch (word)
case pattern1
  command-list1
breaksw
case pattern2
  command-list2
breaksw
default:
  command-list3
breaksw
endsw
```

The **case** control structure can be thought of as a complex **if** control structure. It evaluates a character string and determines which list of commands to execute. If the character string *word* matches *pattern1*, the script executes the commands denoted by *command-list1*. If the character string *word* matches *pattern2*, the script executes the commands denoted by *command-list2*. If the character string *word* does not match any pattern, the commands after default: (in this case *command-list3*) are executed. Note the use of the **breaksw** statement to terminate each command list and the **endsw** statement to terminate the C shell **case** structure.

cd

The **cd** command has the following syntax:

```
cd name
```

The **cd** command is an abbreviation for the command **chdir**.

chdir

The **chdir** command has the following syntax:

```
chdir name
```

The **chdir** command changes the shell's working directory to directory name. If no argument is given, it then changes to the home directory of the user.

continue

The **continue** statement has the following syntax:

continue

The **continue** statement proceeds to execute the nearest enclosing **while** or **foreach**. The rest of the commands on the current line are executed.

default

The **default** statement has the following syntax:

default:

The **default** statement labels the default case in a **switch** statement. The default should come after all **case** labels.

dirs

The **dirs** command has the following syntax:

dirs

The **dirs** command prints the directory stack.

echo

The **echo** command has the following syntax:

echo *wordlist*

The **echo** command writes the specified words to the shell's standard output. A \c causes **echo** to complete without printing a newline. A \n in *wordlist* causes a newline to be printed. Otherwise the words are echoed, separated by spaces. See your system manual for other options or escape characters.

else

The **else** statement has the following syntax:

else

The **else** statement is part of the **if...else...endif** C shell structure. Statements between the **else** and the **endif** are executed if the condition following the **if** is FALSE. **else** statements may be nested.

end

The **end** statement has the following syntax:

end

The **end** statement terminates the **foreach...end** and **while...end** C shell structures. For ease in debugging, the **end** statement should be coded on a separate line.

endif

The **endif** statement has the following syntax:

endif

The **endif** statement terminates the **if...else...endif** C shell structure. Each **if** must have a corresponding **endif**.

endsw

The **endsw** statement has the following syntax:

endsw

The **endsw** statement marks the end of a **switch** C shell structure, used to select among options.

eval

The **eval** command has the following syntax:

    eval *arg*

eval evaluates arguments inputting the result to the shell.

exec

The **exec** command has the following syntax:

    exec *command*

The **exec** command executes the specified command in place of the current shell.

exit

The **exit** command has the following syntax:

    exit
    exit(*expr*)

The **exit** command leaves the shell either with the value of the status variable (first form) or with the value of the specified *expr* (second form).

fg

The **fg** command has the following syntax:

    fg [%*job*...]

The **fg** command places the current job or the specified job in the foreground.

foreach

The **foreach** command has the following syntax:

> foreach *name* (*wordlist*)
>   *command list*
> end

The **foreach** command executes one or a series of commands a predetermined number of times. When the C shell encounters the **foreach** control structure, it sets the variable *name* to the first value in the word list and executes all commands between *foreach* and *end*. It then sets the variable *name* to the next value in the word list and executes all *commands* between *foreach* and *end*. Execution ends when there are no more words in the list.

glob

The **glob** command has the following syntax:

> glob *wordlist*

The **glob** command is like **echo**, but no \ escapes are recognized and words are delimited by null characters in the output. The **glob** command is useful for programs that employ the shell to apply filename expansion to a list of words.

goto

The **goto** command has the following syntax:

> goto *word*

The **goto** command causes the expansion of the specified word to yield a string of the form *label:*. The shell rewinds its input and searches for a line of the form *label:* possibly preceded by blanks or tabs. Execution continues after the specified line.

history

The **history** command has the following syntax:

    history

The **history** command displays the history event list.

if

The **if** control structure has the following syntax:

    if *expression* then
        command-list
    endif

or

    if *expression* then
        command-list1
    else
        command-list2
    endif

The **if** control structure enables you to code different actions to meet different conditions. The first form of the **if** control structure executes all commands between the **then** and the **endif** if the *expression* is TRUE. If the *expression* is FALSE, commands between the **then** and the **endif** are skipped. Indentation is often used to show that the command list "belongs to" the **if...endif** control structure.

The second form of the **if** control structure provides more flexibility. If the *expression* is TRUE, the commands in *command-list1* are executed. If the *expression* is FALSE, the commands in *command-list2* are executed. Notice the use of indentation, as in the first form of the **if** control structure.

jobs

The **jobs** command has the following syntax:

    jobs [-l]

The **jobs** command generates a list of active jobs. Use the option -l to print process IDs.

kill

The **kill** command has the following syntax:

> kill *pid*
> kill [-*sig*] *pid...*

The **kill** command cancels the designated process ID (*pid*). The second form sends the designated signal.

login

The **login** command has the following syntax:

> login

The **login** command replaces the login shell with **/bin/login**. It enables a currently active user to log in with a different user name.

logout

The **logout** command has the following syntax:

> logout

The **logout** command terminates a login shell. It is the only way to log out if *ignoreeof* is set.

newgrp

The **newgrp** command has the following syntax:

> newgrp *group*

The **newgrp** command changes the group ID of the user issuing the command.

nice

The **nice** command has the following syntax:

> nice [+*number*] [*command*]

The **nice** command sets the execution priority, known as the *nice value*. By default, commands have a nice value of 0.

nohup

The **nohup** command has the following syntax:

> nohup [*command*]

The **nohup** command causes hangups to be ignored. The first form is used in shell scripts to cause hangups to be ignored for the remainder of the script. The second form causes the specified command to be run with hangups ignored. Unless the shell is running in the background, **nohup** has no effect. All processes running in the background with & are automatically **nohup**ped.

onintr

The **onintr** command has the following syntax:

> onintr [- | *label*]

The **onintr** command controls the action of the shell on interrupts. The first form restores the default action of the shell on interrupts which is to terminate shell scripts or to return to the terminal command input level. The – causes all interrupts to be ignored. The *label* causes the shell to execute a **goto** *label* when an interrupt is received or a child process terminates because it was interrupted. In any case, if the shell is running in the background, interrupts are ignored whether any form of **onintr** is present or not.

popd

The **popd** command has the following syntax:

popd +*n*

The **popd** command pops the directory stack and returns to the new top directory. The +*n* discards the *n*th entry in the stack.

pushd

The **pushd** command has the following syntax:

pushd [*name*]

or

pushd +*n*

The **pushd** command changes to the designated directory and adds the current directory to the stack. If no name is specified, exchange the two top stack elements.

rehash

The **rehash** command has the following syntax:

rehash

The **rehash** command rebuilds the internal hash table. This is needed if new commands are added to directories in the path while you are logged in. If you don't use it, you won't find these commands.

repeat

The **repeat** command has the following syntax:

repeat *count command*

The **repeat** command causes the specified command to be executed *count* times. I/O redirection occurs exactly once, even if count is 0.

set

The **set** command has the following syntax:

set [*name* | name=word | name[index]=word | name=(wordlist)]
set *name=word*
set *name[index]=word*
set *name=(wordlist)*

The **set** command displays or changes the values of C shell variables. The **set** command shows the value of all shell variables. Variables whose value is other than a single word print as a parenthesized word list. **set** *name* sets the variable *name* to the null string. The **set** *word* command sets the variable *name* to the single designated *word.* The **set** **name**[*index*]=**word** command sets the *index*th component of *name* to *word*; this component must already exist. The **set name=[***wordlist***]** command sets *name* to the list of words in *wordlist.*

setenv

The **setenv** command has the following syntax:

setenv *name value*

The **setenv** command sets the value of the environment variable name. This value must be a single string.

shift

The **shift** command has the following syntax:

shift [*variable*]

The **shift** command moves the contents of *argv*[] one position to the left. After **shift** executes, *argv*[*1*] contains the previous contents of *argv*[*2*], and *argv*[*2*] contains the previous contents of *argv*[*3*], and so on.

source

The **source** command has the following syntax:

    source *name*

The **source** command executes the named C shell script in the current shell. The shell reads commands from *name*. Source commands may be nested, but if they are nested too deeply, the shell may run out of file descriptors. An error in a source at any level terminates all nested source commands, including the **csh** process from which **source** was called. If **source** is called from the login shell, it is logged out. Input during source commands is never placed on the history list.

stop

The **stop** command has the following syntax:

    stop [%*job*...]

The **stop** command cancels the current job or the specified job executing in the background.

switch

The **switch** control structure has the following syntax:

    switch (*word*)
    case *pattern1*
      command-list1
    breaksw
    case *pattern2*
      command-list2
    breaksw
    default:
      command-list3
    breaksw
    endsw

The **switch** control structure is used to introduce a **case control structure**.

time

The **time** command has the following syntax:

>   time [*command*]

The **time** command displays a summary of the time used by the current shell and its children. The **time** *command* command displays a summary of the time used by the designated command.

umask

The **umask** command has the following syntax:

>   umask [*value*]

The **umask** command displays or sets the user's file creation permission mask in octal. Common values are 002, giving all access to the group and read and execute access to others, and 022, giving read and execute access to users in the group and all other users.

unalias

The **unalias** command has the following syntax:

>   unalias *pattern*

The **unalias** command removes all aliases matching the specified pattern.

unhash

The **unhash** command has the following syntax:

>   unhash

The **unhash** command disables use of the internal hash table to speed location of executed programs.

unlimit

The **unlimit** command has the following syntax:

> unlimit [*resource*]

The **unlimit** command removes any limitation placed on the designated resource or, if none is specified, on all resources.

unset

The **unset** command has the following syntax:

> unset *pattern*

The **unset** command removes all variables whose names match the specified pattern.

unsetenv

The **unsetenv** command has the following syntax:

> unsetenv *name*

The **unsetenv** command removes environmental variables matching the designated name.

wait

The **wait** command has the following syntax:

> wait

The **wait** command pauses until the completion of all child processes. If the shell is interactive, then an interrupt can disrupt the wait, at which time the shell prints names and process numbers of all children known to be outstanding.

while

The **while** control structure has the following syntax:

> while *expression*
> *command-list*
> end

The **while** control structure, also known as a *while loop*, repeats a series of commands while (as long as) a given condition is TRUE. This control structure is used when the number of repetitions is not known in advance.

First the *expression* is evaluated. If it is TRUE, the command-list is executed and then *expression* is evaluated again. If the *expression* is FALSE, control passes to the command following the *end* statement. Sooner or later the *expression* must be FALSE; if not, an *infinite loop* occurs and execution stops, perhaps necessitating rebooting the system.

Glossary

Absolute pathnames   Absolute pathnames specify the file location relative to the root directory (/). Backup volumes use absolute pathnames so that they can be restored to the proper directory. This term was introduced in Chapter 7.

Account   Account is all information stored in the computer required for a user to log into a given Unix system. Often the system administrator creates, modifies, and deletes user accounts. This term was introduced in Chapter 1.

Aliasing   Aliasing allows you to identify commonly used commands with a name of your own choice. Aliasing is provided by the Korn shell and the C shell interpreters, but not by the Bourne shell interpreter. This term was introduced in Chapter 3.

Anonymous ftp   This service is the primary means of distributing documents and software on Internet. It relies on the standard File Transfer Protocol, and does not require a specific user password but might require an electronic mail address. This term was introduced in Chapter 11.

Automatic number identification (ANI)   Automatic number identification (ANI) is a service displaying the telephone number of the party making the call over digital telephone lines. This term was introduced in Chapter 12.

Back door   A back door, also known as a trap door, is the part of a program that provides access to system resources, bypassing the normal authorization process. Back doors are a common security threat. This term was introduced in Chapter 12.

Bacteria   Bacteria, also known as rabbits, are programs that make copies of themselves until they take over, monopolizing system resources such as central memory or disk space. The system administrator should set up user quotas to help protect against bacteria. This term was introduced in Chapter 12.

Bang   A bang is the ! character, which tells the system to go ahead and exit **vi** anyway. Use the bang character judiciously! This term was introduced in Chapter 2.

Block device   A block device is a peripheral unit that processes physical data organized in blocks, typically multiples of 512 bytes. The most common block device is a hard disk. This term was introduced in Chapter 1.

Block special files   Block special files, also known as block files, move data a block at a time between the file system and a block device such as a disk drive. This term was introduced in Chapter 8.

Boot routine   A boot routine is the program that takes charge of loading the kernel into memory. It may perform hardware verification. This term was introduced in Chapter 9.

Bootstrapping   Bootstrapping is the traditional name for the process by which a computer system starts working. Its origin lies in the phrase, "To pull oneself up by one's bootstraps." This term was introduced in Chapter 9.

Bootstring   A bootstring is the characters typed at the boot prompt. The bootstring may inform the kernel which peripherals are the root, pipe, and swap devices. This term was introduced in Chapter 9.

Bourne shell   The Bourne shell was the standard command interpreter for System V Unix. This term was introduced in Chapter 1.

Bourne shell input prompt   The Bourne shell input prompt is the $ character; it indicates that the Bourne shell is awaiting your input. This term was introduced in Chapter 2.

Bridge   A bridge is a hardware device connecting local-area networks that apply the same transmission protocol. A bridge does not modify the form or the contents of the data packets that it transmits. This term was introduced in Chapter 11.

C Shell   C Shell is a Unix command interpreter whose syntax resembles the C programming language. This term was introduced in Chapter 1.

C Shell input prompt   The C Shell input prompt is the % character; it indicates that the C shell is awaiting your input. This term was introduced in Chapter 2.

Callback   Callback is a telephone service that requires the caller to provide a user name, after which the system breaks the connection. The system then employs the user name to find the caller's phone number in a stored table and finally attempts to call back the caller. This term was introduced in Chapter 12.

Central processing unit (CPU)   The central processing unit (CPU) is the part of the computer that actually executes the program instructions. Examples of character devices include modems and terminals. This term was introduced in Chapter 4.

Character device   A character device is a peripheral unit that transfers data one or more characters at a time. This term was introduced in Chapter 1.

Character special files   Character special files, also known as character files, move data a character at a time between the file system and a character device such as a terminal. This term was introduced in Chapter 8.

Child process   A child process is a new process created by a **fork**. This term was introduced in Chapter 4.

Class   A class is a collection of printers. In a request to a particular class, the first available printer is activated. This term was introduced in Chapter 10.

Client/server architecture   Client/server architecture divides processing of an application between a client, which processes data locally and maintains a user interface, and a server, which handles database and computing-intensive processing. This term was introduced in Chapter 4.

Client-specific resources   Client-specific resources designate the icon and window frame appearance and behavior for individual clients or groups of clients. This term was introduced in Chapter 13.

Command history   Command history accesses previously typed commands to be repeated, either as they are or with modifications. It is provided by the Korn shell and the C shell interpreters, but not by the Bourne shell interpreter. This term was introduced in Chapter 3.

Command mode   Command mode is used to enter commands, such as searching for a character string or quitting the file. The **vi** editor starts in command mode. This term was introduced in Chapter 2.

Component-appearance resources   Component-appearance resources control the appearance of window manager menus, feedback windows, client window frames, and icons. This term was introduced in Chapter 13.

Configuration file   A configuration file is a text file containing formatted information. An example of a Unix configuration file is **/etc/passwd**, the user account database. This term was introduced in Chapter 1.

Connectors   Connectors attach to the end of the cable; each connector forms a male or female end to which other hardware is attached. This term was introduced in Chapter 11.

Control structures   Control structures are Unix shell programming language features that combine individual instructions or commands to express common programming needs. Examples of control structures include the **if, case,** and **while** structures. This term was introduced in Chapter 3.

Crash dump   A crash dump is an image of kernel memory at the time the computer stopped functioning. In the hands of a technical expert, a crash dump can be a key problem-solving tool. This term was introduced in Chapter 9.

Daemon   A daemon is a Unix process that runs in the background (while other tasks are being processed). An example of a daemon is **init**, the process that initiates user logins and starts other daemons. This term was introduced in Chapter 1.

Data Encryption Standard (DES)   Data Encryption Standard (DES) is a commonly used encryption algorithm developed in the 1970s by the United States Government and IBM. Many people feel that this standard is insufficiently secure for military applications. This term was introduced in Chapter 12.

Default GID number   A default GID (group ID) number is a unique integer between 0 and 32767. It indicates the collection of users or *group* to which the login user belongs. This term was introduced in Chapter 5.

Default group ID number   See "Default GID number."

Destination   A destination is a logical printer name, constituted when the printer was added to the system. This term was introduced in Chapter 10.

Device driver   A device driver is a part of the kernel that manages a particular device type, such as a disk controller. The device driver serves as an interface between the kernel and the users. Developing device drivers requires technical mastery both of the device and of its interface with the kernel. This term was introduced in Chapter 1.

Device file   A device file can be a character file or a block file. Device files are identified by two numbers: the *major device number* and the *minor device number*. This term was introduced in Chapter 1.

Device layer   A device layer consists of the kernel routines called device drivers that control the operation of peripheral devices. This term was introduced in Chapter 4.

Directory   A directory is a special file that contains a list of subordinate directories and filenames, as well as information describing the listed files. This term was introduced in Chapter 4.

Display manager   A display manager is a program, such as **xdm**, that manages one or more output displays, both local and remote. It should be invoked for users who wish to run X Window permanently on their display. This term was introduced in Chapter 13.

Editor   An editor is a software tool for creating and modifying scripts and programs. A widely used Unix editor is **vi**. This term was introduced in Chapter 2.

Editor mode   Editor mode, or state, determines how the editor handles the input it receives. The line editor modes in **vi** are command mask mode and input mode. This term was introduced in Chapter 2.

Encryption   Encryption means coding data to prevent its being read by unauthorized individuals. Some encryption methods rely on special numbers known as keys. This term was introduced in Chapter 12.

Extension   An extension of up to three characters can be appended to a filename, usually to indicate the nature of the file. Unix does not rely on filename extensions as much as MS-DOS does. This term was introduced in Chapter 4.

File   A file is a named collection of data stored on disk. Unix provides the system administrator with substantial control over user files. This term was introduced in Chapter 1.

File descriptor   A file descriptor is an integer in each entry of the file descriptor table that identifies the file. This term was introduced in Chapter 4.

File descriptor table   A file descriptor table is associated with each process and identifies all open files for that process. This term was introduced in Chapter 4.

File hierarchy   File hierarchy is the relationship between Unix files and directories. The file hierarchy resembles an upside-down tree. This term was introduced in Chapter 4.

File subsystem   A file subsystem is responsible for accessing and managing user and system files. It is one of the two basic subsystems of the kernel. This term was introduced in Chapter 4.

File systems   File systems are logical groups that comprise the contents of a given storage unit. Each file system is composed of a series of data blocks whose size is a multiple of 512 bytes. This term was introduced in Chapter 4.

File table   A file table indicates the start address of the next user read or write operation for each file and initial access rights to the file. When a process creates a new file or opens a currently existing file, the kernel allocates an entry in the file table. This term was introduced in Chapter 4.

Font management clients   Font management clients provide various font services. This term was introduced in Chapter 13.

Full backup   Full backup copies the entire file system. This term was introduced in Chapter 7.

Gateway   Gateway is a hardware device connecting networks that do not apply the same transmission protocol. Gateways may be used to connect LANs to LANs, or LANs to mini- or mainframe computers. This term was introduced in Chapter 11.

GCOS field   The GCOS field is part of the password file that contains personal information for each user. The system administrator defines this field according to system needs, and communicates this information to user. This term was introduced in Chapter 5.

Graphics-functions clients   Graphics-functions clients provide graphical services to users, including the system administrator. This term was introduced in Chapter 13.

Group   A group is a collection of users who share files or other system resources. Group membership is defined in the **/etc/group** file. This term was introduced in Chapter 5.

Hard link   Hard link is a term used to signify that an inode contains a directory name. This term was introduced in Chapter 8.

Home directory   The home directory is the directory in which users are placed when they log into the system. The home directory of the superuser is the root. This term was introduced in Chapter 5.

Host   A host is a computer attached to the computer network. The host may be of any size or level of processing power. This term was introduced in Chapter 11.

Host name   A host name is a unique name for each machine on a given network that readily identifies the machine, much as the user name identifies a given user. This term was introduced in Chapter 11.

Incremental backup   An incremental backup is a copy of new files and files that have changed since the last backup. This term was introduced in Chapter 7.

Initialization and configuration clients   Initialization and configuration clients start the X Window system and provide the tools to set it up to meet system default or individual needs. This term was introduced in Chapter 13.

Inode   An inode (short for index node) describes a file in great detail. The inode for a given file indicates the file owner, size, type, permissions (who is allowed to access the file and restrictions on this file access), the list of the physical disk blocks that compose the file, and the number of links. This term was introduced in Chapter 1.

Input focus   The input focus, also called the keyboard focus, is the window associated with the keyboard. This term was introduced in Chapter 13.

Input mode   The input mode of the **vi** editor is used to enter text into the file. This term was introduced in Chapter 2.

Interface   An interface is a shell script or a C language program that generates the information associated with a line printer request. This term was introduced in Chapter 10.

Kernel   A kernel is the part of the operating system that resides in memory after booting (starting) the system. The kernel is a resource manager, handling system hardware efficiently and effectively. This term was introduced in Chapter 1.

Kernel mode   Kernel mode processes may access instructions and data anywhere within the system. This term was introduced in Chapter 4.

Key argument   A key argument is a set of options that can be prefaced with a hyphen, used, for example, with the **tar** command. This term was introduced in Chapter 7.

Keyboard focus   The keyboard focus, also called the input focus, is the window associated with the keyboard. This term was introduced in Chapter 13.

Korn shell   The Korn shell is now the standard command interpreter for System V Unix. It integrates the best aspects of the Bourne shell and the C shell. This term was introduced in Chapter 1.

Korn shell input prompt   The Korn shell input prompt is the $ indicating that the Korn shell is awaiting your input. This term was introduced in Chapter 2.

Local-area network (LAN)   A local-area network (LAN) is a network whose components are directly linked, perhaps by private communications lines, and perhaps by the public telephone system. In general, LANs extend over a distance of a kilometer or less, and do not involve signal boosting or filtering. This term was introduced in Chapter 11.

Logic bomb   A logic bomb is a part of a program that lies quietly waiting for the moment to perform special, perhaps malicious, behavior. This term was introduced in Chapter 12.

Logical disk   A logical disk is a simplified model of the physical (actual) disk. This term was introduced in Chapter 8.

Login name   A login name is the name by which a user identifies herself or himself to the system. It is also known as the user name. This term was introduced in Chapter 5.

Login shell   A login shell is the shell initially available to the user. This term was introduced in Chapter 5.

Loopback address   Data sent to such an address is retransmitted to the sending host. This term was introduced in Chapter 11.

Major device number   A major device number identifies the associated device driver for a device. This term was introduced in Chapter 1.

Medium   The medium is the path over which communications flow. This term was introduced in Chapter 11.

Message A message is a unit of formatted data used in communications. This term was introduced in Chapter 4.

Message header A message header indicates the start of a message and includes control information such as source, destination, date, and time. This term was introduced in Chapter 11.

Message of the day facility The message of the day facility is a feature by which the system administrator composes messages that appear on the screen whenever users log onto the system. This term was introduced in Chapter 6.

Message text The message text is the actual information to be transmitted. This term was introduced in Chapter 11.

Minor device number A minor device number informs the device driver of the actual physical unit. This term was introduced in Chapter 1.

Modem A modem (short for *mo*dulator/*dem*odulator) translates the digital signals found in computers and terminals into the analog signals transmitted over standard telephone lines. Because they open computer systems to the outside world, modems are a potential security risk. This term was introduced in Chapter 12.

Mount point The mount point is the place at which the mounted file system's root directory is inserted into the original file system. This term was introduced in Chapter 8.

Mounting Mounting a disk links its file system with one of the installation's existing file systems. A file system must be mounted before it can be accessed. This term was introduced in Chapter 8.

Multitasking Multitasking means that the computer system can perform several tasks simultaneously. This term was introduced in Chapter 1.

Multi-user A multi-user operating system supports several users simultaneously. This term was introduced in Chapter 1.

Multi-user mode Multi-user mode is the usual Unix operating mode, in which several users share Unix system facilities. It provides a full range of services. This term was introduced in Chapter 9.

Naming conventions   Naming conventions are the specific rules for naming Unix files and directories. The system administrator is responsible for developing and enforcing local naming conventions. This term was introduced in Chapter 4.

Nested subdirectory   A nested subdirectory is a directory within a directory. Unix places no limit on the depth of nested subdirectories. This term was introduced in Chapter 1.

Network   A network is two or more linked computers. Common networks include local-area networks (LANs) and wide-area networks (WANs). This term was introduced in Chapter 11.

Network address   A network address is unique for all hosts on a network. The Network Information Center assigns a network address to all hosts belonging to the Internet network. This term was introduced in Chapter 11.

Operating system   An operating system is the control program that manages the hardware and software resources of a computer system. It provides the interface between the computer hardware and those people, both technical and non-technical, who use the computer. This term was introduced in Chapter 1.

Packet switching   Packet switching is a type of message transmission in which messages are broken up into segments called packets, which are transmitted independently and then reassembled at the destination. This term was introduced in Chapter 11.

Partial backup   A partial backup is a complete copy of any file system or directory tree. This term was introduced in Chapter 7.

Partition   A partition is a segment of the logical disk. Dividing a logical disk into partitions improves its usefulness; for instance, a partition can limit the maximum disk space that a greedy user can reserve. This term was introduced in Chapter 8.

Password   A password is a secret code by which a user identifies himself or herself to the system. For passwords to maintain their security value, they must be changed from time to time. This term was introduced in Chapter 5.

Path   A path is a hierarchical list of subdirectories that indicates where to search for a file. This term was introduced in Chapter 4.

Pipe   A pipe is a commonly used programming technique in which the output of one process becomes the input to another process. This term was introduced in Chapter 4.

Pipeline   A pipeline is a sequence of one or more commands separated by a vertical bar. This term was introduced in Chapter 3.

Port   Each end of a TCP/IP (Transmission Control/Interface Protocol) link is attached to a (software) port, identified by a 16-bit number. This term was introduced in Chapter 11.

Portability   Portability is the ability to move software from one hardware platform to another without major recoding. The Unix operating system offers a high degree of portability. This term was introduced in Chapter 1.

Private key   A private key a special number that may be used to decrypt data. This term was introduced in Chapter 12.

Process-control subsystem   A process-control subsystem is responsible for the management of processes (executing programs) and the resources that these processes require. It is one of the two basic subsystems of the kernel. This term was introduced in Chapter 4.

Process   A process is an executing program. The operating system carefully mediates interaction among processes. This term was introduced in Chapter 1.

Program editor   A program editor is a software tool for creating and modifying scripts and programs. A widely used Unix program editor is **vi**. This term was introduced in Chapter 2.

Protected subsystem   A protected subsystem is a privileged subsystem that does not require global authority to perform actions. Subsystem authorizations associated with each protected subsystem are located in the **/etc/auth/subsystems** directory. This term was introduced in Chapter 12.

Protocol   Protocol is the formal set of rules and conventions used when processes or hosts communicate. Due to the complexity of protocols, they are designed in layers to make them more manageable. This term was introduced in Chapter 11.

Protocol layer   A protocol layer consists of a communications protocol, such as TCP/IP (Transmission Control Protocol/Interface Protocol). This transfers data to or from the socket layer. This term was introduced in Chapter 4.

Public key   Public key is a special number that may be used to encrypt data. This term was introduced in Chapter 12.

Rabbits   Rabbits, also known as bacteria, are programs that make copies of themselves until they take over, monopolizing system resources such as central memory or disk space. The system administrator should set up user quotas to help protect against rabbits. This term was introduced in Chapter 12.

Relative pathnames   Relative pathnames are relative to the current directory. Use relative pathnames when creating a **tar** volume where absolute pathnames are unnecessary. This term was introduced in Chapter 7.

Reliable data transmission   Reliable data transmission is transmission for which the system guarantees that every byte transmitted will reach its destination in the order that it was sent, or you will be notified. This term was introduced in Chapter 11.

Request   Request names files and associated information to be printed. This term was introduced in Chapter 10.

Root   Root is the user name associated with the privileged account *superuser*. The superuser has full permission on all files when using the root password. This term was introduced in Chapter 5.

Root directory   A root directory, also called the root, is the unique Unix directory that is not subordinate to any other directory. This term was introduced in Chapter 1.

Router   A router is a hardware device connecting local-area networks, sending packets to the appropriate network destination. As they do their work, routers may have to reorganize packets. This term was introduced in Chapter 11.

Run levels   Run levels are System V Unix system states such as single-user mode and multi-user mode. This term was introduced in Chapter 9.

Runaway programs   Runaway programs are programs that cannot be stopped from the terminal that started them. The most common example is a program containing an infinite loop. This term was introduced in Chapter 14.

Script   A script is a file containing Unix commands. Scripts are written for one of three shells: the Korn shell, the Bourne shell, and the C shell. This term was introduced in Chapter 1.

Self-auditing program   A self-auditing program records a single entry in the audit log for a specific process such as a **login**. Appropriate use of self-auditing programs reduces file storage requirements. This term was introduced in Chapter 12.

Session   A session is defined by the lifetime of a particular Unix process. For traditional character-based terminals, a session is the user's login shell process. This term was introduced in Chapter 13.

Set group ID (SGID) function   The set group ID (SGID) function temporarily modifies the user's group ID. Carefully monitor the use of programs applying SGID and SUID functions, and do not use SGID or SUID shell scripts. This term was introduced in Chapter 12.

Set user ID (SUID) function   The set user ID (SUID) function is a program that temporarily modifies the user's ID. The use of programs applying SUID functions, while considered necessary in most installations, presents a potential security risk. This term was introduced in Chapter 12.

Shadow password files   Shadow password files are files that store encrypted passwords. They are accessible only by the superuser. This term was introduced in Chapter 5.

Shell escapes   Shell escapes are shell script features that permit the user to leave the shell temporarily to execute another program. They open the door to executing unauthorized programs while the user has root or other temporary privileges. This term was introduced in Chapter 12.

Shell   The shell is the command interpreter program that serves as an interface between users and the operating system itself. The most widely used Unix shells are the Korn shell, the Bourne shell, and the C shell. This term was introduced in Chapter 1.

Simple command   A simple command is a sequence of non-blank words separated by tabs or spaces. The first word specifies the command to be executed. This term was introduced in Chapter 3.

Single-user mode   Single-user mode is the operating mode that provides the system administrator with complete control of the Unix system. The single-user mode runs the Korn shell or the Bourne shell, executing as the user root. This term was introduced in Chapter 9.

Socket   A socket is one end of a communications path. Sockets were originally restricted to BSD Unix, but they have been added to Unix System V. This term was introduced in Chapter 4.

Socket layer   A socket layer provides the interface to system calls. This term was introduced in Chapter 4.

Soft link   A soft link links a file using the **ln** command so that it may be executed from a specified directory. This term was introduced in Chapter 8.

Specific appearance and behavior resources   Specific appearance and behavior resources designate **mwm** features such as window management policies. This term was introduced in Chapter 13.

Spooler   A spooler is a buffer, such as the **/usr/spool/lp** file, that collects output and later sends it to the printer, improving system efficiency. The actual printing of the spooler contents is performed sequentially. This term was introduced in Chapter 10.

String options   String options are strings of characters that are assigned values with the syntax *option=string*. Multiple options may be specified on a line. This term was introduced in Chapter 2.

Subsystem filename   The subsystem filename is the group name associated with the protected subsystem. This term was introduced in Chapter 12.

Superblock   A superblock is a 512-byte area starting at byte number 512 of the file system. It contains system control information. This term was introduced in Chapter 8.

Superuser   A superuser is a privileged account associated with the user name *root*. The superuser has complete access to all commands and files on a given Unix system. This term was introduced in Chapter 5.

Swapping   Swapping is the procedure by which Unix "makes room" in central memory for a given process by removing another process from memory. Inefficient swapping degrades system performance. This term was introduced in Chapter 14.

Switch option   Switch option is an environment option whose value is either on or off. Multiple options may be specified on a line. This term was introduced in Chapter 2.

Symbolic link   Symbolic link links a file using the **ln** command so that it may be executed from a specified directory. This term was introduced in Chapter 8.

Symbolic modes   Symbolic modes express permissions without the bother of bits and remembering the order in which permissions (owner, group, and other) are specified. This term was introduced in Chapter 5.

System call   A system call is a program request addressed to the kernel. Common activities, such as accessing files, require system calls. This term was introduced in Chapter 1.

System parameters   System parameters are special values that enable technically proficient system administrators to increase system performance by modifying them. The optimal settings for system parameters are hardware-dependent, and a function of the installation's specific processing activities and goals. This term was introduced in Chapter 14.

Tilde escape   A tilde escape is a **mailx** command feature that enables the user to leave the **mailx** command, execute an option, and then return to the command. This term was introduced in Chapter 6.

Trap door   A trap door, also known as a back door, is the part of a program that provides access to system resources, bypassing the normal authorization process. Trap doors are a common security threat. This term was introduced in Chapter 12.

Trojan horse   A Trojan horse is a program that seems to be doing one thing, such as a game, but actually does something else, such as deleting files. This term was introduced in Chapter 12.

Trusted host   A trusted host is a linked host onto which a user with the same user name on two (or more) hosts can log in from without entering a password. If you do not ban trusted hosts, at least monitor the **/etc/hosts.equiv** file carefully. This term was introduced in Chapter 12.

Trusted ports   Trusted ports are ports that may be accessed only by the superuser. Their port number ranges from 0 to 1023. This term was introduced in Chapter 11.

UID number   A UID (user ID) number is a unique integer between 0 and 32767. It identifies a login name throughout a network. This term was introduced in Chapter 5.

Unmounting   Unmounting a disk reverses the mount operation; it breaks the link between the unmounted disk and the original larger file system. This term was introduced in Chapter 8.

Unnamed   In **vi**, an unnamed buffer is a special buffer that contains the most recently deleted text. Unnamed buffers are used in cut-and-paste operations. This term was introduced in Chapter 2.

User ID number   A user ID number is a unique integer between 0 and 32767. It identifies a login name throughout a network. This term was introduced in Chapter 5.

User mode   User mode processes may access only instructions and data associated with that given process. This term was introduced in Chapter 4.

User name   A user name is the name by which a user identifies herself or himself to the system. It is also known as the login name. This term was introduced in Chapter 5.

Viewable services clients   Viewable services clients provide system administrators and users with X emulation on selected terminals and other desktop facilities. This term was introduced in Chapter 13.

Virus   A virus is computer code that can be executed only in the presence of another program. (In common language any programmed threat is called a virus.) This term was introduced in Chapter 12.

Wide-Area Network (WAN)   A wide-area network (WAN) is a network whose components are linked over a large distance. This term was introduced in Chapter 11.

Widgets   Widgets are standard on-screen building blocks such as menus, scrollbars, buttons, and dialogue boxes. Meticulous use of widgets simplifies the X Window programming process. This term was introduced in Chapter 13.

Window management clients   Window management clients provide useful information about windows. This term was introduced in Chapter 13.

Window manager   A window manager is a special client responsible for manipulating windows on the screen. Window managers associated with the X Window system include **mwm**, **wm**, and **twm**. Proprietary toolkits apply their own window managers, which may be more sophisticated. This term was introduced in Chapter 13.

Window stacking   Window stacking describes relationships among windows; for example, if Window A covers (obscures) Window B, Window A is said to be higher on the stacking order. This term was introduced in Chapter 13.

Worm   A worm is a program that can travel across a network from one computer to another. This term was introduced in Chapter 12.

X protocol   X protocol defines the exact bytes required to perform all X Window operations including drawing a window, moving a window, or reacting to the click of a mouse button. X Window developers and system administrators need not know the X protocol. This term was introduced in Chapter 13.

X Terminal   X Terminal is a diskless graphical computer terminal that runs a single program, the X Window server program. The rapid expansion of the X Window marketplace has lead to the development of a wide variety of X terminals, some of which rival workstations for memory and CPU. This term was introduced in Chapter 13.

X Toolkit Intrinsics   X Toolkit Intrinsics, also known as Xt Intrinsics, enable programmers to create and use standard on-screen building blocks, called widgets; examples include menus, scroll bars, buttons, and dialog boxes. This term was introduced in Chapter 13.

X Window client/server architecture   X Window client/server architecture is the X Window system model, by which clients, or application programs, communicate with servers, or display units over a network. This architecture applies the division of labor principal to centralize key graphics operations in the server, enabling the client to focus on the application at hand. This term was introduced in Chapter 13.

X Window system   X Window system is the standard windowing system for Unix. X Window systems run on a variety of common hardware devices, including workstations and X terminals. This term was introduced in Chapter 13.

Xlib   Xlib functions provide the power of X protocol with much less pain. Xlib is a library of over 300 C language functions used to generate X protocol. This term was introduced in Chapter 13.

Index

T